604

U·X·L American Decades
Cumulative Index

**Includes indexes for the
complete ten-volume set**

Detroit • New York • San Diego • San Francisco • Cleveland • New Haven, Conn. • Waterville, Maine • London • Munich

U•X•L American Decades, Cumulative Index

Index Coordinator
Julie L. Carnagie

0-7876-6604-1

Printed in the United States of America
10 9 8 7 6 5 4 3 2 1

Cumulative Index

A

AAA (American Abstract Artists), *1930s:* 10

AAA (American Automobile Association), *1900s:* 78

AAA (Agricultural Adjustment Administration), *1930s:* 77

AA (Alcoholics Anonymous), *1930s:* 89, 111

AAFC (All-American Football Conference), *1940s:* 153, 167

AAGBL (All-American Girls Baseball League), *1940s:* 154, 162, 163 (ill.)

AALL (American Association of Labor Legislation), *1910s:* 120

Aalto, Alvar, *1940s:* 92

A&P, *1920s:* 24, 36

Aaron, Hank, *1950s:* 158, 164; *1970s:* 163, 166

AARP (American Association of Retired Persons), *1970s:* 110; *1990s:* 122

AAU (Amateur Athletic Union), *1900s:* 146–48; *1910s:* 155, 173–74

AAUP (American Association of University Professors), *1910s:* 46

ABA (American Basketball Association), *1960s:* 166, 177–78; *1970s:* 160–61, 167; *1980s:* 177–78

ABBA, *1970s:* 16

ABM (Antiballistic Missile) Treaty, *1970s:* 80

Abbott Labs, *1960s:* 135

ABC (Atanasoff Berry Computer), *1940s:* 130

ABC (band), *1980s:* 18

The ABC Powers, *1910s:* 73

Abdul-Jabbar, Kareem, *1960s:* 175; *1980s:* 177

Abel, John J. *1900s:* 104, 104 (ill.)

Abie's Irish Rose, 1920s: 2

ABL (American Basketball League), *1930s:* 160–61

ABMs (Antiballistic missiles), *1980s:* 78

A-bomb. *See* Nuclear weapons

Abortions, *1960s:* 120–21, 133–34, 137
controversy, *1990s:* 119, 128–32, 129 (ill.)
inducing pill, *1990s:* 116
rights, *1990s:* 75
See also Roe v. Wade

Abraham & Straus, *1920s:* 37

Italic type indicates volume; (ill.) indicates illustrations.

Abrahams, Harold, *1920s:* 168–69

Absalom! Absalom!, 1930s: 7

Abstract art, *1910s:* 4

Abstract expressionism, *1940s:* 4,
8–10, 9 (ill.); *1950s:* 8

Abzug, Bella, *1970s:* 102, 102 (ill.)

Academic freedom, *1940s:* 50–51

Academic standards, *1980s:* 48, 50,
55, 58–60; *1990s:* 48

Academics, versus sports, *1900s:* 151;
1940s: 152

Academy Awards, *1930s:* 16; *1940s:* 6,
14
Midnight Cowboy, *1960s:* 9
Poitier, Sidney, *1960s:* 7, 105
Streisand, Barbra, *1960s:* 7
Woodstock, *1960s:* 12

Academy Award winners, *1950s:* 13

Academy of Motion Picture Arts and
Sciences Awards. *See* Oscars

Accelerated programs, *1940s:* 44

Accessories (fashion), *1900s:* 93–94

Accident insurance, employer, *1910s:*
69, 86
See also Worker's compensation

Accidents
airplane crashes, *1900s:* 79
cause of death, *1990s:* 126
cell phones, *1990s:* 156
in space program, *1960s:* 160;
1970s: 146–48
steamboats, *1900s:* 78
Three Mile Island, *1970s:* 35,
141, 154–57

Accommodationists, on race issues,
1900s: 40, 52–53

Ace Publishing, *1950s:* 16

Acetate, *1950s:* 90

Acetylcholine, *1920s:* 109

Acetylene, *1920s:* 108

Achievement tests, *1900s:* 44; *1990s:*
46, 51

Acquired immunodeficiency syndrome (AIDS). *See* AIDS

Acquisitions. *See* Mergers and acquisitions

ACT (American College Test), *1980s:*
59

Actifed, *1970s:* 145

Actinomycin, *1940s:* 119

Action Comics, 1930s: 12

Action painters, *1940s:* 9

Actors and actresses, *1900s:* 3; *1960s:*
9

ADA (Americans with Disabilities
Act), *1990s:* 74

Adagio for Strings, 1930s: 20

Adam and the Ants, *1980s:* 18

The Adams Family Chronicles, 1970s: 59

Adams, Samuel Hopkins, *1900s:* 114

Addams, Jane, *1900s:* 47–48, 80–82,
82 (ill.), 88; *1910s:* 80, 99; *1930s:*
88, 105

Addiction, drug, *1930s:* 111

The Adding Machine, 1920s: 2

Adelie penguins, global warming and,
1990s: 150

Adidas, *1980s:* 106

Adkins v. Children's Hospital, 1920s: 64

Adler, Felix, *1910s:* 50, 50 (ill.)

Adler, Mortimer, *1940s:* 48, 48 (ill.),
53–54

Admissions, college, *1970s:* 59, 63–65

Adobe Pagemaker, *1980s:* 160

Adolescents, *1940s:* 86, 98

Adrian, Gilbert, *1930s:* 102; *1940s:* 96

Adult education, *1910s:* 37, 53–54;
1950s: 52

Advanced Research Projects Agency
(ARPA), *1990s:* 145

The Adventures of Kit Carson, 1950s:
107

The Adventures of Ozzie & Harriet,
1950s: 18

Adventure stories, *1900s:* 5

Advertising, *1900s:* 20, 36–37; *1920s:*
5, 18
automobile racing and, *1940s:*
158–59
Chevrolet, *1950s:* 30
of cigarettes, *1960s:* 125; *1970s:*
122; *1980s:* 122
franchises and, *1960s:* 34–35
pharmaceuticals, *1910s:* 112,
115, 126–28
product placement, *1950s:* 31

store decoration, *1910s:* 42
television, *1950s:* 28, 30–31, 116
Advisory Committee on Smoking and Health, *1960s:* 137
AEA (Aerial Experiment Association), *1900s:* 126
AEC (Atomic Energy Commission), *1930s:* 135
AEF (American Expeditionary Forces), *1910s:* 71, 77
Aegyptopithecus, 1960s: 148
Aerial Experiment Association (AEA), *1900s:* 126
Aerobee rocket, *1960s:* 150
Aerobic exercise, *1970s:* 128
Aerodrome, 1900s: 126
Aerodynamics, *1940s:* 137–38
Aeronautical engineering, *1900s:* 125–27
Aerosmith, *1980s:* 24
Aerospace industry, *1950s:* 25
AES (American Eugenics Society), *1930s:* 142–43
AFDC (Aid to Families with Dependent Children), *1980s:* 111
Affirmative action, *1970s:* 42; *1980s:* 101; *1990s:* 47, 59–60
Affluence, postwar, *1940s:* 89, 99–01
The Affluent Society, 1950s: 94
Afghanistan
    arms to, *1980s:* 75
    Soviet Union invasion, *1980s:* 2, 68, 92
AFL (American Federation of Labor), *1920s:* 25; *1930s:* 27, 38; *1970s:* 170–71
    Beck, Dave, *1950s:* 35
    Ethical Practices Committee, *1950s:* 35
    labor racketeering, *1950s:* 33
    Meany, George, *1950s:* 28, 32
    Reuther, Walter P., *1950s:* 29, 29 (ill.), 32
    teamsters, *1950s:* 25, 32–35, 33 (ill.), 34 (ill.)
    Westinghouse and, *1950s:* 25
    See also American Federation of Labor

AFL (American Football League), *1960s:* 165–66, 179–81
AFL-CIO, *1960s:* 39
AFL-NFL championship, *1960s:* 165
Africa
    AIDS, *1990s:* 126
    aid to, *1980s:* 2, 24–25, 26 (ill.)
    reflected in art, *1970s:* 8
African Americans, *1910s:* 82, 91
    Africa and, *1910s:* 94
    antiwar stance, *1910s:* 19
    in armed forces, *1910s:* 96
    artists, *1940s:* 10
    in arts and entertainment, *1920s:* 10–13, 16, 18; *1970s:* 2–4, 8, 15–16, 19–20, 23, 108
    attacks on, *1910s:* 91
    authors, *1940s:* 5, 13
    in baseball, *1920s:* 157–60
    baseball managers, *1980s:* 168
    beauty products, *1910s:* 36
    Black Arts Movement, *1960s:* 114
    Black Pride, *1970s:* 108
    books by, *1970s:* 10
    civil rights leaders, *1940s:* 68–69, 90
    convicts, *1910s:* 60
    corporate employment, *1990s:* 38
    desegregation and, *1940s:* 86–87
    Du Bois, W. E. B., *1930s:* 93, 93 (ill.)
    educational tests, *1980s:* 59–60
    education and, *1900s:* 40–41, 44, 50–54, 63; *1910s:* 47, 51, 60–62, 61 (ill.), 62 (ill.); *1930s:* 46–47, 49–50, 61–65, 63 (ill.); *1940s:* 44, 49, 58 (ill.), 59–61; *1970s:* 48, 65–66
    employment rights, *1970s:* 26, 42
    executives, *1990s:* 32
    in films, *1930s:* 14–15; *1960s:* 7, 105–06
    firms, *1980s:* 31
    in government, *1940s:* 79
    health care for, *1900s:* 106–07
    history, *1910s:* 51
    homicide statistics of, *1910s:* 82
    housing for, *1940s:* 100

intelligence tests, *1950s:* 46
IQ and, *1960s:* 51
Jim Crow laws, *1900s:* 72, 85;
    1910s: 69, 82, 96
literature by, *1900s:* 8–9; *1920s:* 5,
    10–11
in medicine, *1900s:* 105–06, 109;
    1940s: 112, 115–17
in the military, *1900s:* 79
Million Man March, *1990s:* 95
ministers, *1950s:* 91
Miss America, *1980s:* 101
Motown and, *1960s:* 13–15, 14
    (ill.)
in music, *1900s:* 7, 13–14; *1910s:*
    17; *1930s:* 20
newspapers, *1900s:* 2
Niagara Movement, *1900s:* 59, 85
in politics, *1970s:* 74–75, 98, 103
race riots, *1910s:* 91
racial preferences and, *1990s:* 45
racial violence, *1900s:* 71–72, 85
racism, *1910s:* 17, 36, 96
rock and roll music, *1950s:* 15
role in American history, *1960s:*
    48, 53
sailing around the world, *1990s:*
    92
space flight, *1980s:* 150
in sports, *1900s:* 140, 143–44,
    148; *1910s:* 156; *1930s:* 152,
    155, 157, 160–62, 167–68;
    1940s: 153, 155, 157, 161–65,
    164 (ill.); *1950s:* 158; *1960s:*
    164–65, 167–69, 182; *1970s:*
    160, 163, 166–67, 175–76
syphilis and, *1970s:* 137
in television, *1960s:* 106
television depiction of, *1950s:* 31
in theater, *1900s:* 15; *1930s:* 21
voting rights, *1900s:* 58; *1910s:*
    82; *1940s:* 64, 87, 90, 104
in war industries, *1940s:* 24
World War I, *1910s:* 93, 96
See also Busing; Civil Rights
    movement; Integration; specif-
    ic AfricanAmericans
African safari, *1900s:* 3

African sculpture, *1910s:* 3
AFT (American Federation of Teach-
    ers), *1910s:* 46; *1930s:* 47, 51, 54–56
Agassi, Andre, *1990s:* 179, 181
Age discrimination, *1970s:* 110
Agent Orange, *1970s:* 155
The Age of Innocence, 1900s: 7
Agitprop theater, *1930s:* 58
Agranulocytosis, *1930s:* 111
Agrarian economy, *1910s:* 48
Agricultural Adjustment Act, *1930s:*
    36, 78
Agricultural Adjustment Administra-
    tion (AAA), *1930s:* 77
Agricultural lands, *1950s:* 25, 99–102;
    1980s: 30–31, 40
Agricultural Marketing Act, *1920s:* 75
Agriculture, *1910s:* 48, 56–58; *1920s:*
    27, 32–33, 75; *1960s:* 25–26, 28,
    30, 38 (ill.)
    Agricultural Adjustment Act,
        1930s: 36, 79
    Farm Mortgage Refinancing Act,
        1930s: 26
    federal income tax, *1910s:* 32–33
    Frazier-Lemke Farm Bankruptcy
        Act, *1930s:* 69
    during Great Depression, *1930s:*
        32–34
    loans, *1910s:* 25
    machinery, *1910s:* 56
    science, *1910s:* 148–49
    statistics, *1930s:* 37
    Taylor Grazing Act, *1930s:* 69
    training, *1910s:* 56–58
AHA (American Hospital Associa-
    tion), *1930s:* 113; *1980s:* 112
Ah, Wilderness, 1930s: 2
Aida, 1910s: 2; *1960s:* 31
Aideed, Muhammad Farrah, *1990s:* 69
AIDS, *1980s:* 3, 27, 122–30
    Da-i Ho, David, *1990s:* 117, 120,
        120 (ill.)
    epidemic, *1990s:* 118, 123–28
    memorial quilt, *1990s:* 127 (ill.)
Aid to Families with Dependent Chil-
    dren (AFDC), *1980s:* 111
Aiken, Howard, *1940s:* 140

Ailey, Alvin, *1960s:* 114
AIM. *See* American Indian Movement
Ainge, Danny, *1980s:* 177
Ain't Misbehavin', *1970s:* 3
Airbags, automobile, *1990s:* 117
Air bus. *See* Boeing 747
Aircall Corporation, *1950s:* 143
Air Commerce Act, *1920s:* 135
Air-conditioning, *1920s:* 87
Air conditioning, in automobiles, *1940s:* 86
Aircraft, *1930s:* 131, 135–37; *1940s:* 28, 34, 130, 137–38; *1970s:* 140–41
    design, *1920s:* 133
    jet, *1950s:* 137–38, 151–52
Airlines, *1940s:* 3, 130; *1980s:* 30, 35, 37
    discrimination and, *1970s:* 26–27
    smoking bans, *1990s:* 116
    transatlantic, *1970s:* 30
    See also Air travel
Airline strikes, *1960s:* 24
Airmail, *1920s:* 135–36, 136 (ill.); *1930s:* 89
Airplane flights, global nonstop, *1980s:* 147
Airplanes, *1900s:* 79, 120, 125–27, 126 (ill.)
    all metal, *1910s:* 133
    biplanes, *1910s:* 25, 138
    first, *1910s:* 134, 138–39, 151
    multimotored, *1910s:* 132
Air pollution, *1960s:* 94, 126; *1970s:* 122
Air Quality Act, *1960s:* 126
Air-raid drills, *1940s:* 86
Air-to-Surface Vessel (ASV) radar, *1940s:* 143
Air Traffic Controller strikes, *1980s:* 30, 37
Air travel, *1920s:* 25, 31, 129–30, 132, 134–35; *1930s:* 27, 89, 130, 136–38; *1950s:* 27, 35–36, 137; *1970s:* 27, 30, 140–41, 148
    See also Airlines; Aviation
Akron, *1930s:* 130, 137
Akutsu, Tetsuzu, *1980s:* 130
The Alabama, *1910s:* 172

AL (American League), *1960s:* 164, 174
Alamogordo, New Mexico, *1940s:* 130, 146
Alaska Permanent Fund, *1970s:* 35
Alaska, pipeline, *1970s:* 26, 34–35, 152
Alaska, statehood, *1950s:* 69
Alaska tribal council, *1990s:* 92
Alaska-Yuko-Pacific Exposition, *1900s:* 79
Albee, Edward, *1960s:* 18
Albee, F. H., *1910s:* 128
Albert and Mary Lasker Foundation, *1940s:* 113
Albert Lasker Award, *1940s:* 113
Albert Lasker Public Service Award, *1970s:* 126
Albright, Madeleine, *1990s:* 63, 66, 66 (ill.)
Albright, Tenley, *1950s:* 150
Alcatraz Island, *1970s:* 109
Alcindor, Lew. *See* Abdul-Jabbar, Kareem
Alcoa (Aluminum Company of America), *1900s:* 25; *1950s:* 36–37
The Alcoa Hour, *1950s:* 18
Alcock, John, *1910s:* 133, 139
Alcohol abuse, schools, *1980s:* 49, 63–64
Alcoholic beverages, *1910s:* 25, 69
    health benefits of, *1970s:* 123
Alcoholics Anonymous (AA), *1930s:* 89, 111
Alcoholism, *1950s:* 114
Alcohol prohibition, *1900s:* 83, 86
Aldington, Richard, *1910s:* 12
Aldrich-Vreeland Act, *1900s:* 28, 33
Aldrin, Edwin "Buzz," *1960s:* 159, 159 (ill.)
Alen, William Van, *1930s:* 97
Alexander, Grover Cleveland, *1950s:* 176
"Alexander's Ragtime Band," *1910s:* 2, 17
Alfred P. Murrah Federal Building, *1990s:* 64–65, 81–83, 82 (ill.), 92
Alger, Horatio, *1900s:* 5

Algren, Nelson, *1930s:* 13

Alice Adams, 1920s: 2

Alien, 1970s: 19

Alienation, *1960s:* 4, 12

Alien Registration Act, *1940s:* 78

Aliens, with AIDS, *1980s:* 123

Ali, Muhammed, *1960s:* 164–65, 167–68, 168 (ill.); *1970s:* 160–61, 164, 164 (ill.)

All-American Football Conference (AAFC), *1940s:* 153, 167

All-American Girls Baseball League (AAGBL), *1940s:* 154, 162, 163 (ill.)

Allen, Dick, *1960s:* 173

Allen, Paul, *1970s:* 44–45; *1980s:* 161

Allen, Steve, *1950s:* 17, 19

Allergies, *1940s:* 119

Alliance for Progress, *1960s:* 68

Allied powers, *1910s:* 52, 68, 75, 77
    See also Central powers

All in the Family, 1970s: 2, 6, 21–22

All My Sons, 1940s: 19

All the King's Men, 1940s: 12

All the President's Men, 1970s: 74

Alpert, Richard, *1960s:* 94

Alpo, *1960s:* 41

ALS (Amyotrophic lateral sclerosis), *1920s:* 152; *1940s:* 152

Altair 8800, 42–44, 141

Altamont Music Festival, *1960s:* 12, 95

Alternative energy sources, *1970s:* 32–35

Alternative lifestyles, *1970s:* 49, 98–99, 108–11, 161

Aluminum, *1950s:* 36–37

Aluminum City Terrace Housing, New Kensington, Pennsylvania, *1940s:* 90, 93

Aluminum Company of America (Alcoa), *1900s:* 25

Alvarez, Louis, *1940s:* 130

Alvarez, Luis, *1980s:* 146, 150, 150 (ill.)

Alvin Theater, *1930s:* 3

Alworth, Lance, *1960s:* 180

Alzheimer, Alois, *1980s:* 136

Alzheimer's disease, *1980s:* 125, 136–37, 136 (ill.); *1990s:* 116

AMA (American Medical Association), *1920s:* 111, 118; *1950s:* 125–26; *1990s:* 121
    See also American Medical Association

Amalgamated Clothing Workers of America, *1940s:* 28

Amateur Athletic Union (AAU), *1900s:* 146–48; *1910s:* 155, 173–74

Amateur Athletic Union track meet, *1930s:* 153

Amazon.com, *1990s:* 32, 33, 34 (ill.)

Ambers, Lou, *1930s:* 162

Ambulance ships, *1910s:* 113

Ameche, Alan, *1950s:* 174

Amedure, Scott, *1990s:* 2, 15

Amendments (constitutional), *1950s:* 105–07; *1980s:* 9, 58; *1990s:* 44, 106–09

America, 1940s: 131

America
    contract with, *1990s:* 70–72
    as world police force, *1990s:* 69–70

American Abstract Artists (AAA), *1930s:* 10

American Academy of Arts and Letters, *1940s:* 2

American Academy of Dental Medicine, *1940s:* 109

American Academy of Pediatrics, *1990s:* 116

American Airlines, *1970s:* 27

American Airways, *1930s:* 136

American & Continental Tobacco, *1900s:* 58

American Antivivisection Society, *1900s:* 130

American Association for Cancer Research, *1900s:* 101

American Association for the Hard of Hearing, *1910s:* 113

American Association of Labor Legislation (AALL), *1910s:* 120; *1940s:* 117

American Association of Retired Persons (AARP), *1970s:* 110; *1990s:* 122

American Association of Science Workers, *1940s:* 109

American Association of University Professors (AAUP), *1910s:* 46; *1950s:* 50, 62

American Automobile Association (AAA), *1900s:* 78

American Ballet, *1920s:* 3

American Ballet Caravan, *1930s:* 22

American Ballet Company, *1930s:* 22

American Bandstand, 1950s: 2, 109

American Bank and Trust Company, *1970s:* 27

American Banking Association, *1950s:* 38

American Bar Association, *1950s:* 68

American Basketball Association (ABA), *1960s:* 166, 177–78; *1970s:* 160–61, 167; *1980s:* 177–78

American Basketball League (ABL), *1920s:* 160; *1930s:* 160–61

American Birth Control League, *1920s:* 102

American Bowling Congress, *1900s:* 138; *1950s:* 158

American Brands, *1960s:* 41

American Cancer Society, *1910s:* 112; *1940s:* 109; *1950s:* 115; *1980s:* 122

American Chemical Society, *1940s:* 108

American Child Health Organization, *1920s:* 117

American citizenship, *1910s:* 47

American College of Surgeons, *1910s:* 112–14

American College Test (ACT), *1980s:* 59

American crawl (swimming), *1900s:* 142

American Derby, *1910s:* 172

American Document, 1930s: 22

American Dream, *1920s:* 5

American Education Fellowship, *1940s:* 44

American Education Week, *1920s:* 46

American Eugenics Society (AES), *1930s:* 142–43

American Expeditionary Forces (AEF), *1910s:* 71, 77

American experience, writers on, *1930s:* 12–14

American Export and Isbrandsten Lines, *1960s:* 31

American Express Company, *1950s:* 38; *1980s:* 17; *1990s:* 32

American Federation of Labor (AFL), *1900s:* 40; *1910s:* 29, 36–39, 46, 120; *1920s:* 25; *1930s:* 27, 38; *1940s:* 39

American Federation of Labor and Congress of Industrial Organizations. *See* AFL-CIO

American Federation of Musicians, *1940s:* 2

American Federation of Teachers (AFT), *1910s:* 47; *1930s:* 47, 51, 54–56; *1980s:* 64

American Football League (AFL), *1960s:* 165–66, 179–81; *1970s:* 170–71

American Gothic, 1930s: 8, 9 (ill.)

American Graffiti, 1970s: 18

American Heart Association, *1960s:* 120, 138; *1970s:* 123; *1980s:* 122

The American Heritage Dictionary, 1980s: 9

The American High School Today, 1950s: 50

American Historical Association, *1960s:* 53

American history, in schools, *1940s:* 45; *1960s:* 48, 52–53

American Hospital Association (AHA), *1930s:* 113

American Humane Association (AHA), *1980s:* 112

American Impressionism, *1900s:* 3, 8

American Independent Oil, *1960s:* 41

An American in Paris, 1920s: 6

American Institute of Architects, *1910s:* 94

American Institute of Architects' Gold Medal, *1940s:* 90

American Institue of Psychoanalysis, *1930s:* 114

American Interplanetary Society, *1930s:* 130

Americanism platform, *1910s:* 84

Americanization Movement, *1900s:* 44–45, 47, 61

American Journal of Public Health, *1920s:* 115

American Journal of the Diseases of Childhood, 1930s: 110

American League (baseball), *1900s:* 138, 141, 144; *1910s:* 154–55, 157, 161–62; *1920s:* 154–60; *1930s:* 158; *1960s:* 164, 174

American League pennant, *1940s:* 161

American Legion, *1910s:* 67; *1930s:* 60; *1970s:* 133–34

American Locomotive Company, *1940s:* 25

American Lutheran Church, *1930s:* 88

American Lung Association, *1900s:* 113; *1980s:* 122

American Medical Association (AMA), *1900s:* 100–01, 103, 105, 109–10, 114; *1920s:* 111, 118; *1930s:* 114, 118, 120, 125; *1940s:* 108, 110, 117–18; *1950s:* 125–26; *1960s:* 129–31, 138; *1990s:* 121
   health insurance, *1910s:* 113, 121
   medical schools, *1910s:* 113
   truth in advertising, *1910s:* 115, 127

American modern design, *1950s:* 103

American Mutoscope, *1910s:* 14

American Olympic Association, *1920s:* 148

American Peace League, *1910s:* 50

American Physical Society, *1930s:* 146

American Polar Society, *1930s:* 131

American Professional Football Association (APFA), *1920s:* 163

American Protective League (APL), *1910s:* 98

American Psychiatric Association, *1970s:* 98, 122

American Psychological Association, *1900s:* 123

American Red Cross, *1910s:* 122, 123 (ill.), 122 (ill.); *1940s:* 108, 112

American Rocket Society, *1930s:* 130

American School Citizenship League, *1910s:* 50

American School of the Air, 1930s: 46

Americans for the Republic, *1980s:* 97

American Society for Clinical Investigation, *1900s:* 101

American Society of Composers, Authors, and Publishers (ASCAP), *1910s:* 2

American Society of Orthodontists, *1910s:* 113

Americans with Disabilities Act (ADA), *1990s:* 74

American Symphony Orchestra, *1960s:* 3

American Telephone and Telegraph (AT&T), *1920s:* 38, 128; *1940s:* 25

American Tennis Association (ATA), *1930s:* 168

American Theatre Wing Antoinette Perry Awards. *See* Tony Awards

American Tobacco Company, *1900s:* 58, 65; *1910s:* 24, 66; *1930s:* 36
   See also American Brands

American Top 40, 1970s: 2

An American Tragedy, 1900s: 6

American Viscose Company, *1910s:* 90

American Woman Athlete of the Year, *1930s:* 156; *1940s:* 156

America's Cup, *1930s:* 152

Ames, Joseph S., *1940s:* 137

Amino acids, *1900s:* 104; *1960s:* 148, 151

Amnesty International, *1980s:* 3, 27

Amos and Andy, 1930s: 18

Ampex system, *1950s:* 137

Amphetamines, *1940s:* 108

AMPS (Bell Laboratory's Advance Mobile Phone System), *1990s:* 155

Amtrak, *1970s:* 39

Amundsen, Roald, *1910s:* 132

Amundsen-Scott South Pole Station, *1990s:* 131

Amusement parks, *1910s:* 90

Amyotrophic lateral sclerosis (ALS), *1920s:* 152; *1940s:* 152

Amy Vanderbilt's Complete Book of Etiquette, 1950s: 90

Anaconda Copper Mining Company, *1940s:* 38

Anaheim Amigos, *1960s:* 177

Anaheim Mighty Ducks, *1990s:* 176

"Anarchy in the U.K.," *1970s:* 14

Anchors Aweigh, 1930s: 17

Anderson, Bronco Billy, *1900s:* 11

Anderson, Carl David, *1930s:* 144

Anderson, J. Reid, *1980s:* 44

Anderson, Marian, *1950s:* 3

Anderson, Sherwood, *1910s:* 10; *1930s:* 12

Anderson, W. French, *1990s:* 116

Anderson, Willie, *1900s:* 142

Andreessen, Marc, *1990s:* 142, 142 (ill.)

Andrews, Fannie Fern Phillips, *1910s:* 50

Andromeda, *1920s:* 132

Andropov, Yuri, *1980s:* 90

And The Band Played On, 1980s: 128

And to Think that I Saw It on Mulberry Street, 1930s: 3

The Andy Griffith Show, 1960s: 19

Anemia, *1910s:* 126; *1920s:* 113; *1960s:* 123, 136

Anesthesia, *1900s:* 102, 107
     during childbirth, *1960s:* 134

Anesthetics, *1930s:* 112, 116–17

Angel, 1930s: 15

"Angel Baby," *1960s:* 11

Angelou, Maya, *1990s:* 100

Angels in America, 1980s: 128

Animal research, *1960s:* 125

Animal rights, *1980s:* 133

The Animals, *1960s:* 10

Animal testing, *1900s:* 109, 130

Animal tissue, in medicine, *1950s:* 114

Animated cartoons, *1900s:* 79

Animated films, *1930s:* 3; *1940s:* 13

Anna Christie, 1920s: 7

Anna T. Jeanes Foundation, *1900s:* 41

Annenberg Challenge Grant, *1990s:* 48

Annenberg, Walter H., *1990s:* 48, 48 (ill.)

Annie Get Your Gun, 1930s: 3, 17

Annie Hall, 1970s: 99, 103

Anorexia, *1980s:* 122–23, 125, 138–40

Antabus, *1950s:* 114

Antarctica
     global warming, *1990s:* 150
     ozone layer, *1980s:* 146, 158

An Anthology of Famous English and American Poetry, 1930s: 3

Anthracite Coal Strike, *1900s:* 20, 23, 26–27, 58

Anthropology, *1930s:* 134; *1960s:* 145, 148

Anthropology, human remains, *1980s:* 146

Antiabortion movement, *1970s:* 89–90
     See also Roe v. *Wade*

Antianxiety drugs, *1960s:* 120, 122

Antiapartheid Protest Day, *1980s:* 62

Antiballistic Missile (ABM) Treaty, *1970s:* 80

Antiballistic missiles (ABMs), *1980s:* 78

Antibiotics, *1900s:* 100; *1930s:* 111; *1940s:* 109, 118–19; *1950s:* 114–15, 123

Anticommunism, *1940s:* 67, 79–82, 81 (ill.); *1970s:* 82–83
     education and, *1940s:* 48–51
     motion picture industry and, *1940s:* 3, 5, 14
     Perkins, Frances, *1940s:* 69
     in schools, *1940s:* 50–51
     Sinatra, Frank and, *1940s:* 7
     Trotskyites, *1940s:* 78
     Wright, Richard, *1940s:* 7
     See also House Un-American Activities Committee

Anticonvulsant drugs, *1960s:* 120

Anti-German feelings, *1910s:* 99

Antihistamines, *1940s:* 119

Antinerve gas pill, Gulf War syndrome, *1990s:* 124–25

Antinuclear conference, *1980s:* 96

Antinuclear movement, *1980s:* 96, 113–15, 114 (ill.)

Antiobesity drug, *1990s:* 117

Antioch College, *1930s:* 59

Antiparticle, *1930s:* 143

Antipoverty campaign, *1960s:* 68, 70, 82, 85

Antiquities Act, *1900s:* 68

Anti-Riot Act, *1960s:* 115

Anti-Saloon League (ASL), *1900s:* 86; *1930s:* 92

Anti-Semites, *1940s:* 86

Antiseptics, *1900s:* 102

Antismoking campaigns, *1960s:* 120, 138

Antitrust laws, *1900s:* 32, 34, 64–65, 74; *1910s:* 24, 31; *1940s:* 25; *1990s:* 28–29, 32

    American Tobacco Company, *1910s:* 66

    baseball, *1910s:* 155; *1920s:* 154; *1950s:* 158; *1970s:* 160, 165–66

    football, *1950s:* 158; *1970s:* 161

    Harding, Warren G. and, *1920s:* 33

    IBM, *1980s:* 42–44

    Sherman Anti-Trust Act, *1920s:* 154

Anti-Lynching Bill, *1920s:* 64

Antiviral drugs, *1990s:* 125

Antivivisectionism, *1900s:* 109, 130

Antiwar protests, *1910s:* 19, 53, 96–98; *1960s:* 36, 69, 71, 78–79, 84, 97, 103 (ill.); *1970s:* 2, 6, 48, 76, 79

    Catch-22 as, *1960s:* 19

    on college campuses, *1960s:* 47, 49, 63–65

    at Democratic National Convention, *1960s:* 71, 86, 103, 114–15

    Muhammad Ali, *1960s:* 165, 167–68

    by Spock, Benjamin, *1960s:* 99

AOL Time-Warner, *1990s:* 40

Aortic aneurysms, *1960s:* 124

Aorta transplants, *1950s:* 114

Apartheid, *1980s:* 62

Apartment buildings, *1920s:* 89, 99–100; *1950s:* 90

APFA (American Professional Football Association), *1920s:* 163

Aphadinitrophenol, *1930s:* 110

APL (American Protective League), *1910s:* 98

Aplastic anemia, *1960s:* 123

Apocalypse Now, *1970s:* 6

Apollo 11, *1960s:* 6, 143–44, 159

Apollo missions, *1970s:* 140, 145–46

Apollo 7, *1960s:* 143, 159

Apollo-Soyuz, *1970s:* 141, 146

Apollo 12, *1960s:* 143

Apostoli, Fred, *1930s:* 162

Appalachian Spring, *1930s:* 6

Appendicitis, *1930s:* 110

Apple Computer, *1970s:* 43–44, 141; *1980s:* 43, 146, 160–61; *1990s:* 28

Apple 1, *1970s:* 43

Apple II, *1970s:* 43, 141

AppleWriter, *1970s:* 44

Appliances, *1910s:* 102, 134, 144

Applied science, versus pure, *1940s:* 133

Apps, Syl, *1930s:* 166

"April Showers," *1920s:* 7

The Aquarian Conspiracy, *1980s:* 96, 118

Aqueduct (horseracing), *1920s:* 148, 167

Arbor Day, *1900s:* 79

Arbuckle, Roscoe "Fatty," *1920s:* 104

Arcaro, Eddie, *1940s:* 156, 156 (ill.)

Archaeology, *1940s:* 131, 136–37; *1960s:* 145, 148; *1970s:* 140, 148–51, 151 (ill.)

Arch Award, *1930s:* 162

Archer, Dennis, *1990s:* 100

Architecture, *1900s:* 5, 81, 96–97; *1910s:* 91–92, 94, 100–01; *1920s:* 86; *1930s:* 97–98; *1940s:* 90, 92–93; *1960s:* 99

    art deco, *1920s:* 99

    Bauhaus, *1920s:* 97–98; *1930s:* 133

    Chicago Tribune Company Building, *1920s:* 97, 98 (ill.)

    in Florida, *1920s:* 91

Johnson Wax Building, *1930s:* 89, 93

Oriental theme, *1920s:* 87

Wrigley Building, *1920s:* 86

ziggurat design, *1920s:* 98–99

See also names of architects; names of specific schools of design

Archive of American Folk Song, *1930s:* 20

Arctic ice cap, global warming, *1990s:* 150

Arden, Elizabeth, *1940s:* 28, 28 (ill.)

Arendt, Hannah, *1940s:* 90, 90 (ill.)

Argentina, *1910s:* 73

Argüelles, José, *1980s:* 117

Ariadne auf Naxos, 1910s: 16

Aristide, Jean-Bertrand, *1990s:* 69

Arizona, statehood, *1910s:* 66

Arlington Classic, *1930s:* 165

Armat, George, *1910s:* 11

Armistice Day, *1920s:* 64; *1930s:* 3

Armistice, World War I, *1910s:* 67, 78, 85

The Armory Show, *1910s:* 2, 8, 12

Arms control, *1970s:* 72, 75, 80

Arms race, *1960s:* 75–76

Armstrong, Debbie, *1980s:* 188

Armstrong, Edwin H., *1910s:* 148; *1920s:* 128, 144–45

Armstrong, Henry, *1930s:* 153, 162

Armstrong, Lance, *1990s:* 163, 163 (ill.), 166

Armstrong, Louis, *1920s:* 2, 6, 6 (ill.), 12; *1940s:* 16; *1960s:* 2

Armstrong, Neil A., *1960s:* 144, 159

Army, *1910s:* 96

Army football team, *1940s:* 156, 167

Army Medical Corps, *1940s:* 120

Army-Navy football games, *1900s:* 151

Army-navy surplus stores, *1960s:* 111

Army of the Republic of Vietnam (ARVN), *1970s:* 78

Arnaz, Desi, *1950s:* 17, 19, 30; *1960s:* 2

ARPA (Advanced Research Projects Agency), *1990s:* 145

ARPANET, *1990s:* 145–47

"Arsenal of democracy," *1940s:* 64

Art, *1950s:* 2, 8

Art collections, *1940s:* 2

Art Deco, *1930s:* 90, 95

Arteries, *1950s:* 114–15

Art exhibitions, *1900s:* 3

Art exhibits, *1940s:* 2–3, 8; *1960s:* 113–14; *1970s:* 3, 8

Arthritis, *1970s:* 136

Arthur Murray Party, 1950s: 109

Artificial hearts, *1960s:* 121–22, 124, 126–27; *1980s:* 122–23, 126, 130–34, 132 (ill.)

Artificial insemination, *1960s:* 122, 134

Artificial pneumothorax, *1910s:* 130

Artificial suntanning cream, *1960s:* 142

Artificial sweeteners, *1960s:* 121–23, 135

Artificial valves, heart, *1950s:* 114

Artillery shells, *1910s:* 135, 151

Art nouveau, *1900s:* 83; *1910s:* 103

Art of This Century Gallery, *1940s:* 8

Art Ross Trophy, *1990s:* 177

Arts and crafts movement, *1900s:* 5, 81, 97

Arts and entertainment, *1900s:* 1–17; *1910s:* 1–23; *1920s:* 1–21; *1930s:* 1–24; *1940s:* 1–21; *1950s:* 1–20; *1960s:* 1–21; *1970s:* 1–24; *1980s:* 1–27

Black Arts Movement, *1960s:* 114

chronology, *1900s:* 2–3; *1910s:* 2–3; *1920s:* 2–3; *1930s:* 2–3; *1940s:* 2–3; *1950s:* 2; *1960s:* 2–3; *1970s:* 2–3; *1980s:* 2–3

corporate funding of, *1960s:* 27, 31–32

cultural events spending, *1980s:* 3

headline makers, *1900s:* 6–7; *1910s:* 6–7; *1920s:* 6–7; *1930s:* 6–7; *1940s:* 6–7; *1950s:* 6–7; *1960s:* 6–7; *1980s:* 6–7

impact on sports, *1930s:* 155

National Endowment for the
Arts, *1960s:* 113–14
overview, *1900s:* 4–5; *1910s:* 4–5;
1920s: 4–5; *1930s:* 4–5; *1940s:*
4–5; *1950s:* 4–5; *1960s:* 4–5;
1970s: 4–5; *1980s:* 4–5
versus politics, *1980s:* 8–9
Arts, in education, *1900s:* 40, 48
ARVN (Army of the Republic of Viet-
nam), *1970s:* 78
ASCAP (American Society of Com-
posers, Authors, and Publishers),
1910s: 2
Ascorbic acid. *See* Vitamin C
"Ash Can" paintings, *1910s:* 5
The "Ash Can" School, *1910s:* 4, 8
(ill.), 9; *1920s:* 17
Ashe, Arthur, *1960s:* 165; *1970s:* 161,
176
Ashford, Emmett, *1960s:* 165
Ash, Mary Kay, *1960s:* 28, 28 (ill.), 42
Asian Americans, *1990s:* 38
Asian flu, *1950s:* 116, 120
As I Lay Dying, 1930s: 7
Asimov, Issac, *1950s:* 16
ASL (Anti-Saloon League), *1900s:* 86;
1930s: 92
As Nasty As They Want to Be, 1980s: 24
Aspirin, *1910s:* 128; *1960s:* 120
Assassination attempts, Wallace,
George, *1970s:* 85
Assassinations, *1930s:* 83; *1960s:* 4
Evers, Medgar, *1960s:* 101–02
Kennedy, John F., *1960s:* 6, 20,
68, 70, 72, 85, 94, 96, 100, 104
Kennedy, Robert, *1960s:* 69–72,
86, 96, 100
King, Martin Luther, Jr., *1960s:*
69–72, 96, 100
Malcolm X, *1960s:* 69–70, 97,
99–101, 104–05
McKinley, William, *1900s:* 58, 70
Assault Weapons Ban. *See* Violent
Crime Control and Law Enforce-
ment Act
Assembly lines, *1900s:* 35, 35 (ill.),
91; *1910s:* 26, 34, 36, 101, 132,
134, 141; *1920s:* 29

Assimilation. *See* Americanization
Movement
Assisted suicide, *1990s:* 116–17
Association for the Study of Negro
Life and History, *1910s:* 51
Association of American Medical Col-
leges, *1900s:* 100–01
Association of American Painters and
Sculptors, *1910s:* 2, 12
Astaire, Adele, *1930s:* 2
Astaire, Fred, *1920s:* 9; *1930s:* 2, 18;
1940s: 17
Asteroids, *1980s:* 146, 150
Asthma, *1980s:* 141, 156
Astor, Mary, *1940s:* 15
Astrology, *1980s:* 78, 117
Astronauts, *1960s:* 142–43, 146
women, *1970s:* 99; *1980s:* 150
See also specific astronauts by
name
Astronomy, *1900s:* 133; *1910s:*
133–37, 139; *1960s:* 144, 149–51;
1980s: 146–47
ASV (Air-to-Surface Vessel) radar,
1940s: 143
Asylums, *1910s:* 116
ATA (American Tennis Association),
1930s: 168
Atanasoff Berry Computer (ABC),
1940s: 130
AT&T, *1920s:* 38, 128; *1940s:* 25;
1960s: 25
color television and, *1950s:* 142
FCC and, *1950s:* 24
stockholders, *1950s:* 24, 42
transatlantic cable, *1950s:* 143
Western Union and, *1950s:* 24
ATF (Bureau of Alcohol, Tobacco, and
Firearms), *1990s:* 81
Athletes
drug abuse in, *1990s:* 184
drug-enhanced performance,
1950s: 115
of the century, *1990s:* 165
professional, *1900s:* 141
student, *1980s:* 58–60
top twenty, *1990s:* 184
See also Sports

Athletic programs, for women, *1970s:* 62, 62 (ill.)

Athletic shoes, *1970s:* 30

Atkins, Robert C., *1990s:* 120, 120 (ill.)

Atkin v. Kansas, 20, *1900s:* 34

Atlanta Braves, *1910s:* 163–64; *1960s:* 174–75; *1990s:* 168

"Atlanta Compromise," *1900s:* 52, 63

Atlanta, Georgia
    race riots, *1900s:* 59
    school system, *1900s:* 40

Atlanta Hawks, *1960s:* 176

The Atlantic Monthly, 1910s: 11

Atlantic Ocean, nonstop flights, *1910s:* 133

Atlantis (space shuttle), *1990s:* 142

ATMs (Automatic teller machines), *1980s:* 159

"Atom Bomb Baby," *1930s:* 144

"Atom Buster," *1930s:* 144

Atomic bombs, *1930s:* 131, 135, 140, 144–47; *1940s:* 65, 69, 76–78, 77 (ill.), 80, 109, 130–35, 143–48, 145 (ill.), 147 (ill.)

Atomic Cocktail, *1940s:* 144

Atomic Energy Commission (United Nations), *1910s:* 28; *1930s:* 135; *1940s:* 131; *1960s:* 142–43

Atomic number, *1930s:* 143

Atomic physics, *1910s:* 132, 139–40

Atomic power plants, *1950s:* 25

Atomic weights, *1910s:* 137

"Atom Polka," *1930s:* 144

Atoms, *1930s:* 143

Attendance, at baseball games, *1900s:* 145

Attica State Correctional Facility, *1970s:* 70, 92–93

Attlee, Clement, *1940s:* 79–80

Auden, W. H., *1940s:* 2

Audion, *1900s:* 119, 122, 128

Audrey Rose, 1970s: 18

Auerbach, Arnold "Red," *1960s:* 169, 176

Augusta National Golf Course, *1930s:* 152, 164; *1940s:* 168

Australian Open, *1990s:* 181

Australia II, 1980s: 168

Australopithecus, 1970s: 150

Australopithecus afarensis, 1970s: 151

Austria-Hungary, *1910s:* 66–67, 75, 77–78

Austro-Hungarian Americans, *1910s:* 96

Authority, respect for, *1950s:* 104–05

Autio, Asario, *1900s:* 139

The Autobiography of an Idea, 1920s: 86

Automobile Club of America, *1900s:* 78

Automobile industry, *1900s:* 21, 78, 81, 119–20, 124–25; *1910s:* 91, 103–05, 142–43, 143 (ill.); *1920s:* 26, 28–29, 34–35, 130; *1930s:* 27, 38, 94–95, 130–31; *1940s:* 25, 86–87; *1950s:* 27, 92; *1960s:* 27, 95, 97, 106; *1970s:* 28–29, 32, 40
    advertisements, *1900s:* 20
    advertising, *1940s:* 158–59
    airbags, *1990s:* 117
    birth of, *1900s:* 22, 91
    Chevrolet, *1950s:* 30, 40, 41 (ill.)
    Chrysler, *1950s:* 136
    Durant, William C., *1910s:* 28
    Ford, Henry in, *1900s:* 24, 34–35, 35 (ill.)
    Ford Motor Company, *1950s:* 24–25, 99
    franchises in, *1960s:* 34–35
    hydraulic brakes, *1910s:* 133
    imports, *1960s:* 30–31
    National Highway Act, *1950s:* 40
    new brands in, *1900s:* 78
    passenger cars, *1950s:* 98–99
    postwar technology, *1940s:* 102
    safety, *1960s:* 25, 29
    smog and, *1960s:* 126
    strikes, *1940s:* 24; *1960s:* 24–25
    suburbs and, *1940s:* 102
    unemployment benefits, *1950s:* 24
    windshields, *1940s:* 86
    See also Ford Motor Company

Automobile races, *1900s:* 139

Automobile racing, *1910s:* 154, 156, 160–61; *1930s:* 155; *1940s:* 158–59; *1960s:* 166, 170–72, 171 (ill.)

Auto shows, *1900s:* 78

Autry, Gene, *1930s:* 18

"Avalon," *1920s:* 7

Avalon, Frankie, *1960s:* 10, 108

Avant-garde films, *1960s:* 15–16

Avertin, *1930s:* 116

Aviation, *1900s:* 20, 22, 118–19, 123, 125–27; *1920s:* 26, 34, 128, 134–41; *1930s:* 134–38
> military, *1940s:* 137–38
> *See also* Air travel

Avis, *1960s:* 40

Axis powers, *1940s:* 70

Azidothymidine (AZT), for AIDS, *1980s:* 123, 130

B

BAA (Basketball Association of America), *1940s:* 153, 162; *1950s:* 168

Babies
> cyanosis and, *1940s:* 112
> milk for, *1900s:* 101
> mortality of, *1930s:* 111; *1940s:* 111
> premature, *1960s:* 121
> *See also* Infants

Baboons, heart transplants, *1980s:* 133

Babson Institute and School of Management, *1920s:* 28

Babson, Roger, *1920s:* 28

Baby boom, *1940s:* 87, 96–98

Baby boomers, *1950s:* 62–63, 99; *1960s:* 7

Baby boom generation, *1970s:* 111

Baby Doll, 1950s: 91

Baby Fae, *1980s:* 122, 124, 133

Baby food, *1950s:* 42

"Baby I Love You," *1960s:* 15

"Baby I Need Your Loving," *1960s:* 14

Baby M, *1980s:* 124, 134–35, 135 (ill.)

Baby's Milk Fund, *1900s:* 101

Bacillus Calmette-Guerin vaccine (BCG), *1920s:* 114–15

Back-to-basics. *See* Traditionalism, educational

Back to the Future, 1980s: 7, 9

Bacteria, *1950s:* 123

Bacteria, genome mapping, *1990s:* 138, 142

Bacterial infections, *1910s:* 122; *1940s:* 118

Bacteriological laboratories, *1910s:* 125

Bacteriological warfare, *1940s:* 109

Bad, 1980s: 3

Baekeland, Leo Hendrik, *1910s:* 146

Baer, George F., *1900s:* 27

Baer, Max, *1930s:* 161–62

Baez, Joan, *1930s:* 7; *1960s:* 113

Bahrain, *1990s:* 68

Baikonur Cosmodrome, *1990s:* 159

Bailey, F. Lee, *1990s:* 86

Bailey, Leonard, *1980s:* 133

Baisley, Beth, *1980s:* 59 (ill.)

Baker, Frank "Home Run," *1900s:* 163; *1920s:* 156

Baker, George, *1910s:* 90

Baker House, *1940s:* 92

Baker International Corporation, *1980s:* 62

Baker, Newton D., *1910s:* 70, 70 (ill.), 96

Bakke, Allen, *1970s:* 49, 52, 52 (ill.), 64–65

Bakker, Jim, *1970s:* 102, 102 (ill.); *1980s:* 97, 115–16

Bakker, Tammy Faye, *1970s:* 102, 102 (ill.)

Baldwin, James, *1940s:* 13

Ballantine Publishing, *1950s:* 16

Ballard, Del Jr., *1990s:* 164

Ballard, Robert, *1970s:* 144, 144 (ill.); *1980s:* 146

Ballesteros, Seve, *1980s:* 183

Ballet, *1910s:* 2, 9–10, 10 (ill.)

Ballet Russes, *1910s:* 9

Ballistic Missile Defense Program, *1980s:* 80

Ball, Lucille, *1950s:* 4, 17, 19, 30; *1960s:* 2

Balloon bombs, *1940s:* 137

Ballooning, *1900s:* 125; *1940s:* 131

Balloons, in astronomy, *1960s:* 149

Ballroom dancing, *1910s:* 90, 106; *1950s:* 109

Baltimore Bullets, *1950s:* 169; *1960s:* 176

Baltimore Colts, *1950s:* 159–60, 173–74; *1960s:* 165–66, 179–80; *1980s:* 180–81; *1990s:* 175

Baltimore Orioles, *1910s:* 159; *1950s:* 168; *1960s:* 169, 173, 175

Baltimore Ravens, *1990s:* 175

Balto, *1920s:* 109

Banana Republic, *1980s:* 106

Band Aid (concert), *1980s:* 2, 5, 24

The Bangles, *1980s:* 19

Bank failures, *1970s:* 27

Bank Holding Company Act of 1958, *1950s:* 38

Banking, *1910s:* 24, 32; *1980s:* 30, 36, 38, 159

Banking industry, *1920s:* 24, 27, 29, 38–43, 65; *1930s:* 26, 42 (ill.)
   American Banking Association, *1950s:* 38
   Bank Holding Company Act of 1958, *1950s:* 38
   Bank of America, *1950s:* 37–38
   Chase-Manhattan Bank, *1950s:* 42
   children and, *1930s:* 59
   Morgan, J. P. and, *1930s:* 41
   Roosevelt, Franklin D. and, *1930s:* 41–42, 68, 76, 78–79

Bank of America, *1920s:* 29, 38; *1930s:* 36; *1950s:* 37–38

Bank of the United States, *1930s:* 26, 68

Bankruptcy
   Greyhound, *1990s:* 28
   Pan American World Airways, *1990s:* 28
   saving and loan institutions, *1980s:* 30

Banks, *1910s:* 25
   failure of, *1900s:* 21, 28
   regulation of, *1900s:* 33
   in rural communities, *1900s:* 32

Banks, Ernie, *1950s:* 164

The Bank Street School of Education, *1910s:* 51

Banting, Frederick Grant, *1920s:* 118–19

Baptists, *1940s:* 99

Baraka, Amiri, *1960s:* 114

Bara, Theda, *1920s:* 94

Barber, Samuel, *1930s:* 20

Barbershops, *1900s:* 93, 95

Barberton, South Africa, *1960s:* 148

Bardeen, John, *1950s:* 142

Barker, Fred, *1930s:* 85

Barker, Len, *1980s:* 175

Barker, "Ma," *1930s:* 72, 72 (ill.), 85

Barkley, Charles, *1980s:* 177; *1990s:* 172

Barnard, Christiaan, *1960s:* 121, 127

Barnes, Djuna, *1920s:* 3, 13

Barnett, Dick, *1960s:* 177; *1970s:* 169

Barnett, James H., *1990s:* 128

Barnstorming, *1920s:* 134–35

Barrie, Dennis, *1990s:* 2, 8

Barrow, Clyde, *1930s:* 82; *1960s:* 10

Barr, Stringfellow, *1940s:* 53

Barry, Jack, *1910s:* 163

Barrymore, Ethel, *1910s:* 19

Barrymore, John, *1910s:* 19; *1920s:* 3

Barrymore, Lionel, *1910s:* 19

Barry, Philip, *1920s:* 3–4

Bartók, Béla, *1930s:* 20

Barton, Bruce, *1920s:* 90, 90 (ill.)

Barton, Otis, *1930s:* 131

Barton, Sid, *1920s:* 167

Baruch, Bernard M., *1910s:* 28, 28 (ill.), 31

Barzun, Jacques, *1940s:* 53

Baseball, *1900s:* 138–39, 141, 143–46; *1910s:* 154–55, 157, 160–62; *1920s:* 148–50, 152–60; *1930s:* 152–53, 158–60, 164; *1940s:* 152, 154–55, 157, 159–63, 160 (ill.), 163 (ill.); *1950s:* 158–60, 164–68, 165 (ill.); *1960s:* 164–66, 168–69, 172–75; *1970s:* 160–61, 165–66; *1980s:* 168, 174–77, 175 (ill.)
   record breakers, *1990s:* 168–71
   strikes, *1990s:* 163–64, 168

Baseball commissioners, *1940s:* 152–53

Baseball Hall of Fame, *1900s:* 143; *1910s:* 158; *1940s:* 152, 157

Baseball Writers' Association of America, *1930s:* 152, 160

BASIC (programming language), *1960s:* 152; *1970s:* 44–45

Basie, Count, *1930s:* 3, 5, 20; *1940s:* 16

Basketball, *1900s:* 139, 141, 146–48, 147 (ill.); *1910s:* 156, 164–67, 165 (ill.); *1920s:* 160; *1930s:* 160–61; *1940s:* 152–54, 161–65, 164 (ill.); *1950s:* 168–70; *1960s:* 165–67, 169, 175–78; *1970s:* 160–61, 166–69, 168 (ill.); *1980s:* 168, 170, 172, 177–78; *1990s:* 164, 171–72
    championships, *1990s:* 172
    Dream Team, *1990s:* 172
    Jordan, Michael, *1990s:* 164–67, 166 (ill.), 171–72
    University of Tennessee Lady Volunteers, *1990s:* 163
    women's, *1990s:* 163, 167

Basketball Association of America (BAA), *1940s:* 153, 162; *1950s:* 168

The Basketball Diaries, 1980s: 9

Baskin-Robbins Ice Cream, *1950s:* 41; *1960s:* 35

Basquiat, Jean Michel, *1980s:* 12

Bass Weejuns, *1960s:* 111

Bateson, Gregory, *1940s:* 141

Baths, schools, *1900s:* 40

Bathyscaphes, *1960s:* 154

Bathysphere, *1930s:* 130–31

Batista, Fulgencio, *1930s:* 82; *1960s:* 76

Batman, *1940s:* 10

Batman, 1980s: 9

Batteries, *1900s:* 118

Batting titles, *1960s:* 168

Battle of Leyte Gulf, *1940s:* 73

Battle of Midway, *1940s:* 64, 72

Battle of the Atlantic, *1940s:* 70

Battle of the Bulge, *1940s:* 76

Battle of the Java Sea, *1940s:* 72

"Battle of the Sexes," *1970s:* 130, 160, 163–64, 176

Battle of the Somme, *1910s:* 150

Baugh, Sammy, *1930s:* 163

Bauhaus architecture, *1950s:* 104

Bauhaus design, *1930s:* 133

Baum, L. Frank, *1960s:* 150

Bayer aspirin, *1960s:* 120

Bayer Company, *1910s:* 128

Bay of Pigs, *1960s:* 68, 76–77

Bazaar (store), *1960s:* 111–12

Baziotes, William, *1940s:* 8

BCG (bacillus Calmette-Guerin vaccine), *1920s:* 114–15

BCG vaccine, *1940s:* 109

Beach Blanket Bingo, 1960s: 108

The Beach Boys, *1960s:* 11, 108

Beach Party, 1960s: 108

Beamon, Bob, *1960s:* 181

Beard, Charles, *1930s:* 50, 50 (ill.)

Beard, Charles Austin, *1910s:* 50, 50 (ill.)

Bearden, Romare, *1970s:* 8

Beat generation, *1950s:* 3, 5, 9–10

"Beat It," *1980s:* 19

Beatlemania, *1960s:* 6

The Beatles, *1960s:* 2–3, 5–6, 6 (ill.), 10–12, 108; *1980s:* 21

Beatrice International Foods, *1980s:* 31, 34

Beatty, Jim, *1960s:* 164

Beatty, Warren, *1960s:* 8 (ill.)

Beaux-Arts, *1910s:* 92, 94, 100–01

Bebop, *1940s:* 16–17, 16 (ill.)

Beck, Dave, *1950s:* 34–35, 34 (ill.)

Beckman, Johnny, *1910s:* 166

Beckwith, Jonathan, *1960s:* 150

Becky Sharp, 1920s: 144

Bedtime for Bonzo, 1980s: 80

Beebe, Charles William, *1930s:* 131

Bee Gees, *1970s:* 16

Beer, *1930s:* 131

Beetle (car), *1960s:* 30–31, 95

Begin, Menachem, *1970s:* 71

Behavioral psychology, *1940s:* 113; *1960s:* 125

Behaviorism, *1920s:* 103

Beiderbecke, Bix, *1920s:* 3, 13

Belafonte, Harry, *1980s:* 24

Believe, 1980s: 26

Beliveau, Jean, *1980s:* 169

Bell, Alexander Graham, *1900s:* 126; *1910s:* 133

Belleau Wood battle, *1910s:* 78

Bellevue-Stratford Hotel, *1970s:* 133

Bell, James "Cool Papa," *1930s:* 160

Bell Laboratories, *1920s:* 128–29, 131; *1950s:* 136–37, 142; *1960s:* 143; *1980s:* 146; *1990s:* 33, 154

Bell Laboratory's Advance Mobile Phone System (AMPS), *1990s:* 155

Bellow, Saul, *1940s:* 5, 12; *1970s:* 3

Bellows, George, *1900s:* 3; *1910s:* 8, 12; *1920s:* 2, 17

Bell P59-A, *1940s:* 130

Bell Telephone Company, *1910s:* 132; *1970s:* 152

Bell Telephone Laboratories, *1940s:* 141

Bell Telephone Systems, *1960s:* 25

Bell X-1 rocket, *1940s:* 131

The Belmont Stakes, *1910s:* 172; *1920s:* 166–67; *1930s:* 165

Beloved, 1990s: 19

Benadryl, 1940s: 119

Ben and Jerry's Ice Cream, *1990s:* 39

Ben Casey, 1960s: 19

Benchley, Peter, *1970s:* 10

Bender, Chief, *1910s:* 163

Benedict, Clint, *1930s:* 165

Benedict, Ruth, *1930s:* 134, 134 (ill.); *1940s:* 136–37

Ben Franklin stores, *1980s:* 43

Ben-Hur, 1950s: 106

Bennett, Harry, *1930s:* 38

Bennett, John W., *1940s:* 136

Bennett, Michael, *1970s:* 14

Bennett, William J., *1980s:* 52, 52 (ill.), 63

Bennie Goodman and His Orchestra, *1930s:* 3

Bennington College, *1930s:* 59

Benoit, Joan, *1980s:* 192

Benton, Thomas Hart, *1930s:* 6, 6 (ill.), 8

Benzedrene, *1940s:* 108

Benzedrine inhaler, *1930s:* 110

Benz, Karl, *1900s:* 124

Benzyl alcohol, *1930s:* 116

Berbick, Trevor, *1980s:* 169

Berea College v. Kentucky, 1900s: 41

Bergdorf Goodman, 1920s: 86

Berger, Hans, *1920s:* 115–16

Berg, Patricia "Patty," *1940s:* 154, 156, 156 (ill.), 170

Berkeley, Busby, *1920s:* 10; *1930s:* 18, 19 (ill.)

Berkeley top shot, *1930s:* 16

Berle, Adolf A., *1930s:* 35, 76

Berle, Milton "Uncle Miltie," *1940s:* 18; *1950s:* 4–6, 6 (ill.), 17, 30

Berliner, Emile, *1920s:* 140–41

Berlin, Irving, *1910s:* 2, 5–6, 6 (ill.), 17; *1920s:* 9, 12

Berlin Wall, *1960s:* 68; *1980s:* 91 (ill.)

Bermuda, global warming, *1990s:* 150

Bernstein, Carl, *1970s:* 74, 74 (ill.), 85–86

Bernstein, Leonard, *1940s:* 17; *1950s:* 3, 6, 6 (ill.), *1960s:* 2

Berry, Chuck, *1950s:* 15; *1960s:* 11

Berry, Raymond, *1950s:* 174

Berson, Soloman A., *1970s:* 126

Bertoia, Harry, *1950s:* 104

Berwanger, Jay, *1930s:* 153

Best, Charles, *1920s:* 118–19

Best-sellers, *1970s:* 11

Beta-dimethylaminoethyl benzhydryl ether hydrochloride, *1940s:* 119

Betelgeuse, *1920s:* 133

Bethe, Hans, *1930s:* 144; *1940s:* 133

Bethlehem Steel Company, *1900s:* 25

Bethlehem Steel Corporation, *1940s:* 38

Bethune-Cookman College, *1920s:* 50; *1930s:* 50; *1940s:* 90

Bethune, Mary McLeod, *1900s:* 41; *1920s:* 50, 50 (ill.); *1930s:* 50, 50 (ill.), 79; *1940s:* 90, 90 (ill.)

The Betsy, 1970s: 9

"Bette Davis Eyes," *1980s:* 19

Better Homes & Garden, 1920s: 100

Betty Crocker's Picture Cookbook, 1950s: 90

Bevatrons, *1950s:* 136

Beverages, alcoholic, health benefits of, *1970s:* 123

The Beverly Hillbillies, 1960s: 19

Beverly Hills Hotel, *1910s:* 90

Bezos, Jeff, *1990s:* 32, 32 (ill.)

Bhaktivedanta, A.C., *1970s:* 114

Bible in schools. *See* Church versus state

Bible, reading in school, *1920s:* 47, 87

Bibles, *1940s:* 86

Bicentennial (U.S.), *1970s:* 71

Bic pens, *1950s:* 41

Bicycling, *1930s:* 155

Biennial Survey of Education, 1910s: 58

Bifocal contact lenses, *1950s:* 137

Bigamy, *1930s:* 30

Big bands, *1940s:* 15–16

Big Bang theory, *1920s:* 132; *1940s:* 133; *1960s:* 145, 151; *1970s:* 144

The Big Bopper, *1950s:* 3

The Big Four, *1910s:* 78

Big Little Books, *1930s:* 12

The Big Sleep, 1930s: 15; *1940s:* 14

"Big stick" diplomacy, *1900s:* 73

Big Sulphur Creek, California, *1960s:* 153

Big Ten (college football), *1900s:* 150

Bikini Beach, 1960s: 108

Bikini Islands, *1940s:* 87, 144

Bilateral prefrontal lobotomy, *1930s:* 111

Bilingual education, *1960s:* 48, 52; *1970s:* 48, 50, 55–57; *1980s:* 60–62, 60 (ill.)

Bilingual Education Act of 1968, *1960s:* 55

Bill Haley and The Comets, *1950s:* 3

"Billie Jean," *1980s:* 19

Billionaires, *1980s:* 31

Bill Nye the Science Guy, 1990s: 48

Billy Jack, 1970s: 13

Biltmore Theatre, *1960s:* 3

Biochemistry, *1900s:* 101; *1960s:* 146, 150–52

Biograph Company, *1910s:* 7, 14

Biological sciences, public health and, *1910s:* 144–45, 145 (ill.)

Biological warfare, *1940s:* 137

Biologics Control Act, *1900s:* 100

Biology, *1900s:* 129–32; *1940s:* 139–40; *1960s:* 145, 150–52

Biology, molecular, *1950s:* 141

Biomedical research, *1940s:* 113

Biosphere 2, *1990s:* 138, 151–55, 153 (ill.)

Biplanes, *1910s:* 25, 138

Bird, Larry, *1980s:* 169–70, 172, 172 (ill.), 177; *1990s:* 172

Birdseye, Clarence, *1910s:* 144, 145 (ill.)

Bird's Eye Frozen Foods, *1930s:* 26

Birmingham, Alabama, *1960s:* 74, 102

Birmingham University, *1930s:* 141

Birnbach, Lisa, *1980s:* 96

Birth control, *1910s:* 91, 113, 117; *1920s:* 102, 108; *1930s:* 110–11, 117–18; *1940s:* 109; *1950s:* 91; *1960s:* 94, 120, 122, 133, 134 (ill.), 145, 154–56

    abortion inducing pill, *1990s:* 116

    oral contraception, *1990s:* 117

    See also Oral contraception

Birth Control Clinical Research Bureau, *1920s:* 102

Birth defects, *1940s:* 109; *1960s:* 121, 123, 125, 135–36

Birth defects, Gulf War Syndrome, *1990s:* 124

The Birth of a Nation, 7, 1910s: 14–15, 17; *1920s:* 71

Bishop, Katharine Scott, *1920s:* 123

Bjurstedt, Molla, *1910s:* 175 (ill.), 176

Black Art, 1970s: 8

Black Arts Movement, *1960s:* 114

Black baseball leagues, *1900s:* 145–46

"Black basketball," *1960s:* 176

The Blackboard Jungle, 1950s: 3

"Blackbottom Stomp," *1920s:* 3

Black Caesar, 1970s: 20

Black colleges, *1900s:* 41, 51, 63; *1940s:* 116

Black education. *See* African Americans, education

Black English, *1970s:* 49; *1990s:* 53

Blackenstein, 1970s: 20

Black Face and Arm Unit, 1970s: 8

Blackfather, 1970s: 20

Black history, *1910s:* 51; *1960s:* 53

The Black Hole, 1970s: 19

Black holes, *1910s:* 133; *1960s:* 149
Black, Hugo, *1930s:* 47
Black identity, *1970s:* 108–09
Black Legion, *1960s:* 104
Blacklist, *1940s:* 6, 14–15
Blacklist, Hollywood, *1950s:* 4, 13–15
Blackmail, 1920s: 143
Black Mask, 1920s: 19; *1930s:* 14
Black Mountain College, *1930s:* 59
Black Muslims, *1960s:* 99, 105
Black nationalism, *1960s:* 69
Black Panther Party, *1960s:* 94, 103
The Black Pirate, 1920s: 144
Black Pride, *1970s:* 108
Black Rock Club, *1940s:* 168
Black Scholar, 1970s: 66
Black separatism, *1960s:* 99, 105
Black Sox scandal, *1910s:* 155,
    157–58, 162; *1920s:* 148, 150,
    153–55
Black Star Line, *1910s:* 94
Black studies, *1970s:* 65–66
Black the Ripper, 1970s: 20
Black Tuesday, *1920s:* 40 (ill.), 43, 87
Blacula, 1970s: 20
Blair, Bonnie, *1980s:* 171, 192; *1990s:*
    165, 183, 183 (ill.)
The Blair Witch Project, 1990s: 3
Blake, Eubie, *1910s:* 17; *1920s:* 11
Blake, Toe, *1930s:* 166
Blalock, Alfred, *1940s:* 112, 112 (ill.)
Blanchard, Felix "Doc," *1940s:* 156,
    156 (ill.)
Blanc, Mel, *1930s:* 3
Blanda, George, *1960s:* 180
Blanding, Sarah G., *1940s:* 48, 48 (ill.)
Blatty, William Peter, *1970s:* 2
Blaxploitation films, *1970s:* 4, 20
Blimps, *1920s:* 139, 139 (ill.)
    See also. Dirigibles
Blindness, transplants for, *1950s:* 115
"Blitzkrieg Bop," *1970s:* 14
Blitzstein, Marc, *1930s:* 20–21
Blockade, of Cuba, *1960s:* 77
Blockbuster movies, *1970s:* 5, 17–19
Blondie, *1980s:* 19
Blood, *1950s:* 114–15, 132
Blood banks, *1930s:* 111; *1960s:* 120

Blood Circus, 1990s: 21
Blood diseases, *1940s:* 134
"Blood for Britain" campaign, *1940s:*
    112
Blood tests, AIDS, *1980s:* 123, 126
Blood transfusions, *1910s:* 113, 124;
    1940s: 108, 110, 112; *1960s:* 120
Blood tranfusions, AIDS, *1980s:* 124
Blood types, *1930s:* 115
Bloom, Allan, *1980s:* 52, 52 (ill.)
Bloom, Benjamin S., *1970s:* 52
"Blowin' in the Wind," *1960s:* 113
Bluebird (automobile), *1930s:* 153
Blue-collar workers, labor unions and,
    1950s: 27
Blue Cross insurance, *1930s:* 110,
    113, 118–20
Bluegrass music, *1940s:* 18
Blue-Gray Game, *1930s:* 163
Blue Shield insurance, *1930s:* 113,
    119
Blues music, *1900s:* 5, 13–14; 7, 17;
    1920s: 12; *1930s:* 3, 20; *1940s:* 17
The Bluest Eye, 1970s: 2, 7, 10
Blue, Vida, *1970s:* 166
Bluford, Guion S. Jr., *1980s:* 150, 150
    (ill.)
Blumer, George, *1900s:* 100
Bly, Robert, *1990s:* 92, 96, 96 (ill.),
    100–01
Blythe, William Jefferson IV. *See* Clinton, Bill
Board of Control for Southern Regional Education, *1940s:* 60
Boas, Franz, *1910s:* 132
The Bob Mathias Story, 1950s: 176
Bob Wills and the Texas Playboys,
    1940s: 17
Boca Raton, development of, *1920s:*
    91
Boeing Aircraft, *1910s:* 25; *1920s:* 34
Boeing Airplane Company, *1940s:* 28,
    96
Boeing B-39, *1940s:* 138
Boeing 747, *1970s:* 140, 149
Boeing 314, *1930s:* 137
Boeing 247, *1930s:* 136
Boeing, William, *1920s:* 34

Boeing, William Edward, *1940s:* 28, 28 (ill.)

Boesky, Ivan, *1980s:* 31, 34, 34 (ill.)

Bogart, Humphrey, *1930s:* 16; *1940s:* 2, 6, 6 (ill.), 15

Boggs, Wade, *1980s:* 176

Bohr, Niels Henrik David, *1910s:* 140; *1930s:* 146

Boitano, Brian, *1980s:* 192

Boland, Edward, *1980s:* 68

Bollingen poetry prize, *1940s:* 3

Bombings
    Oklahoma City, *1990s:* 64–65, 67, 81–83, 92–93
    Olympics, *1990s:* 182
    in Vietnam, *1970s:* 78–79
    World Trade Center, *1990s:* 64–65, 83

Bombs, *1910s:* 135, 150–51

Bomb shelters, *1950s:* 75

Bombs, hydrogen, *1940s:* 87, 146, 148
    See also Atomic bombs

Bond drives, *1940s:* 33

Bond, Horace Mann, *1930s:* 50

Bond, James, *1960s:* 9

B-1 bombers, *1980s:* 77, 79 (ill.)

Bonneville Salt Flats, *1930s:* 153

Bonnie and Clyde, 1960s: 8 (ill.), 10

Bontemps, Arna, *1920s:* 11

Bonthron, Bill, *1930s:* 168–69

Bonus Expeditionary Force, *1930s:* 74, 74 (ill.)

Bonus marches, *1930s:* 74, 74 (ill.)

Boogie-woogie, *1940s:* 17

Book publishing, paperbacks, *1940s:* 11

Books, *1950s:* 10, 52; *1970s:* 2, 4–5, 9–11; *1980s:* 12
    Amazon.com, *1990s:* 32
    clubs, *1990s:* 18
    Oprah Winfrey's Book Club, 1990s: 3, 5, 14, 18–20
    sales, *1990s:* 18
    top, *1990s:* 18
    See also specific titles

Boomtown Rats, *1980s:* 24

Boone, Debby, *1970s:* 13

Boorstin, Daniel, *1960s:* 53

Booth, Evangeline Cory, *1900s:* 82, 82 (ill.)

Bootlegging, *1920s:* 68, 72–74, 87; *1930s:* 68, 81, 85

Bop (music). *See* Jazz

Bop Till You Drop, 1970s: 3

Borg, Bjorn, *1980s:* 185

Borges, Jorgé Luis, *1970s:* 10

Bork, Robert H., *1970s:* 87; *1980s:* 69, 72, 72 (ill.)

Born in the USA, 1980s: 7

Borrelia burgdorferi, 1970s: 136

Bosker, Gideon, *1920s:* 95

Bosnia, *1990s:* 71–72

Boston Beaneaters. *See* Boston Red Sox

Boston Braves, *1910s:* 154–55, 163–64; *1950s:* 158, 168

Boston Bruins, *1920s:* 148; *1970s:* 173

Boston, busing in, *1970s:* 48–50, 54

Boston Celtics, *1910s:* 156, 166; *1950s:* 161, 168; *1960s:* 165–66, 169, 176–77; *1970s:* 169; *1980s:* 169, 172

Boston Institute of Contemporary Art, *1950s:* 2

Boston Latin School, *1990s:* 45

Boston Marathon, *1900s:* 138, 152

Boston, Massachusetts public schools, *1990s:* 45

Boston Patriots, *1960s:* 180

Boston police force, *1910s:* 25

Boston Red Sox, *1900s:* 144; *1910s:* 154–55, 157, 163–65; *1920s:* 153, 155; *1940s:* 153; *1950s:* 158, 164; *1960s:* 173; *1990s:* 163

The Boston Strangler, *1960s:* 80

Boston Teachers' Union, *1990s:* 44

Boston University, *1940s:* 152

The Boston Wire Stitcher Company, *1910s:* 133

Botany, *1900s:* 122

Boucher, Frank, *1930s:* 166

Boulanger, Nadia, *1930s:* 20

Boulder Canyon Dam. *See* Hoover Dam

Bow, Clara, *1920s:* 15, 94

Bowerman, Bill, *1970s:* 30

Bowling, *1900s:* 138; *1950s:* 158, 161, 170–71

Bowling Writers Association of America (BWAA), *1950s:* 171

Bowman, Scotty, *1990s:* 177

Boxer, Barbara, *1990s:* 75

Boxing, *1900s:* 138–41, 148, 149 (ill.); *1910s:* 154–56, 158, 166–68; *1920s:* 149–52, 161; *1930s:* 152–53, 161–62; *1940s:* 152–53, 157, 165–66; *1950s:* 158, 171–72, 172 (ill.); *1960s:* 164–65, 167–68; *1970s:* 160–61, 164, 180; *1980s:* 192

Boyce, William Dickson, *1910s:* 90

Boydston, Jo Ann, *1920s:* 54

Boyle, Kay, *1920s:* 13

Boys' Corn Club, *1900s:* 78

Boy Scouts of America, *1910s:* 90; *1980s:* 112

Boys' fashion, *1910s:* 108 (ill.)

Bradbury, Ray, *1950s:* 8, 16

Braddock, James J., *1940s:* 157

Braddock, Jim, *1930s:* 153

Bradford, Perry, *1910s:* 3

Bradham, Caleb D., *1900s:* 37

Bradley, Bill, *1960s:* 177; *1970s:* 169

Bradley, Thomas, *1970s:* 98

Bradshaw, Terry, *1990s:* 164

Brady Handgun Violence Prevention Act, *1990s:* 94, 106–09

Brady, James, *1980s:* 68; *1990s:* 106

Brady Law. *See* Brady Handgun Violence Prevention Act

Brady, Sarah, *1990s:* 106

Bragg, William Henry, *1910s:* 146

Bragg, William Lawrence, *1910s:* 146

Brain implants, *1960s:* 124

Brain Reserve, *1990s:* 97

Brains Trust, *1930s:* 76

Brain surgery, *1940s:* 123

Branca, Ralph, *1950s:* 166

Branch Davidian compound, *1990s:* 64–65, 67, 81

Brancusi, Constantin, *1910s:* 12

Brandeis, Louis D., *1910s:* 70, 70 (ill.)

Brand names, *1900s:* 36–37, 78; *1960s:* 35

Brando, Marlon, *1940s:* 20; *1950s:* 4, 6, 6 (ill.), 12, 110

Brassieres, *1910s:* 91

Brattain, Walter, *1950s:* 142

Braun, Wernher von, *1940s:* 133, 139

Brave New World, 1930s: 133

Brawley, Tawana, *1980s:* 72, 72 (ill.)

Brazil, *1910s:* 73

Break dancing, *1980s:* 22

Breakfast at Tiffany's, 1950s: 9

Breaking the Surface, 1990s: 117

Breast cancer, *1910s:* 112, 114, 124

Breast implants, *1960s:* 120, 122; *1990s:* 132

Breeding, *1900s:* 129

Breedlove, Sara. *See* Walker, Sara

Bremer, Arthur, *1970s:* 89

Brennan, Bill, *1920s:* 161

Brennan, William, *1950s:* 106

Breslin, Jimmy, *1960s:* 80

Brett, George, *1980s:* 176

Bretton Woods Conference, *1940s:* 24–25, 35

Breuer, Marcel, *1940s:* 90, 90 (ill.), 92, 93

Brezhnev, Leonid, *1980s:* 90

Bribes
    corporate, *1970s:* 27
    in sports, *1940s:* 152, 165–66

Brice, Fanny, *1910s:* 5, 18

Bridges, *1930s:* 138–39

The Bridges of Madison County (book), *1990s:* 2, 20

The Bridges of Madison County (movie), *1990s:* 20

Brigham Young University, *1930s:* 134

Brill, Steven, *1990s:* 15

Brinkley, Christie, *1980s:* 100, 100 (ill.)

Brinkley, David, *1950s:* 18

British Amateur (golf), *1920s:* 165

British invasion (music), *1960s:* 10–11

British Open (golf), *1920s:* 165–66; *1980s:* 183; *1990s:* 179

British punk music, *1970s:* 13–14

Britton, John Bayard, *1990s:* 128

Broadacre City, *1930s:* 89

Broadcasting
    radio, *1920s:* 35–36; *1930s:*
        17–20
    television, *1920s:* 129; *1930s:* 147
Broadway Revues. *See* Musicals
Broadway theater, *1900s:* 13–15;
    1960s: 3, 7, 18–19
Broadwood Hotel, *1930s:* 161
Brock, Lou, *1960s:* 173; *1970s:* 166;
    1980s: 176
Brokaw, Irving, *1900s:* 139
Broker's Tip, *1930s:* 152
Bromberg, J. Edgar, *1930s:* 21
Brooklyn Bridge, 1920s: 2
Brooklyn College, *1940s:* 152
Brooklyn Dodgers, *1910s:* 161; *1940s:*
    152, 157, 161; *1950s:* 159–61,
    166–68
Brooklyn Superbas, *1910s:* 161
Brooks Brothers, *1980s:* 104
Brookwood Labor College, *1930s:* 47,
    59
Brotherhood of Locomotive Firemen,
    1900s: 24
Brotherhood of Sleeping Car Porters,
    1920s: 25
Brown & Williamson Tobacco Com-
    pany, *1990s:* 71
Brown Derby, *1930s:* 98
Brown, Edmund G. "Pat," *1960s:* 63,
    73
Browne, Jackson, *1970s:* 11
Browne, Mary K, *1910s:* 176
Brownian motion, *1900s:* 119
Browning, Tom, *1980s:* 175
Brown, Jim, *1950s:* 173–74; *1960s:*
    168, 168 (ill.)
Brown, Joe, *1990s:* 15
Brown, Nicole. *See* Simpson, Nicole
    Brown
Brown Power, *1970s:* 109
Brownsville, New York riots, *1960s:*
    69, 103
Brown v. Board of Education, 1950s:
    46–48, 51, 56–59, 68, 71; *1960s:*
    48, 59; *1970s:* 48, 53
Brown, Wesley A., *1940s:* 60
Browsers, *1990s:* 142

Brubeck, Dave, *1950s:* 15
Brundage, Avery, *1960s:* 182
Bruner, Jerome, *1960s:* 50, 50 (ill.)
Bryan, Charles W., *1920s:* 77
Bryan, William Jennings, *1900s:* 58;
    1910s: 75; *1920s:* 60
Bryn Mawr University, *1900s:* 40
B-29 Superfortress, *1940s:* 28
Bubonic plague, *1900s:* 100, 111–12,
    111 (ill.)
Buchanan, James "Diamond Jim,"
    1910s: 129
Buchanan v. Warley, 1910s: 82
Buck, Carrie, *1920s:* 80
Buck, Pearl, *1990s:* 19
Buck, Pearl S., *1930s:* 13
Buck Rogers, 1930s: 11
Budapest University, *1930s:* 135
Budd, Edward G., *1930s:* 96
Buddhism, *1980s:* 117
Budge, Don, *1930s:* 153, 168
Buffalo Bills, *1960s:* 180
Buffalo Germans, *1910s:* 156, 164
Buffalo Sabres, *1990s:* 176
Buggles, *1980s:* 2
Bugliosi, Vincent, *1960s:* 81
Bugs Bunny, *1930s:* 3
Buick, *1910s:* 142; *1920s:* 28; *1930s:*
    131
Buick-Berle Show, 1950s: 30
Buick, David D., *1900s:* 125
Buicks, *1940s:* 102
Building codes, *1950s:* 91
Buildings, architecture, *1910s:* 91–92,
    100–01
Buildings, glass & steel, *1950s:* 90
Bulgaria, *1910s:* 77
Bulimia, *1980s:* 122–23, 125, 138–40
Bullock's, *1920s:* 37
Bumper Five, *1940s:* 139
Bundy, May Sutton, *1910s:* 175 (ill.)
Bunsen School, Belleville, Illinois,
    1900s: 40
Burbank, Luther, *1900s:* 79, 122, 122
    (ill.)
Burbank potato hybrid, *1900s:* 122
Burbridge, Margaret, *1960s:* 149
Burchfield, Charles, *1920s:* 18

Bureau of Alcohol, Tobacco, and Firearms (ATF), *1990s:* 81

Bureau of Education, *1910s:* 46–47, 58

Bureau of Educational Experiments, *1910s:* 51

Bureau of Indian Affairs, *1970s:* 109–10

Bureau of Research and Efficiency, *1910s:* 46

Burke, Billie, *1910s:* 18

Burns, Arthur, *1970s:* 27

Burns, Tommy, *1900s:* 143, 148

Burroughs, Edgar Rice, *1930s:* 11

Burroughs, William S., *1950s:* 10

Burton, LeVar, *1970s:* 23 (ill.)

Bus boycott, *1950s:* 69, 73

Buses, *1990s:* 28

Bush, Barbara, *1990s:* 75

Bush, George H. W., *1980s:* 31, 63, 83, 86; *1990s:* 64, 66, 66 (ill.), 68, 87, 116, 121

Bushman, Francis X., *1910s:* 16

Bush, Vannevar, *1920s:* 143; *1940s:* 47, 130, 134, 134 (ill.)

Business and the economy, *1900s:* 19–38; *1910s:* 23–40; *1920s:* 23–44; *1930s:* 25–44; *1940s:* 23–42, 36 (ill.); *1950s:* 25–43; *1960s:* 23–43; *1970s:* 25–45; *1980s:* 29–45; *1990s:* 27–42

    business expansion, *1940s:* 36–38

    chronology, *1900s:* 20–21; *1910s:* 24–25; *1920s:* 24–25; *1930s:* 26–27; *1940s:* 24–25; *1950s:* 24–25; *1960s:* 24–25; *1970s:* 26–27; *1980s:* 30–31; *1990s:* 28–29

    education and, *1900s:* 42–43

    globalization, *1990s:* 39–42

    government and, *1910s:* 27, 84

    headline makers, *1900s:* 24–25; *1910s:* 28–29; *1920s:* 28–29; *1930s:* 30–31; *1940s:* 28–29; *1950s:* 28–29; *1960s:* 28–29; *1970s:* 30; *1980s:* 34; *1990s:* 32

    Internet, *1990s:* 30–31, 33–39, 139

    "Military-Industrial Complex," *1940s:* 34–36, 66, 137–38, 140

    Nobel Prize winners in economics, *1970s:* 37; *1990s:* 37

    overview, *1900s:* 22–23; *1910s:* 26–27; *1920s:* 26–27; *1930s:* 28–29; *1940s:* 26–27; *1950s:* 26–27; *1960s:* 26–27; *1970s:* 28–29; *1980s:* 32–34; *1990s:* 30–31

    Reagan economics, *1980s:* 31–32, 71, 81–85

Business education, *1910s:* 57

Businesses, small versus large, *1950s:* 41–43

Business models, *1990s:* 34

Business organizations, *1900s:* 20

Business schools, *1900s:* 50; *1920s:* 24; *1980s:* 105

Busing, *1970s:* 48–49, 51, 53–54, 54 (ill.)

    for school integration, *1960s:* 59–60

    parochial schools, *1950s:* 53

Buster Brown, 1900s: 16

Butenandt, Adolph, *1920s:* 109

Butler, Nicholas Murray, *1910s:* 53; *1920s:* 50, 50 (ill.)

Butler, Pierce, *1920s:* 82

Butler, William, *1920s:* 78

Butte, Montana, shooting, *1990s:* 44

Butterfield, Alexander, *1970s:* 86

Butterworth, Julian, *1920s:* 47

Butz, Earl, *1980s:* 40

BWAA (Bowling Writers Association of America), *1950s:* 171

Bwana Devil, 1950s: 2, 10

Bye Bye Birdie, 1960s: 18

Byrd, Richard E., *1920s:* 129, 137; *1930s:* 134, 134 (ill.)

The Byrds, *1960s:* 10

Byrne, Jane, *1970s:* 98

Byrnes, James F., *1950s:* 58

C

Cabell, James Branch, *1920s:* 14

Cable Act, *1920s:* 86

Cable cars, *1900s:* 21

Cable News Network (CNN), *1980s:* 96, 101

Cable television, *1980s:* 101
See also specific programs

Cadillacs, *1910s:* 103; *1930s:* 94; *1950s:* 98–99

Cadore, Leon, *1920s:* 148

Caesarian section, *1900s:* 100

Caesar, Sid, *1950s:* 4, 17

Caffrey, James, *1900s:* 138

Cage, John, *1940s:* 18

Cagney, James, *1920s:* 10; *1930s:* 16, 83

Cahan, Abraham, *1910s:* 11

Cahill, Thaddeus, *1900s:* 119

The Caine Mutiny, *1950s:* 2, 10

Cain, James M., *1930s:* 14

Calculators, pocket, *1970s:* 140

Calder, Alexander, *1920s:* 3, 13; *1930s:* 10

California Board of Education, *1980s:* 49

California, education, *1910s:* 46

"California Girls," *1960s:* 11

California Institute of Technology, *1930s:* 135, 143; *1960s:* 126

Callahan, T. M., *1900s:* 25

Calley, William, *1970s:* 70, 74, 74 (ill.)

Calley, William L., Jr., *1960s:* 79

Call It Sleep, *1930s:* 13

"Call Me," *1980s:* 19

The Call of the Wild, *1900s:* 5, 7

Calmette, Albert, *1920s:* 114–15

Caltech. *See* California Institute of Technology

Calypso, *1970s:* 144

Camaro SS, *1960s:* 95

Cambodia bombing, *1960s:* 79; *1970s:* 78–79

Camel Caravan, *1950s:* 30

Camel Cigarettes, *1950s:* 31

Camera, microfilm, *1920s:* 128

Cameras, *1940s:* 131

Cameras, television, *1960s:* 143

Camera Work, *1910s:* 2

Campaign contributions, *1900s:* 59; *1910s:* 66

Campanella, Roy, *1950s:* 159

Campbell, Malcolm, *1930s:* 153, 155

Campbell's Soup Company, *1900s:* 37

Camp David peace accord, *1970s:* 71

Campus protests, apartheid, *1980s:* 62

Camp, Walter, *1900s:* 142, 142 (ill.)

Canada Dry Ginger Ale, *1900s:* 79

Canadian Overseas Telecommunications Corporation, *1950s:* 143

Canal Zone, *1900s:* 73–74, 104

Cancer, *1900s:* 100; *1910s:* 112, 114, 124; *1920s:* 108–09; *1940s:* 108–09, 120; *1950s:* 114–16, 122, 129–31; *1960s:* 121, 123; *1970s:* 122; *1990s:* 126
AIDS and, *1980s:* 127
lung, *1930s:* 111

Cancer treatment, *1960s:* 120

Candidates, presidential, *1970s:* 81

"Candle in the Wind '95," *1990s:* 26

"Candy Apples," *1960s:* 16

Cane, *1920s:* 10–11

Canine searches, students, *1980s:* 48

Canned Heat, *1960s:* 12

Canneries, *1990s:* 28

The Cannibal, *1940s:* 12

Canning industry, *1910s:* 85

Cannon, James Jr., *1930s:* 92, 92 (ill.)

Cannon, W. A., *1900s:* 129

Canseco, Jose, *1980s:* 176

Canteen Corporation, *1960s:* 41

Canton Bulldogs, *1900s:* 150; *1910s:* 169

Cantor, Eddie, *1910s:* 18; *1920s:* 9

Canzoneri, Tony, *1930s:* 162

Capek, Karel, *1920s:* 8

Capitalism, Miller, Arthur on, *1940s:* 19

Capitalists, *1900s:* 25

Capone, Alphonse "Al," *1920s:* 68, 68 (ill.), 73–74; *1930s:* 81

Capote, Truman, *1940s:* 5, 12; *1950s:* 9; *1960s:* 80

Capp, Al, *1930s:* 6, 6 (ill.)

Capra, Frank, *1930s:* 16; *1940s:* 14

Capriati, Jennifer, *1990s:* 164

Captain America, *1940s:* 10

Captain Billy's Whiz Bang, *1920s:* 19

Captain Marvel, *1940s:* 10

Carbine, Pat, *1970s:* 2

Carbo, Frankie "Jimmie the Wop,"
   1940s: 165–66

Carbon Company, *1920s:* 24

Carbon dioxide, *1990s:* 141, 150

Carbon-14, *1940s:* 131

Carbon monoxide, *1980s:* 140

The Cardinal of the Kremlin, 1980s: 12

Cardin, Pierre, *1960s:* 94

Cardiopulmonary resuscitation
   (CPR), *1960s:* 128

Cardiovascular medicine, *1950s:*
   114–16, 123–25

Cardiovascular surgery, *1960s:* 127–28
   See also Heart surgery

The Care and Feeding of Children,
   1920s: 117

Career training, *1910s:* 49

"Careless Whisper," *1980s:* 19

Carey, Mariah, *1990s:* 5, 25–26

Caribbean, *1910s:* 68, 72–73

Car industry. *See* Automobile industry

Carlesimo, P. J., *1990s:* 164, 173

Carlos, John, *1960s:* 182

Carlson, Chester F., *1930s:* 131; *1950s:*
   140, 140 (ill.)

Carlton, Steve, *1980s:* 176

Carnaby Street look, *1960s:* 113

Carnegie, Andrew, *1900s:* 2, 24–25, 24
   (ill.), 40–41, 50, 64, 78, 118; *1910s:*
   139

Carnegie, Dale, *1930s:* 3

Carnegie Endowment for International Peace, *1920s:* 50

Carnegie Foundation for the
   Advancement of Teaching, *1900s:*
   41; *1920s:* 47, 60

Carnegie Hall, *1910s:* 3; *1930s:* 3;
   1960s: 2–3

Carnegie, Hattie, *1920s:* 90, 90 (ill.);
   1930s: 92, 92 (ill.)

Carnegie Institution of Washington,
   1900s: 40

Carnegie Report on Intercollegiate
   Athletics, *1920s:* 60–61

Carnegie Steel Corporation, *1900s:*
   24–25, 58

Carnera, Primo, *1930s:* 161

Carnes, Kim, *1980s:* 19

Carney, Art, *1950s:* 18, 18 (ill.)

Carnovsky, Morris, *1930s:* 21

Carolina Hurricanes, *1990s:* 176

Carolina Panthers, *1990s:* 175

Carothers, Wallace, *1930s:* 89

Carousel, 1920s: 8

Carpathia, 1910s: 151

Carpenter, Karen, *1980s:* 138

Carpenter, Scott, *1960s:* 154

Carpentier, George, *1920s:* 161

Car racing. *See* Automobile racing

Carradine, David, *1970s:* 114

Carranza, Venustiano, *1910s:* 73–74

Carrel, Alexis, *1910s:* 112; *1930s:* 114,
   114 (ill.)

Carroll, Dianne, *1970s:* 21

Carruth, Rae, *1990s:* 175

Cars. *See* Automobile industry

Carson, Johnny, *1960s:* 6, 6 (ill.)

Carson, Rachel, *1940s:* 115; *1960s:* 98,
   98 (ill.)

Carter, C. Dana, *1900s:* 100

Carter, Elliott, *1930s:* 20

Carter Family, *1930s:* 18

Carter, Jimmy, *1970s:* 71, 156; *1980s:*
   2, 35, 68, 76, 85; *1990s:* 69
      Cold war and, *1970s:* 72–73
      energy policy, *1970s:* 33–34
      on inflation, *1970s:* 39
      Iranian hostage crisis, *1970s:*
         93–94

Cartoons, *1900s:* 79

Cartwright, Alexander, *1900s:* 144

Caruso, Enrico, *1900s:* 14

Casablanca, 1940s: 6, 13

"The Case Against the Jew," *1940s:* 86

Case, Theodore, *1920s:* 131, 142

Casey, William, *1980s:* 87

Cash, Johnny, *1980s:* 25

Cash, Rosanne, *1980s:* 25

Cassatt, Mary, *1900s:* 3, 8; *1910s:* 12

Cassini, Oleg, *1950s:* 99

Castle, Irene, *1910s:* 18, 90, 106

Castle, Vernon, *1910s:* 90, 106

Castro, Fidel, *1960s:* 76–77

Casualties, Vietnam, *1960s:* 69, 78–79

Catalogs, *1900s:* 81

The Catcher in the Rye, 1950s: 9

Catch-22, 1960s: 4, 19

CAT (Computerized axial tomography) scans, *1970s:* 122, 124, 129

Cater, Danny, *1960s:* 173

Cather, Willa, *1910s:* 6, 6 (ill.), 10

Cathode rays, *1900s:* 119

Catholicism, *1940s:* 86, 99; *1950s:* 91, 141

    changing rules of, *1960s:* 95

    of Kennedy, John F., *1960s:* 83

Catholic schools, *1950s:* 49, 52–53, 63

    federal funding for, *1960s:* 57

    integration in, *1960s:* 46

Catholic University of America, *1910s:* 90

Catholic Worker, 1930s: 88

Cats, 1980s: 13–14

Cat's Cradle, 1960s: 18

Caucasians, illiteracy, *1980s:* 49

CBGB, 1970s: 13

CB radios, *1970s:* 99

CBS (Columbia Broadcasting System), *1920s:* 7; *1930s:* 21–22, 46; *1950s:* 2, 43, 145–46; *1990s:* 16, 29

CCC. *See* Civilian Conservation Corps

CDC (Centers for Disease Control), *1990s:* 44, 123

    See also Centers for Disease Control and Prevention

CDs (compact discs), *1970s:* 156; *1980s:* 23

    Amazon.com, *1990s:* 32

    preferred medium, *1990s:* 2

Cédras, Raoul, *1990s:* 69

Celera Genomics, *1990s:* 139, 142–44

Cellular communications, *1990s:* 154–56

Celtics, Boston, *1970s:* 169

Censorship

    arts, *1980s:* 5, 8–9

    education, *1980s:* 5, 9, 49–50, 54–58, 57 (ill.)

    family television hour, *1970s:* 22

    HUAC and, *1940s:* 45

    in movies, *1900s:* 11

    MPAA ratings and, *1960s:* 9

    Sesame Street, 1970s: 2

    television, *1960s:* 2

    of textbooks, *1950s:* 61; *1970s:* 59–60

Census Bureau, *1950s:* 47, 91, 143

Census reports, *1920s:* 64

Center for Cognitive Studies, Harvard University, *1960s:* 50

Centers for Disease Control and Prevention (CDC), *1940s:* 110, 114–15; *1970s:* 123, 134–35, 137; *1990s:* 44, 123

    AIDS and, *1980s:* 122, 127–28

    radon levels, *1980s:* 141

    toxic shock syndrome, *1980s:* 131

Central High School, *1950s:* 47, 58–60, 59 (ill.), 69

Central Intelligence Agency (CIA), *1940s:* 66; *1960s:* 76; *1990s:* 65, 69

Central Intelligence Agency (CIA), Iran-Contra scandal, *1980s:* 68, 86

Central powers, *1910s:* 52, 68, 75–78

Century of Progress World's Fair, *1930s:* 2, 88, 106, 132

Cepeda, Orlando, *1960s:* 173

Cepheid stars, *1910s:* 137, 139

Cerdan, Marcel, *1940s:* 166

Cereals, nutritional content of, *1970s:* 122

Cerebral palsy, *1950s:* 115; *1960s:* 124

Cermak, Anton J., *1930s:* 83

Cezanne, Paul, *1910s:* 12

CFCs. *See* Chlorofluorocarbons

Chadwick, Florence, *1950s:* 158

Chadwick, James, *1930s:* 144

Chaffee, Roger B., *1960s:* 143, 146, 159

Chagall, Marc, *1940s:* 8

"Chain of Fools," *1960s:* 15

Chain stores, *1900s:* 25; *1960s:* 26, 33–35, 34 (ill.)

Challenger (space shuttle), *1980s:* 147–48, 150–55, 153 (ill.)

The Chamber, 1990s: 20

Chamberlain-Kahn Act, *1910s:* 113, 125

Chamberlain, Wilt, *1960s:* 176–77; *1980s:* 178

Chambers, Whittaker, *1940s:* 68; *1950s:* 78

The Champagne, *1910s:* 172

Chance Vought, *1960s:* 28

Chandler, A. B. "Happy," *1940s:* 152–53

Chandler, Raymond, *1920s:* 19; *1930s:* 5, 14

Chanel, *1930s:* 101

Chanel, Gabrielle "Coco," *1910s:* 91, 107; *1920s:* 86, 90, 90 (ill.), 92, 94; *1950s:* 94, 94 (ill.)

Chanel No. 5, *1920s:* 86

Chaney, James, *1960s:* 102

Chang: A Drama of the Wilderness, 1920s: 16

Chang, Michael, *1990s:* 181

Channel Heights, San Diego, California, *1940s:* 93

Channel One, *1990s:* 44

Chanute, Octave, *1900s:* 126

Chaplin, Charles, *1910s:* 3, 6, 6 (ill.), 15; *1930s:* 133

Chaplin, Charlie, *1940s:* 2, 13
    See also Chaplin, Charles

Chapman, Ray, *1920s:* 110

Chapman, Tracy, *1980s:* 3

Chargoff, Erwin, *1940s:* 133

Chariots of Fire, 1920s: 169

The Charleston, *1920s:* 11, 15 (ill.), 16, 86, 88, 93 (ill.)

Charleston, Oscar, *1920s:* 158

Charter schools, *1990s:* 52–54

Chase Manhattan Bank, *1920s:* 38; *1950s:* 42

Chase, William Merritt, *1910s:* 8

Chastain, Brandi, *1990s:* 163, 165

Chavez, Cesar, *1960s:* 28, 28 (ill.), 38 (ill.); *1970s:* 102, 102 (ill.)

Chavis, Benjamin, *1990s:* 99

Cheating Death: Catastrophes Caught on Tape, 1990s: 16

Cheating, University of Florida, *1950s:* 46

Checker, Chubby, *1960s:* 94, 108

Cheers, 1990s: 16

Chekhov, Anton, *1900s:* 2

"Chelsea" fashions. *See* "Mod" fashions

Chemicals, toxic, *1970s:* 143, 153–54

Chemical weapons, Gulf War syndrome, *1990s:* 124–25

Chemie Gruenenthal, *1960s:* 135–36

Chemistry, *1910s:* 146; *1930s:* 140–42
    Nobel Prizes in, *1970s:* 150

Chemotherapy, *1960s:* 120

Chenault, Ken, *1990s:* 32, 32 (ill.)

Chernenko, Konstantin, *1980s:* 90

Chernobyl nuclear power plant, *1980s:* 147, 154

The Cherry Orchard, 1900s: 2

Chesnutt, Waddell, *1900s:* 8

Chess, *1960s:* 164

Chevrolet, *1910s:* 28; *1920s:* 24, 34, 130, 134; *1930s:* 40; *1950s:* 30, 41 (ill.); *1960s:* 95

Chevrolet Corvair, 1960s: 29

Chevrolet on Broadway, 1950s: 30

Chevrolet Tele-Theatre, 1950s: 30

Chevy Showroom Starring Andy Williams, 1950s: 30

Chewing gum, *1940s:* 29

Chiang Kai-Sheck, *1940s:* 49

Chic, 1970s: 15

Chicago Art Institute, *1930s:* 6

Chicago Bears, *1920s:* 149, 153; *1930s:* 152, 157, 163; *1940s:* 152, 167; *1980s:* 181

Chicago Blackhawks, *1920s:* 149; *1930s:* 165

Chicago Bulls, *1960s:* 176; *1980s:* 168, 172, 178; *1990s:* 163, 166–67

Chicago Cardinals, *1920s:* 149, 153

Chicago Century of Progress Exhibition, *1930s:* 94

Chicago Cubs, *1900s:* 139, 144; *1910s:* 154, 161; *1930s:* 152; *1940s:* 161; *1990s:* 169

Chicago Defender, 1900s: 2

Chicago Grand Opera, *1910s:* 2

Chicago, Judy, *1970s:* 3, 9, 9 (ill.)

Chicago Packers, *1960s:* 176

Chicago (rock band), *1980s:* 19

Chicago Seven, *1960s:* 114–15

Chicago Stags, *1950s:* 168

Chicago style of architecture, *1900s:* 96

Chicago Symphony, *1970s:* 2

Chicago Teachers' Federation (CTF), *1900s:* 40, 44

Chicago Tribune, 1910s: 67; *1930s:* 162–63

Chicago Tribune Building, *1910s:* 101

Chicago Tribune Company Building, *1920s:* 97, 98 (ill.)

Chicago White Sox, *1900s:* 138–39; *1910s:* 155, 157–59, 161–62; *1920s:* 148, 150, 154–56, 155 (ill.); *1990s:* 163

Chicago World's Fair, *1930s:* 2

Chicago Zephyrs, *1960s:* 176

Chicano movement, *1970s:* 98, 109

Chico and the Man, 1970s: 109

The Chiffons, *1960s:* 11

Child abuse, *1980s:* 99, 112–13

Childbirth, *1960s:* 134–35

Childhood development, *1960s:* 125

Child labor, *1900s:* 22, 31 (ill.), 59, 87; *1910s:* 49–50, 60, 69, 83, 85–86, 86 (ill.)
     during the war, *1940s:* 98

Child Labor Law, *1900s:* 59; *1920s:* 64

Child-protective-service (CPS), *1980s:* 112

Children
     with AIDS, *1980s:* 122
     clothing, *1910s:* 90, 108 (ill.); *1950s:* 107, 109
     handicapped, *1910s:* 113
     medical reform for, *1920s:* 116–17
     social services for, *1970s:* 105

Children's Bureau, *1910s:* 112

Children's Defense Fund, *1990s:* 48

Children's television, *1940s:* 18
     The Muppet Show, 1970s: 3, 6
     Sesame Street, 1970s: 2, 6

Childress, Alice, *1970s:* 10

Child's (restaurants), *1920s:* 36

Chile, *1910s:* 73

Chilean copper mines, *1940s:* 38

China Clipper, 1930s: 89

China, relations with U.S., *1970s:* 26, 70, 72–73, 80–83

"Chime Blues," *1920s:* 2

Chisholm Shirley, *1970s:* 74, 74 (ill.)

Chloramphenicol, *1960s:* 123, 136

Chlorine, *1910s:* 123

Chlorofluorocarbons (CFCs), *1970s:* 140–41, 153

Chlorofluorocarbons (CFCs), ozone layer depletion, *1980s:* 147–48, 158

Chloroform, *1930s:* 116

Chloromycetin, *1940s:* 119

Cholesterol, *1980s:* 122

Chopra, Deepak, *1990s:* 95–96, 96 (ill.), 108

Choreography, *1940s:* 19; *1960s:* 114

A Chorus Line, 1970s: 3, 15; *1980s:* 2

Choynsky, Joe, *1900s:* 143

Christa, 1970s: 9

Christian Broadcasting Network, *1980s:* 116

Christian fundamentalism, *1920s:* 102–03; *1970s:* 101–02, 112–14

Christian groups, *1980s:* 54–56, 97, 115–16, 116 (ill.)

Christianity, *1910s:* 93

Christianity and Crisis, 1950s: 30

Christian Mission. *See* Salvation Army

The Christian Science Journal, 1900s: 82

Christian Science movement, *1900s:* 82

Christiansen, Jack, *1950s:* 174

Christie's, *1980s:* 10–11

Christmas bombings, *1970s:* 78–79

Christmas Seals, *1900s:* 113

Chromosomes, *1900s:* 130; *1910s:* 117, 144; *1940s:* 139–40

Chromosomes, map, *1990s:* 138

Chrysler Building, *1910s:* 100; *1930s:* 96–97; *1950s:* 43

Chrysler Corporation, *1920s:* 24–25, 28, 34; *1930s:* 39–41, 94, 130; *1940s:* 87; *1950s:* 136; *1960s:* 30–31; *1970s:* 27, 29; *1980s:* 32

Chrysler, Walter P., *1900s:* 125; *1920s:* 28; *1930s:* 41

Chun King, *1960s:* 41

Church and state, *1940s: 60; 1990s: 44*

Churchill, Winston, *1910s: 150;
1940s: 75–76, 79–80*

Church versus state, *1950s: 46,
52–54; 1980s: 48, 50–51, 54, 58*

CIA (Central Intelligence Agency),
1940s: 66; 1960s: 76; 1990s: 65, 69

CIA (Central Intelligence Agency),
Iran-Contra scandal, *1980s: 68, 86*

Cicotte, Eddie, *1910s: 162; 1920s: 154*

Cigarette advertising, *1980s: 122*

Cigarette packaging, warning labels
on, *1960s: 12, 120, 138*

Cigarettes, *1970s: 122–23*
See also Smoking

Cigars, *1990s: 98–99*

Cincinnati Bengals, *1980s: 181*

Cincinnati, Ohio, continuation school
in, *1900s: 41*

Cincinnati Reds, *1910s: 161–62;
1920s: 154; 1930s: 153; 1940s: 157,
159; 1940s: 157, 159; 1960s: 164,
169; 1980s: 169*

Cincinnati Red Stockings, *1900s: 144*

CIO (Congress of Industrial Organizations), *1930s: 27, 31, 38, 57*
CIO. *See also* Congress of Industrial Organizations

Circuits, theatrical, *1900s: 15*

Circus, 1920s: 3

Cisco Systems, *1990s: 40*

The Citadel, *1990s: 4, 56*

Citizen Kane, 1940s: 7

Citizens' band radios. *See* CB radios

Citizenship, American, *1910s: 47*

City College of New York, *1950s: 168;
1960s: 47*

City Life, 1910s: 3

City Lights, 1910s: 6

City University of New York (CUNY),
1960s: 47

Civil disobedience. *See* Antiwar
protests; Civil Rights movement

Civilian Conservation Corps (CCC),
1930s: 46, 54, 55 (ill.), 73, 77

Civil liberties, *1940s: 78–79*

Civil rights, *1900s: 40; 1930s: 78–79;
1980s: 72*

Civil Rights Act, *1960s: 59, 68–69,
74–75*

Civil Rights Act of 1959, *1950s: 69*

Civil Rights Act of 1964, *1960s: 41*

Civil Rights movement, *1910s: 50;
1960s: 4, 70, 74–75, 99; 1970s: 4*
Africa and, *1910s: 91*
American history classes and,
1960s: 48
courts, *1950s: 68–69*
desegregation, *1950s: 46, 50,
57–60, 57 (ill.), 59 (ill.), 71*
economic factors, *1950s: 102*
education, *1910s: 47, 51, 60–62,
61 (ill.), 62 (ill.)*
The Great White Hope, 1910s: 166
Jim Crow Laws, *1910s: 69, 82,
96; 1950s: 96*
King, Martin Luther, Jr., *1950s:
97*
Marshall, Thurgood, *1950s: 51,
57 (ill.)*
National Educational Association, *1950s: 47*
race riots, *1910s: 91*
racism, *1910s: 14, 36, 96*
Selma, Alabama protest, *1960s:
69, 94*
student protests and, *1960s: 49,
61, 94*
Sweatt, Herman Marion, *1950s:
46*
teachers, *1950s: 91*
Till, Emmett, *1950s: 74*
See also African Americans; Violence; Women

Civil Service Commission, *1920s: 65*

Civil Works Administration (CWA),
1930s: 26, 77

Civil Works Emergency Relief Act,
1930s: 68

Clad, George's, *1910s: 146*

Clairol, *1950s: 90*

The Clansman, 3, 1900s: 5, 79

Clark, Barney, *1980s: 124, 126, 132*

Clark, Dick, *1950s: 2, 109*

Clarke, Bobby, *1970s: 173*

Clark, Joe Louis, *1980s: 52, 52 (ill.)*

Clash, *1970s:* 14

Class consciousness, *1900s:* 4, 29

Class differences, *1900s:* 23

Classical music, *1930s:* 20; *1940s:* 15, 18

Clavell, James, *1970s:* 9

Clay, Cassius. *See* Muhammed Ali

Clayton Antitrust Act, *1910s:* 31

Clear Air Act amendments of 1970, *1970s:* 90

Clear and Present Danger, 1980s: 12

Clearing House Association, *1900s:* 28

Clemenceau, Georges, *1910s:* 78, 79 (ill.)

Clemens, Roger, *1980s:* 176; *1990s:* 163

Clemens, Samuel Langhorne. *See* Twain, Mark

Clemente, Roberto, *1960s:* 168, 168 (ill.)

Clemson College, *1960s:* 46

Cleopatra, 1930s: 15

Cleveland Browns, *1950s:* 173–74; *1960s:* 168; *1990s:* 175

Cleveland Indians, *1920s:* 148; *1930s:* 157; *1940s:* 161; *1950s:* 166–67; *1970s:* 160; *1990s:* 163

Cleveland, Ohio public schools, *1990s:* 45

Cleveland Rebels, *1950s:* 168

Cliff Dwellers, 1910s: 9

Clifford, Camille, *1900s:* 92 (ill.)

Clift, Montgomery, *1950s:* 12

Climatology, *1960s:* 152–54

Climatology, global warming, *1990s:* 150

Clinical depression, *1940s:* 125

Clinics
   for babies, *1910s:* 112
   birth control, *1910s:* 91, 113; *1930s:* 117–18
   Mayo, *1910s:* 112, 114, 116, 118, 120
   psychiatric, *1910s:* 116

Clinton, Bill, *1970s:* 137; *1980s:* 80; *1990s:* 3, 78, 78 (ill.), 110
   black English, *1990s:* 18
   gene cloning, *1990s:* 134

health care, *1990s:* 116, 118, 121–23, 123 (ill.)
   Hussein, Saddam, *1990s:* 66–68
   scandals/impeachment, *1990s:* 62–63, 65, 75–80
   school violence, *1990s:* 49
   Somalia, *1990s:* 68

Clinton, Hillary Rodham, *1990s:* 63, 66, 66 (ill.), 75–76, 79, 118, 121–23, 123 (ill.)

The Cloisters, *1920s:* 91

Cloning
   animal, *1990s:* 117
   fetal stem cells, *1990s:* 117
   human embryo, *1990s:* 116

Closed-chest heart massage, *1960s:* 128

Close Encounters of the Third Kind, 1970s: 3, 10, 18

The Closing of the American Mind, 1980s: 52

Clothes dryers, *1950s:* 137

Clothing, *1950s:* 90
   polyester, *1970s:* 99
   secondhand, *1970s:* 118
   See also Fashion

Cloud seeding, *1940s:* 131, 143

Clurman, Harold, *1930s:* 21

Clutter family, *1960s:* 80

CND (Council of National Defense), *1910s:* 117, 121

CNN (Cable News Network), *1980s:* 96, 101

Coal-burning stoves, *1910s:* 102

Coal miners
   explosions and, *1900s:* 21
   strikes, *1900s:* 20, 23, 26–27, 58; *1950s:* 24; *1970s:* 27

Coal mining, *1910s:* 24, 29, 86 (ill.); *1930s:* 26, 37

Coal mining strikes, *1940s:* 24, 40

Coast Guard, *1910s:* 66

Coastline, oil and gas drilling, *1980s:* 30

Coates, Robert, *1940s:* 8

Cobain, Kurt, *1990s:* 2, 6, 6 (ill.), 22–23, 22 (ill.), 110

Cobb, Lee J., *1930s:* 21

Cobb, Ty, *1900s:* 144; *1910s:* 157–58, 158 (ill.), 161-64; *1920s:* 149

COBOL programming language, *1950s:* 140, 146; *1970s:* 44

Coca-Cola, *1900s:* 78; *1910s:* 107; *1930s:* 36, 88; *1940s:* 37–38; *1950s:* 91

Coca-Cola 600, *1990s:* 166

Cocaine, *1900s:* 78; *1910s:* 83; *1980s:* 64, 97, 108–09

Cochran, Barbara, *1970s:* 177

Cochran, Johnnie, *1990s:* 66, 66 (ill.), 86, 86 (ill.)

Cocker, Joe, *1960s:* 12

Cody, Buffalo Bill, *1900s:* 2

Coeducation, *1950s:* 46

Coeducational schools, *1940s:* 55

Coffee, *1990s:* 94, 98–99, 99 (ill.)

Coffee, Linda, *1970s:* 75, 88–89

Coffee prices, *1970s:* 27

Coffin, Howard E., *1910s:* 28

Cohan, George M., *1910s:* 3, 17

Cohn, Fannie, *1910s:* 40

Colbert, Claudette, *1930s:* 16

Cold, common, *1950s:* 125

Cold war, *1940s:* 14, 27, 34–36, 45, 80–81; *1950s:* 49; *1960s:* 70, 75–77, 156, 181–82; *1970s:* 12–13, 145–46; *1980s:* 74–75, 90–92
    end of, *1990s:* 64, 64
    Hiss, Alger and, *1950s:* 68, 70–71, 77
    Korea, *1950s:* 77
    McCarthyism, *1950s:* 4, 7, 13–15, 32, 68, 79–81
    nuclear weapons, *1950s:* 74–77
    Olympics, *1950s:* 161, 175
    Rosenbergs and, *1950s:* 68, 71, 78–79
    teachers and, *1950s:* 46, 49, 61–62
    See also Anticommunism

Cole, Bob, *1900s:* 13

Cole, Nat King, *1950s:* 5, 15; *1960s:* 106

Cole-Whittaker, Terry, *1980s:* 100, 100 (ill.)

The Colgate Comedy Hour, 1950s: 18

Collating machine, *1930s:* 131

Collazo, Oscar, *1950s:* 81

Collectibles, *1950s:* 93

College basketball, *1940s:* 152, 161; *1960s:* 165, 167, 175–76

College Board Commission on English, *1960s:* 53

College Entrance Examination Board, *1900s:* 40; *1940s:* 44

College football, *1910s:* 155–56, 166–69; *1920s:* 150–53, 161–63; *1940s:* 152, 156, 166–67; *1960s:* 165, 167, 178–79

College of Dental Surgery, Cincinnati, *1910s:* 112

College of Medical Evangelists, *1900s:* 101

College preparatory schools, *1900s:* 48

Colleges. *See* Universities and colleges

College sports
    basketball, *1900s:* 139, 141, 146
    football, *1900s:* 138–39, 148–52
    soccer, *1900s:* 139
    wrestling, *1900s:* 139

Collegiate All-Americans, *1930s:* 152

Collier's, 1910s: 19

Collingswood, Charles, *1950s:* 18

Collins, Eddie, *1910s:* 157, 163

Collins, Francis S., *1990s:* 143–44

Collins, Judy, *1960s:* 113

Collins, Michael, *1960s:* 159

Collip, James B., *1920s:* 108, 119

Colombia, *1900s:* 73–74

Color, 1920s: 10

Colorado Avalanche, *1990s:* 176

Colorado Rockies, *1990s:* 164

Colorado Supreme Court, antigay rights, *1990s:* 92

Colorfast textiles, *1940s:* 86

Color field painting, *1940s:* 9

Color photographs, in newspapers, *1900s:* 2

The Color Purple, 1980s: 7

Colossus, *1940s:* 141

Columbia, 1960s: 159

Columbia Broadcasting System (CBS), *1920s:* 7; *1930s:* 21–22, 46

Columbia Pictures, *1950s:* 11

Columbia-Presbyterian Medical Center, New York, New York, *1960s:* 134

Columbia Records, *1950s:* 152

Columbia River, *1980s:* 164

Columbia (space shuttle), *1980s:* 146, 151; *1990s:* 44

Columbia University, *1910s:* 46, 49, 112; *1920s:* 50; *1930s:* 50, 76, 121, 134; *1960s:* 47, 64

Columbine High School, Littleton, Colorado shootings, *1990s:* 45, 50, 51 (ill.)

Columbus Panhandlers, *1910s:* 169

Comedians, Pryor, Richard, *1970s:* 7

Comic books, *1940s:* 10–11; *1950s:* 90–91

Comic strips, *1900s:* 16, 79; *1930s:* 10–12

Coming Home, 1970s: 6

Coming of Age in Samoa, 1920s: 133; *1940s:* 136

Comiskey Park, *1930s:* 152–53

Commission on Higher Education, *1940s:* 49

Commission on Uniform Laws, *1910s:* 86

Committee for a Sane Nuclear Policy (SANE), *1980s:* 113

Committee for Industrial Organizations. *See* Congress of Industrial Organizations

Committee of One Hundred on National Health, *1900s:* 101

Committee on Medical Research, Office of Research and Development, *1940s:* 121

Committee on Public Information (CPI), *1910s:* 20, 52, 76

Committee to Reelect the President (CREEP), *1970s:* 84–86

Common Business-Oriented Language (COBOL), *1970s:* 44

Common cold, *1950s:* 125

Common Sense Book of Baby and Child Care, 1920s: 117; *1960s:* 99

Commonwealth College, *1930s:* 59

Communes, *1970s:* 48

Communicable Disease Center. *See* Centers for Disease Control and Prevention(CDC)

Communicable diseases, *1920s:* 114–15
    See also Infectious diseases

Communications, *1900s:* 120, 127

Communications Decency Act, *1990s:* 139

Communications industry strikes, *1960s:* 25

Communism, *1930s:* 47, 50–51, 56–58, 60–61; *1980s:* 70–71, 74–75
    in Cuba, *1960s:* 76
    Korea, *1950s:* 77
    McCarthyism, *1950s:* 4, 7, 13–15, 32, 68, 79–81
    Nixon, Richard and, *1970s:* 82–83
    nuclear weapons, *1950s:* 74–77
    Olympics, *1950s:* 161, 175
    postwar economy and, *1920s:* 70–72
    school teachers and, *1920s:* 46
    teachers and, *1950s:* 46, 49, 61–62
    in Vietnam, *1960s:* 77–78
    See also Anticommunism

Communist Party of the U.S.A. (CPUSA), *1940s:* 78, 82

Community colleges, *1940s:* 46, 56

Community Service Organization (CSO), *1960s:* 28

Como, Perry, *1940s:* 16; *1950s:* 5, 15, 18

Compact cars, *1960s:* 30–31, 97, 106; *1970s:* 40

Compact discs (CDs), *1970s:* 156; *1980s:* 2
    Amazon.com, *1990s:* 32
    preferred medium, *1990s:* 2

Competition, in auto industry, *1970s:* 29

The Complete Book of Running, 1970s: 126, 129

Complexity and Contradiction in Architecture, 1960s: 99

Composers, *1900s:* 16; *1910s:* 5, 16–17; *1930s:* 20

Compton, Arthur Holly, *1920s:* 132, 132 (ill.)

Compton effect, *1920s:* 132

Compulsory education, *1910s:* 49, 60, 67

Compulsory MisEducation, 1960s: 56

Compulsory religious education, *1940s:* 60

Computer disks, *1970s:* 140

Computerized axial tomography (CAT) scans, *1970s:* 122, 124, 129

Computer keyboards, *1960s:* 143, 145

Computer programming languages, *1950s:* 140, 146–47; *1970s:* 44–45

Computers, *1940s:* 130, 140–42, 142 (ill.); *1950s:* 143–47, 144 (ill.); *1960s:* 29, 36–37, 145, 152–53
    analog, *1920s:* 143
    animation, *1990s:* 117
    Apple, *1980s:* 43, 146, 160–61
    Burroughs, *1950s:* 136
    first networks, *1990s:* 145
    genome mapping, *1990s:* 143
    IBM, *1950s:* 24, 43; *1980s:* 42–44, 146–47, 160–61
    Machine of the Year, *1980s:* 160
    Mark I, *1950s:* 140
    notebook, *1980s:* 30
    personal, *1970s:* 42–45
    Remington-Rand Corporation, *1950s:* 43
    revolution, *1980s:* 159–61
    teachers use of, *1980s:* 48
    transistorized, *1950s:* 137
    UNIVAC, *1950s:* 136, 138, 140, 143–46, 144 (ill.)
    See also Personal computers

Computer software. *See* Software

Conant, James B., *1910s:* 52; *1950s:* 50, 50 (ill.), 53; *1960s:* 50, 50 (ill.), 57

Concert aid
    African famine, *1980s:* 2, 5, 25–26
    AIDS research, *1980s:* 3
    Amnesty International, *1980s:* 3
    farms, *1980s:* 3–4, 26–27, 26 (ill.)
    rock music, *1980s:* 23–24

Concert halls, *1910s:* 90

Concorde, *1970s:* 141

Conditioned reflexes, *1900s:* 118

Condoms, AIDS and, *1980s:* 130

Conerly, Charlie, *1950s:* 175

Conformity, *1950s:* 99–102

Congenital heart defects, *1960s:* 124

Conglomerates, *1960s:* 26, 28, 40–41

Congress, *1910s:* 66, 70; *1960s:* 84–85

Congressional Medal of Honor, *1920s:* 139

Congressional Space Medal of Honor, *1990s:* 142

Congress of Industrial Organizations (CIO), *1930s:* 27, 31, 38, 57; *1940s:* 25, 39

Congress of Racial Equality (CORE), *1940s:* 90; *1960s:* 102

Connally Hot Oil Act, *1930s:* 26, 43

Conn, Billy, *1930s:* 162; *1940s:* 166

Connecticut Society for Mental Hygiene, *1900s:* 101

Connery, Sean, *1960s:* 9

Connor, Roger, *1920s:* 156

Connors, Jimmy, *1970s:* 161, 176–77

Conolly, Maureen "Little Mo," *1950s:* 161

Conrad, Frank, *1920s:* 145

Conscientious objectors, *1910s:* 98; *1920s:* 82

Conservation, *1900s:* 59, 61, 63, 68, 69 (ill.)

Conservatism, social justice movements and, *1970s:* 100

Conservative education, *1930s:* 60; *1940s:* 47, 50–51

Consolidated Tobacco Company, *1900s:* 58

Constitution, *1910s:* 50

Constitutional amendments, *1900s:* 21; *1980s:* 9, 58; *1990s:* 106–07

Construction, *1920s:* 31–32

Consultation of Older and Younger Adults for Social Change, *1970s:* 110

Consumer credit, *1950s:* 24–25, 27,
38–39

Consumer education, *1980s:* 50

Consumerism, *1900s:* 23; *1930s:*
28–29, 103–04; *1980s:* 102–03;
1990s: 98–102
  advertising and, *1920s:* 5, 18
  of postwar economy, *1920s:* 27;
    1940s: 27, 87–88, 100–03

Consumer price index, *1980s:* 37

Consumer prices, *1960s:* 25, 40

Consumer Product Safety Act of 1972,
1970s: 36

Consumer Product Safety Commission, *1970s:* 36; *1980s:* 35

Consumer protection, *1910s:* 84;
1970s: 30, 36

Consumer protection laws, *1900s:* 32

Consumer safety, *1960s:* 29, 82

Contact lenses, *1950s:* 137

Contagious diseases. *See* Infectious
diseases

Containment, of Soviet Union, *1940s:*
34–36, 65, 80–82
  See also Anticommunism

Contemporary Arts Center, Cincinnati, *1990s:* 2, 8

Contempt of civil court, *1990s:* 63

Context, in scientific research, *1940s:*
136

Continental Baking, *1960s:* 40–41

Continuation schools, *1900s:* 41

The Contours, *1960s:* 13

Contraception. *See* Birth control

Contract Plan, *1920s:* 55

Contract with America, *1990s:* 70–72

Control Data, *1960s:* 37

Controversy, Olympics and, *1900s:*
153

Convertibles (automobiles), *1940s:*
102

Convicts, *1910s:* 87, 126

Cooder, Ry, *1970s:* 3

Cook, Chris, *1930s:* 77

Cook County Hospital, *1930s:* 111;
1960s: 121

Cookman Institute for Men, *1920s:* 50

Cooley, Denton A., *1960s:* 121, 124,
124 (ill.), 126–27

Coolidge, Calvin, *1920s:* 65, 68, 68
(ill.), 118; *1930s:* 77
  agricultural policy, *1920s:* 33
  "Coolidge optimism," *1920s:* 25
  Federal Communications Com-
    mission and, *1920s:* 34
  on government in business,
    1920s: 25, 74
  industry regulation and, *1920s:*
    27, 33
  Lindbergh, Charles and, *1920s:*
    139
  on the McNary-Haugen Bill,
    1920s: 75
  political election of, *1920s:* 67,
    76–78

Coolidge, William D., *1910s:* 129, 151

"Cool jazz," *1940s:* 17

Coombs, Jack, *1910s:* 161–62

Coon-skin caps, *1950s:* 93

Cooper, Alice, *1970s:* 13

Cooper, Ben, *1970s:* 160

Cooper, Charles "Chuck," *1940s:* 162

Cooper, Christin, *1980s:* 188

Cooper, Gary, *1930s:* 16; *1950s:* 13

Cooper, Irving S., *1960s:* 124

Cooper, Kenneth, *1970s:* 128, 130
(ill.)

Copland, Aaron, *1920s:* 12; *1930s:* 20;
1940s: 16

The Copperhead, 1910s: 19

Coppola, Francis Ford, *1970s:* 2, 6, 6
(ill.), 17–18

COPS, 1990s: 16–17

Copy machines, *1950s:* 137, 140, 147

Corbett, James, *1900s:* 138

Corbett, James J., *1900s:* 148

CORE (Congress of Racial Equality),
1940s: 90; *1960s:* 102

Core curriculum, *1940s:* 52–54

Cori, Gerty Theresa, *1940s:* 134, 134
(ill.)

Cornell University, *1910s:* 46; *1960s:*
57

Corning Glass Works, *1910s:* 133

Coronary artery bypass surgery, *1960s:* 122, 127–28

Corporate sponsorship of the arts, *1960s:* 27, 31–32

Corporations
multinational, *1990s:* 31, 39–42
spiritualism and, *1990s:* 95, 108
welfare funds for, *1990s:* 41
See also Business and the economy; specific companies

Correction fluid, *1950s:* 138

Correns, Karl, *1900s:* 129

Correspondence courses, *1940s:* 44–45, 55

Corruption, political, *1900s:* 65–67

Corruption, in sports, *1940s:* 165–66

Corrupt Practices Act, *1920s:* 25

Cortisone, *1910s:* 116

Corvair, *1960s:* 29

Cosby, Bill, *1960s:* 97, 106; *1980s:* 100, 100 (ill.), 111

The Cosby Show, 1980s: 16, 100

Cosmic microwave background, *1970s:* 144

Cosmetics, *1930s:* 89; *1950s:* 103; *1960s:* 28, 42

Cosmetics industry, *1940s:* 28

Cosmic rays, *1920s:* 133

Cosmonauts, *1960s:* 142, 144, 156–58

Costello, Frank, *1950s:* 81

Costello, Maurice, *1910s:* 16

Costs
of consumer goods, *1960s:* 25, 40
of gasoline, *1970s:* 26–27, 32, 35
of goods, *1970s:* 41
health care, *1940s:* 111; *1970s:* 132–33
public education, *1910s:* 46, 53
of separate but equal schools, *1940s:* 60–61
of Vietnam War, *1970s:* 36–37, 76
war, *1940s:* 31–32
World War I, *1910s:* 25, 32–33

Cotton Bowl, *1930s:* 163–64

Cotton industry, *1920s:* 128–29

Coty awards, *1970s:* 103

Coubertin, Pierre de, *1900s:* 141, 152

Coulter, Art, *1930s:* 166

Council of National Defense (CND), *1910s:* 117, 121

Council on Medical Education, *1900s:* 100–01, 109–10

Counterculture, *1960s:* 95, 97, 106–08; *1970s:* 11–12, 111

The Count of Monte Cristo, 1910s: 2

Country Joe and the Fish, *1960s:* 12

Country music, *1940s:* 17–18; *1980s:* 25
See also Farms, concert aid

Country-swing bands, *1940s:* 17

Counts, George S., *1920s:* 46–47, 50, 53; *1930s:* 46–47, 51, 51 (ill.), 56, 58

County training schools, *1910s:* 47

Coupland, Douglas, *1990s:* 110

Couples, Fred, *1990s:* 179

Courier, Jim, *1990s:* 181

Courreges, Andre, *1960s:* 98, 98 (ill.)

Courtroom television, *1990s:* 14–15

Courtroom Television Network, *1990s:* 15

Cousteau, Jacques, *1970s:* 144, 144 (ill.)

Cousy, Bob, *1960s:* 176

The Covenant, 1980s: 12

Cover-ups. *See* Watergate

Covington, Benjamin, *1900s:* 107

Cowboys, Dallas, *1970s:* 172

Cowlings, Al, *1990s:* 85

Cox, Archibald, *1970s:* 74, 86–87

Cox, James M., *1920s:* 76, 145

CPI (Committee on Public Information), *1910s:* 20, 52, 76

CPR (cardiopulmonary resuscitation), *1960s:* 128

CPS (Child-protective-service), *1980s:* 112

CPUSA. *See* Communist Party of the U.S.A.

Crabbe, Buster, *1930s:* 155, 166

Crack, *1980s:* 97, 109

The Cradle Will Rock, 1930s: 21

Craig, Ralph, *1910s:* 174

Cramm, Gottfried von, *1930s:* 168

Crane, Stephen, *1900s:* 8

Crawford, Cheryl, *1930s:* 21

Crawford, Joan, *1920s:* 16; *1930s:* 6, 6 (ill.), 102

Crawford, Michael, *1980s:* 14

Crazylegs, 1950s: 176

Creationism, *1970s:* 140; *1980s:* 48–49, 54, 56–57; *1990s:* 47

Credit cards, *1950s:* 38; *1980s:* 103

Credit, consumer, *1950s:* 24–25, 27, 38–39

Credit, for consumer goods, *1940s:* 25

Creel Committee. *See* Committee on Public Information

Creel, George, *1910s:* 20, 85

CREEP (Committee to Reelect the President), *1970s:* 84–86

Crenshaw, Ben, *1970s:* 174

Crew, D. J., *1990s:* 111 (ill.)

Crick, Francis H. C., *1950s:* 147; *1990s:* 130

Crime, *1950s:* 83, 91; *1960s:* 80–81
  Barker, "Ma," *1930s:* 72
  drug-related, *1980s:* 108–09
  hate, *1990s:* 93, 102
  Immigration Act of 1887, *1910s:* 66
  juvenile, *1990s:* 105
  Mafia, *1930s:* 81–83
  New York, *1910s:* 2
  tribal punishment, *1990s:* 92
  war against, *1930s:* 83–85
  See also Organized crime; Shootings; Violence

Crime Does Not Pay, 1940s: 11

Crime, labor unions and, *1900s:* 21

Crime stories, in comic books, *1940s:* 11

Crime syndicates, *1940s:* 165

Criminal justice, changes in, *1960s:* 81

Crisis in the Classroom, 1970s: 52

Crisler, Fritz, *1940s:* 167

Criticism, of education, *1960s:* 55–57

Cronkite, Walter, *1950s:* 18, 145; *1960s:* 6, 6 (ill.)

Crosby, Bing, *1940s:* 17–18

Crosby, Caresse, *1910s:* 91

Crosby, Stills, Nash and Young, *1960s:* 12

Cross-country skiing, *1900s:* 139

The Crossword Puzzle Book, 1920s: 101

Crossword puzzles, *1920s:* 101

Cryosurgery, *1960s:* 122, 124

The Crystals, *1960s:* 11

CSO (Community Service Organization), *1960s:* 28

CTF (Chicago Teachers' Federation), *1900s:* 40, 44

Cuba, *1910s:* 72

Cuban Giants, *1900s:* 145

Cuban missile crisis, *1960s:* 68, 70, 76–77, 85; *1980s:* 113

Cuban X-Giants, *1900s:* 146

Cuba, skyjackings to, *1960s:* 81

Cubberley, Ellwood P., *1920s:* 46, 53–55, 57

Cubism, *1920s:* 17–18; *1940s:* 4

Cubist Realism, *1920s:* 18

Cubo-Realism, *1920s:* 18

Cullen, Countee, *1920s:* 10

Culligan water filters, *1950s:* 41

Cults, religious, *1970s:* 99, 114–16, 117 (ill.)

Cultural education, *1940s:* 52–54

Cultural protest, through rock music, *1970s:* 12

Cultural revolution
  in music, *1960s:* 11
  in theater, *1960s:* 17–18

Cultural traditionalism, *1970s:* 100–01

Cumberland College, *1910s:* 155

cummings, e.e., *1920s:* 13

Cummings, Homer S., *1930s:* 83

Cunningham, Billy, *1960s:* 177

Cunningham, Glenn, *1930s:* 168–69

Cunningham, Merce, *1960s:* 114

CUNY (City University of New York), *1960s:* 47

"Cupcake," *1960s:* 16

"The Cup of Life," *1990s:* 24

Currency, *1970s:* 38

Currency, national, *1900s:* 20, 32

Currency, World War I, *1910s:* 32

Current Tax Payment Act, *1940s:* 64

Curriculum, *1900s:* 46–48; *1950s:*
   53–55; *1960s:* 52–54; *1980s:* 48
    academic requirements, *1980s:* 50
    agriculture, *1910s:* 56–58
    American history in, *1940s:* 45
    business, *1910s:* 57
    censorship, *1980s:* 54–58
    changes in, *1920s:* 53–55
    core, *1940s:* 52–54
    creationism versus evolution,
      1980s: 48–49, 54, 56–57
    secondary schools, *1910s:* 48
    sports in, *1920s:* 47, 60–61
    women's studies, *1910s:* 58–60
    World War I, *1910s:* 47
Curtis, Charles, *1920s:* 78
Curtiss, Glenn, *1910s:* 138
Curtiss-Wright, *1920s:* 34
Curtis, Tony, *1950s:* 12 (ill.)
Cushing, Harvey Williams, *1910s:*
   129; *1920s:* 112, 112 (ill.)
Cushing's disease, *1920s:* 112
Custody cases, *1950s:* 91
CWA (Civil Works Administration),
   1930s: 26, 77
Cyanide poisonings, Tylenol, *1980s:*
   122, 125
Cyanosis, *1940s:* 112
Cybernetics, *1940s:* 141–42; *1950s:* 136
Cyclamates, *1960s:* 121–23, 135
Cyclotron, *1930s:* 130, 145–46
Cynicism, political, *1970s:* 84
Cystoscopes, *1960s:* 121
Cy Young Award, *1960s:* 168
Czolgosz, Leon, *1900s:* 58, 70

D

Dachau concentration camp, *1940s:*
   101 (ill.)
Dacron fabrics, *1950s:* 91
Da-i Ho, David, *1990s:* 117, 120, 120
   (ill.)
Daily, Dan, *1950s:* 176
Daimler, Gottlieb, *1900s:* 124
Dairy Queen, *1960s:* 35
Dali, Salvador, *1940s:* 8
Dallas, 1980s: 16

Dallas Chaparrals, *1960s:* 177
Dallas Cowboys, *1970s:* 172; *1990s:*
   175
Dallas Stars, *1990s:* 176
Dalton Plan, *1920s:* 46, 55–56
Daly, John, *1990s:* 179
Dam, Carl, *1920s:* 124
Damn Yankees, 1950s: 176
Dams, irrigation, *1900s:* 20, 58
Dance, *1900s:* 6, 15; *1920s:* 11; *1930s:*
   22; *1940s:* 6, 17; *1960s:* 114; *1980s:*
   3, 22
    ballet, *1910s:* 2, 9–10, 10 (ill.)
    ballroom, *1910s:* 90, 106
    censorship and, *1910s:* 59
    Denishawn School of Dancing,
      1910s: 3
    disco, *1970s:* 15–16
    Duncan, Isadora, *1910s:* 3
    Little Renaissance, *1910s:* 4
Dance crazes, *1960s:* 108
Dance Fools Dance, 1930s: 6
Dance marathons, *1920s:* 102
Dance Project, *1930s:* 22
Dance Repertory Theatre, *1930s:* 22
Dancer Series, 1970s: 8
Dancer's Image, 1960s: 165
Dancing, *1950s:* 109
"Dancing in the Street," *1960s:* 15
Dangling Man, 1940s: 12
Daniel, Beth, *1990s:* 179
Daniels, Charles, *1900s:* 139, 142, 142
   (ill.)
Danish modern design, *1950s:* 104
Dante, *1980s:* 55
DAR (Daughters of the American Rev-
   olution), *1900s:* 45; *1930s:* 60, 73
"Dare Progressive Education Be Pro-
   gressive?," *1930s:* 46
Dark Abstraction, 1920s: 2
The Dark Side of the Moon, 1970s: 2
Darling Lili, 1960s: 9
Darrow, Clarence, *1900s:* 27, 30;
   1920s: 59 (ill.), 68, 68 (ill.)
    Leopold and Loeb case, *1920s:* 82
    Scopes Monkey Trial and, *1920s:*
      60
    Sweet, Ossian and, *1920s:* 83

Dartmouth College, *1920s:* 24

Dartmouth Time-Sharing System
(DTSS), *1960s:* 152–53

Darvon, *1950s:* 115

Darwin, Charles, *1900s:* 119, 131;
1910s: 150; *1920s:* 60; *1940s:* 140;
1980s: 56

Darwinism, *1920s:* 103
book banning and, *1920s:* 47
in school, *1920s:* 46–47; *1990s:*
56–59

Dating, high school, *1940s:* 98

Dating systems, radioactive-potassi-
um, *1950s:* 148–49

Datsun, *1960s:* 30–31

Daughters of the American Revolution
(DAR), *1900s:* 45; *1930s:* 60, 73

Daugherty, Harry, *1920s:* 67

The Dave Clark Five, *1960s:* 10

Davenport, Lindsay, *1990s:* 165, 181

Davidson, Donald, *1930s:* 14

Davidson, Henry P., *1900s:* 28

Davidson, Jo, *1920s:* 13

da Vinci, Leonardo, *1960s:* 2–3

Davies, Laura, *1980s:* 183

Davis, Al, *1980s:* 180

Davis Cup, *1900s:* 138; *1910s:* 154

Davis Cup (tennis), *1940s:* 153

Davis, Glenn, *1940s:* 156

Davis, Harry, *1900s:* 3

Davis, Jerome, *1930s:* 56

Davis, John W., *1920s:* 77

Davis, Miles, *1940s:* 5, 17; *1950s:* 15

Davis, Rennie, *1960s:* 115

Davis, Stuart, *1930s:* 5

Dawes, Charles G., *1920s:* 76

Dawes Plan, *1920s:* 65

The Day After, *1980s:* 96, 113

A Day at the Races, *1930s:* 164

Day care, *1970s:* 105

Day, Doris, *1950s:* 13

"A Day in the Life," *1960s:* 11

Daylight Saving Time, *1910s:* 67

A Day of National Solidarity, *1980s:* 62

The Day the Earth Stood Still, *1950s:*
16

Daytona Literary and Industrial Institute for the Training of Negro Girls,
1900s: 41

Daytona Normal and Industrial Institute for Negro Girls, *1920s:* 50

Dayton Triangles, *1910s:* 169

DC-1, *1930s:* 136

DC-3, *1930s:* 135–37

DC-2, *1930s:* 136

D-Day, *1940s:* 68, 75

DDT (dichlorodiphenyl-
trichloroethane), *1940s:* 110,
114–15, 115 (ill.), 130; *1960s:* 121;
1970s: 140, 152–53

Dead Sea Scrolls, *1940s:* 87

Dean, Dizzy, *1930s:* 158

Dean, James, *1950s:* 3, 12

Dean, John, *1970s:* 70, 86

Death, *1980s:* 50, 122, 128
causes of, *1930s:* 112, 121–24;
1970s: 131; *1990s:* 126
infants, *1910s:* 112; *1920s:* 117
pneumonia, *1910s:* 114
right-to-die, *1970s:* 123–24,
127–28
tuberculosis, *1910s:* 114, 129–30

Death at an Early Age, *1970s:* 52

Death of a Salesman, *1940s:* 19

Death of Money parade, *1960s:* 95

DeBakey, Michael E., *1960s:* 124, 124
(ill.), 126–27

Debates, presidential candidates,
1960s: 19–20, 68, 83–84, 83 (ill.)

Debs, Eugene V., *1900s:* 24, 24 (ill.);
1910s: 37, 66; *1920s:* 64

Debt
consumer, *1990s:* 94
government, *1940s:* 31–34
national, *1910s:* 67
school systems, *1990s:* 45
U.S., *1980s:* 30–31, 81–85
war, Germany, *1940s:* 38–39

DeBusschere, Dave, *1960s:* 177;
1970s: 169

Debutantes, *1930s:* 102

Decathlon, *1960s:* 181

Decatur Staleys, *1920s:* 164

Decca Records, *1940s:* 2

Declaration of Independence, *1930s:* 22

Declaration of the United Nations, *1940s:* 64

de Coubertin, Baron, *1920s:* 167

The Deep End of the Ocean, 1990s: 3

Deep-sea exploration, *1970s:* 141–42, 144

Defense Guidance Plan, *1980s:* 68, 76

Defense industry, *1910s:* 76, 135, 150–51

    African Americans in, *1940s:* 103–04

    Office of Production Management, *1940s:* 24

    production in, *1940s:* 30–31

Defense of Marriage Act, *1990s:* 102

Defense spending, *1940s:* 35

The Defiant Ones, 1960s: 105

Deficit, federal, *1970s:* 36–37

Deficit spending, *1990s:* 36

Deficit spending, Reagan administration, *1980s:* 73, 81–85

De Forest, Lee, *1900s:* 119, 122, 128; *1910s:* 3, 5, 20, 148; *1920s:* 131, 142

DeGeneres, Ellen, *1990s:* 96, 96 (ill.)

de Graff, Robert Fair, *1940s:* 11

Dehnert, Henry "Dutch," *1910s:* 165

de Kruif, Paul, *1920s:* 129

De La Beckwith, Byron, *1960s:* 101–02

Dellinger, David, *1960s:* 115

Del Monte, *1960s:* 41

Delta Air Lines, *1970s:* 26

Demaret, Jimmy, *1940s:* 168

Demetrius and the Gladiators, 1950s: 106

DeMille, Cecil B., *1910s:* 3, 15; *1930s:* 15

Democracy and Education, 1910s: 48

Democratic National Committee. *See* Watergate

Democratic National Convention, *1960s:* 71, 86, 103, 114–15

Democratic Party, *1910s:* 68, 84

Dempsey, Jack, *1910s:* 155, 167; *1920s:* 149, 151–52, 152 (ill.), 161; *1950s:* 171

Dempster, Jeffrey, *1930s:* 140

Demuth, Charles, *1920s:* 18

Denby, Edwin, *1920s:* 67, 78–79

Dengue fever, *1940s:* 114

Denishawn School of Dancing, *1910s:* 3, 10

Denkanesh. See Lucy (fossil)

Dental checkups, *1910s:* 51

Dental instruments, *1950s:* 136

Dentistry, *1910s:* 112–13

Denver Broncos, *1990s:* 175

Denver Nuggets, *1950s:* 169; *1960s:* 178

Denver Rockets, *1960s:* 177

Deoxyribonucleic acid (DNA), *1960s.* 150–52

    See also DNA

DePalma, Ralph, *1910s:* 160

Department of Agriculture, *1910s:* 148

Department of Commerce, *1930s:* 130

Department of Commerce and Labor, *1900s:* 45, 64

Department of Defense, *1940s:* 66

Department of Education, *1980s:* 50

Department of Energy, *1970s:* 30, 34

Department of Health and Human Services, *1980s:* 123

Department of Health, Education, and Welfare, *1950s:* 46, 114; *1960s:* 121

Department of Immigration Education, *1920s:* 52

Department of Justice, *1940s:* 2, 5, 14, 25

Department of Labor, *1910s:* 86

Department of the Interior, *1930s:* 3

Department stores, *1900s:* 25, 81; *1910s:* 42; *1950s:* 25; *1960s:* 35

Depression (economic)

    See also Great Depression

Deregulation, *1980s:* 32, 34–37

    airlines, *1980s:* 35

    banking, *1980s:* 30, 36, 38

    phone service, *1970s:* 27

    railroads, *1980s:* 35

savings and loan associations, *1980s:* 33, 37

trucking, *1980s:* 30, 35

Derham, James, *1900s:* 105

Der Rosenkavalier, 1910s: 16

Dershowitz, Alan M., *1990s:* 86

DeSalvo, Albert, *1960s:* 80

Desegregation, *1950s:* 46–47, 50, 57–60, 57 (ill.), 59 (ill.), 71

   See also Integration; Segregation

Desertion, *1910s:* 122

Desert Storm. *See* Persian Gulf War

de Sitter, Willem, *1910s:* 133

The Desk Set, 1950s: 145

Desktop computers, *1960s:* 36–37

Desktop publishing, *1980s:* 160

DeSoto, *1920s:* 25

DeSoto Airflow, *1930s:* 94, 95 (ill.), 130

Desserts, frozen, *1950s:* 90

Detective fiction, *1920s:* 19

Détente, *1970s:* 80–81; *1980s:* 75

Detroit Cougars, *1920s:* 149

Detroit Falcons, *1950s:* 168

Detroit Lions, *1950s:* 173; *1990s:* 175

Detroit, Michigan race riots, *1940s:* 86, 104; *1960s:* 95

Detroit Pistons, *1950s:* 169; *1980s:* 169

Detroit Public Library, *1910s:* 94

Detroit Tigers, *1900s:* 139, 144; *1910s:* 162; *1960s:* 173

Deuterium, *1930s:* 135

Deuteron rays, *1950s:* 114

Developmental psychology, *1900s:* 123

Dever, Paul A., *1950s:* 53

Devers, Gail, *1990s:* 183

De Vries, Hugo, *1930s:* 142

DeVries, William, *1980s:* 126, 126 (ill.)

Dewey, Evelyn, *1910s:* 50

Dewey, John, *1910s:* 46–48, 54, 58; *1920s:* 46, 50–51, 54–55; *1930s:* 46, 56, 58; *1940s:* 50, 54; *1950s:* 50

Dewey Stakes, *1920s:* 148, 167

Dewey, Thomas E., *1930s:* 82; *1940s:* 45, 67–68, 68 (ill.); *1950s:* 130 (ill.)

Dewson, Mary Williams, *1930s:* 92, 92 (ill.)

Dexter, Edwin, *1900s:* 41

Diabetes, *1920s:* 117–19; *1990s:* 126

Diaghilev, Sergey, *1910s:* 9

Dialysis machines, *1960s:* 122, 128, 129 (ill.)

Diamond, David, *1930s:* 20

Diapers, disposable, *1950s:* 136

Diaz, Porfirio, *1910s:* 73

Dichlorodiphenyltrichloroethane. *See* DDT

Dick, George, *1920s:* 112, 114

Dick, Gladys, *1920s:* 112, 114

Dick test, *1920s:* 112

Dick Tracy, 1930s: 11–12, 11 (ill.)

The Dick Van Dyke Show, 1960s: 19

Dictatorships, *1940s:* 2

Didrikson, Mildred "Babe," *1930s:* 155–56, 156 (ill.), 166

   See also. Zaharias, Mildred "Babe" Didrikson

Diem, Ngo Dinh, *1960s:* 68, 78

Diesel engine, development of, *1920s:* 135

Diet, *1910s:* 112

Diet, high fat, *1950s:* 125

Dietrich, Marlene, *1930s:* 15, 102

Differential analyzers, *1940s:* 134

The Diggers, *1960s:* 95

Digital computers, *1940s:* 130, 140–42

Digital video discs (DVDs), *1990s:* 151

Dinah Shore Classics, *1990s:* 179

Dine, Jim, *1960s:* 16

The Dinner Party, 1970s: 3, 9

Diode vacuum tubes, *1900s:* 118

Dioxin, *1970s:* 156

Dihigo, Martín, *1920s:* 160

Dilling, Elizabeth, *1930s:* 60

Dillinger, John, *1930s:* 82–84, 95

DiMaggio, Joe, *1930s:* 154, 158; *1940s:* 152, 156, 156 (ill.), 159, 160 (ill.), 161; *1950s:* 158, 164

Dime Detective, 1930s: 14

The Dinah Shore Chevy Show, 1950s: 30

Diners Club, *1950s:* 38

Ding Dong School, 1950s: 64, 64 (ill.)

Dinosaurs, *1980s:* 146, 150

Dionne and Friends, *1980s:* 19

Dionne quintuplets, *1930s:* 88

Dior, Christian, *1940s:* 96; *1950s:* 99

Diothane, *1930s:* 116

Diphtheria, *1910s:* 132; *1950s:* 115

Diptheria vaccine, *1920s:* 109

Diplomacy, *1910s:* 72–73

Director's Liability Act, *1910s:* 173

Dirigibles, *1900s:* 118, 125; *1920s:* 139–40; *1930s:* 136–37

Disabled employees, *1990s:* 28

Disarmament, *1930s:* 69

Discipline, schools, *1980s:* 48

Disco music, *1970s:* 2–3, 5, 7, 15–16

Discotheques, *1970s:* 99, 112

Discount rate, *1960s:* 25

Discount stores, *1960s:* 26, 34 (ill.), 35

Discovery (space shuttle), *1980s:* 147, 154; *1990s:* 138–39, 156, 158

Discrimination
educational, *1900s:* 50–51
gays and lesbians, *1990s:* 92
immigrants, *1900s:* 84
See also specific types of discrimination

Discus throwing, *1960s:* 169, 181

Disease prevention, *1900s:* 102

Diseases, *1900s:* 110–15; *1920s:* 110–11, 114–15
genome mapping, *1990s:* 143
See also specific diseases

Dishwashers, *1960s:* 142

Disinfectants, *1910s:* 132

Disk drives, *1970s:* 43–44, 141

Disks, computer, *1970s:* 140

Disneyland, *1950s:* 91

Disney (television show). *See* Walt Disney (television show)

Disney, Walt, *1920s:* 142; *1930s:* 3, 17, 122; *1940s:* 2, 13

Disney World, *1970s:* 152

Displaced Persons Act, *1940s:* 65

Dissenters, war, *1910s:* 19, 53

Distinguished Flying Cross, *1920s:* 139

"Divine Right" letter, *1900s:* 27

Divorce, *1900s:* 78

Divorce Court, 1990s: 15

Divorce laws, *1970s:* 106

Dixon, Thomas, *1900s:* 3, 5

Dizzy Dean, *1950s:* 176

DNA (deoxyribonucleic acid), *1940s:* 130, 133; *1960s:* 150–52
gene therapy and, *1990s:* 130–34
genome mapping, *1990s:* 143–44
molecule, *1990s:* 144 (ill.)
testing, *1990s:* 86

Dochez, Alphonse Raymond, *1930s:* 121

"Dock of the Bay," *1960s:* 15

Doctors
background information, *1990s:* 117
salaries, *1970s:* 132; *1980s:* 137
shortage of, *1970s:* 133
strikes by, *1970s:* 122–23
See also Physicians

Documentaries
rock concerts, *1960s:* 12
shock, *1990s:* 14, 16, 18
war, *1940s:* 14

Dodge automobiles, *1910s:* 142

Dodge, Horace, *1910s:* 103

Dodge, John, *1910s:* 103

Doheny, Edward L., *1920s:* 78–79

Doisy, Edward, *1920s:* 109

Dollar diplomacy, *1910s:* 68, 72–73

Dolls, Raggedy Ann, *1910s:* 91

Dolly (cloned sheep), *1990s:* 133–34

Dolores Claiborne, 1990s: 20

Dolphins, communication of, *1960s:* 151

Dolphins, Miami, *1970s:* 160, 171

Dolphins, protection of, *1990s:* 28

Domagk, Gerhard, *1930s:* 120; *1940s:* 118

Domestic partners, *1990s:* 92

Domestic servants, *1910s:* 102

Domino, Fats, *1950s:* 15

Donahue, Phil, *1990s:* 13–14

Donald Duck, *1930s:* 17, 122

Donaldson, Walter, *1910s:* 5, 17; *1930s:* 2

Donath, W. F., *1920s:* 123

Don Juan, 1920s: 3, 16, 129, 142

Donovan, Art, *1950s:* 175

Donovan, Marion, *1950s:* 136

Doobie Brothers, *1970s:* 13

Dooley, Thomas A., *1950s:* 118, 118 (ill.)

Doolittle, Hilda, *1910s:* 12; *1920s:* 13

Doolittle, James H., *1920s:* 137

The Doors, *1960s:* 11–13

Doorway to Hell, 1930s: 16

Doppler navigation, *1950s:* 137

Dorais, Gus, *1910s:* 168; *1920s:* 153

Dorsey, Jimmy, *1930s:* 2

Dorsey, Thomas, *1930s:* 20

Dorsey, Tommy, *1930s:* 20

Dorsey, Susan Miller, *1920s:* 46

Dos Passos, John, *1920s:* 14; *1930s:* 4, 12–13; *1940s:* 12

"Do They Know It's Christmas," *1980s:* 24

Douglas Aircraft, *1920s:* 34

Douglas, Carl, *1970s:* 114

Douglas, Donald W., *1920s:* 28

Douglas, Kirk, *1950s:* 15

Dove, Robert, *1900s:* 105

Dow Chemical, *1930s:* 140; *1960s:* 36, 64

Dow Corning, *1990s:* 132

Dow Jones Industrial Average, *1920s:* 65; *1930s:* 26; *1960s:* 25–26, 32–33; *1990s:* 28–29

"Down Hearted Blues," *1920s:* 2

Downsizing, *1990s:* 38–39

Down's syndrome, *1950s:* 148

"Do You Love Me," *1960s:* 13

Dozier, Lamont, *1960s:* 13

Draft evaders, *1970s:* 71

Draft, military, *1940s:* 44, 64; *1950s:* 60–61; *1960s:* 49, 54–55

Drake, Frank, *1960s:* 150

Drama, *1920s:* 4, 7–9; *1940s:* 5–6, 18–20

DRAM (dynamic random access memory), *1980s:* 147

Dr. Atkins' New Diet Revolution, 1990s: 120

Dr. Dre, *1990s:* 23

Dreams, *1900s:* 131–32

Dream Team (basketball), *1990s:* 172

Dreier, Katherine, *1920s:* 2

Dreiser, Theodore, *1900s:* 5, 6, 6 (ill.), 8; *1910s:* 10; *1930s:* 12; *1980s:* 2

Dresden, bombing of, *1940s:* 75

Drew, Charles R., *1940s:* 112, 112 (ill.)

Drew, Howard P., *1910s:* 174

Drexel Burnham Lambert, *1980s:* 30, 42

Drexler, Clyde, *1990s:* 172

Dr. Goldfoot and the Bikini Machine, 1960s: 108

Drilling equipment, *1950s:* 136

Drinker, Philip, *1920s:* 119, 129

Drinkwater, John, *1930s:* 133

Driscoll, Paddy, *1920s:* 148

Drive-in theaters, *1930s:* 88

Driver education, *1980s:* 50

Driving speed limits, *1970s:* 26

Dr. Kildare, 1960s: 19

Dr. No, 1960s: 9

Dropouts, *1940s:* 58–59; *1980s:* 63

Dropouts, high school, *1970s:* 57

Drosophila melanogaster, 1900s: 130

Dr. Seuss, *1930s:* 3

    See also Geisel, Theodore S.

Drug abuse, *1980s:* 49

    AIDS, *1980s:* 123–24, 129–30

    baseball and, *1980s:* 174

    basketball and, *1980s:* 177

    crime and, *1980s:* 108–09

    Reagan, Nancy campaign against, *1980s:* 63, 96

    schools, *1980s:* 48–49, 63–65

    trafficking, *1980s:* 69

Drug addiction, *1930s:* 111

Drug culture, *1960s:* 107

    LSD, *1960s:* 95, 99

    in rock music, *1960s:* 11–13

Drug education, *1980s:* 50

Drugs

    abortion inducing pill, *1990s:* 116

    abuse of, *1990s:* 164

AIDS, *1990s:* 126
antiobesity, *1990s:* 117
antiviral, *1990s:* 125
for enhanced athletic performance, *1950s:* 115
pharmaceutical companies,
1990s: 126
Drugs (pharmaceuticals), for AIDS,
1980s: 123, 130
Dryers, clothes, *1950s:* 137
DTSS (Dartmouth Time-Sharing Sys-
tem), *1960s:* 152–53
Dubinsky, David, *1930s:* 30–31 30
(ill.)
Du Bois, W. E. B., *1900s:* 40, 52–53,
59, 82, 85; *1910s:* 50, 61–62; *1920s:*
11; *1930s:* 93, 93 (ill.)
Duchamp, Marcel, *1910s:* 12; *1920s:* 2
Duck Soup, 1930s: 15 (ill.), 17
Dudley, Bill, *1940s:* 167
Duesenberg, *1920s:* 34, 87; *1930s:* 41
Duesenberg Model J, *1920s:* 87
Dukakis, Michael, *1920s:* 83; *1980s:*
73
Duke, James B., *1920s:* 47
Duke University, *1920s:* 47
Dumas, Charles, *1950s:* 159
Dunaway, Faye, *1960s:* 8 (ill.)
Duncan, Isadora, *1900s:* 6, 6 (ill.);
1910s: 3
Dunlop Rubber Company, *1920s:* 129
Dunn, Johnny, *1910s:* 3
Dunwoody, Henry, *1900s:* 128
DuPont Chemicals, *1970s:* 153
Du Pont Company, *1920s:* 28; *1930s:*
89, 130–31, 141–42; *1950s:* 42,
90–91
Du Pont de Nemours, E. I., *1950s:* 90
Du Pont, Pierre S., *1920s:* 28, 28 (ill.)
Duprene. *See* Neoprene
Duran Duran, *1980s:* 18
Durant, William "Billy" C., *1910s:* 28,
28 (ill.)
Duval, David, *1990s:* 179
DVD (digital video discs), *1990s:* 151
Dwyer Classic, *1930s:* 165
Dying Swan, 1910s: 9

Dylan, Bob, *1930s:* 7; *1960s:* 2, 5–6, 6
(ill.), 113
Dymaxion House, *1920s:* 87
Dynamic random access memory
(DRAM), *1980s:* 147
Dynasty, 1980s: 16

E

EABA (Eastern Amateur Basketball
Association), *1900s:* 148
Eagle, 1960s: 159
Eagle Forum, *1970s:* 103
Eames, Charles, *1950s:* 104
Earhart, Amelia, *1930s:* 89, 130, 134,
134 (ill.), 136
Ear infections, genome mapping,
1990s: 142
Earl Carroll Theater, *1930s:* 2
The Earl Carroll Vanities, 1920s: 9;
1930s: 2
Earl's Court, *1910s:* 132
Early childhood education, *1960s:* 56
Earth, *1970s:* 147 (ill.), 151–53
age and origin of, *1960s:* 145,
148, 151
Earth Day, *1960s:* 130; *1970s:* 140,
151–52
Earthquake measurement, *1930s:* 143
Earthquakes, *1900s:* 3, 21, 118
Earth science, *1930s:* 143; *1960s:*
152–54
Earth Summit, *1990s:* 138, 152–53
Eastern Airlines, *1920s:* 29
Eastern Amateur Basketball Associa-
tion (EABA), *1900s:* 148
Eastern Colored League, *1920s:* 158
Eastern European Jews, *1910s:* 98
Eastern Europeans, *1910s:* 99
Eastern League (college basketball),
1900s: 146
Eastern religions, *1970s:* 114
Eastern religious traditions, *1980s:*
116–17
"Easter Parade," *1910s:* 6
East London Revival Society. *See* Sal-
vation Army
Eastman, Charles Alexander, *1900s:* 9

Eastman, George, *1920s:* 128

East Village, New York, New York, *1960s:* 107

East-West All-Star Games, *1930s:* 152

Eastwood, Clint, *1990s:* 20

Easy Rider, 1960s: 4–5, 10

Easy Street, 1910s: 6

Eating disorders, *1980s:* 122–23, 138–40

Ebbets Field, 1910s: 154

The Ebert Prize, *1910s:* 119

Ebonics, *1990s:* 53

Ebony Concerto, 1940s: 16

Echo satellite, *1960s:* 151

Eckert, J. Presper, *1940s:* 141

Eclipses, solar, *1900s:* 133

Ecole des Beaux Arts, *1910s:* 100

E-commerce
    Amazon.com, *1990s:* 32, 33, 34 (ill.)
    economic growth, *1990s:* 30–31, 33–36, 139

Economic development, federal funding for, *1960s:* 82

An Economic Interpretation of the Constitution of the United States, 1910s: 50

Economic recession, *1980s:* 122

Economic restrictions, on Germany, *1910s:* 76

Economic sanctions, *1980s:* 62

Economic Wage Stabilization Act of 1970, *1970s:* 26

Economy. *See* Business and the economy

ECT. *See* Electroconvulsive therapy

Eddy, Mary Baker, *1900s:* 82

Edelin, Kenneth C., *1970s:* 126, 126 (ill.)

Edelman, Marian Wright, *1990s:* 48, 48 (ill.)

Ederle, Gertrude, *1920s:* 149, 151, 168 (ill.), 169

Edison, Thomas Alva, *1900s:* 3, 118, 122, 122 (ill.), 128; *1910s:* 13; *1920s:* 141–42; *1970s:* 156

Edmonton Oilers, *1980s:* 168–69, 172, 184–85

EDS. *See* Electronic Data Systems

Edsel automobile, *1950s:* 99

The Ed Sullivan Show, 1950s: 19; *1960s:* 2–3

Education, *1900s:* 39–56; *1910s:* 45–63; *1930s:* 45–66; *1940s:* 43–62; *1950s:* 45–65; *1970s:* 47–66; *1980s:* 47–65; *1990s:* 43–61
    academic freedom, *1940s:* 50–51
    affect of Red Scare, *1920s:* 49
    annual expenditures, *1920s:* 57
    business schools, *1900s:* 50; *1920s:* 24
    Carnegie, Andrew and, *1900s:* 24
    child labor and, *1910s:* 85–86
    chronology, *1900s:* 40–41; *1910s:* 46–47; *1920s:* 46–47; *1930s:* 46–47; *1940s:* 44–45; *1950s:* 46–47; *1960s:* 46–47; *1970s:* 48–49; *1980s:* 48–49; *1990s:* 44–45
    Darwinism in, *1920s:* 46–47
    enrollment, *1920s:* 46–48, 55
    extension programs, *1910s:* 53–54
    federal funding, *1940s:* 54–55
    foreign languages in, *1920s:* 46, 52–53
    headline makers, *1900s:* 44; *1910s:* 50–51; *1920s:* 50–51; *1930s:* 50–51; *1940s:* 48–49; *1950s:* 50–51; *1960s:* 50–51; *1970s:* 52; *1980s:* 52; *1990s:* 48
    overview, *1900s:* 42–43; *1910s:* 48–49; *1920s:* 48–49; *1930s:* 48–49; *1940s:* 46–47; *1950s:* 48–49; *1960s:* 48–49; *1970s:* 50–51; *1980s:* 50–51; *1990s:* 46–47
    Reagan, Ronald, *1980s:* 50
    school clothes, *1960s:* 111
    See also Medical schools

Educational Amendments Act of 1972, *1970s:* 62

Educational Equality League, *1930s:* 46, 65

Educational films, *1940s:* 44–45

Educational reform, *1900s:* 40, 42, 53–55; *1910s:* 50, 54–56; *1920s:*

53–55; *1940s:* 52–54; *1950s:* 50;
1970s: 52; *1990s:* 51
Educational television, *1950s:* 49,
63–64, 64 (ill.); *1960s:* 31–32;
1990s: 48
   ban on *Sesame Street, 1970s:* 2
   in schools, *1970s:* 59
Educational Testing Service, *1970s:* 49
Educational tests, *1980s:* 50, 59–60
The Education Commission of the
States, *1980s:* 49
Education for All Handicapped Chil-
dren Act of 1975, *1970s:* 56
Education for Freedom, 1940s: 54
Edward, Prince of Wales, *1920s:*
95–96
Edwards with the News, 1950s: 3
Edward VII, *1900s:* 78
EEG (electroencephalogram), *1920s:*
115
E! Entertainment Television, 1990s: 3,
13
EEOC (Equal Employment Opportu-
nity Commission), *1990s:* 28
   See also Equal Employment
      Opportunity Commission
Egypt, *1990s:* 68
Egyptian relics, *1970s:* 99
Ehrlichman, John, *1970s:* 70, 86
Ehrlich, Paul, *1910s:* 114
E. I. Du Pont de Nemours and Com-
pany, *1960s:* 24
"The Eight," *1900s:* 6; *1910s:* 9
Eighteenth Amendment, *1910s:* 25,
69, 82–83
Eijkman, Christiaan, *1920s:* 111, 123
Einstein, Albert, *1900s:* 119, 121, 123,
132–33; *1910s:* 133, 135–36, 136
(ill.); *1930s:* 130–31, 146–47;
1940s: 132, 144, 146; *1960s:* 146
Einthoven, Willem, *1920s:* 110, 116
Eisenhower, Dwight D., *1940s:* 65, 68,
68 (ill.); *1950s:* 72, 72 (ill.); *1960s:*
76, 84, 96; *1970s:* 83; *1980s:* 77;
1990s: 145
   on atomic bombs, *1940s:* 77
   corporate taxation, *1950s:* 25
   desegregation, *1950s:* 57

   education, *1950s:* 46
   elections, *1950s:* 68, 71, 83–86,
      146
   heart attack, *1950s:* 117, 124
   "Military-Industrial Complex,"
      1950s: 40
   Operation Torch, *1940s:* 75
   physical fitness, *1950s:* 131
   Pledge of Allegiance, *1950s:* 69
   televised press conference, *1950s:*
      3
Eisenhower, Mamie Doud, *1950s:* 94,
94 (ill.)
Eisenstadt v. *Baird, 1970s:* 89
El Alamein, *1940s:* 74
Elderly, *1940s:* 111
Elderly health care, *1960s:* 82,
120–21, 123, 131
Elderly rights, *1970s:* 110
Elder, Robert Lee, *1970s:* 175
Elders, Joycelyn, *1990s:* 116, 120, 120
(ill.)
"Eleanor Rigby," *1960s:* 11
Elections, *1920s:* 67, 70, 75–78
   congressional, *1990s:* 74
Elections, presidential, *1910s:* 68,
83–85, *1930s:* 77; *1940s:* 68; *1950s:*
83–86; *1970s:* 81; *1990s:* 75
   computers and, *1950s:* 145–46
   See also Presidential elections
Elective system, in universities, *1900s:*
44
Electric guitars, *1960s:* 113
Electricians, *1960s:* 24
Electricity, *1910s:* 102, 134; *1960s:*
152–54
Electricity industry, *1930s:* 31, 131
Electricity, nuclear power, *1950s:* 136
Electric knives, *1930s:* 131
Electric locomotives, *1940s:* 25
Electric razors, *1900s:* 119
Electric Theater, *1900s:* 9–10
Electroconvulsive therapy (ECT),
1940s: 108, 122–25, 124 (ill.)
Electrocutions. *See* Executions
Electrolytic radio detector, *1900s:* 118
Electronic circuits, *1960s:* 142, 145

Electronic Data Systems (EDS), *1960s:* 29

Electronic Industries' Association, *1990s:* 17

Electronic Numerical Integrator and Calculator (ENIAC), *1940s:* 130, 141, 142 (ill.)

Electronics, *1950s:* 142

Electronics industry, *1960s:* 27, 29, 36–37, 39

Electrons, *1900s:* 119; *1930s:* 143

Electron tubes, *1910s:* 148

Electrocardiograph, *1920s:* 116

Electroencephalogram (EEG), *1920s:* 115

Electroplating, *1900s:* 118

Electroshock therapy (EST), *1950s:* 27, 114, 116, 124–25

Elementary and Secondary Education Act, *1960s:* 52; *1970s:* 55–56

Elementary schools, *1980s:* 50, 54

Elementary schools, California, *1910s:* 46

Elementary school shootings, Butte, Montana, *1990s:* 44

Element 103. *See* Lawrencium

Elements, *1930s:* 143

Eliot, Charles William, *1900s:* 44, 44 (ill.), 103

Eliot, T. S., *1920s:* 2; *1940s:* 3; *1980s:* 14

Elkins Act, *1900s:* 32, 65

Ellen, 1990s: 96

Ellington, Duke, *1930s:* 3; *1940s:* 16

Elliot, Jack "Ramblin'," *1960s:* 113

Ellis, Dale, *1980s:* 177

Ellis Island, *1900s:* 46 (ill.)

El Salvador, *1980s:* 75

Els, Ernie, *1990s:* 179

Elvis. *See* Presley, Elvis

Elway, John, *1990s:* 175

Embargoes
    economic, *1970s:* 94
    oil, *1970s:* 26, 30–32

"Embraceable You," *1930s:* 2

Embryo implantation, *1950s:* 136

Embryonic cells, *1990s:* 133

Emergency Banking Act, *1930s:* 76

Emergency Needs of Women, *1930s:* 88

Emergency Relief Appropriations Act, *1930s:* 27

Emily Post Institute, *1920s:* 91

Emission standards, *1960s:* 126

Emmy awards, *1990s:* 17

Emory University, *1900s:* 40

The Emperor Jones, 1920s: 2, 7–9

Empire, 1960s: 15

Empire State Building, *1910s:* 100; *1920s:* 32; *1930s:* 96–98, 99 (ill.), 147

The Empire Strikes Back, 1980s: 9

Employee benefits, health insurance, *1970s:* 131–32

Employers
    accident insurance, *1910s:* 69, 86
    health care costs, *1990s:* 121–22

Employment, *1950s:* 27
    of African Americans, *1940s:* 86, 103–04
    wartime, *1940s:* 86, 88, 93, 96
    women, *1910s:* 93, 102

Employment discrimination, *1970s:* 26–27, 29, 41–42, 49, 104–05
    gender-based, *1960s:* 42

Employment Opportunity Commission (EEOC), *1990s:* 28

Employment tests, discrimination in, *1970s:* 26

Encyclopaedia Britannica Company, *1970s:* 27

Encyclopedia of the Social Sciences, 1920s: 50

Endarterectomy, *1960s:* 128

Endeavour (space shuttle), *1980s:* 154; *1990s:* 158

Enders, John, *1960s:* 131

Enders, John Franklin, *1940s:* 122; *1950s:* 118, 118 (ill.)

Endorsements, *1950s:* 31

Energy conservation, *1970s:* 30–33

Energy consumption, *1970s:* 31

Energy-efficient cars, *1970s:* 40

Energy policy, *1970s:* 31–35

Engineering, *1910s:* 28

The Engineers and the Price System,
  1910s: 149

England, punk music in, *1970s:* 13–14

English-as-a-second-language instruction, *1970s:* 48

English Channel, *1950s:* 158

English, in schools, *1980s:* 50, 61

English language, *1960s:* 53

ENIAC (Electronic Numerical Integrator and Calculator), *1940s:* 130, 141, 142 (ill.)

Enigma code, *1940s:* 141

Enoch Arden, 1910s: 15

Enola Gay, 1930s: 145 (ill.), 146

Enovid, *1960s:* 155

Enterprise, 1930s: 152

Entertainment and Sports Programming Network (ESPN), *1990s:* 163

Entertainment industry. *See* Arts and entertainment

Entertaining, *1980s:* 101

Enter the Dragon, 1970s: 114

Entrance examinations, *1900s:* 40

Environment, *1990s:* 28, 138
    coastline oil drilling, *1980s:* 30
    Earth summit, *1990s:* 138
    federal control and, *1980s:* 35
    global warming, *1990s:* 139, 141,
      148–53, 153 (ill.)
    oil spills, *1980s:* 147–48, 156–57
    pollution dangers, *1980s:* 148
    protected lands/oil exploration,
      1980s: 35–36
    Superfund, *1980s:* 148, 155
    World Trade Organization, *1990s:*
      41

Environmentalism, *1960s:* 94, 98,
  123, 130; *1970s:* 151–53

Environmental law, *1970s:* 90

Environmental medicine, *1980s:*
  140–42

Environmental protection, *1900s:* 59,
  61, 63, 68, 69 (ill.)

Environmental Protection Agency
  (EPA), *1960s:* 98, 130; *1970s:* 30,
  140, 152–53; *1980s:* 35, 140, 146

Environmental science, *1960s:* 145

Environment, DDT and, *1940s:*
  114–15

Environment Programme, *1980s:* 158

Enzymes, role of, *1920s:* 129

EPA (Environmental Protection
  Agency), *1960s:* 98, 130

Epidemics, *1940s:* 114

Epilepsy, *1920s:* 108; *1960s:* 124

Equal Employment Opportunity
  Commission (EEOC), *1970s:* 42,
  104; *1980s:* 96

Equal employment opportunity laws,
  1970s: 40–42

Equal Opportunity act, *1960s:* 69

Equal rights
    gender-based, *1900s:* 40
    race-based, *1900s:* 40
    women in workforce, *1960s:* 42
    See also African Americans;
      Women

Equal Rights Amendment, *1910s:* 95,
  1930s: 73; *1970s:* 41, 98–99, 103,
  105–07, 105 (ill.); *1980s:* 96,
  104–05

Equitable Savings and Loan building,
  Portland, Oregon, *1940s:* 92

Ergonomics, *1980s:* 141

Erikson, Erik, *1960s:* 50

Erlanger, John, *1900s:* 100

Erlanger, Joseph, *1920s:* 108

Ernst, Max, *1940s:* 8

Erving, Julius, *1970s:* 167, 168 (ill.),
  169

Ervin, Sam, *1970s:* 86

Escalante, Jaime, *1980s:* 52, 52 (ill.)

Escalators, *1910s:* 132

Esch-Cummins Act, *1920s:* 24

Escobedo v. *Illinois, 1960s:* 81

ESEA (Elementary and Secondary
  Education Act), *1970s:* 55–56

Espionage, *1900s:* 24; *1910s:* 67;
  1940s: 68; *1990s:* 29
    Rosenbergs and, *1950s:* 68, 71,
      78–79

Espionage Act, *1910s:* 19, 37–38, 76;
  1920s: 64

ESPN (Entertainment and Sports Programming Network), *1990s:* 163

Esposito, Phil, *1970s:* 173
EST. *See* Electroshock therapy
Estrogen, *1960s:* 120
Estrone, *1920s:* 109
Ethan Frome, 1900s: 7; *1910s:* 11
Ether, *1930s:* 116, 117 (ill.)
Ethical Culture Movement, *1910s:* 50
Ethical Idealism, *1910s:* 95
Ethical Practices Committee, AFL-CIO, *1950s:* 35
Ethics, *1910s:* 50, 95
Ethics, medical, *1900s:* 130
Ethics violations, *1990s:* 63
Ethnic Heritage Studies Act of 1972, *1970s:* 98
Ethnic identity, *1970s:* 109
Ethnicities, in high schools, *1900s:* 49
    See also Immigrants
Ethnic neighborhoods, *1900s:* 84
Ethyl Corporation, *1920s:* 24
Ethyl gasoline, *1920s:* 128
Etiquette, *1920s:* 91
eToys Inc., *1990s:* 33
E.T.: The Extra-Terrestrial, 1970s: 19; *1980s:* 2, 7, 9, 12
Eucaine, *1930s:* 116
EU (European Union), *1990s:* 40
Eugenics, *1910s:* 150; *1920s:* 80, 109; *1930s:* 142–43
Eurocentric arts, *1900s:* 8
European art, *1910s:* 12
European composers, *1910s:* 16
European educational systems, *1910s:* 48
Evangelical movement, *1980s:* 115–16, 116 (ill.)
Evan, Gil, *1940s:* 16
Evans, Herbert McLean, *1920s:* 123
Evans, Mathilde A., *1900s:* 109
Evans, Walker, *1930s:* 4
Evergood, Philip, *1930s:* 8
Evers, Medgar, *1960s:* 101–02
Evert, Chris, *1970s:* 161, 176–77
"Every Breath You Take," *1980s:* 19
Evipan, *1930s:* 110
Evolution, *1900s:* 131; *1910s:* 137, 150; *1980s:* 48–49, 54, 56–58
    in school, *1930s:* 47

versus creationism, *1970s:* 140
    See also Darwinism
Evolutionary biology, *1940s:* 140
Evolutionary theory, *1990s:* 45, 47
Ewing, James, *1900s:* 101
Executions, of Rosenbergs, *1950s:* 68, 71, 78–79
Executive Order 8802, *1940s:* 86, 103
Executive privilege, *1970s:* 70, 86–88
Exercise, *1970s:* 124–25, 128–31
Exeter, *1900s:* 48
The Exhibition of Independent Artists, *1910s:* 9
Exile, as crime punishment, *1990s:* 92
Existentialism, *1940s:* 5
Exodus, 1950s: 15
The Exorcist, 1970s: 2, 18
Expansion, business, *1940s:* 36–38, 36 (ill.)
Expatriates, *1900s:* 6
Expatriation, *1920s:* 13–14, 50
Expedition Act, *1900s:* 32
Expeditions, polar, *1920s:* 129, 137; *1930s:* 134
Experimental College, *1920s:* 47
Experimental Sociology, Descriptive and Analytical: Delinquents, 1900s: 62
Exploration, North Pole, *1900s:* 123
Explorer IV satellite, *1950s:* 137
Explosives, *1910s:* 151
Exports. *See* Imports and exports
Expressionism, *1920s:* 8
Expressionism, abstract, *1950s:* 8
Extension programs, *1910s:* 53–54
Extracurricular activities, grades and, *1980s:* 48
Extraterrestrials, *1960s:* 150–51; *1990s:* 93
Exxon, *1990s:* 29, 40
Exxon Corporation, *1970s:* 27
Exxon Valdez, 1980s: 147–48, 156–57
Eyeglass shortages, *1940s:* 31
Ezzard, Charles, *1950s:* 171

F

FAA (Federal Aviation Administration), *1950s:* 35

Fab Four. *See* The Beatles

Fabian, *1960s:* 10

A Fable, 1950s: 9–10

Fabolous, *1990s:* 111 (ill.)

Fabry, Charles, *1910s:* 132

Face molds, *1910s:* 129

Factories, *1910s:* 26–27, 29, 33–36, 40, 49

Factories, design of, *1920s:* 90

Fads, *1920s:* 88–89, 100–02; *1950s:* 93; *1960s:* 108

Fairbanks, Douglas, *1910s:* 3, 13 (ill.), 15; *1920s:* 3

Fairbanks, Douglas, Jr., *1940s:* 14

Fair Employment Practices Committee (FEPC), *1940s:* 86, 103–04

Fair Labor Standards Act, *1930s:* 27, 69; *1940s:* 24; *1960s:* 24

Fairness and Accuracy in Reporting (FAIR), *1990s:* 12

Fairs, *1930s:* 105–07

"Faith," *1980s:* 19

Fall, Albert, *1920s:* 67, 78–79

Fallingwater Building, *1930s:* 93, 96

Falwell, Jerry, *1970s:* 99, 112–14; *1980s:* 100, 100 (ill.), 116
    homosexuals and, *1990s:* 93

Family
    affect of war on, *1940s:* 96–99
    extended, *1990s:* 100–05, 103 (ill.)

Family hour, on television, *1970s:* 22

Family life, *1930s:* 103–04
    See also Lifestyles and social trends

Family Limitation, 1910s: 66

Family planning, *1920s:* 108; *1960s:* 94
    See also Birth control

The Famous Players Film Company, *1910s:* 2

Fan magazines, *1920s:* 18–19

Fanny Farmer, *1920s:* 36

Fantasia, 1940s: 2, 13

FAP (Federal Arts Project), *1930s:* 9–10; *1940s:* 8

Farian, Frank, *1980s:* 17

Farm Credit Act, *1930s:* 26

Farmer, James, *1940s:* 90, 90 (ill.)

Farming. *See* Agriculture

Farmland. *See* Agricultural lands

Farm Mortgage Refinancing Act, *1930s:* 26

Farms
    bankruptcy, *1980s:* 30
    concert aid, *1980s:* 3–4, 26–27, 26 (ill.), 42 (ill.)
    crisis, *1980s:* 33, 40–42
    land, *1980s:* 30–31, 40

Farm Security Administration, *1930s:* 120

Farnsworth, Philo T., *1930s:* 134, 134 (ill.)

Farrakhan, Louis, *1990s:* 93, 95–96, 96 (ill.), 99–101, 100 (ill.)

Farrell, James T., *1930s:* 4–5

Fascism, *1940s:* 4, 70, 79

Fashion, *1900s:* 79, 81, 91–96, 92 (ill.), 93 (ill.); *1910s:* 92, 105–08; *1930s:* 88, 90, 92–93, 101–03, 141, 158; *1940s:* 88–89, 91, 93–96, 94 (ill.); *1950s:* 90, 101 (ill.), 102–03, 107, 108 (ill.), 109–10; *1960s:* 94–95, 97, 108–11, 109 (ill.), 110 (ill.); *1970s:* 101, 103, 116–19, 118 (ill.); *1990s:* 93, 97, 109–12, 111 (ill.)
    automobiles and, *1900s:* 91
    exercise clothing, *1980s:* 106
    men's, *1920s:* 86, 95–97
    Miami Vice, 1980s: 96–97
    preppy/street fashion, *1980s:* 107–09
    prices, *1900s:* 94
    street style, *1980s:* 97, 107–08
    women's, *1920s:* 86–87, 90, 92–95
    yuppies, *1980s:* 103–06, 106

Fashion boutiques, *1960s:* 112

Fashion designers, *1960s:* 94, 98

Fashion models, *1960s:* 113

Fast food, *1990s:* 28

Fast food restaurants, *1950s:* 90, 97; *1960s:* 26, 35

Father Divine, *1910s:* 90

Father Knows Best, 1950s: 18

"Fat Man," *1940s:* 77, 146

Fats Domino, *1950s:* 15

Fats, saturated, *1980s:* 122

Faubus, Orval E., *1950s:* 50, 50 (ill.), 59–60

Faulkner, Shannon, *1990s:* 45, 56 (ill.)

Faulkner, William, *1920s:* 14; *1930s:* 4–5, 7, 7 (ill.), 13–14; *1940s:* 12; *1950s:* 5, 9, 54

Fauset, Jessie, *1920s:* 11

Fawcett, Wilford H., *1920s:* 19

Fayum desert, Egypt, *1960s:* 148

FBI (Federal Bureau of Investigation), *1920s:* 64; *1930s:* 72, 83; *1950s:* 105; *1970s:* 107
   See also Federal Bureau of Investigation

FBVE (Federal Board for Vocational Education), *1910s:* 47, 57

FCC (Federal Communications Commission), *1920s:* 34; *1930s:* 130; *1940s:* 2; *1950s:* 24
   See also Federal Communications Commission

FDA. *See* Food and Drug Administration

FDA (Federal Drug Administration), *1930s:* 121; *1950s:* 122

FDIC (Federal Deposit Insurance Corporation), *1930s:* 68, 77–78, 83

Fear of Flying, *1970s:* 2, 10

Federal aid to education, *1910s:* 47–48, 57; *1960s:* 46–48, 57–59, 82

Federal aid to the arts, *1930s:* 9–10, 20–21; *1960s:* 113–14

Federal Aid to the Arts Bill, *1960s:* 3

Federal Arts Project (FAP), *1930s:* 9–10; *1940s:* 8

Federal Aviation Act, *1950s:* 35

Federal Aviation Administration (FAA), *1950s:* 35

Federal Board for Vocational Education (FBVE), *1910s:* 47, 57

Federal Bureau of Education, *1920s:* 52

Federal Bureau of Investigation (FBI), *1900s:* 21; *1920s:* 64; *1930s:* 72, 83; *1950s:* 105; *1970s:* 107
   Columbine High School shootings, *1990s:* 50
   Unabomber, *1990s:* 80–81

Federal Children's Bureau, *1930s:* 111

Federal Communications Commission (FCC), *1920s:* 34; *1930s:* 130; *1940s:* 2; *1950s:* 24; *1960s:* 25
   Stern, Howard, *1990s:* 13
   television industry, *1990s:* 17
   wireless communications, *1990s:* 155

Federal Council of Churches, *1930s:* 110; *1940s:* 86

Federal Council of Churches of Christ, *1920s:* 87

Federal deficit, *1940s:* 33–34; *1970s:* 36–38

Federal Deposit Insurance Corporation (FDIC), *1930s:* 68, 77–78, 83

Federal Drug Administration (FDA), *1930s:* 121

Federal Emergency Relief Act, *1930s:* 26

Federal Emergency Relief Administration (FERA), *1930s:* 76–77

Federal Energy Office. *See* Department of Energy

The Federal Farm Loan Act, *1910s:* 25

Federal funding, schools, *1990s:* 45, 47–48, 51, 54–55

Federal Highway Act, *1910s:* 66

Federal Housing Authority (FHA), *1940s:* 101

Federal income tax. *See* Taxes

Federal League, *1910s:* 154, 157, 161; *1920s:* 154

Federal loans, *1970s:* 27, 29

Federal Music Project (FMP), *1930s:* 20

Federal Narcotics Control Board, *1920s:* 64, 108

Federal Radio Commission, *1920s:* 129

Federal Railroad Administration, *1910s:* 76

Federal Reserve, *1910s:* 24, 32; *1920s:*
    29; *1930s:* 42
        interest rates and, *1940s:* 25
Federal Reserve Act, *1910s:* 24, 32, 66
Federal Reserve Bank, *1900s:* 28–29
Federal Reserve Board, *1960s:* 25;
    1990s: 32
Federal Savings and Loan Insurance
    Corporation, *1980s:* 38
Federal Theater Project (FTP), *1930s:*
    21–22
Federal Trade Commission (FTC),
    1910s: 31–32, 66, 83; *1950s:* 125;
    1960s: 120, 138
Federal Trade Commission Act,
    1910s: 25
Federal workers, *1910s:* 67
Federal Writers' Project, *1940s:* 7
Federated Department Stores, *1920s:*
    37
Feinberg Law, *1950s:* 61
Feinstein, Dianne, *1990s:* 75
Feller, Bob, *1940s:* 159, 161
Felsch, Happy, *1910s:* 162; *1920s:* 154
Felton, Rebecca, *1920s:* 64
The Feminine Mystique, 1960s: 98
Feminism, *1960s:* 42, 95, 97–98, 112
    (ill.); *1970s:* 98, 100, 104–08;
    1980s: 96, 104–05
        artwork, *1970s:* 3, 8–9
        books, *1970s:* 10
        Schlafly, Phyllis and, *1970s:* 98,
            103, 105–07
        Steinem, Gloria, *1970s:* 7
        See also Women
Fences, 1980s: 7
Feng Shui, *1990s:* 109
Fenway Park, *1910s:* 154
FEPC. *See* Fair Employment Practices
    Committee
FERA (Federal Emergency Relief
    Administration), *1930s:* 76–77
Ferber, Edna, *1920s:* 9
Ferdinand, Franz, *1910s:* 75
Ferguson, Marilyn, *1980s:* 96, 118
Fermi Award, *1940s:* 135
Fermi, Enrico, *1940s:* 130, 133–34,
    134 (ill.), 144

Fermi National Accelerator Laborato-
    ry, *1970s:* 140
Ferraro, Geraldine, *1980s:* 72, 72 (ill.)
Ferriss, Hugh, *1920s:* 86
Fertility drugs, *1960s:* 122, 134
Fertilizers, *1910s:* 134, 148–49
Fessenden, Reginald Aubrey, *1900s:*
    79, 118, 128; *1910s:* 148
Fetal disorders, genome mapping,
    1990s: 143–44
Fetal stem cells, cloning, *1990s:* 117
Fetuses, ultrasound tests and, *1950s:*
    115
FHA (Federal Housing Authority),
    1940s: 101
Fiat, *1960s:* 30
Fiber optics, *1970s:* 152
Fiction, *1920s:* 6–7, 13, 19; *1940s:*
    11–12
        See also Books
Fiddler on the Roof, 1900s: 18
Fidelity Capital Fund, *1960s:* 33
Field-Ion microscopes, *1950s:* 136
Fields, W. C., *1910s:* 5, 18; *1920s:* 9
Fifteenth Amendment, *1910s:* 80–81
Fifty Million Frenchmen, 1920s: 3
Fignon, Laurent, *1980s:* 189
Figure skating, *1900s:* 139; *1950s:*
    158; *1960s:* 164; *1970s:* 179 (ill.);
    1980s: 190
Filas for Sale, 1970s: 8
Filene department store, *1910s:* 42;
    1920s: 37
Filibuster, Civil Rights Act and, *1960s:*
    74–75
Film distribution, *1940s:* 2, 5, 14
Film industry. *See* Motion picture
    industry
Film noir, *1940s:* 2, 5, 14–15
Films, *1900s:* 10–11; *1910s:* 13–16, 13
    (ill.); *1920s:* 4–5, 14–16; *1940s:* 7,
    12–15; *1960s:* 4–5, 7–9, 8 (ill.), 19
    (ill.); *1970s:* 5, 16–20
        Academy Award winners, *1950s:*
            13
        African Americans in, *1960s:*
            105–06
        AIDS, *1990s:* 128

animated, *1930s:* 3

avant-garde, *1960s:* 15–16

beach, *1960s:* 108

Biblical, *1950s:* 106

blaxploitation, *1970s:* 4, 20

from books, *1970s:* 10

censorship, *1980s:* 5

Chaplin, Charlie, *1930s:* 133

color, *1900s:* 3

communism and, *1940s:* 82

computer animation, *1990s:* 147

computerized effects, *1980s:* 159

content regulations, *1930s:* 2

dancing in, *1940s:* 19

directors, *1910s:* 7, 14

drive-in theater, *1930s:* 88

educational, *1940s:* 44–45

feature length, *1910s:* 4

gangster, *1930s:* 16

history, *1990s:* 10 (ill.)

Hollywood blacklist, *1950s:* 4

home movies, *1920s:* 128, 131,
    141–43

martial arts, *1970s:* 114

Marx Brothers, *1930s:* 15 (ill.),
    17, 164

politics, *1990s:* 10

Porter, Edwin Stanton and,
    1900s: 7

product placement, *1950s:* 31

ratings of, *1960s:* 3, 10

record gross earnings, *1980s:* 3

science fiction, *1900s:* 2

short movies, *1910s:* 4

silent, *1910s:* 13

slapstick comedies, *1910s:* 15

with sound, *1920s:* 5, 16–17, 129,

technicolor, *1920s:* 128, 131,
    143–44

3-D, *1950s:* 2, 4, 10, 11 (ill.)

top, *1980s:* 9

top 1990s, *1990s:* 10

versus television, *1950s:* 4, 10–11

violence, *1990s:* 4, 9–11, 10 (ill.)

war, *1940s:* 5

women in, *1950s:* 102

Financial panics, *1900s:* 21, 23, 27–29

Financing, of World War I, *1910s:*
    32–33

Fingers, Rollie, *1980s:* 176

Finlay, Carlos, *1900s:* 114

Finley, Karen, *1990s:* 6, 6 (ill.)

Finnegan's Wake, 1960s: 146

Fires, *1900s:* 3; *1910s:* 40, 41 (ill.), 90,
    106

Fireside Chats, *1930s:* 2, 68, 76

Firestone Tire and Rubber Company,
    1900s: 23; *1960s:* 25

The Firm, 1990s: 2, 5

Firpo, Luis, *1920s:* 161

First amendment, *1950s:* 105–07;
    1980s: 9; *1990s:* 44

First Lady of the World, *1930s:* 73

First Symphony, 1930s: 20

Fischer, Bobby, *1960s:* 164

Fishbein, Morris, *1920s:* 120; *1930s:*
    114

Fish Committee. *See* House Un-Amer-
    ican Activities Committee

Fishing, *1930s:* 152

Fisk University, *1900s:* 52; *1950s:* 46

Fists of Fury, 1970s: 114

Fitch, Clyde, *1900s:* 2

Fitness movement, *1970s:* 124–25,
    128–31, 130 (ill.)

Fitzgerald, Ella, *1930s:* 7, 7 (ill.)

Fitzgerald, F. Scott, *1920s:* 2, 6, 6
    (ill.), 13; *1930s:* 4; *1940s:* 2, 11;
    1980s: 9

Fitzgerald, Zelda, *1920s:* 6

The Fixx, *1980s:* 18

Fixx, James F., *1970s:* 126, 126 (ill.),
    128–29

Flag day, *1910s:* 47

Flagler, Henry M., *1920s:* 38

Flagpole sitting, *1920s:* 102

Flaherty, Robert, *1920s:* 2

Flamethrowers, *1910s:* 135, 150

Flanagan, Hallie, *1930s:* 21

Flanner, Janet, *1920s:* 13

Flappers, *1910s:* 59; *1920s:* 92, 93
    (ill.); *1930s:* 101

The Flash, *1940s:* 10

Flashdance, 1980s: 22, 106

Flash Gordon, *1930s:* 12, 166

Flash Gordon, 1930s: 11

Fleming, Alexander, *1920s:* 109, 111, 120–21; *1940s:* 118; *1950s:* 123

Fleming, John, *1900s:* 118

Fleming, Peggy, *1960s:* 164

Fleming, Peter, *1980s:* 185

Fletcher Henderson Orchestra, *1920s:* 12

Flexner, Abraham, *1910s:* 112; *1920s:* 112, 112 (ill.)

Flexner, Simon, *1900s:* 101, 109–10; *1920s:* 112

Flickers. *See* Films

Flick, Lawrence, *1900s:* 113

Flight of Europa, 1920s: 3

Flights around the world, *1940s:* 131

Floch, Felix, *1940s:* 133

A Flock of Seagulls, *1980s:* 18

Flood, Curt, *1920s:* 154; *1970s:* 160, 162, 165

Floppy disks, *1970s:* 110

Florida
    architecture in, *1920s:* 91
    Boca Raton, *1920s:* 91
    land speculation and, *1920s:* 37–38

Florida Marlins, *1990s:* 168

Florida Panthers, *1990s:* 176

Flowers, Gennifer, *1990s:* 75

Floyd, "Pretty Boy," *1930s:* 82, 85

Flu epidemics, *1970s:* 123, 125, 135–38

Fluorescent lighting, *1930s:* 27, 131

Fluoride, *1940s:* 109
    tooth decay and, *1960s:* 121

"The Flying Dutchman," *1900s:* 143, 143 (ill.)

Flynn, Elizabeth Gurley, *1910s:* 24

Flyers, Philadelphia, *1970s:* 173

FMP (Federal Music Project), *1930s:* 20

Fokine, Michel, *1920s:* 3

Fokker, F32, *1920s:* 25

Folkers, Karl, *1940s:* 131

Folk music, *1930s:* 3, 7, 20; *1960s:* 6, 112–13

Folk schools, *1930s:* 57

Folks, Homer, *1900s:* 100

Follies, 1910s: 18; *1920s:* 9

Follow the Sun, 1950s: 176

"Follow the Yellow Brick Road," *1930s:* 3

Follow Through, *1960s:* 58–59

Folsom, James, *1950s:* 69

Fonck, Rene, *1910s:* 138

Fonda, Jane, *1970s:* 2, 6, 6 (ill.)

Fonda, Peter, *1960s:* 5, 9

Food
    in art, *1960s:* 16
    companies, *1960s:* 41
    labeling of, *1970s:* 36
    organic, *1970s:* 115

Food and Drug Administration (FDA), *1950s:* 122; *1960s:* 123, 125, 133, 135, 136–37, 155
    AIDS drugs, *1980s:* 130; *1990s:* 126
    artificial hearts, *1980s:* 126, 131, 133
    breast implants, *1990s:* 132
    on CFCs, *1970s:* 153
    chlorofluorocarbons, *1980s:* 158
    on contact lenses, *1970s:* 122
    on equipment safety, *1970s:* 123
    on food labeling, *1970s:* 36
    RU-484 abortion inducing pill, *1990s:* 116
    tamper-resistant packaging, *1980s:* 129

Food, Drug, and Cosmetic Act, *1930s:* 27, 112–13, 121

Food, frozen, *1950s:* 90, 92, 99

Food industry, *1930s:* 31

Food preservation, *1910s:* 134, 144

Food Resource and Action Center, *1980s:* 122

Food safety regulations, *1900s:* 21, 32–33

Food Sticks, *1970s:* 145

Football, *1900s:* 41, 138, 142, 148–52; *1910s:* 155–56, 159 (ill.), 166–69; *1920s:* 149–53, 161–64; *1930s:* 152–53, 162–64; *1940s:* 152, 155–56, 166–67; *1950s:* 158–59, 161, 173–75; *1960s:* 165–69, 178–81, 180 (ill.); *1970s:* 160–61,

164, 169–72, 171 (ill.); *1980s:* 168, 170, 178–81, 179 (ill.); *1990s:* 165, 173–75, 174 (ill.)

Football Hall of Fame, *1910s:* 159

Ford Foundation, *1960s:* 31

Ford, Gerald R., *1970s:* 26–27
    energy policy, *1970s:* 32–33
    on health insurance, *1970s:* 122
    Nixon, Richard M. and, *1970s:* 86–88
    swine-flu and, *1970s:* 136–37

Ford, Glenn, *1950s:* 176

Ford, Henry, *1900s:* 24, 24 (ill.), 34–35, 91, 120, 124–25; *1910s:* 34, 67, 132, 134, 141; *1920s:* 29, 29 (ill.), 32, 129–30, 134; *1930s:* 41, 89, 95

Ford, John, *1940s:* 14

Ford Motor Company, *1900s:* 21, 24, 34–35, 35 (ill.), 78–79, 119, 125; *1910s:* 34–36, 35 (ill.), 92, 104 (ill.), 132, 134, 140–41; *1920s:* 24–25, 34, 90, 134; *1930s:* 26, 38–41, 88, 94, 106, 130, 154; *1940s:* 24, 38, 153; *1950s:* 24–25, 99; *1960s:* 30–31, 39, 94

Ford Mustang, *1960s:* 31, 94, 106

Fordney-McCumer Tariff Act, *1920s:* 24

Foreign aid, postwar, *1940s:* 38–39

Foreign cars, *1970s:* 40

Foreign car sales, *1960s:* 30–31

Foreign language classes, *1960s:* 52

Foreign language, in school, *1920s:* 52–53

Foreign policy, *1900s:* 72–74; *1910s:* 68, 72–75; *1970s:* 75, 80–83; *1980s:* 70–71, 74–75
    See also Containment

Foreman, George, *1960s:* 168; *1970s:* 161, 164

Forest Hills, *1930s:* 168

Forest Service, *1900s:* 68

Formaldehyde, *1980s:* 140

"For Once in My Life," *1960s:* 14

Forrest Gump, 1990s: 10–11

Forsaking All Others, 1930s: 6

For the Record, 1980s: 78

FORTRAN programming language, *1950s:* 146; *1970s:* 44

"Fortress America," *1940s:* 70

Fort Valley State College, *1930s:* 50

42nd Street, 1930s: 19 (ill.)

For Whom the Bell Tolls, 1940s: 12

Fosbury, Dick, *1960s:* 181

Fossil dating, *1950s:* 148–49

Fossil fuels, global warming and, *1990s:* 150–51

Fossils, *1970s:* 140, 148–51

Foster, Andrew, *1920s:* 158

Foster, Bill, *1920s:* 158–59

Foster, Harold, *1930s:* 11

Foster, Vincent W., Jr, *1990s:* 64

4-H clubs, *1900s:* 78

The Four Horsemen of the Apocalypse, 1920s: 162

Four Saints in Three Acts, 1930s: 22

Fourteen Points, *1920s:* 80

Fourteen Points peace proposal, *1910s:* 67, 78

Fourteenth Amendment, *1940s:* 59; *1970s:* 89

The Four Tops, *1960s:* 14

Fox network, shock documentaries, *1990s:* 16–18

Fox Studios, *1920s:* 142

Foxx, Jimmy, *1920s:* 156

Foyt, A. J., *1960s:* 170

France, *1910s:* 25, 75, 77–78, 96
    invasion of, *1940s:* 76
    loans to, *1940s:* 25

France, Bill, *1940s:* 158

Franchises, *1960s:* 34–35

Frankensteen, Richard, *1930s:* 38, 39 (ill.)

Frankenstein, 1930s: 15

Frank, Glenn, *1920s:* 47

Franklin, Aretha, *1960s:* 15

Franklin Life Insurance, *1960s:* 41

Franklin, Rosalind, *1950s:* 147–48

Franks, Robert, *1920s:* 80–82

Frawley, William, *1950s:* 19

Frazee, Harry, *1910s:* 155, 164; *1920s:* 155

Frazier-Lemke Farm Bankruptcy Act, *1930s:* 69

Frazier, Walt, *1960s:* 177; *1970s:* 169

Frederick G. Robie House, *1900s:* 96

Free agency, *1970s:* 161, 165–66

Freed, Alan, *1950s:* 15

Freedom of Information Act of 1974, *1970s:* 30

Freedom of speech, *1970s:* 22, 48
  See also First amendment

Freedom of the press. *See* First amendment

Freedom Riders, *1960s:* 68, 74, 94, 102

Freedom School, Indianola, Mississippi, *1960s:* 47

Freedom 7, 1960s: 157

Freeman, Walter, *1940s:* 123

Free speech, *1940s:* 79
  on campuses, *1960s:* 47, 49, 61–63, 61 (ill.), 62 (ill.)

Freestyle education, *1910s:* 54

Free substitution rule, *1940s:* 166–67

Free Synagogue of New York, *1930s:* 93

Freeth, George Douglas, *1900s:* 139

Free trade, *1940s:* 35, 39, 78–79

Free universities, *1960s:* 57

Freezers, home, *1950s:* 136

Freezing, for preservation, *1910s:* 144

Frémont, John C., *1980s:* 162

French, Chester, *1920s:* 86

French, Marilyn, *1970s:* 10

French Ministry of Public Health, *1930s:* 114

French Open, *1990s:* 181

Freon, *1930s:* 130, 141

Freud, Sigmund, *1900s:* 118–19, 121, 131–33, 132 (ill.); *1910s:* 135, 146–47; *1930s:* 114

Frick, Ford, *1960s:* 164, 172

Frick, Henry Clay, *1900s:* 83

Friedan, Betty, *1960s:* 95, 98, 98 (ill.)

Friendship, 1960s: 146

Friendship 7, 1960s: 157

Friml, Rudolf, *1920s:* 3

Frisch, Frankie, *1930s:* 152

Froines, John, *1960s:* 115

From Here to Eternity, 1950s: 8

From Russia with Love, 1960s: 9

Frost, Robert, *1910s:* 6, 6 (ill.); *1920s:* 2; *1960s:* 2

Frozen dinners, *1950s:* 90, 92, 99

Frozen food, *1910s:* 144

Fruit flies, *1900s:* 130

FTC (Federal Trade Commission), *1950s:* 125; *1960s:* 120, 138

FTP (Federal Theater Project), *1930s:* 21

Fuel efficiency, of cars, *1960s:* 31

Fuel emissions, *1960s:* 126

Fuel shortages, *1970s:* 31

Fuentes, Carlos, *1970s:* 10–11

Fulbright Act, *1940s:* 45

Fulbright-Hays Act, *1940s:* 52

Fulbright, J. William, *1950s:* 54

Fulks, Joe, *1940s:* 165

Fuller, Hoyt, *1960s:* 114

Fuller, R. Buckminster, *1920s:* 87; *1930s:* 59; *1950s:* 90, 94, 94 (ill.)

Full Square Gospel Church, *1920s:* 91

Functionalism, *1930s:* 96

Fundamentalism, *1980s:* 54–56, 97, 115–16, 116 (ill.)
  Christian, *1970s:* 101–02, 112–14
  Islamic, *1970s:* 92–94

Funding
  for the arts, *1940s:* 8; *1990s:* 2–4, 8–9
  of the arts, corporate, *1960s:* 27, 31–32
  education, *1990s:* 48
  federal, antipoverty, *1960s:* 82
  government, for education, *1920s:* 57–58, 57 (ill.); *1930s:* 46–50, 52–56; *1940s:* 54–55; *1950s:* 49, 52, 63
  government, for research, *1940s:* 113, 120, 132
  See also Federal aid to education; Federal aid to the arts; Great Society

Funerals, *1910s:* 120

Funicello, Annette, *1960s:* 108

Funk, Casimir, *1910s:* 132

Funnies on Parade, 1930s: 12

Funny Girl, 1960s: 7, 18

A Funny Thing Happened on the Way to the Forum, 1960s: 18

Furniture, *1910s:* 102; *1950s:* 91, 103–04

G

Gable, Clark, *1930s:* 3, 16, 103

Gabler, Mel and Norma, *1970s:* 59–60

Gabriel, Peter, *1980s:* 3

Gaedel, Eddie, *1950s:* 166

Gaia hypothesis, *1970s:* 153

Gagarin, Yuri A., *1960s:* 142, 144, 156

Galanos, James, *1950s:* 103; *1980s:* 96

Galapagos Islands, *1970s:* 141, 144

Galaxies, *1990s:* 138

Galbraith, John Kenneth, *1950s:* 94, 94 (ill.)

Gallant Fox, *1930s:* 152, 165

Gallant Man, 1950s: 159

Gallico, Paul, *1930s:* 154

Gallo, Robert, *1980s:* 126, 126 (ill.)

Gallo, Robert C., *1990s:* 125

Galsworthy, John, *1910s:* 19

Gambling, *1910s:* 172–73; *1980s:* 169, 174; *1990s:* 98–99

Games, *1950s:* 107

Gamma globulin, for polio, *1940s:* 122

Gamows, George, *1940s:* 133

Gandil, Chick, *1910s:* 162; *1920s:* 155

Gangs, *1980s:* 108–09

Gangster films, *1930s:* 16

"Gansta's Paradise," *1990s:* 26

Gantt, Harvey, *1960s:* 46

The Gap, *1980s:* 108

Garage bands. *See* Punk rock

Garbo, Greta, *1920s:* 3; *1930s:* 93, 102

Garden and Home, 1920s: 100

Gardiner, Charlie, *1930s:* 165

Garfield, John, *1930s:* 21

Garland, Hamlin, *1900s:* 8; *1910s:* 11

Garment industry, *1910s:* 24, 39–41, 39 (ill.), 41 (ill.), 85

Garment industry strikes, *1900s:* 21

Garn-St. Germain Act, *1980s:* 39

Garrity, Arthur, *1970s:* 48–49

Garvey, Marcus, *1910s:* 94, 94 (ill.); *1960s:* 104

Gary, Elbert H., *1910s:* 38

Gary, William, *1900s:* 40

Gases, poisonous, *1910s:* 135, 151

Gashouse Gang, *1930s:* 153, 158

Gasohol, *1970s:* 34

Gasoline, *1950s:* 90
    leaded, *1980s:* 146
    oil crisis and, *1970s:* 26–27, 32, 33 (ill.), 35
    unleaded, *1970s:* 26

Gasoline rationing, *1940s:* 24–25, 30–31

Gas ranges, *1910s:* 102

Gasser, Herbert, *1920s:* 108

Gates, Bill, *1980s:* 44, 161, 161 (ill.); *1990s:* 32, 32 (ill.)

GATT. *See* General Agreement on Tariffs and Trade

Gauguin, Paul, *1910s:* 12

Gay community, AIDS backlash, *1980s:* 128

Gaye, Marvin, *1960s:* 13

Gayle, Addison, Jr., *1960s:* 114

Gay liberation movement, *1960s:* 97, 103–04

Gay rights, *1970s:* 49, 98–99, 108–09, 122; *1990s:* 92, 94–95
    Ellen, 1990s: 96
    hate crimes, *1990s:* 93, 102
    marriage, *1990s:* 93

Gehrig, Lou, *1920s:* 149, 152, 152 (ill.), 156–57; *1930s:* 152–53, 156, 156 (ill.), 158; *1940s:* 152; *1990s:* 162–63, 169

Geisel, Theodore S., *1950s:* 51

Geldof, Bob, *1980s:* 5, 24

Gell-Mann, Murray, *1960s:* 146, 146 (ill.)

Gelsinger, Jesse, *1990s:* 132

Gemini 4, 1960s: 158

Gemini 7, 1960s: 158

Gender discrimination, *1970s:* 26–27, 29, 41–42, 49, 98, 104–05
    See also Women

The Gene Autry Show, 1950s: 107

Gene cloning, *1990s:* 133–34

Gene map. *See* Genome mapping

Genentech, *1970s:* 141

General Agreement on Tariffs and Trade (GATT), *1940s:* 25, 27, 35

General Assembly of the Presbyterian Church, *1920s:* 46

General Council of Congregational and Christian Churches, *1930s:* 88

General Education Board, *1900s:* 40

General Electric Company, *1900s:* 25, 79, 118, 129; *1910s:* 56; *1920s:* 128–29; *1930s:* 27; *1940s:* 25, 139; *1960s:* 24, 37; *1990s:* 29, 40

General Electric Theatre, 1950s: 30

General Medical Society for Psychotherapy, *1920s:* 109

General Motors (GM) Corporation, *1900s:* 23, 125; *1920s:* 24–25, 28, 34, 38, 135; *1930s:* 27, 32, 38–41, 59, 94; *1940s:* 25, 38; *1950s:* 24, 29, 42; *1960s:* 24–25, 29–31; *1990s:* 28–29

General Motors Training Center, Warren, Michigan, *1940s:* 92

General-Purpose vehicles. *See* Jeeps

The General Slocum, 1900s: 78

General stores, *1960s:* 33

General theory of relativity, *1900s:* 133; *1960s:* 146

Generation X, *1990s:* 2, 110

Genes, *1900s:* 119, 129; *1930s:* 143

Gene therapy, *1990s:* 116, 119, 130–34

Genetic engineering, *1970s:* 140–41

Genetic mutations, *1900s:* 118

Genetics, *1900s:* 118, 121, 129–32; *1910s:* 117, 134, 137, 144–45; *1930s:* 142–43; *1940s:* 130, 133, 139–40; *1960s:* 51, 145–46, 150–52

Geneva Convention, *1920s:* 109

The Genius, 1900s: 6

Genome mapping, *1990s:* 117, 138–40, 142–45

Genotypes, *1900s:* 119

Genteel tradition, *1900s:* 4

Geodesic domes, *1950s:* 90, 94

Geology, *1910s:* 134, 147

George, David Lloyd, *1910s:* 78, 79 (ill.)

George-Deen Act, *1930s:* 47

George Washington Bridge, *1930s:* 138

George Washington University Medical School, *1930s:* 110

George White's Scandals, 1920s: 2, 9

Georgia Tech, *1910s:* 155; *1920s:* 149

Geothermal power, *1960s:* 153

Gerber baby food, *1950s:* 41

Gerber, David, *1920s:* 25

Gerde's Folk City, *1960s:* 2

German Americans, *1910s:* 93, 96

German measles. *See* Rubella

German U-boats, *1910s:* 30, 66, 68, 75–77, 142–43, 151

Germany, *1930s:* 69, 71; *1960s:* 68
    after World War I, *1940s:* 70
    declaration of war on, *1910s:* 67–68, 75–76
    Olympics, *1910s:* 174
    rockets, *1940s:* 139
    surrender of, *1940s:* 76
    troop mobilization against, *1910s:* 70
    See also World War II

Gernreich, Rudi, *1950s:* 103

Gerry and the Pacemakers, *1960s:* 10

Gershwin, George, *1920s:* 2–3, 6, 6 (ill.), 9, 12; *1930s:* 2–3, 20, 22–23

Gershwin, Ira, *1920s:* 9; *1930s:* 2

Gettysburg Memorial, *1930s:* 89

Gertie the Dinosaur, 1900s: 79

Ghostbusters, 1980s: 9

Giannini, Amadeo Peter, *1920s:* 25, 29, 29 (ill.)

Giant slalom, *1980s:* 188

Gibbon, John H., *1950s:* 118, 118 (ill.)

Gibbons, Fred, *1980s:* 44

Gibbons, Leeza, *1990s:* 14

Gibbons, Tom, *1920s:* 161

Gibbs, Lois, *1970s:* 141

GI Bill, *1940s:* 27, 44, 47, 56, 100; *1950s:* 26

Gibson, Althea, *1950s:* 158, 161–62, 162 (ill.)

Gibson, Bob, *1960s:* 173; *1970s:* 166

Gibson, Charles Dana, *1900s:* 93

Gibson Girl, *1900s:* 81, 92 (ill.), 93

Gibson, Josh, *1920s:* 160

Gideon v. *Wainright, 1960s:* 81

"The Gift Outright," *1960s:* 2

Gilbert, Cass, *1910s:* 94, 94 (ill.), 100

Gilbreth, Frank B, *1910s:* 28–29, 28 (ill.), 34

Gilbreth, Lillian Moller, *1910s:* 28–29, 29 (ill.), 34

Gilbert, John, *1920s:* 3

Gilchrist, Cookie, *1960s:* 180

Gillespie, Dizzy, *1950s:* 15

Gillette Cavalcade of Sports, 1950s: 176

Gillette Safety Razor, *1940s:* 153

Gilliam, Jim, *1950s:* 164

Gilman, Charlotte Perkins, *1900s:* 83, 83 (ill.)

Gimbel Brothers, *1920s:* 37, 86

Ginevra dei Benci, 1960s: 3

Ginger Ale, *1900s:* 79

Gingrich, Newt, *1990s:* 63, 67, 67 (ill.), 72

Ginsberg, Allen, *1950s:* 3, 5, 9

Giovanni, Nikki, *1960s:* 114

Gipp, George "The Gipper," *1920s:* 162, 162 (ill.)

Girl Crazy, 1930s: 2

Girl groups, *1960s:* 11

Girls' Home Club, *1900s:* 78

Girl You Know It's True, 1980s: 17

Gish, Lillian D., *1910s:* 15

Gladys Knight and the Pips, *1960s:* 13

Glackens, William, *1910s:* 8

Glasgow, Ellen, *1920s:* 14

Glaspie, April C., *1990s:* 68

Glass, *1910s:* 85, 133

Glass, Carter, *1920s:* 76

Glass House, *1940s:* 92

The Glass Menagerie, 1940s: 19

Glass, Philip, *1960s:* 16

Glass-Steagall Credit Expansion Act, *1930s:* 26, 68, 77

Glaucoma, *1950s:* 115

Gleason, Jackie, *1950s:* 4, 17, 18 (ill.)

The Glebe, 1910s: 12

Glengarry Glen Ross, 1980s: 14–15

Glenn, John, *1960s:* 146, 146 (ill.), 157; *1990s:* 139, 156

Globalization
business, *1990s:* 39–42
in scientific research, *1900s:* 120–21

Global warming, *1960s:* 145, 154; *1990s:* 139, 141

Glomar Challenger, 1960s: 153

GM. *See* General Motors

G-Men, 1930s: 15, 83

Glyn, Elinor, *1920s:* 15

GNP (Gross National Product), *1910s:* 76

"God Bless America," *1930s:* 3

God Bless America rally, *1970s:* 99

God Bless You, Mr. Rosewater, 1960s: 18

Goddard, Paulette, *1920s:* 10

Goddard, Robert, *1910s:* 136

Goddard, Robert H., *1920s:* 129

The Godfather, 1970s: 2, 5–6, 17–18

The Godfather: Part II, 1970s: 6, 18

"God Save the Queen," *1970s:* 14

Godspell, 1970s: 2, 13

Goering, Hermann, *1930s:* 167

Goetz, Bernhard, *1980s:* 72–73, 72 (ill.)

Goldberger, Joseph, *1910s:* 126; *1920s:* 122

Gold Diggers of 1933, 1930s: 16

The Golden Bear. *See* Nicklaus, Jack

Golden Gate Bridge, *1930s:* 139

Golden Gate's International Exposition, *1930s:* 89, 106

Golden Gloves tournament, *1930s:* 152

Goldfinger, 1960s: 9

Gold Gloves, *1960s:* 168

Goldman, Emma, *1900s:* 83, 83 (ill.); *1910s:* 98

Goldman, Ronald, *1990s:* 2, 14–15, 63, 85, 88

Goldman Sachs, *1930s:* 35–36

Goldmark, Peter, *1940s:* 131

Gold Reserve Act, *1930s:* 68

The Gold Rush, 1910s: 6

Gold Standard Act, *1900s:* 20, 32

Goldwater, Barry, *1960s:* 85

Golf, *1900s:* 139, 142; *1910s:* 156, 159, 159 (ill.), 169–70, 171 (ill.); *1920s:* 148–49, 151–52, 164–66; *1930s:* 152, 164; *1940s:* 152, 155–56, 168–70, 169 (ill.); *1950s:* 158, 163; *1960s:* 165; *1970s:* 160, 174–76; *1980s:* 181–83; *1990s:* 165, 177–79

Golub, Harvey, *1990s:* 32

Gompers, Samuel, *1910s:* 29, 29 (ill.), 37, 40–41, 120

Gone With the Wind, 1930s: 3, 14

Gonorrhea, *1930s:* 123; *1960s:* 120; *1970s:* 123

Goodbye Columbus, 1950s: 9

The Good Earth, 1930s: 13

Gooden, Dwight, *1980s:* 176

Goodman, Andrew, *1960s:* 102

Goodman, Benny, *1930s:* 2–3, 5, 20; *1940s:* 16; *1960s:* 2

Goodman, Paul, *1930s:* 59; *1960s:* 55–57

Good Neighbor Policy, *1930s:* 80

Goodrich, Gail, *1960s:* 175

Good Times, 1970s: 108

Googie architecture, *1950s:* 92, 94, 96

Gorbachev, Mikhail, *1980s:* 70, 81, 90–92, 114

Gordon, Jeff, *1990s:* 166, 166 (ill.)

Gordon, Robert W., *1930s:* 20

Gordy, Berry, Jr., *1960s:* 13

Gore, Albert, *1980s:* 9

Gore, Tipper, *1980s:* 9

Gorgas, WIlliam Crawford, *1900s:* 104, 104 (ill.)

Gospel music, *1930s:* 20; *1940s:* 18; *1960s:* 15

Gothic architecture, *1910s:* 94, 100

Gothic art, *1910s:* 100

Gottlieb, Adolph, *1940s:* 9

Gottlieb, Eddie, *1930s:* 161

Gould, Chester, *1930s:* 11; *1950s:* 143

Government loans, corporations, *1990s:* 41

Government, politics and law, *1900s:* 57–75; *1910s:* 65–88; *1920s:* 63–84; *1930s:* 67–86; *1940s:* 63–83; *1950s:* 67–86; *1960s:* 67–91; *1970s:* 69–95; *1980s:* 67–93; *1990s:* 61–89

  big business and, *1960s:* 37

  business and government, *1940s:* 26–27, 30

  chronology, *1900s:* 58–59; *1910s:* 66–67; *1920s:* 64–65; *1930s:* 68–69; *1940s:* 64–65; *1950s:* 68–69; *1960s:* 68–69; *1970s:* 70–71; *1980s:* 68–69; *1990s:* 62–63

  elections, *1950s:* 83–86, 82 (ill.)

  equal opportunities, *1970s:* 40–42

  farmers and the government, *1960s:* 30

  headline makers, *1900s:* 62–63; *1910s:* 70–71; *1920s:* 68–69; *1930s:* 72–73; *1940s:* 68–69; *1950s:* 72–73; *1960s:* 72–73; *1970s:* 71–75; *1980s:* 72–73; *1990s:* 66–67

  intervention in labor strikes, *1900s:* 26–27

  "Military-Industrial Complex," *1940s:* 34–36, 66, 137–38, 140

  Olympics and, *1970s:* 178–80

  Olympics and politics, *1960s:* 181–82

  overview, *1900s:* 60–61; *1910s:* 68–69; *1920s:* 66–67; *1930s:* 70–71; *1940s:* 66–67; *1950s:* 70–71; *1960s:* 70–71; *1970s:* 72–73; *1980s:* 70–71; *1990s:* 64–65

  See also Civil Rights movement; Cold war; specific laws and legislation

Gowdy, Hank, *1910s:* 155; *1920s:* 158

GP vehicles. *See* Jeeps

Grades, extracurricular activities and, *1980s:* 48

The Graduate, 1960s: 4, 9

Grady Gammage Auditorium, *1950s:* 96

Graf, Steffi, *1990s:* 181

Graham, Billy, *1940s:* 87, 99; *1950s:* 91, 95, 95 (ill.); *1980s:* 96

Graham, David, *1980s:* 183

Graham, Martha, *1910s:* 10; *1920s:* 3; *1930s:* 4, 22, 59; *1940s:* 6, 6 (ill.); *1960s:* 114

Graham, Otto, *1950s:* 173, 175

Granatelli, Andy, *1960s:* 170

Grand Central Station, *1910s:* 24, 100

Grand Challenge Cup, *1910s:* 154

Grand Cross of the Supreme Order of the German Eagle, *1930s:* 89

Grand Hyatt Hotel, *1980s:* 34

Grand Ole Opry, *1930s:* 18

Grand Slam, *1920s:* 165

Grand Slam (golf), *1930s:* 152, 164

Grand Slam (tennis), *1930s:* 168; *1980s:* 173, 185

Grange, Harold "Red," *1920s:* 95, 149–50, 152, 152 (ill.), 161–62, 164

Grant, Horace, *1990s:* 171

Grants
    arts, *1990s:* 2–4, 8–9
    corporate welfare, *1990s:* 41
    school, *1990s:* 45

Graphics, Apple computers, *1980s:* 160

Grate American Sleep-Out, *1980s:* 97

Grauman's Chinese Theater, *1920s:* 87

Gravitation, *1910s:* 136

Gray, Hannah H., *1970s:* 99

Gray Panthers, *1970s:* 110

Gray, Pete, *1940s:* 161

Grayson, Kentucky high school shooting, *1990s:* 44

Graziano, Rocky, *1940s:* 165

Grease, 1980s: 2

Greasers, *1950s:* 110

"Great Books," *1940s:* 48–49, 52–54, 54 (ill.)

Great Books Foundation, *1950s:* 52

Great Britain, *1910s:* 75, 77–78
    See also England

Great Depression, *1920s:* 27, 43, 89; *1930s:* 32–43, 70, 74, 90–91
    family life, *1930s:* 103–04
    religion and, *1930s:* 100

The Great Dictator, 1940s: 2, 13

The Great Gatsby, 1920s: 6

Great Society, *1960s:* 27, 70, 72, 81–82, 86
    education and, *1960s:* 57
    health care and, *1960s:* 130–31
    labor and, *1960s:* 38–40

The Great Train Robbery, 1900s: 7, 11, 78

The Great War. *See* World War I

The Great White Hope, 1910s: 166; *1970s: 20*

Green Acres, 1960s; 19

Green Bay Packers, *1920s:* 163–64; *1930s:* 164; *1960s:* 165, 169, 180–81; *1980s:* 169; *1990s:* 175

Greene, Charles, *1900s:* 97

Greene, Henry, *1900s:* 97

Greenfield Village, *1920s:* 32

Greenglass, David, *1950s:* 78–79

Greenhouse effect, *1960s:* 145, 154

Greenhouse gas emissions, *1990s:* 139

Greenhouses, Biosphere 2, *1990s:* 151–52

Greenland, *1900s:* 123

Green Lantern, *1940s:* 10

Green Party, *1960s:* 29

Green, Paul, *1930s:* 21

Green, Pumpsie, *1950s:* 164

Greenspan, Alan, *1990s:* 32, 32 (ill.)

Greenstreet, Sidney, *1940s:* 15

The Greenwich Village Follies, 1920s: 9

Greenwich Village, New York, *1960s:* 2

Greer, Hal, *1960s:* 177

Grenada, *1980s:* 75

Gretzky, Wayne, *1970s:* 174; *1980s:* 168–69, 171–72, 172 (ill.), 184–85; *1990s:* 177

Greyhound Corporation, *1920s:* 25

Greyhound Lines Inc., *1990s:* 28

Grey, Zane, *1900s:* 9

GRID (Gay-related immune deficiency). *See* AIDS

Grier, Roosevelt, *1950s:* 174

Griffin, Michael Frederick, *1990s:* 128

Griffith, D. W., *1910s:* 2, 7, 7 (ill.), 14–15

Grimstead, Swede, *1910s:* 166

Grisham, John, *1990s:* 2, 5–6, 6 (ill.), 20

Grissom, Virgil "Gus," *1960s:* 143,
146, 146 (ill.), 157, 159

Griswold v. Connecticut, 1970s: 89

G. R. Kinney Company, *1950s:* 42

Grocery stores, *1910s:* 42

Grohl, Dave, *1990s:* 22 (ill.)

Gropius, Walter, *1920s:* 97; *1930s:* 96;
1940s: 92–93; *1950s:* 96, 104

Gross National Product (GNP), *1910s:*
76; *1960s:* 35

Groton, *1900s:* 48

Group Health Association, Inc.,
1940s: 108

Group Theatre, *1930s:* 21

Grove, Andrew, *1980s:* 44

Groves, Leslie R., *1940s:* 144

Groza, Lou, *1950s:* 173

Grunge rock music, *1990s:* 2, 5,
21–23

Guadalcanal, *1940s:* 72–73

Guam, *1900s:* 72; *1910s:* 72

Guerin, Camille, *1920s:* 114–15

A Guest of Honor, 1900s: 2; *1910s:* 17

Guess Who's Coming to Dinner, 1960s:
7, 105–06

Guffey, J. M., *1900s:* 29

Guffey Oil, *1900s:* 29

Guggenheim, Daniel, *1920s:* 137

Guggenheim Fund for the Promotion
of Aeronautics, *1920s:* 137

Guggenheim Museum of Non-objective Art, *1930s:* 10; *1950s:* 9

Guggenheim, Peggy, *1940s:* 8

Guiding Light, 1930s: 3

Guild Theater, *1930s:* 2

The Gulf Between, 1920s: 143–44

"Gulf Coast Blues," *1920s:* 2

Gulf of Tonkin Resolution, *1960s:* 78

Gulf Oil Corporation, *1900s:* 25, 29

Gulf War Syndrome, *1990s:* 124–25
See also Persian Gulf War

Gum, chewing, *1940s:* 29

Gun Control Act of 1946, *1940s:* 105

Gunn, David, *1990s:* 128

Gunsmoke, 1950s: 2

Guns
in America, *1990s:* 92, 94,
105–08

control, *1990s:* 92, 105–08

manufacturers, *1990s:* 93

schools, *1980s:* 64; *1990s:* 44,
49–50

Guston, Philip, *1940s:* 9

Gutenberg, Beno, *1910s:* 147; *1930s:*
143

Guthrie, Arlo, *1930s:* 7

Guthrie, C. C., *1900s:* 101

Guthrie Theatre, *1960s:* 2

Guthrie, Woody, *1930s:* 3, 7, 7 (ill.);
1960s: 6

Guyot, Arnold, *1960s:* 146

Guyots, *1960s:* 146

Gwynn, Tony, *1980s:* 176

Gymnastics, *1930s:* 155; *1970s:* 178
(ill.); *1980s:* 189

Gym shoes. *See* Athletic shoes

H

Hackman, Gene, *1960s:* 10

Haddix, Harvey, *1950s:* 159

Haemophilus influenzae, 1990s. 138

Hagen, Walter "The Haig," *1910s:*
156, 170, 171 (ill.); *1920s:* 151–52,
165–66

Hahn, Otto, *1930s:* 144; *1940s:* 132

Haight-Ashbury, *1960s:* 95, 97, 107

Hair, 1960s: 3–4, 18–19

Hair coloring, *1950s:* 90

Haircut 100, *1980s:* 18

Hairstyles, *1960s:* 94, 108, 110–11;
1970s: 118

Haiti, *1910s:* 72; *1990s:* 69

Halas, George, *1920s:* 164; *1990s:* 164

Haldeman, H. R., *1970s:* 70, 86

Hale American Open (golf), *1940s:*
168

Hale, George Ellery, *1900s:* 119, 122,
122 (ill.); *1910s:* 139

Hale telescope, *1940s:* 131

Hale v. Henkel, 1900s: 34

Haley, Alex, *1970s:* 4–5, 23, 108

Haley, Bill, *1950s:* 3

Haley, Margaret A., *1900s:* 40, 44

Hall, Edward Wheeler, *1920s:* 80

Halley's Comet, *1910s:* 132

Hall, Granville Stanley, *1900s:* 47,
123, 123 (ill.)

Hall, George C., *1900s:* 107

Hall, Jerry, *1990s:* 116

Hall of Fame
baseball, *1930s:* 160; *1960s:* 168,
173
basketball, *1960s:* 176
football, *1960s:* 169
hockey, *1930s:* 166
Paige, Leroy "Satchel," *1920s:* 157

Hallucinogenic drugs, *1960s:* 94–95,
107

Hamill, Dorothy, *1970s:* 118, 179
(ill.), 180

Hamilton, Scott, *1980s:* 188

Hamlin College, *1900s:* 146

Hammer, Armand, *1930s:* 30, 30 (ill.)

Hammerstein, Oscar II, *1920s:* 8

Hammett, Dashiell, *1920s:* 19; *1930s:*
13–14; *1940s:* 14–15

Hamm, Mia, *1990s:* 165–66, 166 (ill.)

Hammond, Laurens, *1930s:* 2

Hammond Pros, *1980s:* 169

Hampton Institute, *1900s:* 51

*Handbook on Formative and Summative
Evaluation of Student Learning,
1970s:* 52

Handicapped accommodations, *1970s:*
49, 56

Handicapped, children, *1910s:* 113;
1960s: 46

Hand-pump heart massage, *1960s:*
128

H & R Block, *1960s:* 35

Hands Across America, *1980s:* 97, 111

Handy, W. C., *1900s:* 14; *1910s:* 5, 7, 7
(ill.), 17; *1920s:* 11

Hanks, Tom, *1990s:* 11

Hanna, Mark, *1900s:* 70

Hard-boiled fiction, *1920s:* 19; *1930s:*
14

Hardbound books, *1950s:* 10

Harding, Warren G., *1910s:* 80; *1920s:*
64, 68, 68 (ill.), 86, 145
agricultural policy, *1920s:* 33
election of, *1920s:* 67, 70, 76
on government in business,
1920s: 74
industry regulation and, *1920s:*
27, 33
Teapot Dome Scandal and, *1920s:*
67, 78–79

Harding, Tonya, *1990s:* 164, 183

Hare Krishna, *1970s:* 114

Haring, Keith, *1980s:* 4, 6, 6 (ill.)

Harlan County labor strike, *1930s:* 26,
37

Harlem Globetrotters, *1920s:* 160;
1930s: 161; *1940s:* 162–65, 164
(ill.); *1950s:* 176

The Harlem Globetrotters, 1950s: 176

Harlem, New York riots, *1960s:* 69,
103

Harlem Renaissance, *1920s:* 5, 10–11

Harley-Davidson, *1900s:* 23

Harlow, Harry F., *1960s:* 125, 125 (ill.)

The Harmonic Convergence, *1980s:*
117

Harriman, Averell, *1950s:* 85

Harris, Bucky, *1920s:* 158

Harris, Eric, *1990s:* 50

Harris, Franco, *1970s:* 171 (ill.)

Harris, Margaret, *1970s:* 2

Harrison, George, *1960s:* 6, 6 (ill.),
11–12; *1970s:* 13

The Harrison Narcotic Act, *1910s:* 82

Harrison, Pat, *1930s:* 47

Harris, Roy, *1930s:* 20

Harris, Seale, *1920s:* 108

Harroun, Ray, *1910s:* 154, 160

*Harry Potter and the Chamber of
Secrets, 1990s:* 21

*Harry Potter and the Prisoner of Azka-
ban, 1990s:* 21

Harry Potter and the Sorcerer's Stone
(book), *1990s:* 21

Harry Potter and the Sorcerer's Stone
(movie), *1990s:* 21

Hartford Fire Insurance, *1960s:* 41

Hart, Frederick, *1980s:* 83

Hart, George S., *1930s:* 22

Hartley, Marsden, *1910s:* 12

Hart Trophy, *1930s:* 166; *1980s:* 185

Hart, William S., *1910s:* 16

Harvard College, *1930s:* 2

Harvard Divinity School, *1950s:* 47

Harvard Mark 1, *1940s:* 130, 140

Harvard Stadium, *1900s:* 138

Harvard University, *1900s:* 44, 50,
52–53; *1910s:* 46; *1920s:* 24; *1930s:*
93; *1960s:* 51, 63–64; *1980s:* 62

Harvard University Law School,
1950s: 46

Harvard University School of Architecture, *1930s:* 96

Hassam, Childe, *1910s:* 12

Hastie, William, *1930s:* 79, 89

Hatch, Orrin, *1990s:* 102

Hate crimes, *1990s:* 93, 102

Hats, for women, *1900s:* 93

Hattiesburg, Mississippi, school segregation in, *1900s:* 41

Haughton, Percy, *1900s:* 151

Havlicek, John, *1960s:* 177

Hawaii, *1900s:* 50, 72
global warming, *1990s:* 150
statehood, *1950s:* 69

Hawes, Elizabeth, *1930s:* 102

Hawkes, E. Z., *1900s:* 101

Hawkes, John, *1940s:* 12

Hawkman, *1910s:* 10

Hawks, Howard, *1930s:* 7

Haworth, Norman, *1930s:* 141

Hayden, Tom, *1960s:* 115

Haydon, Murray, *1980s:* 132

Hayes, Bob, *1960s:* 181

Hayes, George E. C., *1950s:* 57 (ill.)

Hays, Arthur Garfield, *1920s:* 82

Hays Office, *1930s:* 2

Hays, Will, *1920s:* 104

Hays, Will H., *1930s:* 15

Haywood, William "Big Bill" D.,
1900s: 21, 24, 24 (ill.), 29–30;
1910s: 98

Hayworth, Rita, *1940s:* 87; *1980s:* 137

Hazardous Substance Response Trust
Fund, *1980s:* 155

Hazardous wastes, *1980s:* 148

Hazelwood, Joseph, *1980s:* 156

Hazzard, Walt, *1960s:* 175

H-bomb. *See* Nuclear weapons

Head Start program, *1960s:* 58; *1970s:*
105

Health. *See* Medicine and health

Health benefits, temporary employees, *1990s:* 36

Health care, *1990s:* 116, 118, 121–23

Health care costs, *1930s:* 118; *1940s:*
111; *1950s:* 120

Health clubs, *1970s:* 130–31; *1980s:*
106, 107 (ill.)

Health education, *1980s:* 130

Health insurance, *1910s:* 113; *1930s:*
110, 113, 118–20; *1940s:* 108, 110,
117–18; *1960s:* 82, 120–21, 123,
131; *1970s:* 122; *1990s:* 28
AIDS and, *1980s:* 130
See also Health maintenance
organizations

Health Maintenance Organization Act
of 1973, *1970s:* 122, 133

Health maintenance organizations
(HMOs), *1970s:* 122, 125, 131–33;
1990s: 121

Health reform. *See* Medical reform

Hearing impaired, *1910s:* 113

Hearst newspapers, *1930s:* 50, 60

Hearst, Patricia, *1970s:* 98, 102, 102
(ill.)

Hearst, William Randolph, *1900s:* 16;
1910s: 3, 19–20, 19 (ill.), 91; *1930s:*
53, 60; *1940s:* 2; *1970s:* 102

Heart disease, *1940s:* 120; *1950s:*
122–25; *1990s:* 126
See also Cardiovascular medicine

Heart-lung machine, *1950s:* 114;
1960s: 124

Heart, mechanical, *1930s:* 111, 114

Heart surgery, *1960s:* 124, 126–28

Heart transplants, *1960s:* 121–22,
124, 127; *1980s:* 122–24, 126,
130–34, 132 (ill.)

Heaven's Gate cult, *1990s:* 93

Heavy metal music, *1990s:* 5

Heavyweight boxing, *1900s:* 138–39,
141, 148, 149 (ill.); *1940s:* 152–53,
157, 165–66; *1960s:* 164–65,
167–68
See also Boxing

Hecht, Ben, *1920s:* 4

Hecktoen, Ludvig, *1900s:* 100

Hefner, Hugh, *1950s:* 95, 95 (ill.)

Heiden, Eric, *1980s:* 171, 186

Heifetz, Jascha, *1910s:* 3

Heimlich maneuver, *1970s:* 122

Heinkel 179, *1930s:* 131

Heinlein, Robert, *1950s:* 16

Heinsohn, Tom, *1960s:* 177

Heisman, John, *1910s:* 168

Heisman Trophy, *1930s:* 153; *1940s:* 156; *1960s:* 178

Helicopters, *1900s:* 119; *1920s:* 140–41; *1930s:* 131; *1940s:* 130

Helium, liquid, *1900s:* 119

Heller, Joseph, *1960s:* 4, 19

Hellman, Lillian, *1940s:* 6, 6 (ill.), 20; *1950s:* 14

"Hello, Dolly!," *1920s:* 6; *1960s:* 18

Hell's Angels, 1930s: 30; *1960s:* 95

Hellzapoppin', 1930s: 22

Helms, Jesse, *1980s:* 9; *1990s:* 8

Helter Skelter, 1960s: 81

Hemingway, Ernest, *1920s:* 3, 6–7, 6 (ill.), 13–14; *1940s:* 12; *1950s:* 5, 9

Henderson, Donald A., *1970s:* 126

Henderson, Rickey, *1980s:* 176

Hendrix, Jimi, *1960s:* 10, 12–13

Henie, Sonje, *1930s:* 155

Henning, Anne, *1970s:* 177

Henri, Robert, *1900s:* 6, 6 (ill.); *1910s:* 8–9

Henry Phipps Psychiatric Clinic, *1910s:* 116

Henry Street Settlement, *1900s:* 87; *1910s:* 18

Henson, Jim, *1970s:* 6, 6 (ill.)

Heparin, *1920s:* 128

Hepburn Act, *1900s:* 32–33, 65

Hepburn, Audrey, *1950s:* 13

Hepburn, Katharine, *1930s:* 89

Herbicides, *1970s:* 155

Heredity, *1910s:* 117, 134; *1950s:* 147–48; *1960s:* 145

Hereditary determinants, *1900s:* 129–31

Heresis, 1970s: 9

Heritage USA, *1970s:* 102

Herman, Woody, *1940s:* 16

Hermitage Museum, *1980s:* 2

A Hero Ain't Nothin' but a Sandwich, 1970s: 10

Heroes for Sale, 1930s: 15

Heroin, *1920s:* 108

Hershey, *1900s:* 23

Hershiser, Orel, *1980s:* 176

Hertz, Heinrich R., *1900s:* 127; *1910s:* 147

Hertzian waves, *1900s:* 127

Hesburgh, Theodore M., *1960s:* 60

Hess, Harry H., *1960s:* 147, 153

Hess, Victor, *1910s:* 140

Heston, Charlton, *1990s:* 97, 97 (ill.)

Hewlett-Packard, *1930s:* 27; *1970s:* 140; *1980s:* 30, 160–61

Heyburn Bill, *1900s:* 32

Heydler, John, *1920s:* 149

HGT. *See* Gene therapy

Hickel, Walter, *1970s:* 152

Hickock, Richard, *1960s:* 80

The Hidden Persuaders, 1950s: 30–31

Higginbotham, Willy, *1950s:* 150

Higher education, *1950s:* 46–47

  yuppies, *1980s:* 105–06

  See also Universities and colleges

Higher Education Facilities Act, *1960s:* 47, 57

High fat diets, *1950s:* 125

High jump, *1950s:* 159

Highlander Folk School, *1930s:* 57

High school drop-outs, *1980s:* 63

High schools, *1940s:* 57–59

  African Americans in, *1930s:* 46

  dating in, *1940s:* 98

  desegregation, *1950s:* 50, 57–60, 57 (ill.), 59 (ill.)

  diplomas, *1970s:* 48

  dropouts, *1970s:* 57

  equivalency diploma, *1940s:* 56

  shootings, *1990s:* 44–45

  weapons in, *1990s:* 44

High-tech industries, *1960s:* 36–37

Hilfiger, Tommy, *1990s:* 92, 97, 97 (ill.)

Hill, Anita, *1990s:* 64, 87, 87 (ill.)

Hillbilly music, *1930s:* 18–20

Hill-Burton Act. *See* Hospital Survey and Construction Act

Hill, George, *1930s:* 53

Hill, Joe, *1910s:* 94, 94 (ill.), 98

Hillman, Sidney, *1940s:* 28, 28 (ill.)

Hillquit, Morris, *1910s:* 98

Himes, Chester, *1940s:* 12–13

Hindenberg, 1930s: 131, 137–38

Hines, Lewis, *1900s:* 87

Hinckley, John W., Jr., *1980s:* 68, 78, 81

Hip-hop music, *1990s:* 7, 23–24, 109–12

Hippies, *1960s:* 107

Hirsch, Elroy "Crazylegs," *1950s:* 176

Hiroshima, Japan, *1940s:* 65, 75, 77 (ill.), 109, 131, 145 (ill.), 146; *1950s:* 75, 139

His Family, 1910s: 11

Hispanic Americans, *1960s:* 168; *1980s:* 48, 60–62, 60 (ill.)
  bilingual education for, *1970s:* 55 (ill.), 56–57
  Brown Power, *1970s:* 108–09
  in school, *1930s:* 51

Hispanics, *1990s:* 38, 45

Hiss, Alger, *1940s:* 68, 68 (ill.); *1950s:* 68, 70–71, 77; *1970s:* 83

Histamine, *1940s:* 119

History, African Americans, *1910s:* 51

The History of Education, 1920s: 46

His Trust/His Trust Fulfilled, 1910s: 14

Hitchcock, Alfred, *1920s:* 143

Hitchcock, Henry-Russell, *1930s:* 88

Hitler, Adolf, *1930s:* 71, 88–89, 100, 166–67; *1940s:* 13, 65, 70, 76

HIV, *1980s:* 124–26, 130; *1990s:* 117–20, 121, 126
  See also AIDS

HMO Act of 1973, *1970s:* 122, 133

HMOs (Health maintenance organizations), *1990s:* 121
  See also Health maintenance organizations

Hockey, *1920s:* 148–49; *1930s:* 165–66; *1960s:* 164–65; *1970s:* 161, 172–74; *1980s:* 161, 183–85; *1990s:* 176–77
  Gretzky, Wayne, *1980s:* 168–69, 171–72, 172 (ill.), 184–85

Olympics, *1980s:* 186–87, 187 (ill.)

Hodgkin's disease, *1900s:* 109

Hoffa, James R., *1950s:* 28, 28 (ill.)

Hoffman, Abbie, *1960s:* 115

Hoffman, Dustin, *1960s:* 9

Hoffman, Hans, *1950s:* 8

Hoffman, Julius, *1960s:* 115

Hoff, Theodore, *1970s:* 146

Hofstadter, Richard, *1940s:* 59

Hogan, Ben, *1950s:* 158, 162, 162 (ill.), 176; *1990s:* 167

Hogan's Alley, 1900s: 16

Hogshead, Nancy, *1980s:* 192

Holden, William, *1950s:* 13

"Hold On," *1990s:* 26

Holiday, Billie, *1940s:* 2–3, 6, 6 (ill.), 16

Holiday Inn, *1950s:* 36; *1960s:* 34

Holiday Inn, 1940s: 17

Holiday, King, Martin Luther Jr., *1990s:* 92

Holland, Bill, *1940s:* 158

Holland, Brian, *1960s:* 13

Holland, Eddie, *1960s:* 13

Hollingshead, Richard M., Jr., *1930s:* 88

Holly, Buddy, *1950s:* 3; *1960s:* 10

Hollywood, *1930s:* 14–18; *1940s:* 7, 13–15; *1960s:* 8–9
  immorality of, *1920s:* 104
  See also Films; motion picture industry

Hollywood blacklist, *1950s:* 4, 13–15

Hollywood Ten, *1940s:* 3, 6, 13–15, 81–82, 81 (ill.)

Holman, Nat, *1910s:* 165

Holm, Eleanor, *1930s:* 167

Holmes, Oliver Wendell, Jr., *1910s:* 70, 70 (ill.); *1920s:* 154

Holt, Andrew David, *1940s:* 48

Holt Company, *1900s:* 119

Holt, L. Emmett, *1920s:* 117

Holum, Dianne, *1970s:* 177

Holyfield, Evander, *1990s:* 163

Home Alone, 1990s: 10

Home appliances, *1900s:* 79, 81

Home decorating, *1980s:* 101

Home economics, *1910s:* 58

Home furnishings, *1900s:* 97

Home kidney dialysis machines, *1960s:* 122

Homeless population, *1980s:* 96–97, 99, 109–12, 110 (ill.)

Home of the Brave, 1960s: 105

Homeowners' Loan Act, *1930s:* 68–69

Homer, Winslow, *1910s:* 8

Homes, *1980s:* 55

Homeschools, *1990s:* 51–52, 52 (ill.)

Home Shopping Network, *1980s:* 103

Home to Harlem, 1920s: 11

Homicides, *1910s:* 36, 82

Homosexuality, *1990s:* 92, 102–04, 103 (ill.), 125–26, 128
  See also Gay rights

Homosexuals, AIDS and, *1980s:* 122, 127–29

The Honeymooners, 1950s: 18, 18 (ill.)

Honeywell, *1960s:* 37

Honky-tonk, *1940s:* 17

Hood, Raymond, *1920s:* 97, 99

Hooker Company, *1970s:* 153–54

Hooker Telescope, *1910s:* 133

Hooks, Valerie Briscohy, *1980s:* 192

Hookworm, *1900s:* 114–15; *1910s:* 126; *1920s:* 122

Hooper, Harry, *1910s:* 164

Hoovercarts, *1930s:* 34

Hoover Company, *1950s:* 137

Hoover Dam, *1930s:* 131, 138, 139 (ill.); *1940s:* 29

Hooverflags, *1930s:* 34

Hoover, Herbert, *1920s:* 67, 69, 69 (ill.), 128; *1930s:* 46, 68, 72, 72 (ill.), 76, 80, 92, 98
  Agricultural Marketing Act and, *1920s:* 75
  economic policy of, *1930s:* 70, 76
  election of, *1920s:* 78
  on government in business, *1920s:* 74
  Great Depression and, *1930s:* 32–34
  health education and, *1920s:* 117
  Smoot-Hawley Tariff, *1930s:* 26

"The Star Spangled Banner" and, *1930s:* 68

television and, *1920s:* 129

Transbay Bridge Project and, *1930s:* 138–39

World War I veterans and, *1930s:* 76

Hoover, J. Edgar, *1920s:* 64; *1930s:* 72, 72 (ill.); *1950s:* 105

Hooverville, *1930s:* 34, 35 (ill.)

Hope, John, *1900s:* 41, 44, 44 (ill.)

Hopkins, Frederick, *1920s:* 108, 111, 123

Hopkins, Harry, *1930s:* 79

Hopkins, Sam "Lightnin," *1940s:* 17

Hopkins, Samuel, *1910s:* 124

Hopper, Dennis, *1960s:* 5, 9

Hopper, Edward, *1900s:* 3; *1910s:* 12; *1920s:* 18; *1930s:* 4, 8–9

Hopper, Grace Murray, *1950s:* 140, 140 (ill.)

Horine, George, *1910s:* 174

Horizontal integration, in business, *1900s:* 23

Hormones, *1900s:* 119

Horner, Bob, *1980s:* 175

Horney, Karen, *1930s:* 114, 114 (ill.)

Hornsby, Roger, *1920s:* 149, 156

Horowitz, Vladimir, *1960s:* 3

Horror fiction, *1990s:* 20

Horror movies, *1970s:* 18

Horse racing, *1910s:* 155–56, 172–73; *1920s:* 148, 166–67; *1930s:* 152, 164–65; *1940s:* 152–53, 156; *1960s:* 165; *1970s:* 161

Horton Hears a Who, 1950s: 50

Horwich, Frances, *1950s:* 64, 64 (ill.)

Hospitals, *1900s:* 106–07, 109; *1910s:* 114; *1940s:* 110–11
  evaluation, *1910s:* 113
  Johns Hopkins Hospital, *1910s:* 129
  mental, *1910s:* 116
  Rockefeller Institute hospital, *1910s:* 112
  St. Mary's, *1910s:* 119

Hospital Survey and Construction Act, *1940s:* 110–11

Hostages, *1980s:* 32, 69, 71
    in Attica prison riot, *1970s:*
      92–93
    in Iran, *1970s:* 71, 73, 91–94, 91
      (ill.)
Hotchkiss, Hazel V., *1900s:* 48; *1910s:*
    174
Hotels, *1950s:* 36
Hot Five, *1920s:* 6, 12
Hot pants, *1970s:* 98, 116
Hours of work, *1900s:* 20, 34
House Beautiful, *1920s:* 100
House by the Railroad, *1920s:* 18
House calls, by doctors, *1960s:*
    128–30, 129 (ill.)
House, Edward M., *1910s:* 71, 71 (ill.)
Household appliances, *1900s:* 79, 118
Houseman, John, *1930s:* 21
House of Mystery, *1920s:* 18
House of Wax, *1950s:* 10
Houses
    interior design, *1900s:* 96–97
    mail-order, *1900s:* 96
The House Science and Technology
    Committee, *1980s:* 154
House Un-American Activities Com-
    mittee (HUAC), *1930s:* 69; *1940s:*
    3, 14–15, 81–82, 81 (ill.); *1950s:* 4,
    13–15
    Hellman, Lillian, *1940s:* 6
    Miller, Arthur, *1940s:* 19
    on textbooks, *1940s:* 45, 51
    See also Anticommunism
Housing, *1910s:* 101–06; *1990s:* 94,
    104
    construction, *1950s:* 24
    designs, *1940s:* 90
    low-income, *1960s:* 82
    suburban, *1940s:* 100–03; *1950s:*
      90
    solar-powered, *1960s:* 143
    wartime, *1940s:* 93
Houston Astrodome, *1960s:* 94
Houston, Charles, *1940s:* 68, 68 (ill.)
Houston Colt .45s, *1960s:* 164, 174
Houston Mavericks, *1960s:* 177
Houston Oilers, *1960s:* 180
Houston, Whitney, *1980s:* 3, 6, 6 (ill.)

Howard, Frank, *1960s:* 173
Howard Johnson Company, *1930s:* 31
Howard, Sidney, *1920s:* 3
Howard University, *1930s:* 62
Howe, Gordie, *1950s:* 162, 162 (ill.)
Howells, John Mead, *1920s:* 97
Howells, William Dean, *1900s:* 8
Howell, William, *1920s:* 128
Howl and Other Poems, *1950s:* 3, 9–10
How Long Brethren, *1930s:* 22
How the Grinch Stole Christmas, *1950s:*
    50
How to Stuff a Wild Bikini, *1960s:* 108
*How to Succeed in Business Without
    Really Trying,* *1960s:* 18
*How to Win Friends and Influence Peo-
    ple,* *1930s:* 3
Hoxsey, Harry M., *1950s:* 122
HTLV-III (Human T-cell lymphotropic
    virus type III), *1980s:* 126–27
HTML (HyperText Markup Lan-
    guage), *1990s:* 142
HUAC (House Un-American Activi-
    ties Committee), *1930s:* 69
    See also House Un-American
      Activities Committee
Hubble, Edwin P., *1920s:* 132, 132
    (ill.); *1930s:* 144
Hubble Space Telescope, *1990s:* 138,
    141, 156–58, 157 (ill.)
Huckleberry Finn, *1980s:* 56, 57 (ill.)
Hudson, *1920s:* 34
Hudson, Rock, *1950s:* 13; *1980s:* 129
Huerta, Victoriano, *1910s:* 73
Huggins, Miller, *1910s:* 155
Hughes, Charles Evans, *1900s:* 62, 62
    (ill.); *1910s:* 84
Hughes, Holly, *1990s:* 8
Hughes, Howard, *1930s:* 30, 30 (ill.),
    136–37; *1940s:* 34
Hughes, Langston, *1920s:* 3, 10
Hugo, Victor, *1980s:* 14
Huie, William Bradford, *1950s:* 74
Hula hoops, *1950s:* 93, 108 (ill.)
Hull, Bobby, *1960s:* 164; *1970s:* 172
Hull House, Chicago, Illinois, *1900s:*
    48, 81–82, 87, 88 (ill.); *1910s:* 80
Hull, Cordell, *1930s:* 80

Hulman, Tony, *1940s:* 158

Human Be-In, *1960s:* 95

Human gene therapy (HGT), *1990s:* 116, 119, 130–34

Human Genome Project (HGP), *1990s:* 117, 138–40, 143–45

Human immunodeficiency virus. *See* HIV

Human Nature and Conduct, 1920s: 46

Human rights, *1910s:* 36

Humans, first, *1970s:* 148–51

Human T-cell lymphotropic virus type III (HTLV-III), *1980s:* 126–27

Humphrey, Doris, *1930s:* 22

Humphrey, Hubert, *1960s:* 71, 83, 86–87; *1970s:* 83

Hungary. *See* Austria-Hungary

"Hungry Like the Wolf," *1980s:* 18

Hunter, Catfish, *1960s:* 173

Hunt, Haroldson Lafayette, Jr., *1930s:* 30

Hunt, H. L., *1950s:* 25

Huntley, Chet, *1950s:* 18

Hunt, Nelson Bunker, *1980s:* 34, 34 (ill.)

Hunt, William Herbert, *1980s:* 34

Hupmobile, *1930s:* 41

Hurst, Fannie, *1920s:* 92

Hurston, Zora Neale, *1920s:* 11; *1930s:* 4; *1940s:* 13

Hussein, Saddam, *1990s:* 64, 66–68

"The Hustle," *1970s:* 15

Huston, John, *1940s:* 2, 14–15

Hutchins, Robert Maynard, *1940s:* 49, 49 (ill.), 52–53; *1950s:* 52

Hutson, Don, *1930s:* 164

Huxley, Aldous, *1930s:* 133

Hybridization, *1900s:* 122

Hyde amendment, *1970s:* 90

Hydraulic brakes, *1910s:* 133

Hydrogen bombs, *1940s:* 87, 146, 148
    See also Atomic bombs; nuclear weapons

Hyland, Lawrence, *1940s:* 142

Hyperinsulinism, *1920s:* 108

Hypertension, *1950s:* 125

HyperText Markup Language (HTML), *1990s:* 142, 147–48

Hypnosis, *1900s:* 123

Hypochloride, *1910s:* 123

Hysterectomies, *1960s:* 121

I

IAA (Intercollegiate Athletic Association), *1900s:* 152

Iba, Hank, *1940s:* 162

IBC (International Boxing Club), *1940s:* 166

IBM Automatic Sequence Controlled Calculator, *1940s:* 130, 140

IBM (International Business Machines), *1930s:* 36, 131; *1940s:* 140; *1950s:* 29, 43; *1960s:* 37, 142; *1990s:* 28, 93
    antitrust laws, *1980s:* 42–44
    computers, *1980s:* 42–44, 160–61
    first personal computer, *1980s:* 146–47
    MS-DOS, *1980s:* 30

"I Can't Help Myself," *1960s:* 14

ICBMs (Intercontinental ballistic missiles), *1980s:* 77–78
    See also Intercontinental Ballistic Missiles

ICC (Interstate Commerce Commission), *1900s:* 33, 65

Ice Bowl, *1930s:* 163

"Ice Bowl," *1960s:* 181

Iceboxes, *1910s:* 102

Ice cream, *1940s:* 87; *1960s:* 35

Ice Cube, *1990s:* 23

Ice Follies of 1939, 1930s: 6

Ice hockey, *1990s:* 165, 176–77

The Iceman Cometh, 1940s: 20

Ickes, Harold, *1940s:* 38, 40

Identity: Youth and Crisis, 1960s: 50

"I Do It for You," *1990s:* 26

IFGA (International Game Fish Association), *1930s:* 152

"If You Change Your Mind," *1980s:* 25

"If You Had My Love," *1990s:* 25

Iggy Pop, *1970s:* 13

"Igloos," *1940s:* 93

"I Got Rhythm," *1930s:* 2

"I Have a Dream" speech, *1960s:* 68, 72

"I Heard It Through the Grapevine," *1960s:* 13

ILGWU (International Ladies' Garment Workers Union), *1900s:* 21, 86; *1930s:* 22, 30–31

Illinois Institute of Technology, *1940s:* 92

Illinois Institute of Technology in Chicago, *1950s:* 96

Illiteracy, *1920s:* 52

Illiteracy, caucasians, *1980s:* 49

I'll Say She Is!, 1920s: 9

I'll Take My Stand, 1930s: 14

I Love Lucy, 1950s: 2, 19, 30, 142

IMF (International Monetary Fund), *1990s:* 40

    See also International Monetary Fund

"I'm Just Wild About Harry," *1920s:* 11

"Immaculate Reception," *1970s:* 171–72, 171 (ill.)

The Immigrant, 1910s: 6

Immigrants, *1900s:* 22, 42, 46 (ill.), 61, 80, 84; *1910s:* 150; *1940s:* 65; *1970s:* 109

    American citizenship, *1910s:* 47

    architecture and, *1940s:* 92

    bilingual education for, *1960s:* 52

    birth control for, *1910s:* 91

    discrimination against, *1900s:* 72; *1910s:* 93; *1940s:* 116–17

    education for, *1900s:* 41, 43, 45–47; *1920s:* 52

    immigration pattterns, *1910s:* 98–100

    Japanese, *1900s:* 59; *1920s:* 64

    restrictions of, *1920s:* 66, 71–72

    scientific research by, *1940s:* 132–33

    theater and, *1900s:* 15

    with AIDS, *1980s:* 123

    white slave trafficking, *1910s:* 87

    workers, *1910s:* 26, 34, 36, 39

Immigration Act, *1900s:* 59

Immigration Act of 1887, *1910s:* 66

Immigration and Naturalization Service, *1920s:* 52

Immorality, in movies, *1900s:* 11

Immorality, of Hollywood, *1920s:* 104

Immunization, *1910s:* 126

Impeachment, Nixon, Richard, *1970s:* 70, 86

Imperial Hotel Building, *1930s:* 93

Implosion bombs, *1940s:* 146

Imports, *1970s:* 29

    cars, *1970s:* 29, 40

    oil, *1970s:* 26–28, 30–32

Imports and exports, *1940s:* 37; *1960s:* 24, 30–31

Impressionism, *1900s:* 3, 8; *1910s:* 8

In All Countries, 1930s: 12

"In a Mist," *1920s:* 3

Incendiary bombs, *1910s:* 135, 150

In Cold Blood, 1960s: 80

Income

    personal, *1950s:* 25–26, 47

    U.S economy, *1950s:* 24

Income taxes, *1900s:* 21, 59; *1910s:* 32, 66; *1940s:* 32–33; *1960s:* 24

Incubators, *1960s:* 121

In Dahomey, 1900s: 15

Independence Day, 1990s: 10

Indiana Pacers, *1960s:* 177–78

Indiana Packers, *1950s:* 169

Indiana Pistons, *1950s:* 169

Indianapolis 500, *1910s:* 154, 156, 160–61; *1940s:* 158–59; *1950s:* 159; *1960s:* 170, 171 (ill.), 172

Indianapolis Jets, *1950s:* 169

Indianapolis Motor Speedway, *1910s:* 160

Indianapolis Olympians, *1950s:* 169

Indian-head pennies, *1900s:* 79

Indian Health Service, *1970s:* 123

Indians (American). *See* Native Americans

Indian Self-Determinatioin Act of 1974, *1970s:* 109

Individualism, *1930s:* 104–05

Industrial economy, *1910s:* 48

Industrial education, *1910s:* 46, 60

    See also Vocational education

Industrialization, *1910s:* 26, 33–36, 92

Industrial wastes, *1960s:* 130; *1970s:* 153–54

Industrial Workers of the World (IWW), *1900s:* 20–21, 24, 29, 58–59, 61; *1910s:* 94, 97–98

Industry, 1920s: 18

Industry regulation, *1920s:* 27, 74–75

Infantile paralysis. *See* Polio

Infant mortality, *1920s:* 117; *1930s:* 111; *1940s:* 111

Infants, *1910s:* 112, 115; *1950s:* 42, 115, 127–28

Infants, AIDS and, *1980s:* 122, 127

Infectious diseases, *1910s:* 66, 121, 124–25; *1940s:* 111, 114, 118
    See also specific diseases; *1960s:* 131–33

INF (Intermediate Nuclear Forces Treaty), *1980s:* 69, 91

Inflation, *1950s:* 38–40; *1960s:* 25–26; *1970s:* 26–28, 37–39; *1990s:* 29, 31–32, 35–36

Influenza, *1940s:* 108; *1990s:* 126, 138

Influenza, epidemic, *1910s:* 85, 113–14, 117–19, 122

Information Age, *1960s:* 27, 36–37, 39

Informational war booklets, *1910s:* 52

Infrared astronomy, *1960s:* 149

Inherited characteristics, *1940s:* 139–40

Inkster, Juli, *1990s:* 179

Inland Steel Corporation, *1940s:* 24

In Living Color, 1990s: 5

Inner-city schools, segregation and, *1970s:* 51, 53

In Old Arizona, 1920s: 142

The Inquiry, *1910s:* 71

Insect control, *1910s:* 144

Insecticides, *1940s:* 110, 114–15

Insect repellents, Gulf War syndrome, *1990s:* 124–25

Insects, genetically engineered, *1990s:* 139

Insider trading, *1980s:* 31, 34

Insight and Responsibility, 1960s: 50

Insull, Samuel, *1930s:* 31, 31 (ill.)

Insulin, *1920s:* 108–09, 118–19

Insurance, health, *1970s:* 122

Insurance organizations, *1910s:* 30, 112; *1940s:* 122

Integrated circuits, *1960s:* 145, 152

Integration, *1960s:* 74
    gender, *1960s:* 95
    race, *1960s:* 46–48, 58 (ill.), 59–60, 96, 102
    See also Desegregation; Segregation

Integration, school, *1930s:* 64–65
    See also Segregation

Intel Corporation, *1970s:* 140, 146; *1980s:* 44; *1990s:* 40

Intelligence, *1910s:* 150

Intelligence tests, *1930s:* 62; *1950s:* 46

Intelsat-6 satellite, *1990s:* 138

Interchange, 1980s: 3

Intercollegiate Athletic Association (IAA), *1900s:* 152

Intercontinental Ballistic Missiles (ICBMs), *1950s:* 139, 150–51; *1980s:* 77–78

Interest rates, *1940s:* 25; *1980s:* 30, 40; *1990s:* 32, 36, 41

Interferometers, *1900s:* 123

Intergalactic distances, *1910s:* 136–37, 139

Interior design, *1900s:* 83, 96–97; *1920s:* 100

Intermediate Nuclear Forces (INF) Treaty, *1980s:* 69, 91

International agreements, *1940s:* 27
    See also specific agreements

International Association of Psychoanalysis, *1910s:* 147

International Bank of Reconstruction and Development. *See* World Bank

International Bible Students Association. *See* Jehovah's Witnesses

International Boxing Club (IBC), *1940s:* 166

International Brotherhood of Teamsters. *See* Teamsters Union

International Bureau of Education, *1910s:* 50

International Business Machines (IBM), *1930s:* 36, 131; *1940s:* 140
    See also IBM
International Congress of Women, *1910s:* 80
International Court of Justice, *1980s:* 68
International debt, U.S., *1980s:* 31
International education, *1940s:* 45
The International Exhibition of Modern Art, *1910s:* 2
International expansion, *1940s:* 36–38
International Game Fish Association (IFGA), *1930s:* 152
International Geophysical Year, *1950s:* 137
International Harvester, *1900s:* 25
International Ladies' Garment Workers Union (ILGWU), *1900s:* 21, 86; *1910s:* 39; *1930s:* 22, 30–31
International Longshoremen's Association, *1930s:* 26
International Meeting of Physical Training and Sport. *See* Olympics
International Monetary Fund (IMF), *1940s:* 24–25, 27, 35, 37; *1990s:* 40
International Olympic Committee (IOC), *1900s:* 152; *1910s:* 173; *1920s:* 167; *1950s:* 175
International Planned Parenthood Federation, *1950s:* 141
International police force, *1990s:* 69–70
International relations education, *1940s:* 47, 51–52
International Space Station (ISS), *1990s:* 141, 158–60
International Style (architecture), *1940s:* 92–93
International Telephone and Telegraph (ITT), *1960s:* 39–41
International Women's Year Conference, *1970s:* 99
International Workers of the World (IWW), *1910s:* 37
Internet
    Amazon.com, *1990s:* 32–33, 34 (ill.)
    beginnings, *1990s:* 33, 140, 142, 144–50, 148 (ill.)
    browsers, *1990s:* 142
    Communications Decency Act, *1990s:* 139
    email, *1990s:* 146
    hate crimes, *1990s:* 93
    multinational use, *1990s:* 35
    new economic growth, *1990s:* 30–31, 33–36, 34 (ill.)
    protocols, *1990s:* 146
    school grants, *1990s:* 45
    violence, *1990s:* 129–30
    World Wide Web, *1990s:* 142
Internment camps, Japanese American, *1940s:* 64, 79, 103, 103 (ill.)
Interplanetary exploration, *1930s:* 130
Interstate commerce, *1900s:* 32–33, 61; *1910s:* 24, 83
Interstate Commerce Commission (ICC), *1900s:* 33, 65; *1910s:* 24
Interstate road systems, *1920s:* 30–31
Interventionists, *1940s:* 70, 72
In the Court of Public Opinion, 1940s: 68
In the Heat of the Night, 1960s: 7, 105
Intolerance, 1910s: 7, 15
Intrauterine devices (IUDs), *1960s:* 122, 133
Intravenous drug users, AIDS and, *1980s:* 123–24, 129–30
An Introduction to the Study of Education and to Teaching, 1920s: 57
Intruder in the Dust, 1960s: 105
Inventions, *1900s:* 122, 126–29; *1940s:* 134
    See also specific products
Investments, foreign, *1940s:* 36–38
IOC (International Olympic Committee), *1900s:* 152; *1910s:* 173; *1920s:* 167; *1950s:* 175
Iodine, *1910s:* 132
IQ tests. *See* Intelligence tests
Iran
    hostages in, *1970s:* 71, 73, 91–94, 91 (ill.)
    oil exports and, *1970s:* 27

Iran-Contra scandal, *1980s:* 68–69,
71, 73, 80–81, 85–90; *1990s:* 64
Iraq, *1990s:* 64, 66–68
Irish, Ned, *1930s:* 161
Iron Curtain, *1940s:* 27, 80
Iron (element), *1920s:* 128
Iron John: A Book About Men, 1990s:
92, 100
Iron lung, *1920s:* 119, 129
Iron ore deposits, *1940s:* 38
Irrigation dams, *1900s:* 20, 58
Irsay, Robert, *1980s:* 180
Irwin, James, *1960s:* 159 (ill.); *1970s:*
145
Irwin, Will, *1910s:* 19
The Isadorables, *1910s:* 3
Islamic extremists, *1990s:* 64
Islamic fundamentalism, *1970s:* 92–94
Isolationism, *1910s:* 72, 85; *1930s:* 71,
80–81
Isolationism, postwar economy and,
1920s: 66, 70; *1940s:* 13, 26, 38, 64,
67, 70
Isotope, *1930s:* 143
I Spy, 1960s: 106
ISS (International Space Station),
1990s: 141, 158–60
It, 1920s: 15
Italy, *1910s:* 78
It Can't Happen Here, 1930s: 21
"The It Girl," *1920s:* 15
It Happened One Night, 1930s: 16
I, The Jury, 1940s: 11
Ito, Lance, *1990s:* 14–15
ITT. *See* International Telephone and
Telegraph
IUDs (Intrauterine devices), *1960s:*
122, 133
"I've Got a Crush on You," *1930s:* 2
Ives, Charles, *1910s:* 16–17; *1960s:* 3
"I Wanna Hold Your Hand," *1960s:* 11
"I Want Your Sex," *1980s:* 3
"I Was Made to Love Her," *1960s:* 14
"I Will Always Love You," *1990s:* 26
Iwo Jima, *1940s:* 65, 73
IWW (Industrial Workers of the
World), *1900s:* 24; *1910s:* 94, 97–98

IWW (International Workers of the
World), *1910s:* 37
Izmira, *1960s:* 41
Izod clothing, *1950s:* 90

J

The Jack Benny Show, 1930s: 2
The Jackie Robinson Story, 1950s: 176
Jackson, Jesse, *1970s:* 98, 103, 103
(ill.); *1980s:* 73, 73 (ill.); *1990s:* 55,
100
Jackson, Mahalia, *1930s:* 20; *1940s:* 18
Jackson, Maynard, *1970s:* 98
Jackson, Michael, *1980s:* 2–3, 18–21,
20 (ill.), 24
Jackson, Phil, *1990s:* 171
Jackson, Reggie, *1960s:* 173
Jackson, "Shoeless" Joe, *1910s:*
157–58, 158 (ill.), 162; *1920s:*
154–55
Jackson, Travis, *1920s:* 158
Jacksonville Jaguars, *1990s:* 175
Jacob, Mary Phelps, *1910s:* 91
Jacobs, Helen, *1930s:* 153, 156
Jager, Peter de, *1990s:* 138
Jagr, Jaromir, *1990s:* 9
James, Bruce, *1900s:* 47
James Buchanan Brady Urological
Institute, *1910s:* 129
James, Henry, *1910s:* 11
James Sullivan Award, *1940s:* 156
Jan and Dean, *1960s:* 108
Janiro, Tony, *1940s:* 166
Jansen, B.C.P., *1920s:* 123
Jansen, Dan, *1990s:* 165, 183
Jannus, Tony, *1910s:* 138–39
Janzen, Lee, *1990s:* 179
Japan, anthropological studies of,
1940s: 136–37
See also Pacific campaign
Japanese American internment camps,
1940s: 64, 79, 103, 103 (ill.)
Japanese immigrants, *1900s:* 59
Jarvik, Robert K., *1980s:* 130–31
Jarvik-7 artificial heart, *1980s:*
131–32, 132 (ill.), 134
Jarvis, Gregory B., *1980s:* 152

Jaworski, Leon, *1970s:* 74, 74 (ill.), 87–88

Jaws, 1970s: 5, 10, 18

Jazz, *1900s:* 13–14; *1910s:* 17, 59; *1920s:* 11–13; *1930s:* 3, 5, 7, 20; *1940s:* 2, 4–6, 16–17, 16 (ill.); *1960s:* 2

Jazz Age, *1920s:* 4–5, 14

The Jazz Singer, 1920s: 3, 7, 16, 129, 142

J.C. Penney Company, *1900s:* 23; *1920s:* 36–37; *1980s:* 108

J. Crew, *1980s:* 108

Jeans, *1990s:* 93

Jeans, designer, *1970s:* 103, 118–19

Jeeps, *1940s:* 31

The Jefferson Airplane, *1960s:* 11–12

Jefferson, Blind Lemon, *1930s:* 20

The Jeffersons, 1970s: 22

Jeffries, James J., *1910s:* 154, 167

Jeffries, Jim, *1900s:* 138

Jehovah's Witnesses, *1930s:* 88

Jenkins, Fats, *1930s:* 161

Jenkins, Ferguson, *1960s:* 173; *1980s:* 176

Jenkins, Martin D., *1930s:* 62

Jenkins Television Corporation, *1930s:* 147

Jenner, Bruce, *1970s:* 180

Jenny Jones Show, 1990s: 3, 5, 13, 15

Jensen, Arthur, *1960s:* 51, 51 (ill.)

Jerry Maguire, 1990s: 164

Jerry Springer, 1990s: 13–16

The Jesse Lasky Feature Play Company, *1910s:* 2

Jesus Christ Superstar, 1970s: 2, 13

"Jesus Is Just Alright," *1970s:* 13

Jet aircraft, *1950s:* 137–38, 151–52

Jet engines, *1940s:* 130, 137–38

Jet Propulsion Laboratory (JPL), *1940s:* 139; *1990s:* 156

Jewish Anti-Defamation League, *1910s:* 90

Jewish immigrants, *1910s:* 40

Jewish Institute of Religion, *1920s:* 87

Jews, *1940s:* 86, 99–100, 101 (ill.), 116; *1950s:* 46

JFK, 1990s: 10

Jim Beam, *1960s:* 41

Jim Crow laws, *1900s:* 72, 85; *1910s:* 69, 82, 96; *1940s:* 59–60, 69; *1950s:* 96; *1960s:* 53

Jim Dandy, *1930s:* 165

Jim Thorpe: All American, 1950s: 176

Job discrimination. *See* Employment discrimination

Jobs, Steven, *1970s:* 43–44, 43 (ill.); *1980s:* 43, 160

Joel, Billy, *1980s:* 100

Joe Louis Promotions, *1940s:* 166

The Joe Louis Story, 1950s: 176

Joe Turner's Come and Gone, 1980s: 7

Jogging, *1970s:* 125, 129–30, 130 (ill.)

Jogging suits, *1970s:* 118

Johannsen, Wilhelm, *1900s:* 119, 129

Johanson, Donald, *1970s:* 149–51, 151 (ill.)

Johansson, Ingemar, *1950s:* 171

John Hancock Building, *1960s:* 93

"Johnny Angel," *1960s:* 11

John P. Grier (horse), *1920s:* 148, 167

Johns Hopkins Hospital, *1910s:* 129

Johns Hopkins Medical School, *1900s:* 101

Johns Hopkins University, *1920s:* 128

Johns Hopkins University Hospital, *1930s:* 120

Johns Hopkins University School of Medicine, *1910s:* 116

Johns, Jasper, *1960s:* 16, 16 (ill.)

Johnson, Alvin Saunders, *1920s:* 50, 50 (ill.)

Johnson & Johnson, *1980s:* 129

Johnson, Ben, *1980s:* 192

Johnson, Byron Bancroft "Ban," *1900s:* 138, 141, 144; *1910s:* 162

Johnson, Cornelius, *1930s:* 167

Johnson, Earvin "Magic," *1980s:* 168, 170, 172, 172 (ill.), 177; *1990s:* 116, 172

Johnson, Howard, *1930s:* 31

Johnson, Hugh S., *1930s:* 36, 78

Johnson, Jack, *1900s:* 139–40, 143, 148, 149 (ill.); *1910s:* 154–58, 158 (ill.), 166–67

Johnson, James P., *1920s:* 11

Johnson, James Weldon, *1900s:* 13
Johnson, J. Rosamund, *1900s:* 13
Johnson, Lyndon B., *1950s:* 85; *1960s:* 3, 25, 68, 70–72, 72 (ill.), 87 (ill.); *1970s:* 36; *1980s:* 109
    campaign of 1960, *1960s:* 83
    campaign of 1964, *1960s:* 85
    on civil rights, *1960s:* 74–75
    on education, *1960s:* 47–48, 57–59
    on federal aid to arts, *1960s:* 113–14
    Great Society, *1960s:* 27, 38–40, 57, 70, 81–82
    on health care, *1960s:* 130–31
    1968 elections and, *1960s:* 86
    satellites and, *1960s:* 158 (ill.)
    Vietnam War and, *1960s:* 70–71, 78, 86–88, 96
Johnson, Michael, *1990s:* 165, 183
Johnson, Philip, *1940s:* 92; *1950s:* 96; *1960s:* 94
Johnson, Rafer, *1960s:* 181
Johnson, Robert, *1930s:* 20
Johnson, Russell, *1930s:* 88
Johnson's Wax, *1960s:* 31
Johnson, Walter, *1910s:* 157, 159, 159 (ill.); *1920s:* 158
Johnson Wax Building, *1930s:* 89, 93
Johnson, William "Judy," *1930s:* 160
Johnston, William M., *1910s:* 176
Joiner, Columbus "Dad," *1930s:* 42–43
Jolson, Al, *1910s:* 5, 18; *1920s:* 3, 7, 7 (ill.), 9, 12, 16, 142
Jones, Ben, *1970s:* 8
Jones, Bobby, *1910s:* 171 (ill.); *1920s:* 95, 151–52, 152 (ill.), 165–66; *1930s:* 152, 154, 164
Jonesboro, Arkansas school shootings, *1990s:* 45
Jones, Casey, *1900s:* 2
Jones, Dorothy, *1910s:* 40
Jones, James, *1950s:* 8
Jones, James Earl, *1910s:* 166; *1970s:* 20, 23
Jones, James Warren ("Jim"), *1970s:* 99, 115–16
Jones, Jenny, *1990s:* 14

Jones, John Paul, *1910s:* 174
Jones, K. C., *1950s:* 168
Jones, LeRoi. *See* Baraka, Amiri
Jones, Paula Corbin, *1990s:* 62–63, 76–77
Jones, Tom, *1960s:* 177
Jonestown massacre, *1970s:* 115–16, 117 (ill.)
Jong, Erica, *1970s:* 2, 10
Joplin, Janis, *1960s:* 12–13
Joplin, Scott, *1900s:* 2, 7, 14, 14 (ill.); *1910s:* 17
Jordan, Michael, *1980s:* 168, 170, 172, 172 (ill.), 178; *1990s:* 162–63, 165–67, 166 (ill.), 171–72
Jorgensen, Christine, *1950s:* 136
Jorgensen, George, *1950s:* 136
Joss, Addie, *1900s:* 139
Journalism, *1900s:* 3, 15–16, 59–60; *1910s:* 19–20
    New, *1960s:* 80
Journal of the American Medical Association, 1910s: 121; *1920s:* 120
Joyce, James, *1920s:* 2, 14; *1960s:* 146
Joyce, Thomas W., *1900s:* 28
Joyner, Florence Griffith, *1980s:* 169, 171, 192
Joyner-Kersee, Jackie, *1980s:* 169, 171, 173, 173 (ill.), 192; *1990s:* 182
JPL (Jet Propulsion Laboratory), *1940s:* 139; *1990s:* 156
J. P. Morgan and Company, *1900s:* 25
Judaism, *1930s:* 100
Judd, Naomi, *1980s:* 25, 25 (ill.)
Judd, Wynonna, *1980s:* 25, 25 (ill.)
Judges, television courtroom, *1990s:* 15
"Jugheads," *1940s:* 57
Jukeboxes, *1930s:* 18
Juke joints, *1930s:* 18
Julia, 1970s: 21
Julius Caesar, 1930s: 21
Julliard Foundation, *1920s:* 2
Jumbo jets, *1970s:* 140, 149
"Jumping genes," *1940s:* 139–40
Jung, Carl, *1920s:* 108
The Jungle, 3, *1900s:* 65
Junior Davis Cup, *1930s:* 168

Junior high school, *1910s:* 46

Junior high school shootings, *1990s:* 45

Junior Wightman Cup, *1930s:* 168

Junk bonds, *1980s:* 30

Jupiter, *1900s:* 118; *1910s:* 137

Jurassic Park, 1990s: 10

Justice, *1950s:* 68–69, 81–83, 82 (ill.)
     See also specific court cases

Justice, 1910s: 19

Justice Department. *See* Department
     of Justice

Just Say No campaign, *1980s:* 63, 96

Juvenile delinquency, *1950s:* 83, 91

J. Walter Thompson, *1920s:* 18

K

Kaczynski, Theodore "Ted," *1990s:*
     63, 80–81

Kahanamoku, Duke, *1910s:* 174,
     1920s: 167

Kahn, Albert, *1910s:* 101; *1920s:* 32,
     90, 90 (ill.)

Kahn, Gus, *1910s:* 17

Kahn, Reuben Leon, *1920s:* 110, 113,
     115

Kaiser Aluminum, *1950s:* 36

Kaiser, Henry, *1940s:* 29, 29 (ill.);
     1970s: 132

Kaiser Permanente, *1970s:* 132

Kalmus, Herbert T., *1920s:* 143–44

Kamenshek, Dorothy "Dottie," *1940s:*
     162

Kamikaze missions, *1940s:* 73

Kane, Bob, *1940s:* 10

Kansas City A's, *1930s:* 157

Kansas City Athletics, *1960s:* 164, 174

Kansas City Chiefs, *1960s:* 165, 180

Kansas City Royals, *1960s:* 174;
     1980s: 174

Kansas State Board of Education,
     1990s: 45

Kantner, Dee, *1990s:* 163

Kantrowitz, Adrian, *1960s:* 126

Kaposi's sarcoma, *1980s:* 126

Karloff, Boris, *1930s:* 15

Kármán, Theodore von, *1930s:* 135,
     135 (ill.)

Karpis, Alvin "Creepy," *1930s:* 85

Karrer, Paul, *1930s:* 141

Kasem, Casey, *1970s:* 2

Kasper (designer), *1950s:* 103

The Katzenjammer Kids, 1900s: 16

Kaufman, George S., *1920s:* 4

Kaufman, Irving R., *1950s:* 79

Kaufman, Moss, *1930s:* 22

Kaufman's, *1920s:* 37

Kazan, Elia, *1930s:* 21; *1950s:* 14

KDKA, *1920s:* 35, 128, 145

Kearney, Michael, *1990s:* 44

Kearsley, James, Jr., *1900s:* 105

Keating, Charles, *1980s:* 39–40, 39
     (ill.)

Keaton, Diane, *1970s:* 99, 103

Keck telescope, *1990s:* 138

Keeler, Leonarde, *1920s:* 141

Keeler, Ruby, *1920s:* 10

Kefauver, Estes, *1950s:* 72, 72 (ill.),
     81, 82 (ill.), 85

Keith Haring, Keith, *1980s:* 12

Keller, Helen, *1900s:* 2

Kelley, Daniel J., *1900s:* 139

Kellogg-Briand Pact, *1920s:* 65

Kellogg Company, *1950s:* 90

Kellor, Frances (Alice), *1900s:* 62, 62
     (ill.); *1910s:* 99

Kelly Act, *1920s:* 31, 34

Kelly, Florence, *1930s:* 105

Kelly, Gene, *1940s:* 17

Kelly, Grace, *1950s:* 13

Kelsey, Frances Oldham, *1960s:* 125,
     125 (ill.)

Kelvinator, *1960s:* 142

Kemeny, John, *1960s:* 152–53

Kemphy Roth tax cuts, *1980s:* 84

Kemp, Jack, *1960s:* 180

Kendall, Edward Calvin, *1910s:* 116,
     116 (ill.)

Kennan, George F., *1940s:* 34, 80

Kennedy family, *1930s:* 102

Kennedy, Jacqueline Bouvier, *1960s:*
     94, 98, 98 (ill.), 108

Kennedy, John F., *1950s:* 53, 105;
     1960s: 2, 72, 72 (ill.); *1970s:* 83
     assassination of, *1960s:* 6, 20, 70,
     72, 85, 94, 96, 100, 104

campaign of 1960, *1960s:* 19–20,
68, 82–84
on civil rights, *1960s:* 74
Cuba and, *1960s:* 76–77
on education, *1960s:* 46, 48, 57
on minimum wage, *1960s:* 24
space program of, *1960s:* 156
steel industry and, *1960s:* 37
televised debates, *1960s:* 19–20,
68, 83–84, 83 (ill.)
Vietnam and, *1960s:* 78
Kennedy, Robert, *1950s:* 105; *1960s:*
68, 72, 72 (ill.); *1990s:* 105
assassination of, *1960s:* 69–72,
86, 96, 100
Cuban missile crisis and, *1960s:*
77
presidential campaign of, *1960s:*
86
Kenny, Elizabeth, *1940s:* 112, 112
(ill.), 122
Kent, Rockwell, *1900s:* 3
Kent State University, *1960s:* 65
Kent State University shootings,
1970s: 48, 70, 79
Kentucky, civil rights law, *1960s:* 69
Kentucky Colonels, *1960s:* 177
Kentucky Derby, *1910s:* 172; *1920s:*
166; *1930s:* 152, 156, 165; *1950s:*
159; *1960s:* 165
Kentucky Wildcats, *1940s:* 162
Keppel, Francis, *1960s:* 51, 57
Kerensky, Aleksandr, *1910s:* 80
Kerouac, Jack, *1950s:* 5–6, 6 (ill.), 9
Kerr, Clark, *1960s:* 63
Kerrigan, Nancy, *1990s:* 164, 183
Kesey, Ken, *1960s:* 4, 18–19
Kettering, Charles F., *1910s:* 103;
1920s: 135
Kevadon. *See* Thalidomide
Kevorkian, Jack, *1990s:* 116–18, 120,
120 (ill.)
Keystone, *1910s:* 15
The Keystone Cops, *1910s:* 15
Khomeini, Ayatollah Ruhollah, *1970s:*
92; *1980s:* 86
Khrushchev, Nikita, *1950s:* 69; *1960s:*
76

Kickbacks, *1900s:* 65–66
Kidnappings, Hearst, Patricia, *1970s:*
98, 102
Kidney dialysis, *1950s:* 115
Kidneys
artificial, *1900s:* 104
research on, *1900s:* 100
Kidney transplants, *1960s:* 120–21,
127
The Killers, *1940s:* 14
Kilpatrick, William Heard, *1910s:* 54;
1920s: 50–51, 54–55
Kimberley-Clark Corporation, *1910s:*
127
Kindergarten, *1930s:* 51
Kindergarten, Americanization in,
1900s: 47
Kindergartens, *1910s:* 50
Kinescope, *1920s:* 143; *1950s:* 142
King, Betsy, *1990s:* 165
King, Billie Jean, *1970s:* 130, 160,
163–64, 164 (ill.), 176
King Camp Gillette, *1900s:* 78
King, Carole, *1970s:* 11
King, Martin Luther, Jr., *1950s:* 97;
1960s: 72, 72 (ill.), 74, 97; *1980s:*
62; *1990s:* 92, 105
assassination of, *1960s:* 69–72,
96, 100
"I Have a Dream" speech, *1960s:*
68, 72
on segregation, *1960s:* 53
Selma, Alabama protest, *1960s:*
94
on Vietnam War, *1960s:* 79
King, Muriel, *1930s:* 89; *1940s:* 96
King Oliver's Creole Jazz Band, *1920s:*
2, 12
King, Rodney Glen, *1990s:* 64–65,
83–84, 85 (ill.), 87
King, Stephen, *1980s:* 6, 6 (ill.);
1990s: 20
King Tut, *1970s:* 99
Kinsey, Alfred, *1950s:* 140, 140 (ill.)
Kipling, Rudyard, *1930s:* 13
Kirkpatrick, Jeanne, *1970s:* 112
Kirstein, Lincoln, *1930s:* 22
Kissathons, *1960s:* 108

Kissinger, Henry, *1970s:* 70, 75, 75
  (ill.), 80, 82
Kiss Me Kate, 1950s: 10
Kiss (rock band), *1970s:* 12 (ill.), 13
Kite, Harold, *1960s:* 171
Kite, Tom, *1970s:* 174; *1990s:* 179
Kitsch, *1950s:* 104
Kitty Hawk, North Carolina, *1900s:*
  118, 126; *1910s:* 138
Kiviat, Abel, *1910s:* 174
KKK (Ku Klux Klan), *1910s:* 14
Klebold, Dylan, *1990s:* 50
Klein, Anne, *1950s:* 103
Klein, Calvin, *1970s:* 103, 103 (ill.),
  119
Kleindienst, Richard, *1970s:* 86
Kleine, George, *1910s:* 14
Kline, Franz, *1950s:* 8
Kmart, *1960s:* 34, 34 (ill.); *1980s:* 101
Knickerbocker Trust Company, *1900s:*
  21, 23, 26
Knicks, New York, *1970s:* 169
Knight, Gladys, *1960s:* 13
Knight, Philip, *1970s:* 30, 30 (ill.)
Knives, in schools, *1990s:* 44
Knoll, Florence, *1950s:* 104
Knoll, Hans, *1950s:* 104
Knox, James Hall Mason, Jr., *1900s:*
  101
Knudsen, William S., *1940s:* 24, 30
Kodak, *1960s:* 39
Kolff, Willem, *1980s:* 130
Kooning, Willem de, *1930s:* 10, 59;
  1940s: 3, 8–9; *1950s:* 5, 8–9; *1980s:*
  3
Koop, C. Everett, *1980s:* 126, 126
  (ill.)
Koprowski, Hilary, *1950s:* 114
Korean War, *1950s:* 68, 70, 76 (ill.),
  83
    aircraft, *1950s:* 151–52
    draft, *1950s:* 60–61
Koresh, David, *1990s:* 81
Korn, Arthur, *1900s:* 118
Kornberg, Arthur, *1950s:* 141, 141
  (ill.)
Kotex, *1910s:* 127
Koufax, Sandy, *1960s:* 168, 168 (ill.)

Kovacs, Ernie, *1950s:* 17
Kozol, Jonathan, *1970s:* 52, 52 (ill.)
Kraenzlein, Alvin, *1900s:* 143, 152
Kramer, Jack, *1940s:* 170
Krannert Center for Performing Arts,
  University of Illinois, *1960s:* 54
Krasner, Lee, *1940s:* 8
Kroc, Raymond A., *1950s:* 28, 28 (ill.)
Kroger, *1920s:* 36; *1950s:* 42
Kruger, Barbara, *1980s:* 6
Krupp steel mills, *1900s:* 36 (ill.)
Kubrick, Stanley, *1960s:* 10
Kuhn, Maggie, *1970s:* 110
Ku Klux Klan, *1900s:* 79; *1910s:* 14;
  1920s: 64–66, 70–72, 73 (ill.), 77;
  1930s: 72; *1990s:* 80
Kundla, John, *1950s:* 170
Kunen, James Simon, *1960s:* 64
Kung Fu, 1970s: 114
"Kung Fu Fighting," *1970s:* 114
Kurland, Bob "Foothills," *1940s:* 162
Kurtz, Thomas, *1960s:* 152–53
Kuwait, *1990s:* 64, 68–69
Kyoto Protocol, *1990s:* 139

L

Labeling, food, *1970s:* 36
La Belle Paree, 1910s: 18
Labor, child. *See* Child labor
Labor Department, *1920s:* 24
Labor disputes, *1990s:* 164, 164, 168
    baseball, *1970s:* 160, 165–66;
      1980s: 170, 174
    basketball, *1980s:* 170
    coal miners, *1970s:* 27
    doctors, *1970s:* 122–23
    football, *1980s:* 170, 179–81, 179
      (ill.)
    postal workers, *1970s:* 26
    teachers, *1970s:* 48
    See also Strikes
Labor leaders, *1950s:* 28; *1960s:* 28
    Debs, Eugene, *1900s:* 24
    Haley, Margaret, *1900s:* 40, 44
    Haywood, William D., *1900s:* 21,
      24
    Lewis, John L., *1940s:* 29

Labor reform
  Brandeis, Louis D., *1910s:* 70
  child labor, *1910s:* 69, 83
  safety, *1910s:* 69
  workers' compensation, *1910s:*
    69, 83
Labor unions, *1900s:* 23; *1910s:*
  24–25, 36–38, 46; *1920s:* 87; *1930s:*
  37–39; *1940s:* 28–29, 39–41, 40
  (ill.); *1950s:* 24–27; *1960s:* 24,
  26–27, 37, 38–40; *1970s:* 102;
  1990s: 41
    agricultural, *1960s:* 25, 28, 38
      (ill.)
    automobile, *1930s:* 27, 31, 38, 39;
      1940s: 24; *1960s:* 24–25
    baseball, *1960s:* 164, 174
    collective bargaining, *1930s:* 36
    factories, *1910s:* 26
    formation of, *1930s:* 27
    government and, *1940s:* 24, 39
    labor colleges and, *1930s:* 47,
      58–59
    Lewis, John L., *1930s:* 31
    mining, *1930s:* 31, 37
    murder of Steunenberg, Frank,
      1900s: 21, 24, 29–30
    musicians, *1940s:* 2
    National Industrial Recovery Act,
      1930s: 69, 76
    NFL Players Association, *1980s:*
      178, 180
    PATCO, *1980s:* 30, 37
    Reagan, Ronald and, *1980s:*
      36–37
    rubber, *1930s:* 27; *1960s:* 25
    steel, *1940s:* 24; *1960s:* 24–25
    teachers, *1900s:* 40; *1940s:* 48;
      1960s: 47
    Triangle Shirtwaist Company,
      1900s: 59
    United Mine Workers, *1900s:* 20,
      26–27; *1910s:* 29, 38; *1940s:* 25
    Wagner Act, *1930s:* 29, 78–80
    women, *1910s:* 40
    See Also AFL-CIO; American
      Federation of Labor; Industrial
      Workers of the World; Strikes;
      Teamsters Union
Laboratory research. *See* Medical
  research
Lac genes, *1960s:* 150
Lacoste, René, *1920s:* 87, 169
Lacoste tennis shirts, *1950s:* 90
La Cucaracha, *1920s:* 144
Ladewig, Marion, *1950s:* 161, 171
Ladies' Home Journal, *1900s:* 2; *1910s:*
  105, 124
Ladies' Professional Golfers' Associa-
  tion (LPGA), *1940s:* 170; *1950s:*
  158, 163; *1970s:* 161, 175; *1980s:*
  183
Lady Chatterly's Lover, *1950s:* 107
Lady Sings the Blues, *1970s:* 20
Lady Soul, *1960s:* 15
Lafleur, Guy, *1970s:* 173
La Follette, Robert M., *1900s:* 62, 62
  (ill.); *1920s:* 69, 69 (ill.), 77
La Guardia, Fiorello, *1940s:* 50
Lahr, Bert, *1920s:* 9
Laissez-faire, *1920s:* 27, 33
Lajoie, Napoleon, *1910s:* 161
Lake Mead, *1930s:* 131
Laker, Freddie, *1970s:* 27, 30, 30 (ill.)
Lake, Ricki, *1990s:* 13–14
Lamarr, Hedy, *1940s:* 33
Lamaze, Fernand, *1960s:* 135
La Motta, Jake, *1940s:* 152, 165–66;
  1950s: 158, 173
Lancaster, Burt, *1950s:* 176
Land, *1980s:* 35–36, 40
Land conservation, *1900s:* 59
Land, Edwin Herbert, *1930s:* 2; *1940s:*
  131
Landis, Kenesaw Mountain, *1910s:*
  155; *1920s:* 148, 155; *1930s:* 154;
  1940s: 152, 160
Landon, Alf, *1930s:* 72, 72 (ill.)
Landrum-Griffin Act, *1950s:* 35
Landry, Tom, *1970s:* 172
Landscape painting, *1900s:* 6
Land speculation, Florida and, *1920s:*
  37–38
Landsteiner, Karl, *1920s:* 113, 113
  (ill.); *1930s:* 110, 113, 115, 115 (ill.)

Lane, Allen, *1940s:* 11

Lane, Mills, *1990s:* 15

Lange, Dorothea, *1930s:* 4

Langevin, Paul, *1910s:* 146

Langley Memorial Aeronautical Laboratory, *1930s:* 130

Langley, Samuel P., *1900s:* 125

Langmuir, Irving, *1910s:* 136, 136 (ill.), 140; *1940s:* 143

Language, *1950s:* 110; *1980s:* 98

Lansky, Meyer, *1930s:* 81–82

Lapchick, Joe, *1910s:* 166

LAPD. *See* Los Angeles Police Department

Laptop computers, *1980s:* 30

Larderello, Italy, *1960s:* 152

Lardner, Ring, *1930s:* 158

Larned, William A., *1910s:* 176

Larsen, Don, *1950s:* 159, 164

Larson, John Augustus, *1920s:* 141

Larson, Nella, *1920s:* 11

LaRue, John, *1900s:* 100

Lasers, *1950s:* 136; *1960s:* 142

Laserwriter, *1980s:* 160

Lasker, Albert, *1930s:* 105

Lasker, Mary, *1940s:* 113, 113 (ill.)

"Last Dance," *1970s:* 7, 16

Lastex, *1930s:* 101

Las Vegas Invitational, *1990s:* 178

Latin America, *1910s:* 68, 72
    iron ore deposits, *1940s:* 38
    U.S. relations with, *1960s:* 68

Latin American authors, *1970s:* 10–11

Latin music, *1990s:* 24–25

Latinos, *1990s:* 3, 24–25

Lattimore, Owen, *1940s:* 49, 49 (ill.)

Laue, Max von, *1910s:* 146

Laughlin, Tom, *1970s:* 114

Lauren, Ralph, *1970s:* 103, 103 (ill.)

Laver, Rod, *1970s:* 176; *1980s:* 185

"La Vida Loca," *1990s:* 24

Law. *See* Government, politics and law

Law enforcement
    changes in, *1960s:* 81
    Chicago Seven and, *1960s:* 115
    social protests and, *1960s:* 96–97, 102–04

Law enforcement shows, *1990s:* 16–17

Lawrence, D. H., *1950s:* 107

Lawrence, Ernest O., *1930s:* 130, 145–46

Lawrence, Florence, *1910s:* 15

Lawrence, Jacob, *1940s:* 10

Lawrencium, *1960s:* 142

Law, Ruth, *1910s:* 135, 138

Laws and regulations
    on abortion, *1960s:* 121
    on antibiotics and vaccines, *1900s:* 100
    antitrust laws, *1910s:* 24, 31, 66, 155; *1920s:* 33, 154; *1930s:* 33–34, 43; *1940s:* 25; *1960s:* 24
    on banking practices, *1900s:* 28–29
    on business, *1900s:* 30, 32–34; *1910s:* 84
    on business trusts, *1900s:* 64–65, 74
    Chamberlain-Kahn Act, *1910s:* 113, 125
    on child labor, *1900s:* 59, 87; *1920s:* 64
    on conservation, *1900s:* 68
    environmental, *1960s:* 94
    on federal discrimination, *1940s:* 86, 103
    on food safety, *1900s:* 3, 33, 59, 65, 101, 105
    on industry, *1920s:* 27, 74–75
    Jim Crow, *1900s:* 72; *1960s:* 53
    loyalty, *1920s:* 46, 52
    medical profession, *1930s:* 114, 118, 120, 125–26
    price controls, *1940s:* 24
    worker's compensation, *1900s:* 20
    on workweek, *1940s:* 24
    See also specific laws and legislation

Lawson, Ernest, *1910s:* 8

Lawson, John Howard, *1940s:* 14

Lawsuits, patent, *1900s:* 3

Layne, Bobby, *1950s:* 174–75

Lazarus Brothers, *1920s:* 37

Lazarus, Emma, *1900s:* 2

LBK (Little Below-the-Knee) club, *1940s:* 95

League of Broke Husbands, *1940s:* 95

League of Colored Baseball Clubs, *1900s:* 145–46

League of Nations, *1910s:* 67, 78-79; *1920s:* 109

A League of Their Own, 1940s: 162

League of Women Voters, *1920s:* 77

Leahy, William D., *1940s:* 77

Leaky, Louis S. B., *1960s:* 148; *1970s:* 148

Leaky, Mary, *1960s:* 148; *1970s:* 151

Leakey, Richard, *1970s:* 148, 150

Learning, during sleep, *1950s:* 114

Learning theory, *1900s:* 44; *1960s:* 50–51, 54

Lear, Norman, *1970s:* 2, 6–7, 6 (ill.), 22–23

Leary, Timothy, *1960s:* 94, 99, 99 (ill.); *1990s:* 139

Leave It to Beaver, 1950s: 18

Leavitt, Henrietta, *1910s:* 135–39, 136 (ill.), 139

Lebanon, *1980s:* 75

Ledbetter, Huddie "Leadbelly," *1980s:* 20

Lee, Bruce, *1970s:* 114

Lee, Rebecca, *1900s:* 105

Lee, Spike, *1990s:* 92

Legal profession, *1950s:* 68

Legionella pneumophilia, 1970s: 134–35

Legionnaires' disease, *1970s:* 123, 125, 133–35

Leigh, Vivien, *1930s:* 3

Lejeune, Jerome, *1950s:* 148

LeMay, Curtis, *1960s:* 89

Lemieux, Mario, *1990s:* 177

LeMond, Greg, *1980s:* 169, 171, 189; *1990s:* 166

Lemmon, Jack, *1950s:* 12 (ill.)

Lenard, Philipp, *1900s:* 119

Lencek, Lena, *1920s:* 95

Lend-Lease program, *1940s:* 25, 71

Lendl, Ivan, *1980s:* 186

Lenglen, Suzanne, *1920s:* 149, 151, 169–70; *1930s:* 167

Lenin, Vladimir, *1910s:* 7, 80

Lennon, John, *1960s:* 3, 6, 6 (ill.), 11

Leonard, Benny, *1920s:* 151, 161

Leonard, Chris, *1910s:* 166

Leonard, Dutch, *1910s:* 163

Leonard, Sugar Ray, *1970s:* 180

Leonard, Walter "Buck," *1920s:* 160

Leopold, Nathan, *1920s:* 80–82, 81 (ill.)

Le Sacre du Printemps, 1920s: 3

Lesbianism. *See* Gay rights

Les Misérables, 1980s: 14 (ill.), 15

"Let It Be," *1960s:* 12

"Let's Spend the Night Together," *1960s:* 11

Let There Be Light, 1940s: 14

Leukemia, *1960s:* 120

Leukemia, genome mapping, *1990s:* 143

Levan, Albert, *1950s:* 148

Levi's jeans, *1990s:* 93

Levi Strauss Company, *1910s:* 90

Levitt, Abraham, *1940s:* 100–02

Levitt and Sons, *1940s:* 87, 100; *1960s:* 41

Levitt, William, *1940s:* 100

Levitt, William J., *1950s:* 90, 98

Lewinsky, Monica, *1990s:* 63, 77–78

Lewis, Carl, *1980s:* 171, 189–90; *1990s:* 165, 182–83

Lewis, Duffy, *1910s:* 164

Lewis, Jerry, *1950s:* 13

Lewis, John Henry, *1930s:* 162

Lewis, John L., *1930s:* 31, 31 (ill.), 38; *1940s:* 25, 29, 29 (ill.), 40

Lewis, Reginald F., *1980s:* 34, 34 (ill.)

Lewis, Sam M., *1910s:* 17

Lewis, Sinclair, *1930s:* 13, 21

Libby, Willard, *1940s:* 131

Liberal Education, 1940s: 53–54

Liberty, 1980s: 168

Liberty Bell 7, 1960s: 157

Liberty Bonds, *1910s:* 96–97

Liberty Loan Act, *1910s:* 25

"Liberty Ships," *1940s:* 29

Libraries, public, *1900s:* 2, 24; *1910s:* 2, 94

Library books, censorship, *1980s:* 54–58

Libya, *1980s:* 75

License plates, *1900s:* 78

Lichtenstein, Roy, *1960s:* 16

Licklider, Joseph C. R., *1990s:* 145

Liddell, Eric, *1920s:* 168–69

Lie detectors, *1920s:* 131, 141

A Lie of the Mind, 1980s: 15

Life expectancy, *1940s:* 109

Life Extension Institute, *1910s:* 112

The Life of a Fireman, 1900s: 7

The Life of Reason, 1910s: 95

Life, origins of, *1970s:* 144

Lifestyle Adjustment Curriculum, *1940s:* 59

Lifestyle investigations, Ford Motor Company, *1910s:* 34–36

Lifestyles and social trends, *1900s:* 77–98; *1910s:* 89–109; *1920s:* 85 105, *1930s:* 87–108, *1940s:* 85–106; *1950s:* 89–111; *1960s:* 93–117; *1970s:* 97–120; *1980s:* 95–118; *1990s:* 89–113
    authority, *1950s:* 104–05
    chronology, *1900s:* 78–79; *1910s:* 90 91; *1920s:* 86–87; *1930s:* 88–89; *1940s:* 86–87; *1950s:* 90–91; *1960s:* 94–95; *1970s:* 98–99; *1980s:* 96–97; *1990s:* 92–93
    conformity, *1950s:* 99–102
    headline makers, *1900s:* 82–83; *1910s:* 94–95; *1920s:* 90–91; *1930s:* 92–93; *1940s:* 90–91; *1950s:* 94–95; *1960s:* 98–99; *1970s:* 102–03; *1980s:* 100–01; *1990s:* 96–97
    materialism, *1950s:* 90, 107
    nuclear family, *1950s:* 91
    overview, *1900s:* 80–81; *1910s:* 92–93; *1920s:* 88–89; *1930s:* 90–91; *1940s:* 88–89; *1950s:* 92–93; *1960s:* 96–97; *1970s:* 100–01; *1980s:* 98–99; *1990s:* 94–95
    prosperity, *1950s:* 93
    values, *1950s:* 93, 102

Life With Father, 1930s: 22

"Lift Every Voice and Sing," *1900s:* 13

Liggett and Myers, *1960s:* 41

Light
    fiber optics and, *1970s:* 152
    speed of, *1900s:* 119, 123

Light bulbs, *1900s:* 122; *1910s:* 136

Lighting, fluorescent, *1930s:* 27, 131

Lights of New York, 1920s: 142

"Like a Prayer," *1980s:* 21

"Like a Virgin," *1980s:* 2, 21

Li'l Abner, 1930s: 6

Lilies of the Field, 1960s: 7, 105

Liliom, 1920s: 8

Lilly, John C., *1960s:* 151–52

Limbaugh, Rush, *1990s:* 4, 12–13, 13 (ill.)

Limb reattachments, *1960s:* 120, 122, 127

Lincoln, Blanche Lambert, *1990s:* 75

Lincoln Center for the Performing Arts, *1960s:* 2

Lincoln Hospital, Durham, North Carolina, *1900s:* 107

Lincoln Memorial, *1920s:* 86

Lincoln pennies, *1900s:* 79

Lincoln University, *1930s:* 50

Lindbergh Act, *1920s:* 132

Lindbergh, Anne Morrow, *1930s:* 136

Lindbergh, Charles A., *1920s:* 25, 31, 38, 87, 95, 129, 131–32, 132 (ill.), 136 (ill.), 137–39; *1930s:* 114, 134, 136; *1940s:* 70

Lindbergh Middle School, Long Beach, California, *1980s:* 64

Linkletter, Art, *1950s:* 17

Lin, Maya Ying, *1980s:* 82

Lipton, Thomas, *1930s:* 152

Lindsay, Vachel, *1910s:* 12

Lindsey, Ben, *1910s:* 85

Lindstrom, Freddie, *1920s:* 158

Lindy hop, *1920s:* 87

Ling Electric Company, *1960s:* 28

Ling, James, *1960s:* 28, 28 (ill.)

Ling-Temco-Vought (LTV), *1960s:* 28

Linux operating system, *1990s:* 138

Liotta, Domingo, *1960s:* 127

Lipinski, Tara, *1990s:* 165, 184

Liquid-fueled rockets, *1910s:* 136
Liquid helium, *1900s:* 119
Liquid Paper, *1950s:* 138
Lisa computer, *1980s:* 146, 160
LISP programming language, *1950s:* 146
Listening devices, *1910s:* 135, 151
Lister, Joseph, *1900s:* 102
Liston, Sonny, *1960s:* 164, 168
Literacy, *1910s:* 69, 82, 99; *1940s:* 44, 46, 57; *1960s:* 46; *1970s:* 57–59; *1980s:* 48–49
   draft and, *1950s:* 60–61
Literacy tests, for voting, *1960s:* 75
Literary canon, *1980s:* 55
Literary journals, *1900s:* 5
Literary movements, *1920s:* 13–14
Literature, *1900s:* 5, 8–9; *1910s:* 4–6, 10–13; *1940s:* 5, 7, 11–12, 12 (ill.); *1950s:* 5, 8–10; *1960s:* 4, 18–19; *1990s:* 18–20
   American experience in, *1930s:* 12–14
   censorship, *1980s:* 54–58
   hard-boiled, *1930s:* 14
   Nobel Prize, *1930s:* 13
   proletarian novels, *1930s:* 12–14
   pulp, *1930s:* 14
   southern, *1930s:* 14
Little Below-the-Knee (LBK) club, *1940s:* 95
"Little Boy," *1940s:* 76, 146
Little Caesar, 1930s: 16
The Little Foxes, 1940s: 6
Little, Lawson, *1940s:* 168
Little, Lawson, Jr., *1930s:* 164
Little League baseball, *1930s:* 153
Little Lord Fauntleroy, 1910s: 7
Little, Malcolm. *See* Malcolm X
Little Nemo in Slumberland, 1900s: 79
Little Orphan Annie, *1930s:* 12
The Little Renaissance, *1910s:* 4
Little Richard, *1950s:* 15; *1960s:* 11
Little, Sally, *1980s:* 183
The Little Theater Movement, *1910s:* 18
Liuzzo, Viola, *1960s:* 102

Live Aid concert, *1980s:* 2, 25–26, 26 (ill.)
Liver disease, *1990s:* 126
Liver transplants, *1960s:* 120, 122, 127
L.L. Bean, *1980s:* 106, 108
LL Cool J, *1990s:* 23
Lloyd, John Henry "Pop," *1920s:* 160
Lloyd Wright, Frank, *1910s:* 90
Loans, *1910s:* 25
   federal, *1970s:* 27, 29
   See also Farms
Lobbying, American Medical Association, *1940s:* 117–18
Lobotomy, *1930s:* 111
Lochner v. *New York, 1900s:* 74
"LOCI," *1960s:* 36
Locke, Alain, *1900s:* 41; *1920s:* 10–11
Lockheed, *1920s:* 34
Lockheed F-80 Shooting Star, *1940s:* 138
Lodge, Oliver, *1900s:* 128
Loeb, Jacques, *1900s:* 129
Loeb, Richard, *1920s:* 80–82, 81 (ill.)
Loews motion picture theaters, *1960s:* 41
Lombardi, Vince, *1960s:* 169, 169 (ill.)
Lonacher, Charlie, *1930s:* 166
London Daily Illustrated Mirror, 1900s: 2
London, Jack, *1900s:* 5, 7, 7 (ill.)
The Lone Ranger, 1930s: 2; *1950s:* 107
Lone Wolf v. *Hitchcock, 1900s:* 58
Long Day's Journey into Night, 1920s: 7
Long-distance telephone services, *1940s:* 86; *1960s:* 25
Long, Huey P., *1930s:* 73, 83
Long Island, *1940s:* 87
Long jump, *1980s:* 189
The Longman Handbook of Modern American History 1763–1996, 1930s: 77
Long, Perrin H., *1930s:* 120
Longshoremen's strike, *1960s:* 24
Look, 1950s: 74
"Look Away," *1980s:* 19
Looking for Mr. Goodbar, 1970s: 10

Loomis, Alfred L., *1940s:* 142

Lopcz, Jennifer, *1990s:* 3, 6–7, 6 (ill.), 25

Lopez, Nancy, *1970s:* 161, 175–76

Lopez, Vincent, *1920s:* 12

"The Lord's Prayer," *1970s:* 3

Lorillard Tobacco Company, *1990s:* 71

Lorre, Peter, *1940s:* 15

Los Alamos, New Mexico, *1940s:* 146

Los Angeles, 1920s: 140

Los Angeles Angels, *1960s:* 164, 174

Los Angeles aqueduct, *1910s:* 132

Los Angeles, California, *1900s:* 90–91 smog in, *1960s:* 126

Los Angeles Chargers, *1960s:* 180

Los Angeles (dirigible), *1930s:* 137

Los Angeles Dodgers, *1980s:* 174

Los Angeles Kings, *1980s:* 184–85

Los Angeles Lakers, *1950s:* 169–70, *1960s:* 176–77; *1980s:* 168, 172, 177

Los Angeles Police Department (LAPD), *1990s:* 64–65, 83–84, 85 (ill.), 86

Los Angeles Raiders, *1980s:* 169

Los Angeles Rams, *1950s:* 173

Los Angeles riots, *1990s:* 64

Lost Boundaries, 1960s: 105

The Lost Generation, *1920s:* 6, 13–14; *1940s:* 11

Lotteries, first, *1970s:* 3

Lotus software, *1980s:* 161

Louganis, Greg, *1980s:* 192; *1990s:* 117

Lou Gehrig's disease, *1920s:* 152; *1940s:* 152

Louisiana Purchase Exposition, *1900s:* 20

Louis, Joe, *1930s:* 153–55, 161–62; *1940s:* 152–53, 157, 157 (ill.), 165–66; *1950s:* 171

Love, 1920s: 3

Love Canal, *1970s:* 141, 155–56

Love, Davis, III, *1990s:* 179

The Love for Three Oranges, 1920s: 2

Loveless, Patti, *1980s:* 25

Lovelock, James, *1970s:* 153

"Love Me Do," *1960s:* 11

Love of Life, 1950s: 2

"The Love Song of J. Alfred Prufrock," *1910s:* 12

"Love to Love You Baby," *1970s:* 7, 16

"Love Will Find a Way," *1920s:* 11

"Love You To," *1960s:* 12

Lowell, Abbott Lawrence, *1920s:* 51, 51 (ill.)

Lowell, Percival, *1910s:* 137

Low-income housing, *1960s:* 82

Loyalty laws, *1920s:* 46, 52

Loyalty oaths, *1930s:* 47, 61; *1940s:* 51

for teachers, *1950s:* 61–62

LPGA (Ladies' Professional Golfers' Association), *1940s:* 170; *1950s:* 158; *1970s:* 161, 175; *1980s:* 183

LP records, *1950s:* 138, 152

LSD (lysergic acid diethylamide), *1960s:* 95, 99, 107

LTV (Ling-Temco-Vought), *1960s:* 28

Lubitsch, Ernst, *1930s:* 15

Lucas, George, *1970s:* 3, 5, 19

Luce, Henry, *1960s:* 182

Luciano, "Lucky," *1930s:* 81–82, 82 (ill.)

Lucid, Shannon, *1990s:* 139, 142, 142 (ill.)

Luckman, Sid, *1930s:* 163

Lucky Lady, 1940s: 131

The Lucy-Desi Comedy Hour, 1960s: 2

"Lucy in the Sky with Diamonds," *1960s:* 12

Lucy (fossil), *1970s:* 141, 149–50, 151 (ill.)

Ludwig and Piech, *1950s:* 131

Luks, George, *1910s:* 8

Lumière, Auguste, *1900s:* 3

Lumière, Louis, *1900s:* 3

Lunar landings. *See* Moon, exploration of

Lunch programs, schools, *1980s:* 48

Lung cancer, *1930s:* 111; *1940s:* 109; *1950s:* 115; *1980s:* 141

Lung disease, *1990s:* 126

Lung surgery, *1900s:* 100

Lung transplants, *1960s:* 120, 122, 127

Lunik III, 1950s: 154

Lusitania, 1900s: 79; *1910s:* 66, 75

Lusk, Clayton R., *1920s:* 52

Lusk laws, *1920s:* 46, 52

Lux Video Theatre, 1950s: 30

Lyme disease, *1970s:* 122, 125, 136

Lynchings, *1900s:* 71–72, 71 (ill.), 85; *1940s:* 2

Lysergic acid diethylamide. *See* LSD

M

Mabel's Strange Predicament, 1910s: 3

"Macarena," *1990s:* 26

MacArthur, Charles, *1920s:* 4

MacArthur, Douglas, *1930s:* 76

"MacArthur Park," *1970s:* 16

Macdonald, Dwight, *1960s:* 53

Mace, Nancy, *1990s:* 57

MacFadden, Bernarr, *1900s:* 101

Machine age, *1930s:* 132–33

Machine guns, *1910s:* 135, 150

Machine of the Year, *1980s:* 160

Mack, Cecil, *1920s:* 11

Mack, Connie, *1910s:* 163

Macintosh computer, *1980s:* 146, 160

MacLaine, Shirley, *1980s:* 118

MacLeish, Archibald, *1920s:* 13

MacLeod, John J. R., *1920s:* 118–19

MacMillan, Donald B., *1920s:* 137

Macon, 1930s: 137

MacPhail, Larry, *1940s:* 152, 157, 157 (ill.)

Macrocontext, *1940s:* 136

Macy's department store, *1910s:* 42

Maddux, Greg, *1990s:* 167, 167 (ill.)

Madero, Francisco, *1910s:* 73

Madison Square Garden, *1920s:* 149; *1930s:* 161, 168

Madonna, *1980s:* 2, 21–22, 102

Mafia, *1930s:* 81–83

Magaw, Alice, *1900s:* 107

Magazines, *1900s:* 2, 5; *1920s:* 18–19
   Better Homes & Garden, 1920s: 100
   Black Art, 1970s: 8
   Black Mask, 1930s: 14
   Captain Billy's Whiz Bang, 1920s: 19
   Catholic Worker, 1930s: 88
   Dime Detective, 1930s: 14
   Heresis, 1970s: 9
   House Beautiful, 1920s: 100
   Ms., 1970s: 2, 7
   New Yorker, 1930s: 2
   People, 1970s: 3
   Photoplay, 1920s: 19
   pulp, *1940s:* 13
   Rolling Stone, 1960s: 3, 7
   Screenland, 1920s: 19
   Screen Romances, 1920s: 19
   Sports Illustrated, 1960s: 182–83
   Vanity Fair, 1920s: 99–100
   Variety, 1920s: 42–43, 142

"Magic," *1940s:* 73

Magnetic resonance imaging (MRIs), *1970s:* 123–24, 129

Magnetrons, *1940s:* 142

The Magnificent Ambersons, 1910s: 11

M. A. Hanna Company, *1940s:* 38

Maharishi Mahesh Yogi, *1970s:* 114

Mah-jongg, *1920s:* 101–02

Mahre, Phil, *1980s:* 168, 188

Mahre, Steve, *1980s:* 188

Maidenform, *1920s:* 94

Maid of Harlem, 1910s: 3

Mailer, Norman, *1940s:* 5, 12, 12 (ill.)

Mail-order houses, *1900s:* 96

Major League Baseball Players Association (MLBPA), *1960s:* 164, 174; *1970s:* 160, 165–66

Making Waves: Swimsuits and the Undressing of America, 1920s: 95

Malaria, *1940s:* 109–10, 114

Malcolm X, *1960s:* 69–70, 97, 99, 99 (ill.), 100–01, 104–05

Malcolm X, (movie) *1990s:* 92

The Mall of America, *1990s:* 92

Mallon, Mary, *1900s:* 112

Mallon, Meg, *1990s:* 179

Mallory, Molla Bjurstedt, *1920s:* 151, 170

Malnutrition, *1900s:* 100, 110; *1960s:* 121

Malone, Karl, *1990s:* 172

Malpractice, *1930s:* 125

Malpractice, medical, *1990s:* 117

"Malpractice Protection," *1930s:* 125

The Maltese Falcon, 1930s: 15; *1940s:* 2, 6, 14–15

"Mama He's Crazy," *1980s:* 25

The Mamas and the Papas, *1960s:* 12

Mamet, David, *1980s:* 14

Mammography, *1910s:* 112

The Mammoth Hunters, 1980s: 12

Mammoth Oil Company, *1920s:* 79

Manabe, Syukuro, *1960s:* 154

Man Against Crime, 1950s: 31

Managed health care. *See* Health maintenance organizations (HMOs)

Management Reporting and Disclosure Act of 1961, *1960s:* 35

Manet, Edouard, *1910s:* 12

Mangrove forests, global warming, *1990s:* 150

Manhattan Project, *1940s:* 78, 130, 132–35, 145–46; *1950s:* 78, 149

    See also Atomic bombs

Manhattan Transfer, 1920s: 14

Mann Act, *1900s:* 143

Mann Act of 1890, *1910s:* 69, 87, 158, 167

Mann-Elkins Act, *1910s:* 24

The Man Nobody Knows, 1920s: 90

Mannock, Edward "Mick," *1910s:* 138

Man o' War, *1910s:* 155; *1920s:* 148, 151, 166–67; *1940s:* 33

Mansfield Theater, *1930s:* 2

Manship, Paul, *1920s:* 3

Manson, Charles, *1960s:* 80–81

Mantle, Mickey, *1950s:* 158, 163–64 163 (ill.), 167; *1960s:* 172

Manufacturing, *1910s:* 26–29, 33–36; *1960s:* 26–27, 39–40; *1980s:* 31, 159

"Maple Leaf Rag," *1900s:* 7

Mapplethorpe, Robert, *1990s:* 2, 9 (ill.)

Mapp v. *Ohio, 1960s:* 81

Maps, road, *1900s:* 78

Ma Rainey's Black Bottom, 1980s: 7

Maranzano, Salvatore, *1930s:* 81–82

Marble, Alice, *1930s:* 168

Marchetti, Gino, *1950s:* 175

March, Harold "Mush," *1930s:* 165

March of Dimes, *1930s:* 113, 122

March on Washington, *1960s:* 58 (ill.), 74, 79

    gay rights, *1990s:* 92

    Million Man, *1990s:* 93, 95–96, 99–102, 101 (ill.)

Marciano, Rocky, *1950s:* 158, 161, 171–72, 172 (ill.)

Marconi Company, *1900s:* 129; *1910s:* 21

Marconi, Guglielmo, *1900s:* 2, 118, 127–28, 128 (ill.); *1910s:* 147–48; *1920s:* 144

Marconi Wireless Company, *1910s:* 20

Mariana Trench, *1960s:* 154

Marichal, Juan, *1960s:* 173

Marijuana, *1980s:* 64

Marijuana Traffic Law, *1930s:* 89

Marine personnel, Tailhook convention, *1990s:* 92

Mariner 8, 1970s: 140

Mariner 4, 1960s: 143

Mariner 2, 1960s: 142

Marines, *1910s:* 78, 96

Marin, John, *1910s:* 12

Marino, Dan, *1980s:* 181; *1990s:* 175

Maris, Roger, *1920s:* 157; *1960s:* 164, 166, 172

Mark 1, *1940s:* 130, 140

Marlowe, Jean, *1940s:* 163 (ill.)

Marmon, *1930s:* 41

Marquette University, *1930s:* 164, 168

Márquez, Gabriel García, *1970s:* 11

Marriages, *1940s:* 86, 96

Mars, *1910s:* 137; *1960s:* 143; *1970s:* 140–41

Marsalis, Wynton, *1980s:* 7, 7 (ill.)

Marshall Field department store, *1910s:* 42

Marshall, George, *1950s:* 60

Marshall, George C., *1940s:* 25, 38, 69, 69 (ill.), 73, 78

Marshall Plan, *1940s:* 25, 27, 38–39, 52, 69

Marshall, Thurgood, *1950s:* 51, 51 (ill.), 57 (ill.)

Marsh, Reginald, *1930s:* 8

Martha and The Vandellas, *1960s:* 14–15

Martial arts, *1970s:* 114

The Martian Chronicles, 1950s: 8

Martin Clippers, *1930s:* 137

Martin, Dean, *1950s:* 5, 15

Martin, Glenn L., *1920s:* 34

Martin Luther King Elementary, *1970s:* 49

Martin, Pepper, *1930s:* 158

Martin, Slater, *1950s:* 170

The Marvelettes, *1960s:* 11, 13

Marx Brothers, *1920s:* 9; *1930s:* 15 (ill.), 17, 164

Marxist Sandinista government, *1980s:* 68

Marx, Karl, *1910s:* 80

Mary Kay Cosmetics, *1960s:* 28, 42

Maryland Law School, *1930s:* 47

The Mary Pickford Company, *1910s:* 7

"Mary's a Grand Old Name," *1900s:* 16

Masers, *1960s:* 150

M.A.S.H. (Mobile Army Surgical Hospital), *1960s:* 124

Mason, Max, *1910s:* 151

Massachusetts Commission on Industrial and Technological Education, *1900s:* 41

Massachusetts Institute of Technology (MIT), *1910s:* 46; *1940s:* 46–47, 130, 142

Massacres, religious, *1910s:* 98

Massage, heart, *1950s:* 114; *1960s:* 128

Massage treatment, for polio, *1940s:* 112, 121

Masseria, Joe, *1930s:* 81–82

Massillon Tigers, *1900s:* 150

Mass production, *1900s:* 34–36, 35 (ill.), 36 (ill.), 81, 91

Master Lock, *1960s:* 41

Master of Arts in Teaching (MAT), Harvard University, *1960s:* 51

Masters, Edgar Lee, *1910s:* 10

Masters Tournament (golf), *1920s:* 165; *1930s:* 152, 164; *1960s:* 165; *1980s:* 183

Master teachers, *1980s:* 53–54

Matas, Rudolph, *1920s:* 108

"Material Girl," *1980s:* 21, 102

Maternity leave, *1970s:* 98

Mathematics, *1980s:* 49–50

Mathematics textbooks, *1970s:* 60

Mathias, Bob, *1940s:* 168

Matisse, Henri, *1910s:* 12

Mattea, Kathy, *1980s:* 25

Matthau, Walter, *1960s:* 10

Mauchly, John, *1940s:* 141

Maude, 1970s: 22

Maxwell, James Clerk, *1910s:* 147

Maxwell Motor Company. *See* Chrysler Corporation

Maynard, Don, *1960s:* 180

Mayo, Charles H., *1900s:* 107; *1910s:* 116, 116 (ill.), 118–19

Mayo Clinic, *1910s:* 112, 114, 116, 118, 120

Mayo Foundation, *1910s:* 119

Mayo, William W., *1900s:* 107; *1910s:* 116, 116 (ill.), 118

Mayo, William Worrall, *1910s:* 119

Mays, Carl, *1920s:* 148

Mays, Willie, *1950s:* 158–59, 163, 163 (ill.), 165 (ill.), 167

Mazeroski, Bill, *1960s:* 164

MCA, *1960s:* 13

McAdoo, William, *1920s:* 76–77

McAndrew, William, *1920s:* 46, 53

McArthur, Douglas, *1950s:* 68

McAuliffe, Sharon Christa, *1980s:* 152

McCall Pattern Company, *1980s:* 34

McCall's patterns, *1920s:* 94

McCardell, Claire, *1940s:* 91, 91 (ill.); *1950s:* 103

McCarthy, Eugene, *1960s:* 73, 73 (ill.), 86

McCarthyism, *1950s:* 7, 32, 68, 79–81

McCarthy, Joseph R., *1940s:* 67, 82; *1950s:* 4, 13–15, 69, 72, 72 (ill.), 79

McCartney, Paul, *1960s:* 6, 6 (ill.), 11; *1980s:* 19

McClellan committee, *1950s:* 33, 81

McClellan, John, *1950s:* 33, 81

McClintock, Barbara, *1940s:* 139–40; *1980s:* 150, 150 (ill.)

McCollum, Elmer, *1920s:* 123

McCollum, Vashti, *1940s:* 60

McCollum v. Board of Education, 1940s: 45, 47, 60

McCord, James W., *1970s:* 85–86

McCormack Institute for Infectious Diseases, *1900s:* 100; *1920s:* 112

McCorvey, Norma, *1970s:* 88

McCovey, Willie, *1960s:* 173

McCoy, Horace, *1930s:* 5, 14

McCoy, Van, *1970s:* 15

McCullers, Carson, *1940s:* 7, 7 (ill.), 12

McCullough, Colleen, *1970s:* 9

McDonald, Patrick J., *1910s:* 174

McDonald's, *1950s:* 41, 90, 96, 98 (ill.); *1960s:* 34–35

McDuffie, Arthur, *1980s:* 84–85

McEnroe, John, *1970s:* 177; *1980s:* 171

McEntire, Reba, *1980s:* 23

McFarlane, Robert, *1980s:* 86–87

McGovern, George, *1970s:* 75, 75 (ill.), 84

McGrath, Earl James, *1950s:* 61–63

McGraw-Electric, *1930s:* 26

McGraw, John, *1910s:* 159, 159 (ill.); *1920s:* 156

McGwire, Mark, *1990s:* 169–71, 170 (ill.)

McInnis, Stuffy, *1910s:* 163

McKay, Claude, *1920s:* 11

McKay, John, *1960s:* 178

McKay, Winsor, *1900s:* 79

McKinley, William, *1900s:* 58, 68, 70

McLain, Denny, *1960s:* 173

McLarnin, Jimmy, *1930s:* 162

McLaurin, G. W., *1940s:* 58 (ill.)

McLoughlin, Maurice E., *1910s:* 176

MC Lyte, *1980s:* 24

McMartin Preschool sexual abuse case, *1980s:* 112

McMillen Inc., *1940s:* 8

McMullen, Fred, *1910s:* 162; *1920s:* 155

McNair, Ronald E., *1980s:* 152

McNally, Dave, *1960s:* 173

McNamara, Robert, *1960s:* 64

McNary-Haugen Bill, *1920s:* 33, 75

McNeely, Earl, *1920s:* 158

McPharlan, James, *1900s:* 30

McPherson, Aimee Semple, *1920s:* 91, 91 (ill.)

McQueen, Steve, *1950s:* 17

McSorley's Bar, 1910s: 9

MCWA (Office of Malaria Control in War Areas), *1940s:* 114

Mead, Janet, *1970s:* 13

Mead, Margaret, *1920s:* 133, 133 (ill.); *1940s:* 136, 141

Meadows, Audrey, *1950s:* 18, 18 (ill.)

Meany, George, *1950s:* 28, 28 (ill.), 32, 33 (ill.)

Measles, *1900s:* 100; *1910s:* 112, 117, 122; *1940s:* 108; *1950s:* 115, 123; *1960s:* 120, 122, 131–33, 132 (ill.), 145

The Measure of Intelligence, 1920s: 109

Meat Inspection Act, *1900s:* 3, 33, 59, 65, 101

Meatpacking industry, *1900s:* 3, 65, 101; *1910s:* 30, 38

Meat rationing, *1940s:* 24

Meat, trichinosis from, *1900s:* 100

Mechanical heart, *1930s:* 111, *1950s:* 114, 124

"Me Decade," *1970s:* 113

Media guidelines, wartime, *1910s:* 5

Medicaid, *1960s:* 82, 123, 131

Medical equipment, *1900s:* 102; *1960s:* 121–22, 128

Medical equipment, safety of, *1970s:* 123

Medical ethics, *1900s:* 130

Medical Information Telephone System (MIST), *1960s:* 121

Medical malpractice, *1990s:* 117

Medical reform, *1920s:* 112, 116–17; *1930s:* 113, 117–20

Medical research, *1900s:* 100–02, 109; *1910s:* 119, 125; *1940s:* 110, 113, 120; *1950s:* 114–15, 128; *1960s:* 125; *1970s:* 137

Medical schools, *1900s:* 101–02, 106–10; *1910s:* 112–13; *1930s:* 110; *1940s:* 115–17, 120–21

Medical technology, *1920s:* 115–16
Medicare, *1960s:* 82, 121, 123, 131; *1990s:* 121
Medicare and Medicaid, *1970s:* 132
Medicine and health, *1900s:* 99–116; *1910s:* 111–30; *1920s:* 107–25; *1930s:* 109–27; *1940s:* 107–27; *1950s:* 113–33; *1960s:* 119–39; *1970s:* 121–38; *1980s:* 121–43; *1990s:* 115–35
    biological sciences and, *1910s:* 144–45, 145 (ill.)
    chronology, *1900s:* 100–01; *1910s:* 112–13; *1920s:* 108–09; *1930s:* 110–11; *1940s:* 108–09; *1950s:* 114–15; *1960s:* 120–21; *1970s:* 122–23; *1980s:* 122–23; *1990s:* 116–17
    government and, *1910s:* 124–26
    headline makers, *1900s:* 104; *1910s:* 116–17; *1920s:* 112–13; *1930s:* 114–15; *1940s:* 112–13; *1950s:* 118–19; *1960s:* 124–25; *1970s:* 126; *1980s:* 126; *1990s:* 120
    health care costs, *1950s:* 120
    health education, *1910s:* 56, 117
    medical checkups, *1910s:* 51, 112
    Nobel Prizes in, *1970s:* 135; *1990s:* 133
    overview, *1900s:* 102–03; *1910s:* 114–15; *1920s:* 110–11; *1930s:* 112–13; *1940s:* 110–11; *1950s:* 116–17; *1960s:* 122–23; *1970s:* 124–25; *1980s:* 124–25; *1990s:* 118–19
    physical fitness, *1910s:* 54, 56, 121
    poisons and, *1970s:* 154–57; *1990s:* 152–55
    tobacco industry and, *1960s:* 41
Medicines. *See* Pharmaceuticals
Meditation, *1980s:* 117
Medwick, Joe, *1930s:* 153
Meese, Edwin, *1980s:* 69, 87
Mefipristone. *See* RU-484
Meiklejohn, Alexander, *1920s:* 47
Meitner, Lise, *1930s:* 145; *1940s:* 132

Méliès, Georges, *1900s:* 2
Mellencamp, John, *1980s:* 3, 26–27
Mellon, Andrew William, *1900s:* 25, 25 (ill.); *1920s:* 69, 69 (ill.), 74
Mellon Institute of Industrial Research, *1920s:* 69
Melodramas, *1900s:* 15
The Melting Pot, 1900s: 3
The Member of the Wedding, 1940s: 7
Memorial Day Massacre, *1930s:* 27
Memorials, Vietnam, *1980s:* 68, 82–83
Memphis, 1920s: 139
"The Memphis Blues," *1910s:* 17
Men
    in education, *1900s:* 41
    fashions for, *1900s:* 94–96, 95 (ill.) *1910s:* 108; *1920s:* 86, 95–97; *1930s:* 103; *1940s:* 89, 93–95; *1960s:* 94, 110; *1970s:* 117–19, 118 (ill.)
    roles of, *1900s:* 22; *1950s:* 90, 102–03
Mendel, Gregor, *1900s:* 121, 129–31
Mendenhall, Dorothy R., *1900s:* 109
Menendez, Erik, *1990s:* 15
Menendez, Lyle, *1990s:* 15
Meningitis, *1910s:* 122–23
Meningitis, genome mapping, *1990s:* 142
Meningitis vaccine, *1960s:* 121–22
Menninger Clinic, *1920s:* 108
Menninger, William Claire, *1940s:* 113, 113 (ill.)
Men's movement, *1990s:* 99–102
Menstruation, *1910s:* 127
Mental disorders, *1940s:* 108, 110, 113, 120, 123–25, 124 (ill.); *1960s:* 56
Mental health, *1900s:* 101
Mental health costs, *1990s:* 122
Mental hospitals, *1910s:* 116; *1950s:* 126–27
Mental illness, *1950s:* 126–27
Menudo, *1990s:* 24
Mercantile National Bank, *1900s:* 28
Merchant ship construction, *1940s:* 24
Mercury-Atlas rocket, *1960s:* 146
Mercury Theatre, *1930s:* 21

Mercy Hospital, Philadelphia, Pennsylvania, *1900s:* 107

Meredith, James, *1960s:* 46–47, 102

Mergers and acquisitions, *1900s:* 23, 64–65; *1950s:* 42; *1960s:* 25–26, 40–41

Mergers, Warner Bros/Time Inc., *1990s:* 28

Meridian, 1970s: 10

Merion Cricket Club, *1930s:* 152

Merman, Ethel, *1920s:* 9; *1930s:* 2

"Merry Oldsmobile," *1900s:* 125

Mesa, Joe, *1990s:* 163

Messerschmitt Me-262, *1940s:* 138

Metachloride, *1940s:* 109

Metal detectors, *1990s:* 46

Metal detectors, schools, *1980s:* 64

Metcalfe, Ralph, *1930s:* 166, 168

Method acting, *1930s:* 21

Methodist Episcopal Church, *1930s:* 92, 100

Methodists, *1940s:* 100

Methotrexate, *1990s:* 130

Metrazol, *1940s:* 122

Metro-Goldwyn-Mayer (M-G-M), *1930s:* 6, 15–18

Metropolitan Life Insurance Tower, *1900s:* 79

Metropolitan Museum of Art, *1940s:* 3

Metropolitan Opera, *1940s:* 3; *1950s:* 3

Metropolitan Opera Company, *1930s:* 18, 22, 98

Metropolitan Opera House, New York City, *1910s:* 2, 16

Meuse-Argonne offensive, *1910s:* 78

Mexico

    Germany and, *1910s:* 77

    illegal activity, *1920s:* 65

    Mexican Revolution, *1910s:* 70–73, 74 (ill.)

    NAFTA, *1990s:* 40

    U.S. relations with, *1910s:* 68, 85

Meyer, Adolf, *1910s:* 116, 116 (ill.)

Meyer v. Nebraska, 1920s: 46, 53

M-G-M (Metro Goldwyn Meyer), *1930s:* 6, 15–18; *1950s:* 11

Miami Dolphins, *1970s:* 160, 171; *1980s:* 181; *1990s:* 175

Miami Vice, 1980s: 96

Michael, George, *1980s:* 3

Michelson, Albert Abraham, *1900s:* 119, 123, 123 (ill.); *1920s:* 133, 133 (ill.)

Michigan, school desegregation in, *1950s:* 60

Michigan State University, *1960s:* 178

Mickey Mouse, *1920s:* 142; *1930s:* 17, 122

Michols, Mike, *1960s:* 9

Microbe Hunters, 1920s: 129

Microcontext, *1940s:* 136

Microevolution, *1900s:* 131

Micro Instrumentation and Telemetry Systems (MITS), *1970s:* 42

Microminis, *1960s:* 108

Microprocessors, *1970s:* 140, 146

Microscopes, *1930s:* 142

Microscopes, field-Ion, *1950s:* 136

Microsoft Corporation, *1970s:* 44–45; *1980s:* 30–31, 44, 146, 161; *1990s:* 28–29, 40

Microsoft Disk Operating System. *See* MS-DOS

Microwave ovens, *1950s:* 136

Midas Muffler, *1960s:* 35

Mid-Channel, 1910s: 19

Middle class, emergence of, *1940s:* 33, 57, 66, 89

Middle East, *1990s:* 64

    Camp David peace accord, *1970s:* 71

    wars in, *1970s:* 26, 31–32

Middle East oil reserves, *1940s:* 38

Middle West Utilities Company, *1930s:* 31

Midgley, Thomas, *1930s:* 141

Midgley, Thomas Jr., *1920s:* 128

Midnight Cowboy, 1960s: 9

Mid-Oceanic Ridge, *1950s:* 137

Midway Gardens, *1910s:* 90

Midwest Industrial League, *1930s:* 161

Miesian architecture, *1940s:* 92

Mies van der Rohe, Ludwig, *1940s:* 92

The Migration of the Negro, 1940s: 10
Mikan, George, *1940s:* 165; *1950s:* 170; *1960s:* 177
Mikkelson, Vern, *1950s:* 170
Milam Building, *1920s:* 87
Military
    airplanes for, *1910s:* 138–39
    aviation, *1940s:* 28, 34, 137–38
    changing views on, *1960s:* 96
    computer network research, *1990s:* 33
    defense industry, *1910s:* 76, 135, 150–51
    desegregation of, *1940s:* 60, 86
    education in, *1960s:* 49, 55
    housing for, *1940s:* 93
    increased power of, *1940s:* 66
    intelligence, *1940s:* 140
    isolationism, *1910s:* 72
    manufacture of supplies, *1940s:* 30–31
    racial discrimination in, *1940s:* 104
    schools, *1940s:* 55
    training, *1910s:* 52
    troop mobilization, *1910s:* 70
    uniforms, *1940s:* 93, 95
    See also World War I
Military build-up, *1980s:* 70–71, 74–81, 113
Military draft, *1940s:* 44, 64
"Military-Industrial Complex," *1940s:* 34–36, 66, 137–38, 140; *1950s:* 39–40; *1960s:* 84
Military medicine, *1960s:* 124
Milken, Michael, *1980s:* 30, 34, 38, 38 (ill.)
Milk pasteurization, *1910s:* 112, 144
Millay, Edna St. Vincent, *1920s:* 2
Millennialism, *1900s:* 88–89
Miller, Arthur, *1940s:* 5, 19
Miller Brewing Company, *1960s:* 41
Miller, Glenn, *1930s:* 2, 20; *1940s:* 2
Miller, Johnny, *1970s:* 174
Miller, Marvin, *1970s:* 165
Miller, Shannon, *1990s:* 165, 183
Miller, Tim, *1990s:* 8
Miller, William Snow, *1900s:* 101

Millikan, Robert A., *1910s:* 140; *1920s:* 133, 133 (ill.); *1930s:* 135, 135 (ill.)
Milliken v. Bradley, 1970s: 53
Millionaires, *1980s:* 31
Million Man March, *1990s:* 93, 95–96, 99–102, 101 (ill.)
Milli Vanilli, *1980s:* 17
Mills, Eleanor, *1920s:* 80
Milwaukee Braves, *1950s:* 158, 164, 168; *1960s:* 174
Milwaukee Bucks, *1960s:* 176
Milwaukee Hawks, *1950s:* 169
The Mind of Primitive Man, 1910s: 132
Mine Owners' Association, *1900s:* 21
Minh, Duong Van, *1970s:* 71
Minicomputers, *1970s:* 146
    See also Personal computers
Minidress, *1960s:* 109 (ill.)
Minimalism, *1960s:* 16–17
Minimum wage, *1930s:* 27, 69; *1950s:* 24; *1960s:* 24
Mining, *1910s:* 86 (ill.), 135
Mining, strip, *1980s:* 36
Miniseries, *1970s:* 22
Miniskirts, *1960s:* 98, 108
Minneapolis Lakers, *1950s:* 161, 169
Minnesota Mining and Manufacturing (3M), *1920s:* 129
Minnesota School of Agriculture and Mining, *1900s:* 146
Minnesota Vikings, *1990s:* 175
Minorities, *1980s:* 52, 59; *1990s:* 31, 38, 47
    as authors, *1970s:* 10–11
    on Broadway, *1900s:* 15
    college education for, *1900s:* 50
    discrimination, *1900s:* 87
    education and, *1970s:* 50, 64–65
    employment of, *1970s:* 39–42
    in high schools, *1900s:* 49
    in medical schools, *1940s:* 115–17
    literature by, *1900s:* 8–9
    See also African Americans; specific minorities; Women
Minoso, Minnie, *1950s:* 164
Minot, George, *1930s:* 110

Minot, George Richards, *1920s:* 113

Minow, Newton, *1960s:* 5

Minstrel shows, *1900s:* 13

Mir, 1990s; 139, 142

The Miracle, 1950s: 106

The Miracles, *1960s:* 13

Miranda v. Arizona, 1960s: 81

MIRVs (Multiple independently targetable reentry vehicles), *1980s:* 78, 80

Miske, Billy, *1920s:* 161

Miss America, *1980s:* 101

Miss America pageant, *1920s:* 86; *1960s:* 95

Missiles, *1950s:* 141; *1960s:* 143

Missiles, to Iran, *1980s:* 69

Missionaries, *1910s:* 93, 95

Mission: Impossible, 1960s: 19

Mission-style furniture, *1910s:* 102

Mississippi Delta field songs, *1900s:* 14

MIST (Medical Information Telephone System), *1960s:* 121

Mitchard, Jacquelyn, *1990s:* 3

Mitchell, John, *1900s:* 26; *1910s:* 29, 29 (ill.); *1970s:* 70, 86

Mitchell, Joni, *1960s:* 113

Mitchell, Lucy Sprague, *1910s:* 51

Mitchell, William, *1920s:* 130, 136–37

Mitchell, William D., *1930s:* 85

MIT (Massachusetts Institute of Technology), *1910s:* 46; *1940s:* 46–47, 130, 142

MITS (Micro Instrumentation and Telemetry Systems), *1970s:* 42

Mix, Tom, *1910s:* 16

Mizner, Addison, *1920s:* 91, 91 (ill.)

MLBPA (Major League Baseball Players Association), *1960s:* 164, 174

Mobil, *1990s:* 29, 40

Mobile Army Surgical Hospital (M.A.S.H.), *1960s:* 124

Mobile telecommunications switching office (MTSO), *1990s:* 154

Model A automobiles, *1900s:* 78, 91

Model A Ford, *1920s:* 25, 34, 129–30, 134; *1930s:* 40, 88, 130

Model T automobiles, *1900s:* 21, 24, 34–35, 35 (ill.), 79, 119, 124 (ill.), 125

Model T Ford, *1910s:* 25, 34, 92, 101, 102 (ill.), 103, 134, 140–43, 143 (ill.); *1920s:* 29, 34, 87, 90

Modern art, *1900s:* 5–6; *1910s:* 2; *1950s:* 2, 8

Modern dance, *1960s:* 114

Modernism, *1900s:* 5, 81
   in architecture, *1940s:* 92
   in art, *1940s:* 4
   in literature, *1940s:* 12

Modernism, literary, *1920s:* 14

Modernism versus tradition, in art, *1930s:* 5, 8–9

Modern Languages Association, *1930s:* 20

Modern Negro Art, 1940s: 10

Modern Times, 1910s: 6; *1930s:* 131

"Mod" fashions, *1960s:* 94, 97, 111–13

Modzelewski, Dick, *1950s:* 174

Moe, Tommy, *1990s:* 182

Moffitt, John C., *1930s:* 21

Mohole, *1960s:* 153

Moholy-Nagy, László, *1910s:* 92

Mohorovicic Discontinuity (Moho), *1960s:* 153

Molecular biology, *1950s:* 141

Moley, Raymond, *1930s:* 35, 76

Molnar, Ferenc, *1920s:* 8

Mona, 1910s: 16

Mona Lisa, 1960s: 2

Monarch, 1950s: 137

Mondale, Walter, *1980s:* 72

Monday Night Football, 1970s: 170

Mondrian, Piet, *1940s:* 2, 8

Monetary policy, *1990s:* 36

Monet, Claude, *1910s:* 12

Money, *1970s:* 38

"Money," *1960s:* 13

Money Train, 1990s: 5

Monk, Thelonious, *1950s:* 15

Monopolies, *1900s:* 60; *1910s:* 31; *1990s:* 28, 32
   Alcoa, *1950s:* 36–37

American Tobacco Company, *1910s:* 66

baseball, *1920s:* 154; *1970s:* 160, 165–66

Federal Trade Commission, *1910s:* 66

football, *1970s:* 161

IBM, *1980s:* 42–44

in motion picture industry, *1940s:* 2–3, 5, 14

railroads, *1920s:* 30

Monroe, Marilyn, *1950s:* 2, 7, 7 (ill.), 12 (ill.), 13, 95, 102; *1960s:* 2, 5, 15

Monroe, Vaughn, *1940s:* 16; *1950s:* 30

Montagnier, Luc, *1990s:* 125

Montana, Joe, *1980s:* 169, 171, 173, 173 (ill.), 181; *1990s:* 164, 175

Monterey International Pop Festival, *1960s:* 3, 12

Monterey Pop, 1960s: 12

Montessori, Maria, *1920s:* 55; *1960s:* 56

Montessori schools, *1960s:* 56

Montgomery, Bernard, *1940s:* 74

Montgomery Lake, *1930s:* 152

Montgomery Ward, *1920s:* 37

Montreal Canadiens, *1930s:* 166; *1960s:* 165; *1970s:* 161, 173

Montreal Expos, *1960s:* 174

Montreal Protocol, *1980s:* 158

Mood rings, *1970s:* 98

Moody, Helen Wills, *1930s:* 153, 156, 156 (ill.), 168, 168 (ill.)

Moondog Rock and Roll Party, 1950s: 15

Moon exploration, *1960s:* 143–44, 156, 159–60, 159 (ill.); *1970s:* 140, 142, 145–46, 148

Moons, Jupiter, *1900s:* 118

Moon, Sun Myung, *1970s:* 99, 114–15

Moore, Alice, *1970s:* 60

Moore, Gordon, *1980s:* 44

Moore, Lenny, *1950s:* 174

Moral education, *1980s:* 50

Morality, *1920s:* 4–5, 14–16

Moral Majority, *1970s:* 99, 112–13; *1980s:* 97, 116

The Moral Majority, *1980s:* 100

Moran, Gertrude Augusta "Gorgeous Gussie," *1940s:* 170–71

Morehouse College, *1900s:* 41, 44

Morely, Edward, *1900s:* 123

Moreno, Manuel Antonio Noriega, *1990s:* 64

Morenz, Howie "Stratford Streak," *1930s:* 166

Morgan, Helen, *1920s:* 9

Morgan, J. P., *1910s:* 24; *1930s:* 76
  See also Morgan, J. Pierpont

Morgan, J. Pierpont, *1900s:* 21, 23, 25, 25 (ill.), 28, 64

Morgan, Julia, *1910s:* 91

Morgan, T. H., *1930s:* 110

Morgan, Thomas Hunt, *1900s:* 130; *1910s:* 117, 117 (ill.), 144

Morrill Act of 1842, *1910s:* 53

Morris, Jack, *1980s:* 177

Morrison, Jim, *1960s:* 12–13

Morrison, Toni, *1970s:* 2, 7, 7 (ill.), 10; *1990s:* 2, 5, 18–19, 19 (ill.)

Morse Code, *1910s:* 132, 151

Mortality, *1980s:* 122, 128
  See also Death

Morton, Ferdinand "Jelly Roll," *1900s:* 14; *1920s:* 3, 12–13

Morton Foods, *1960s:* 41

Morton, William, *1900s:* 107

Morton, William T. G., *1930s:* 116

Morvan, Fabrice, *1980s:* 17

Mosaic, *1990s:* 142, 149
  See also Netscape Navigator

Moscow State Symphony, *1960s:* 2

Moseley, Carol, *1990s:* 75

Moses, Robert, *1940s:* 91, 91 (ill.)

Mosquitoes, yellow fever and, *1900s:* 100, 104, 114

Most Valuable Player (MVP)
  in baseball, *1940s:* 153, 157, 159, 161; *1960s:* 168–69
  in basketball, *1960s:* 169
  in football, *1960s:* 168

Mother Earth, 1900s: 83

Motherhood, surrogate, *1980s:* 134–35, 135 (ill.)

Mother's Day, *1910s:* 91

Motherwell, Robert, *1950s:* 8

Motion Picture Association of America (MPAA), *1960s:* 3, 9

The Motion Picture Association of America Institutes, *1980s:* 2

Motion picture directors, *1910s:* 7, 14

Motion picture industry, *1900s:* 9–11, 12 (ill.), 81; *1950s:* 24; *1960s:* 8–9
 HUAC and, *1940s:* 81–82, 81 (ill.)
 monopolies in, *1940s:* 2–3, 5, 14
 See also Films

Motion Picture Producers and Distributors of America, Inc., *1920s:* 104; *1930s:* 2

Motion pictures. *See* Films

Motley, Archibald Jr., *1920s:* 18

Moton, Robert Russa, *1910s:* 51, 51 (ill.)

The Motor Carrier Act, *1980s:* 30

Motorola, *1980s:* 62

Motor Vehicle Air Pollution Control Act, *1960s:* 94, 126

Motown, *1960s:* 13–15, 14 (ill.)

Mott, John R., *1910s:* 95, 95 (ill.)

Moulton, Forest Ray, *1910s:* 150–51

Mount Palomar Observatory, *1940s:* 131

Mount St. Helens, *1980s:* 146, 149, 161–65, 162 (ill.)

Mount Wilson Observatory, *1910s:* 133, 139

Mourning Becomes Electra, 1920s: 7

Movie industry. *See* Motion picture industry

Movies. *See* Films

Movie stars, *1900s:* 11

Movie studios, *1930s:* 15

Movie theaters, *1900s:* 2–3, 9–10; *1910s:* 2; *1960s:* 41

Movietone, *1920s:* 16

The Moving Picture Experts, *1990s:* 150

Moyer, Charles, *1900s:* 30

Moynihan, Daniel Patrick, *1970s:* 112

Mozert v. *Hawkins County Public Schools, 1980s:* 54–55

MPAA ratings, *1960s:* 3, 9

MPPC (Motion Picture Patents Company), *1900s:* 10; *1910s:* 14

MPPDA (Motion Picture Producers and Distributors of America), *1930s:* 2

MP3, *1990s:* 150

MRIs. *See* Magnetic resonance imaging

MRIs (Magnetic resonance imaging), *1970s:* 123–24, 129

Mrs. Wiggs of the Cabbage Patch, 1900s: 5

Ms., 1970s: 2, 7

MS-DOS, *1980s:* 30, 161

MTSO (Mobile telecommunications switching office), *1990s:* 154

MTV, *1980s:* 2, 4–5, 15–18

MTV Unplugged, 1990s: 23

Muckraking journalism, *1900s:* 3, 59–60

Mudhoney, 1990s: 22

Mueller, Peter, *1970s:* 180

Muhammad, Elijah, *1960s:* 105

Muir, John, *1900s:* 69 (ill.)

Mulligan, Gerry, *1950s:* 15

Multiculturalism, *1970s:* 110

Multinational corporations, *1990s:* 31, 39–42

Multiple independently targetable reentry vehicles (MIRVs), *1980s:* 78, 80

Mumps, *1910s:* 122

Munich Olympics. *See* Summer Olympics

Muon, *1930s:* 144

The Muppet Show, 1970s: 3, 6

Murakami, Masanori, *1960s:* 164

Murder Incorporated, *1940s:* 165

Murders, *1960s:* 80–81, 102–03
 Hall-Mills, *1920s:* 79–80
 Leopold and Loeb, *1920s:* 80–82
 Lindbergh baby, *1920s:* 132
 Sacco and Vanzetti, *1920s:* 83
 See also Assassinations; Homicides

Murder trials, *1900s:* 21, 24

Murphy, William Parry, *1920s:* 113; *1930s:* 110

Murray, Arthur, *1950s:* 109
Murray, Donald, *1930s:* 47, 65
Murray, Kathryn, *1950s:* 109
Murray, Patty, *1990s:* 75
Murray v. Maryland, 1930s: 47
Murray, William H., *1930s:* 26
Murrow, Edward R., *1950s:* 2, 7, 7
    (ill.), 18
Muscle Beach Party, 1960s: 108
Museum of Living Art, *1930s:* 10
Museum of Modern Art, *1930s:* 88;
    1940s: 3; *1960s:* 3, 94
Museum of Non-Objective Painting,
    1940s: 8
Musial, Stan, *1940s:* 155, 161
Music, *1900s:* 5, 13–14, 16; *1910s:* 3,
    7, 15–17; *1920s:* 11–13; *1930s:* 3, 5,
    7, 18–20; *1940s:* 4–7, 15–18, 16
    (ill.), 19 (ill.); *1950s:* 15–16, 152;
    1960s: 5–16, 14 (ill.), 112–13;
    1970s: 11–16, 157
    Amazon.com, *1990s:* 32
    censorship, *1980s:* 9
    computerized effects, *1980s:* 159
    fashion and, *1990s:* 109–12, 111
        (ill.)
    grunge, *1990s:* 2, 5, 21–23
    hip-hop, *1990s:* 7, 23–24
    Latin, *1990s:* 24–25
    MP3, *1990s:* 150
    obscenity, *1980s:* 24
    punk, *1990s:* 5
    rap, *1980s:* 23–24; *1990s:* 3, 5, 7,
        23
    rock and roll, *1990s:* 3, 5
    Rock and Roll Hall of Fame,
        1980s: 3
    videos, *1980s:* 16
    top songs, *1990s:* 25
    See also Concert aid; specific
        types of music
Musicals, *1900s:* 13; *1910s:* 10, 19;
    1920s: 6–7, 9–10; *1930s:* 2, 18;
    1940s: 19; *1950s:* 3; *1960s:* 7,
    18–19; *1970s:* 2–3, 13, 15–16
    See also Revues; specific musicals
The Music Box Revue, 1920s: 9
Music industy, *1900s:* 13

The Musketeers of Pig Alley, 1910s: 2
Muslims, *1980s:* 10
Mussolini, Benito, *1940s:* 75
Mustang (car), *1960s:* 31, 94, 106
Mustard gas, *1910s:* 151
Muste, A. J., *1940s:* 99
Mutations, genetic, *1900s:* 118
Mutoscope, *1910s:* 7
Mutual funds, *1960s:* 33
MVP. *See* Most Valuable Player
My Antonia, 1910s: 6, 11
"My Cherie Amour," *1960s:* 14
"My Day," *1930s:* 73
My Egypt, 1920s: 18
"My Girl," *1960s:* 13
"My Guy," *1960s:* 11
Myhra, Steve, *1950s:* 174
My Lai Massacre, *1960s:* 69, 71, 79;
    1970s: 70, 74
My Kind of Country, 1980s: 25
"My Mammy," *1920s:* 7
Mysticism, *1970s:* 115
"My Sweet Lord," *1970s:* 13

N

NAACP (National Association for the
    Advancement of Colored People),
    1900s: 82, 85; *1910s:* 50, 60, 82, 90;
    1920s: 47, 82–83; *1930s:* 65, 93;
    1960s: 74, 101; *1970s:* 137
    See also National Association for
        the Advancement of Colored-
        People
NABBP (National Association of Base
    Ball Players), *1900s:* 145
Nabor, John, *1970s:* 180
Nabrit, James M., *1950s:* 57 (ill.)
NACA (National Advisory Committee
    on Aeronautics), *1930s:* 136–37;
    1940s: 137–38
Nader, Ralph, *1960s:* 25, 29, 29 (ill.);
    1970s: 30, 30 (ill.)
"Nader's Raiders," *1960s:* 29
NAEP (National Assessment of Edu-
    cational Progress), *1960s:* 51
NAFTA (North American Free Trade
    Agreement), *1990s:* 28, 36, 40

Nagasaki, Japan, *1940s:* 65, 77, 109, 131, 146; *1950s:* 75, 139

Nagurski, Bronko, *1930s:* 157, 157 (ill.)

Naismith, James, *1900s:* 141, 146, 147 (ill.); *1910s:* 164

The Naked and the Dead, 1940s: 5, 12

Naked Lunch, 1950s: 10

Namath, Joe, *1960s:* 166, 180, 180 (ill.)

NAM (National Association of Manufacturers), *1910s:* 86–87

Nanook of the North, 1920s: 2, 16

Napalm, *1940s:* 130; *1960s:* 36

Napster, *1990s:* 150

Narcotics, *1910s:* 69, 83, 113, 127

NASA (National Aeronautics and Space Administration), *1960s:* 142, 156; *1990s:* 141, 156–60

   See also National Aerospace and Space Administration

NASCAR (National Association for Stock Car Racing), *1940s:* 158–59; *1960s:* 166, 170

NASCAR races, *1990s:* 166

Nash, Ogden, *1930s:* 2

Nashville Predators, *1990s:* 175

Nastase, Ilie, *1900s:* 185

National Abortion Federation, *1990s:* 130

National Academy of Design, *1910s:* 8

National Academy of Sciences, *1970s:* 122; *1980s:* 123

National Advisory and Coordinating Council on Bilingual Education, *1980s:* 61

National Advisory Committee on Aeronautics (NACA), *1930s:* 136–37; *1940s:* 137–38

National Advisory Committee on Education, *1930s:* 46

National Aeronautics and Space Administration (NASA), *1960s:* 142, 156

National Aerospace and Space Administration (NASA), *1950s:* 25, 153; *1970s:* 99, 145–48; *1980s:* 151–55, 153 (ill.); *1990s:* 141, 156–60

National American Women Suffrage Association, *1910s:* 81

National Assessment of Educational Progress (NAEP), *1960s:* 51; *1980s:* 48

National Association for Stock Car Racing (NASCAR), *1940s:* 158–59

National Association for the Advancement of Colored People (NAACP), *1900s:* 82, 85; *1910s:* 50, 60, 82, 90; *1920s:* 47, 82–83; *1930s:* 65, 93; *1940s:* 47, 60, 69; *1950s:* 46, 50–51, 58; *1960s:* 74, 101; *1970s:* 137

National Association for the Study and Prevention of Infant Mortality, *1910s:* 112

National Association for the Study and Prevention of Tuberculosis, *1900s:* 113

National Association of Base Ball Players (NABBP), *1900s:* 145

National Association of Broadcasters, *1970s:* 22

National Association of Colored Women, *1900s:* 86

National Association of Manufacturers (NAM), *1910s:* 86–87

National Association of Radio and Television Broadcasters, *1950s:* 125–26

National Association of Stock Car Auto Racing (NASCAR), *1960s:* 166, 170

National Basketball Association (NBA), *1940s:* 153–54, 162; *1950s:* 158–59, 168–70; *1970s:* 160–61, 167, 169; *1980s:* 168, 170, 172, 177–78; *1990s:* 164, 166–67, 171–72, 182

National Basketball League (NBL), *1930s:* 161; *1940s:* 153, 162; *1950s:* 168

National Birth Control League, *1910s:* 117

National Board for Historical Service, *1910s:* 52

National Board of Censorship, *1900s:* 11

National Board of Medical Examiners, *1910s:* 113; *1940s:* 116

National Board of the CPUSA, *1940s:* 78

National Boxing Association (NBA), *1930s:* 162

National Broadcasting Company (NBC), *1920s:* 77, 128; *1930s:* 147

National Cancer Act of 1971, *1970s:* 122

National Cancer Institute, *1930s:* 111; *1940s:* 109; *1980s:* 126; *1990s:* 125

National Canning Association (NCA), *1910s:* 144

National Cash Register, *1910s:* 56

National Center for Superconducting Applications, *1990s:* 142

National Child Labor Committee (NCLC), *1900s:* 87

National Collegiate Athletic Association (NCAA), *1900s:* 139, 146; *1950s:* 168; *1960s:* 165, 175–76, 178; *1980s:* 50, 58; *1990s:* 178

National Commission (baseball), *1900s:* 144

National Commission of Fine Arts, *1910s:* 94

National Commission on Technology, Automation and Economic Progress, *1960s:* 142–43

National Committee on Federal Legislation for Birth Control, *1930s:* 118

National Committee on Pay Equity, *1990s:* 37

National Committee to Stop the ERA, *1970s:* 98, 107

National Conference of Catholic Charities, *1910s:* 90

National Conference of Collegiate Athletics (NCAA), *1940s:* 162

National Conference on Air Pollution, *1950s:* 115

National Conference on Pellagra, *1900s:* 110

National Congress of Mothers, *1900s:* 86

National Council for Financial Aid to Education, *1950s:* 46

National Council of Churches, *1960s:* 94

National Council of Negro Women, *1920s:* 50

National Council of Teachers, *1960s:* 53

National debt, *1910s:* 67; *1970s:* 36–38; *1980s:* 30–31, 81–85

National Defense Act, *1910s:* 76

National Defense Education Act, *1960s:* 52, 57

National Defense Mediation Board (NDMB), *1940s:* 30

National Defense Research Committee (NDRC), *1940s:* 130, 142

National Education Act, *1950s:* 47, 54

National Education Association (NEA), *1900s:* 40; *1920s:* 52; *1930s:* 53–56, 60; *1940s:* 45, 48, 51; *1950s:* 47, 61

National Endowment for the Arts (NEA), *1960s:* 113–14; *1990s:* 2–4, 8–9

National Endowment for the Arts (NEA), cuts to, *1980s:* 5, 9

National Endowment for the Humanities (NEH), *1960s:* 114

National Environmental Policy Act, *1960s:* 130

National Environmental Policy Act of 1970 (NEPA), *1970s:* 90

National Fine Arts Commission, *1960s:* 94

National Football League (NFL), *1920s:* 148–49, 163–64; *1930s:* 77, 153, 155, 162–64; *1940s:* 152–53, 167; *1950s:* 158, 161, 173–75; *1960s:* 165–66, 179–81; *1970s:* 160–61, 170–71; *1980s:* 168, 170, 178–81, 179 (ill.); *1990s:* 165, 173–75, 174 (ill.)

National Foundation for Infantile Paralysis (NIFP), *1930s:* 111, 122; *1940s:* 108; *1950s:* 127–28

National Gallery of Art, *1920s:* 69; *1960s:* 3

National Health Security Plan, *1990s:* 122–23

National Heart Institute, *1940s:* 110

National Highway Act, *1950s:* 25, 40

National Hockey League (NHL), *1920s:* 148–49; *1930s:* 165–66; *1950s:* 161; *1960s:* 164; *1970s:* 161, 172; *1980s:* 161, 168–69, 171–72, 172 (ill.), 183–85; *1990s:* 176–77

National Human Genome Research Institute (NHGRI), *1990s:* 143

National Industrial Recovery Act (NIRA), *1930s:* 26, 36, 68–69, 73, 78, 140

National Institute of Education, *1970s:* 57

National Institute of Mental Health, *1940s:* 110

National Institutes of Health, *1950s:* 122; *1980s:* 123; *1990s:* 132, 143

National Interagency Council on Smoking and Health, *1960s:* 138

National Invitation Tournament (NIT), *1950s:* 168

Nationalism, *1930s:* 3

National Kindergarten Association (NKA), *1900s:* 47

National Labor Relations Act (NLRA), *1930s:* 38

National League (baseball), *1900s:* 138, 141, 144; *1910s:* 154–55, 157, 161, 164; *1920s:* 149, 154–60; *1930s:* 158–59; *1960s:* 164, 174

National League of Professional Basketball (NLPB), *1900s:* 148

National League pennant, *1940s:* 161

National Liberty Journal, 1990s: 93

National Medical Association, *1900s:* 106

National Mental Health Act, *1940s:* 125

National Monetary Commission, *1900s:* 28

National Monuments Act, *1900s:* 68

National Organization for Public Health Nursing, *1910s:* 112

National Organization for Women (NOW), *1960s:* 95, 98; *1990s:* 12, 56–57

National Periodical Publications, *1940s:* 10

National Railroad Passenger Corporation. *See* Amtrak

National Rainbow Coalition, *1990s:* 99–100

National Reclamation Act, *1900s:* 20

National Recovery Administration (NRA), *1930s:* 36, 78

National Research Council, *1980s:* 49

National Rifle Association (NRA), *1990s:* 94, 97, 107

National Science Foundation, *1950s:* 54; *1990s:* 131

National Security Act, *1980s:* 87

National Security Council, *1940s:* 66

National Ski Association, *1900s:* 138

National Society for the Scientific Study of Education, *1900s:* 41

National Tuberculosis Association, *1910s:* 130

National War Labor Board (NWLB), *1910s:* 25; *1940s:* 30, 39–41, 64

National Women's Political Caucus, *1970s:* 7

National Youth Administration (NYA), *1920s:* 50; *1930s:* 26, 47, 50, 65, 78

Nation, Carry, *1900s:* 81, 83, 83 (ill.), 86

Nation of Islam, *1960s:* 99, 105

Native Americans, *1970s:* 98, 109–10, 111 (ill.), 123; *1990s:* 38
   in American history classes, *1960s:* 48, 52–53
   land, *1900s:* 58
   literature by, *1900s:* 9

Native Son, 1930s: 21; *1940s:* 7, 13

The Nat King Cole Show, 1960s: 106

NATO (North Atlantic Treaty Organization), *1990s:* 70
   See also North Atlantic Treaty Organization

Natural Born Killers, 1990s: 9

Natural childbirth, *1960s:* 135

Natural disasters, shock documentaries, *1990s:* 16–18

Naturalism, in literature, *1900s:* 6

Natural resources, international sources of, *1940s:* 38

Natural selection, *1900s:* 131

Nautilus, 1950s: 137

Naval Consulting Board, *1910s:* 28

Naval Officers' Training Corps, *1940s:* 57

Navarro, Theodore "Fats," *1940s:* 17

Navin, Frank, *1910s:* 162

Navratilova, Martina, *1980s:* 168, 173

Navy, *1910s:* 96

Navy personnel, Tailhook convention, *1990s:* 92

Nazis, *1990s:* 4, 11

Nazis, psychology of, *1940s:* 90
    See also Third Reich; World War II

NBA (National Basketball Association), *1960s:* 165–66, 176–78; *1970s:* 160–61, 167, 169; *1980s:* 168, 170, 172, 177–78; *1990s:* 164, 166–67, 171–72

NBA (National Boxing Association), *1930s:* 162

NBC (National Broadcasting System), *1920s:* 77, 128; *1930s:* 147
    color telecasts, *1950s:* 43, 142

NBL (National Basketball League), *1930s:* 161; *1940s:* 153, 162; *1950s:* 168

NCAA (National Collegiate Athletic Association), *1900s:* 139, 146; *1940s:* 162; *1950s:* 168; *1980s:* 50, 58; *1990s:* 178

NCA (National Canning Association), *1910s:* 144

NCI (National Cancer Institute), *1980s:* 126

NCLC (National Child Labor Committee), *1900s:* 87

NCR, *1960s:* 37

NDMB (National Defense Mediation Board), *1940s:* 30

NDRC (National Defense Research Committee), *1940s:* 130, 142

Neal, Larry, *1960s:* 114

NEA (National Education Association), *1920s:* 52; *1930s:* 53–56, 60; *1960s:* 113–14
    See also National Education Association

NEA (National Endowment for the Arts), cuts to, *1980s:* 5, 9

Nebulae, *1910s:* 137

Neddermayer, Seth, *1930s:* 144

Neglect, child, *1980s:* 112

Negligence cases, *1990s:* 28

Negri, Pola, *1920s:* 94

Negro Baseball League, *1920s:* 157–60; *1930s:* 152, 155, 158; *1940s:* 153

Negro National League, *1920s:* 148, 158; *1930s:* 160

Negro Theatre Project, *1930s:* 21

NEH (National Endowment for the Humanities), *1960s:* 114

Nelson, Byron, *1930s:* 164; *1940s:* 169–70, 169 (ill.)

Nelson, Donald, *1940s:* 30

Nelson George, *1950s:* 104

Nelson, George "Baby Face," *1930s:* 82, 85

Nelson, Ricky, *1960s:* 10

Nelson, Willie, *1980s:* 3, 26

Neocaine, *1930s:* 116

Neoconservatism, *1970s:* 100, 111–13

Neon signs, *1910s:* 146

Neoprene, *1930s:* 141

NEPA (National Environmental Policy Act of 1970), *1970s:* 90

Nervous system disorder, genome mapping, *1990s:* 143–44

Nestor, Agnes, *1910s:* 40

Netscape Communications, *1990s:* 28, 39, 138, 142

Netscape Navigator, *1990s:* 138, 142

Neumann, John von, *1930s:* 135, 135 (ill.)

Neumann, Liselotte, *1980s:* 183

Neutrality Act, *1930s:* 81

Neutra, Richard, *1940s:* 93

Neutrons, *1930s:* 144

"Never Be You," *1980s:* 25

Nevermind, *1990s:* 2, 22–23, 110

Nevers, Ernie, *1920s:* 149–50, 153, 153 (ill.), 162, 164

New Age movement, *1980s:* 96, 99–100, 116–18

New age spiritualism, *1990s:* 95, 108–09
Newark, New Jersey riots, *1960s:* 95
"The New Colossus," *1900s:* 2
Newcombe, Don, *1950s:* 164
New Deal, *1930s:* 4, 68, 70–71, 91, 104; *1940s:* 67
    civil rights and, *1930s:* 77–78
    crime and, *1930s:* 83–85
    economy and, *1930s:* 29, 35–37, 76–77
    education and, *1930s:* 53–54, 65
    health care and, *1930s:* 113
    Landon, Alf on, *1930s:* 72
    Long, Huey on, *1930s:* 73
    railroads and, *1930s:* 140
New England Journal of Medicine, *1980s:* 123; *1990s:* 156
New Freedom, *1910s:* 26–27, 30–32, 84; *1920s:* 33
New Hampshire, 1920s: 2
New Jersey Americans, *1960s:* 177
New Journalism, *1900s:* 16; *1960s:* 80
Newlands Reclamation Act, *1900s:* 58
New Look (fashion), *1940s:* 89, 95–96
Newman, Barnett, *1940s:* 9
Newman, Paul, *1950s:* 176
Newman, Pauline, *1910s:* 40
New math, *1970s:* 61
New Mexico, statehood, *1910s:* 66
New Nationalism platform, *1910s:* 84
The New Negro, 1920s: 10
New Orleans Buccaneers, *1960s:* 177
New Orleans, Louisiana
    jazz in, *1900s:* 14
    school integration in, *1960s:* 46
Newport Folk Festival, *1960s:* 113
Newport Jazz Festival, *1950s:* 3
New Republic, 1910s: 52; *1920s:* 50
Newscasters, *1960s:* 6
New School for Social Research, *1910s:* 47, 50; *1920s:* 50
News, in journalism, *1900s:* 15–16
Newspapers, *1910s:* 3, 5, 19–20, 19 (ill.), 52; *1930s:* 50, 60; *1960s:* 24
Newspapers, black, *1900s:* 2
News programs, *1990s:* 44
Newsreels, *1910s:* 2

News, televised, *1960s:* 19–20
New wave music, *1970s:* 15
Newsweek, 1950s: 107
Newton-John, Olivia, *1980s:* 19
New York American, 1910s: 20
New York Automobile Salon, *1920s:* 87
New York Blood Center, *1960s:* 120
New York Central railroad, *1960s:* 25
New York Central Reserve Bank, *1920s:* 29
New York City, *1910s:* 2–3, 5
    Board of Education, *1950s:* 47
    bridges, *1960s:* 142
    communism and teachers, *1950s:* 61–62
    desegregation, *1950s:* 60
    education and, *1900s:* 41
    libraries in, *1900s:* 2
    music industry in, *1900s:* 13
    school integration in, *1960s:* 47
    skyscrapers, *1900s:* 79
    subway system, *1900s:* 20, 78
    Tammany Hall, *1900s:* 66
    theater in, *1900s:* 14–15
    Tin Pan Alley, *1900s:* 16
New York City Board of Health, *1900s:* 113
New York City College, *1940s:* 50
New York City parks and highways, *1940s:* 91
New York City schools, *1980s:* 123
New York Dolls, *1970s:* 13
New York Drama Critics' Circle, *1940s:* 2, 6–7
New Yorker, 1930s: 2
New York Giants, *1900s:* 139; *1910s:* 159, 162; *1920s:* 149, 156, 158; *1930s:* 152, 163; *1940s:* 167; *1960s:* 179, 181; *1990s:* 175
    football, *1950s:* 159–60, 173–74
New York Highlanders, *1900s:* 144; *1910s:* 154
New York Islanders, *1980s:* 168
New York Jets, *1960s:* 165–66, 180
New York Journal, 1900s: 16
New York Knickerbockers, *1950s:* 168

New York Knicks, *1960s:* 177; *1970s:* 169

New York Marathon, *1900s:* 152

New York Metropolitan Opera, *1960s:* 2, 31

New York Metropolitan Opera House, *1910s:* 16

New York Metropolitan Museum of Art, *1950s:* 2

New York Mets, *1950s:* 167; *1960s:* 164–66, 174–75

New York Nets, *1960s:* 178

New York Philharmonic, *1920s:* 142; *1950s:* 3; *1960s:* 2

New York Public Library, *1910s:* 2

New York Rangers, *1920s:* 149; *1930s:* 165–66; *1990s:* 176

New York Rens, *1930s:* 161

New York School (artistic movement), *1940s:* 8

New York Societé Anonyme, *1920s:* 2

New York Society for the Suppression of Vice, *1950s:* 141

New York State Athletic Commission, *1910s:* 154

New York, state constitution, *1910s:* 67

New York State Economic Council, *1930s:* 60

New York State Federation of Labor, *1950s:* 28

New York State Hospital Commission, *1940s:* 108

New York State university system, *1940s:* 45

New York Stock Exchange, *1920s:* 24, 40 (ill.), 42; *1930s:* 32; *1960s:* 24, 32 (ill.), 33, 143

New York Times, 1900s: 15–16

New York Times, Unabomber and, *1990s:* 81

New York Times v. *Sullivan, 1960s:* 81

New York Titans, *1960s:* 180

New York University Settlement, *1900s:* 87

New York Whirlwinds, *1910s:* 165

New York World, 1900s: 16

New York World's Fair, *1930s:* 106–07, 131, 147

New York Yankees, *1900s:* 144; *1910s:* 154–55, 157, 163; *1920s:* 148–49, 152, 155–57; *1930s:* 152–53, 156, 158; *1940s:* 157, 159, 161; *1950s:* 158–61, 164, 166; *1960s:* 164, 172–73; *1970s:* 166; *1990s:* 168

NFL (National Football League), *1920s:* 148–49, 163–64; *1930s:* 153, 155, 162–64

    See also National Football League; *1960s:* 165–66, 179–81; *1970s:* 160–61, 170–71; *1980s:* 168, 170, 178–81, 179 (ill.); *1990s:* 165, 173–75, 174 (ill.)

NFL championship, *1940s:* 152

NFL Players Association (NFLPA), *1980s:* 178, 180

NHGRI (National Human Genome Research Institute), *1990s:* 143

NHL (National Hockey League), *1920s:* 148–49; *1930s:* 165–66; *1950s:* 161; *1960s:* 164; *1970s:* 161, 172; *1980s:* 161, 168–69, 171–72, 172 (ill.), 183–85; *1990s:* 176–77

Niacin deficiency, *1910s:* 112

Niagara Movement, *1900s:* 59, 85

Nicaragua, *1910s:* 72; *1980s:* 68–69, 75, 86

Nicholas II, *1910s:* 7, 79–80

Nicholson, Jack, *1960s:* 9

Nichols, Terry Lynn, *1990s:* 83

Nicklaus, Jack, *1960s:* 165; *1970s:* 160–61, 174–75; *1980s:* 171, 181–83; *1990s:* 178

Nickel alkaline batteries, *1900s:* 118

Nickelodeons, *1900s:* 3, 10, 79

Nielsen, Jerri, *1990s:* 131

Nike, *1970s:* 30; *1980s:* 96, 106

Nikolais, Alwin, *1960s:* 114

Nicotinamide, *1900s:* 110

Niebuhr, H. Richard, *1940s:* 100

Niebuhr, Reinhold, *1940s:* 91, 91 (ill.), 99; *1950s:* 95, 95 (ill.)

NIFP (National Foundation of Infantile Paralysis), *1950s:* 128

A Night at the Opera, 1930s: 18

Night Journey, 1940s: 6

Night schools, *1910s:* 46

NIH (National Institutes of Health), *1990s:* 132, 143

Nijinsky, Vaslav, *1910s:* 9

Nimoy, Leonard, *1960s:* 19 (ill.)

Nineteenth Amendment, *1910s:* 80, 95; *1970s:* 98

Nippon, 1990s: 40

NIRA. *See* National Industrial Recovery Act

Nirenberg, Marshall W., *1960s:* 147

Nirvana, *1990s:* 2, 21–22, 22 (ill.), 110

NIT (National Invitation Tournament), *1950s:* 168

Nitrogen dioxide, *1980s:* 140

Nitrous oxide, *1930s:* 116

Nixon, 1990s: 10

Nixon, Richard M., *1930s:* 30; *1940s:* 67; *1950s:* 78, 84–85; *1960s:* 3, 73, 73 (ill.), 86; *1970s:* 26, 70–71, 82–88, 82 (ill.), 87 (ill.); *1980s:* 75–76

    campaign of 1960, 19–20, 68, 82–84

    energy policy, *1970s:* 31–32

    on the environment, *1960s:* 130

    on health care, *1970s:* 132–33

    National Cancer Act, *1970s:* 122

    1966 elections and, *1960s:* 85

    presidential election of, *1960s:* 69, 71, 86–89

    Soviet Union and, *1970s:* 72

    televised debates, *1960s:* 19–20, 68, 83–84, 83 (ill.)

    Vietnam War and, *1960s:* 79, 96; *1970s:* 76–79

    wage and price controls, *1970s:* 28, 38

    Watergate, *1970s:* 73, 84–88

    women appointments, *1970s:* 107

NKA (National Kindergarten Association), *1900s:* 47

NL (National League), *1960s:* 174

NLPB (National League of Professional Basketball), *1900s:* 148

NLRA (National Labor Relations Act), *1930s:* 38

Nobel, Alfred, *1990s:* 19

Nobel Foundation, *1990s:* 19

Nobel Prizes, *1990s:* 2, 19

    Addams, Jane, *1930s:* 88

    Banting, Frederick Grant, *1920s:* 119

    Bellow, Saul, *1970s:* 3

    Best, Charles, *1920s:* 119

    Carrel, Alexis, *1930s:* 114

    chemistry, *1910s:* 133, 136–37

    in chemistry or physics, *1970s:* 150

    Collip, James B., *1920s:* 119

    Compton, Arthur Holly, *1920s:* 132

    Cori, Gerty Theresa, *1940s:* 134

    economics, *1910s:* 35; *1980s:* 39; *1990s:* 37

    economists, *1970s:* 37

    Eijkman, Christiaan, *1920s:* 111

    Einstein, Albert, *1900s:* 133

    Einthoven, Willem, *1920s:* 110–11, 116

    Eliot, T. S., *1940s:* 3

    Enders, John F., *1940s:* 122

    Faulkner, William, *1940s:* 12

    Fermi, Enrico, *1940s:* 134

    first, *1900s:* 2

    Gell-Mann, Murray, *1960s:* 146

    genetics, *1980s:* 150

    Haworth, Norman, *1930s:* 141

    Hemingway, Ernest, *1920s:* 6

    Hopkins, Frederick, *1920s:* 111

    Karrer, Paul, *1930s:* 141

    King, Martin Luther, Jr., *1960s:* 72

    Kissinger, Henry, *1970s:* 75

    Landsteiner, Karl, *1930s:* 113, 115

    in literature, *1900s:* 9; *1930s:* 13

    MacLeod, John J. R., *1920s:* 119

    Marshall, George C., *1940s:* 69

    McClintock, Barbara, *1940s:* 140

    medicine, *1910s:* 112, 117, 119; *1980s:* 139

Michelson, Albert Abraham, *1900s:* 123

Millikan, Robert A., *1920s:* 133; *1930s:* 135

Minot, George, *1930s:* 110, 113

Morgan, T. H., *1930s:* 110, 113

Morrison, Toni, *1970s:* 7

Murphy, William P., *1930s:* 110, 113

Nirenberg, Marshall W., *1960s:* 146

O'Neill, Eugene, *1920s:* 7

peace, *1900s:* 59, 73

Penzias, Arno, *1970s:* 144

physics, *1900s:* 119; *1980s:* 163

in physiology or medicine, *1970s:* 135

science, *1990s:* 159

Singer, Issac Bashevis, *1970s:* 3

Urey, Harold C., *1930s:* 135

Whipple, George Hoyt, *1930s:* 110, 113

Wilson, Robert W., *1970s:* 144

Yalow, Rosalyn S., *1970s:* 126

Noguchi, Isamu, *1930s:* 10

Nongraded schools, *1910s:* 46

Nonviolent protests, *1940s:* 90, 99

Nonviolent resistance, *1960s:* 63–64, 72, 74, 94

Norfolk jackets, *1910s:* 107

Noriega, Manuel, *1980s:* 69

Normal schools, *1910s:* 54–55, 58

Normand, Mabel, *1910s:* 15

Norman, Greg, *1980s:* 183

Norris, Chuck, *1970s:* 114

Norris, Frank, *1900s:* 8

North Africa, World War II in, *1940s:* 75

North American Free Trade Agreement (NAFTA), *1990s:* 28, 36, 40

North Atlantic Treaty Organization (NATO), *1940s:* 65, 68, 81; *1990s:* 70

Northern Securities Company, *1900s:* 64

Northern Securities v. *United States, 1900s:* 34, 74

North Korea, relations with U.S., *1960s:* 71

North, Oliver, *1980s:* 69, 73, 73 (ill.), 87, 89

North Pole, *1900s:* 119, 123

North, segregation in, *1970s:* 51–52

The North Star, 1940s: 6

Northwestern University School of Medicine, *1930s:* 110

Nostalgic films, *1970s:* 18

Notebook computers, *1980s:* 30

Notorious B.I.G., *1990s:* 3, 24

Notre Dame, *1920s:* 153, 162; *1940s:* 167

Notre Dame football, *1950s:* 159

Novello, Antonia, *1990s:* 116

Novels, *1940s:* 11–12
    See also Books

Novocaine, *1900s:* 79; *1930s:* 116

Novoselic, Kris, *1990s:* 22 (ill.)

Novy, Frederick George, *1900s:* 100

No Way Out, 1960s: 105

"Now I Wanna Sniff Some Glue," *1970s:* 14

NOW (National Organization for Women), *1990s:* 12, 56–57
    See also National Organization for Women

Noyce, Robert, *1980s:* 44

NRA (National Recovery Association), *1930s:* 36, 78

NRA (National Rifle Association), *1990s:* 94, 97, 107

Nuclear arms race, *1940s:* 80

Nuclear energy
    dangers of, *1960s:* 121
    explosions, *1960s:* 142
    submarines, *1960s:* 142

Nuclear fallout, *1940s:* 148

Nuclear fission, *1930s:* 144; *1940s:* 132

Nuclear power, *1940s:* 131, 143–48, 145 (ill.), 147 (ill.); *1950s:* 136; *1970s:* 35, 141, 154–57
    See also Atomic bombs

Nuclear power plants
    accidents, *1980s:* 146–47

Three Mile Island, *1980s:* 114
(ill.)
Nuclear submarines, *1950s:* 136
Nuclear weapons, *1960s:* 68, 70,
75–77; *1970s:* 80; *1980s:* 69, 75, 99
A-bomb, *1950s:* 69, 149–50
Cold war, *1950s:* 74–77
H-bomb, *1950s:* 139, 149–50
Rosenbergs and, *1950s:* 68, 71,
78–79
See also Atomic bombs; Strategic
Defense Initiative
Number 23, 1940s: 9 (ill.)
Nunn, Sam, *1990s:* 69
Nuremberg Files, *1990s:* 129
Nuremburg trials, *1940s:* 65
Nurmi, Paavo, *1920s:* 168; *1930s:* 168
Nursing, *1910s:* 49, 59, 112
Nutritional cereals, *1970s:* 122
NWLB. *See* National War Labor Board
NYA. *See* National Youth Administra-
tion
Nye, Bill, *1990s:* 48, 48 (ill.)
Nye, Gerald, *1930s:* 81
Nye Investigating Committee, *1930s:*
81
Nylon, *1930s:* 131, 141–42; *1950s:* 90,
115
Nylon stockings, *1940s:* 31, 95; *1950s:*
90

O

Oakland A's, *1910s:* 163; *1960s:* 174
Oakland Athletics, *1980s:* 174; *1990s:*
164
Oakland Oaks, *1960s:* 177
Oakland Raiders, *1960s:* 180; *1980s:*
180
O'Brien, Lawrence, *1970s:* 84
Obscenity, *1990s:* 2–4, 8–9
Observatories, *1990s:* 138
Obsidian, *1960s:* 148
Obstruction of justice, Nixon,
Richard, *1970s:* 84–86
Occult, *1970s:* 115
Occupational Safety and Health Act of
1970, *1970s:* 122

Occupational Safety and Health
Administration, *1980s:* 35
Ocean (musical group), *1970s:* 13
Oceanography, *1960s:* 142, 144–46,
153–54, 155 (ill.)
Oceans, exploration of, *1970s:*
141–42, 144
Ochoa, Severo, *1940s:* 133
Ochs, Phil, *1960s:* 113
O'Connor, Basil, *1930s:* 122
O'Connor, Carroll, *1970s:* 22
O'Connor, Sandra Day, *1980s:* 68, 73,
73 (ill.)
October War, *1970s:* 31–32
Odets, Clifford, *1930s:* 4, 21
Oerter, Al, *1960s:* 169, 169 (ill.), 181
Oeschger, Joe, *1920s:* 148
Office of Advocacy, *1990s:* 37
Office of Education, *1930s:* 53; *1970s:*
56–57
Office of Malaria Control in War
Areas (MCWA), *1940s:* 114
Office of Management and Budget,
1980s: 73
Office of National Drug Control Poli-
cy, *1980s:* 109
Office of Price Administration and
Civilian Supply (OPA), *1940s:* 24,
27
Office of Production Management
(OPM), *1940s:* 24, 30
Office of Scientific Research and
Development (OSRD), *1940s:* 130,
134
Office of War Information (OWI),
1940s: 13–14, 136
Officiating, basketball, *1990s:* 164
"Of Mr. Booker T. Washington and
Others," *1900s:* 53
Of Thee I Sing, 1920s: 6; *1930s:* 20
O. Henry Awards, *1910s:* 3
Ohio Players, *1970s:* 15
Ohio State University, *1930s:* 168;
1960s: 178–79
Oil
embargoes, *1970s:* 26, 30–32
in Iran, *1970s:* 91–92
prices, *1970s:* 27–28, 31

Oil and gas industry
  California offshore oil tracts,
    1980s: 36
  coastline, *1980s:* 30
  federal lands, *1980s:* 35–36
  world prices, *1980s:* 30
Oil companies, *1940s:* 38
Oil drilling equipment, *1950s:* 136
Oil industry, *1910s:* 30, 32–33; *1930s:*
  26, 30, 42–43
Oil spills, *Exxon Valdez, 1980s:*
  147–48, 156–57
Oil strikes, *1930s:* 42–43
Oingo Boingo, *1980s:* 18
Okamoto, Ayako, *1980s:* 183
O'Keeffe, Georgia, *1920s:* 2, 18; *1930s:*
  4
Okinawa, *1940s:* 65, 73
Oklahoma!, 1940s: 3, 17
Oklahoma City bombing, *1990s:*
  62–63, 65, 81–83, 92–93
Oklahoma Sooners, *1950s:* 161
Oklahoma, statehood, *1900s:* 59
Olajuwon, Hakeem, *1980s:* 177;
  1990s: 172
Oldenburg, Claes, *1960s:* 16
The Old Man and the Sea, 1920s: 6;
  1950s: 8–10
Oldsmobile, *1900s:* 125; *1930s:* 131;
  1940s: 87
Olds, Ransom Eli, *1900s:* 91, 125
Olduvai Gorge, Tanzania, *1960s:* 148
Oliva, Tony, *1960s:* 173
Oliver, Joe "King," *1900s:* 14
Olympics, *1900s:* 141, 152–53; *1910s:*
  154, 156–57, 159, 165, 173–74;
  1920s: 148, 167–69; *1930s:* 152–53,
  155, 157, 166–67; *1940s:* 152–53,
  168; *1950s:* 175; *1960s:* 167, 169,
  181–82; *1970s:* 160–61, 163,
  177–80; *1980s:* 22, 68, 168–69,
  173, 183, 186–90, 187 (ill.), 188
  (ill.); *1990s:* 164–65, 171, 177,
  181–84
    Albertville, *1990s:* 164, 181–84
    Athens, Greece, *1900s:* 139
    Atlanta, *1990s:* 65, 163, 165
    Barcelona, *1990s:* 164

Bombing, Atlanta, Georgia,
  1990s: 184
Lillehammer, *1990s:* 163
London, England, *1900s:* 139
Nagano, *1990s:* 163
Paris, France, *1900s:* 138, 152
St. Louis, Missouri, *1900s:* 138,
  152
Omaha (horse), *1930s:* 165
Oman, *1990s:* 68
O.M.D. (Orchestral Maneuvers in the
  Dark), *1980s:* 18
O'Meara, Mark, *1990s:* 179
The Omen, 1970s: 10, 18
O'Neal, Shaquille, *1990s:* 172
One Flew Over the Cuckoo's Nest,
  1960s: 4, 18–19
One Hundred Years of Solitude, 1970s:
  11
O'Neill, Eugene, *1910s:* 18; *1920s:* 4,
  7–9, 7 (ill.); *1930s:* 2, 4, 13; *1940s:*
  20
O'Neill, J. A., *1920s:* 129
O'Neill, James, *1910s:* 2
One of Ours, 1910s: 6
One Potato Two Potato, 1960s: 106
One-step, *1910s:* 106
"One Tin Soldier," *1970s:* 13
On Human Nature, 1970s: 144
Onizuka, Ellison S., *1980s:* 152
Onnes, Heike Kamerlingh, *1900s:*
  119; *1910s:* 146
On the Interpretation of Dreams, 1900s:
  118, 131
On the Origin of Species, 1900s: 119;
  1920s: 60
On the Town, 1940s: 17
On the Waterfront, 1950s: 13–14
OPA (Office of Price Administration
  and Civilian Supply), *1940s:* 24, 27
Op Art, *1960s:* 16–17
OPEC. *See* Organization of Petroleum
  Exporting Countries
Opel, *1920s:* 25
Open heart surgery, *1960s:* 124
Opera, *1900s:* 7, 13–14; *1910s:* 16;
  1930s: 22–23; *1940s:* 3; *1960s:* 2, 31
Operating systems, *1970s:* 45

Operation Desert Storm. *See* Persian Gulf War

Operation Menu, *1970s:* 78

Operation Overlord, *1940s:* 68, 75

Operation Rescue, *1990s:* 128

Operation Restore Hope, *1990s:* 68

Operations (medical). *See* Surgery

Operation Torch, *1940s:* 64, 68, 75

O Pioneers!, 1910s: 6, 11

Opium, *1910s:* 113

OPM (Office of Production Management), *1940s:* 24, 30

Oppenheimer, J. Robert, *1940s:* 135, 135 (ill.), 146; *1950s:* 139, 149

Oprah, 1990s: 108

Optical fibers, *1970s:* 152

Optics, *1910s:* 112

Optoelectronics, *1970s:* 156

Optometry, *1910s:* 112

Oral contraception, *1950s:* 137–38, 141; *1960s:* 120, 122, 133, 134 (ill.), 145, 154–56; *1990s:* 117

Orange Bowl, *1930s:* 163

Orange juice, powdered, *1960s:* 142

Orchard, Harry, *1900s:* 30

Orchestral Maneuvers in the Dark (O.M.D.), *1980s:* 18

Orchestras, *1910s:* 16

Order L-85, *1940s:* 93–95

Organic foods, *1970s:* 115

Organization of Petroleum Exporting Countries (OPEC), *1970s:* 26, 31, 34

Organized crime
    AFL-CIO, *1950s:* 32
    boxing and, *1940s:* 165
    Hoffa, James, *1950s:* 28
    investigations, *1950s:* 68, 81–82, 82 (ill.)

Organized labor. *See* Labor unions

Organ, pipeless, *1930s:* 2

Original Celtics, *1920s:* 160

Original Independent Show, *1900s:* 3

Origins of the universe, Hubble Telescope and, *1990s:* 141

The Origins of Totalitarianism, 1940s: 90

Orlon, *1950s:* 90

"Ornithology," *1940s:* 17

Orphan Annie, *1930s:* 12

Orr, Bobby, *1970s:* 173

Ortiz-DelValle, Sandhi, *1990s:* 164

Orton, Samuel Torrey, *1920s:* 108

Oscars, *1920s:* 15, 135, 142
    See also Academy Awards

Oscar winners. *See* Academy Award winners

Oscilloscope, *1920s:* 108

OSRD. *See* Office of Scientific Research and Development

Osteoporosis, *1960s:* 120

Oswald, Lee Harvey, *1960s:* 2, 94, 100, 104

Otello, 1940s: 3

Others, 1910s: 12

Ottawa Senators, *1990s:* 176

Ouimet, Francis, *1910s:* 156, 159, 159 (ill.), 170

Our Dancing Daughters, 1920s: 15

Our Miss Brooks, 1940s: 18

Outcault, Richard, *1900s:* 16

Out of Sight, 1990s: 3, 5

Out of the Past, 1940s: 14

Over-the-counter drugs, *1910s:* 115, 127

"Over There," *1910s:* 3

Owen-Keating Bill, *1910s:* 86

Owens, Jesse, *1930s:* 153, 155, 157, 157 (ill.), 167–68

OWI. *See* Office of War Information

Oxford University, *1930s:* 50

Ozone depletion, *1980s:* 146–47, 155–5, 158 (ill.)

Ozone, destruction of, *1970s:* 140–41, 153

Ozone layer, *1910s:* 132

P

Paar, Jack, *1950s:* 17; *1960s:* 2, 6

Pacemakers, *1950s:* 114, 116

Pacific campaign, *1940s:* 72–73, 76–78, 77 (ill.), 137

Pacific Gas and Electric, *1960s:* 153

Pacific, U.S. territories in, *1900s:* 72–73

Pacifism, *1940s:* 99
    See also Antiwar protests

Packard, *1920s:* 34; *1930s:* 41
Packard, Vance, *1950s:* 30
Pact of Paris, *1920s:* 50
Paddock, Charley, *1920s:* 167
Pagers, *1950s:* 143
Pahlavi, Muhammad Reza (Shah of Iran), *1970s:* 71, 91–93
Paige, Leroy "Satchel," *1920s:* 158–59, 159 (ill.); *1930s:* 157, 157 (ill.), 160; *1960s:* 164
Painting, *1920s:* 17–18; *1930s:* 6, 8–9
Painting, 1940s: 3
Palace Theatre, *1910s:* 2
Palestine Liberation Organization (PLO), *1970s:* 71, 75
Paley, William S., *1920s:* 7, 7 (ill.)
Palmer, A. Mitchell, *1920s:* 70, 76
Palmer, Arnold, *1970s:* 174
Palmer, Jim, *1960s:* 173
Palmer, Violet, *1990s:* 163
Panama, *1900s:* 74
Panama Canal, *1900s:* 58–59, 73–74, 73 (ill.), 118; *1910s:* 24
Panama, U.S. invasion, *1980s:* 69
Pan-American Airlines, *1950s:* 137
Pan-American Airways, *1930s:* 27; *1940s:* 131
Pan-American games, *1960s:* 165
Pan-American Petroleum and Transport Company, *1920s:* 79
Pan American World Airways (Pan Am), *1990s:* 28
Panics, financial, *1900s:* 21, 23, 27–29
Pantyhose, *1960s:* 108
"Papa Don't Preach," *1980s:* 21
Papanicolaou, George N., *1920s:* 116
Paperback books, *1940s:* 11; *1950s:* 10
Pap smears, *1920s:* 115; *1950s:* 122
Paquin, Mademoiselle, *1910s:* 107
Paralysis
    from polio, *1940s:* 122, 123 (ill.)
    post-stroke, *1960s:* 124
Paramount Pictures, *1910s:* 2; *1930s:* 15
Paraphernalia (store), *1960s:* 94
Parapsychology, *1970s:* 115
Parasites, *1990s:* 139
Parathormone, *1920s:* 109
Pardee, George C., *1900s:* 111–12

Pardons, Nixon, Richard, *1970s:* 88
Pardue, Jim, *1960s:* 171
Parents' Music Resource Center, *1980s:* 9
Paris Bound, 1920s: 3
Paris, influence on fashion, *1920s:* 90, 92–94
Paris Peace Conference, *1910s:* 67
Parke, Davis and Company, *1960s:* 136
Parker, Bonnie, *1960s:* 10
Parker, Charlie, *1940s:* 5, 16 (ill.), 17; *1950s:* 15
Parker, Fess, *1950s:* 107
Parker, Francis, *1900s:* 40; *1910s:* 54
Parker, Horatio, *1910s:* 16
Parker, Jim, *1950s:* 174
Parker, Robert B., *1990s:* 5
Parkinson's disease, *1960s:* 124
Parks, *1930s:* 89
Parks, Gordon, *1970s:* 20
Parks, Rosa, *1950s:* 69, 73; *1990s:* 100
Parnell, Johnny, *1910s:* 171 (ill.)
Parnis, Mollie, *1930s:* 101–02
Parochial schools
    federal funding for, *1960s:* 57
    integration in, *1960s:* 46
Parran, Thomas, *1930s:* 115, 115 (ill.), 123; *1940s:* 114
Parthenogenesis, *1900s:* 129
Partial Nuclear Test Ban Treaty, *1960s:* 68
Particle accelerators, *1970s:* 140
The Partner, 1990s: 20
Passing Show, 1910s: 18
Pasteurization, milk, *1910s:* 112, 144
PATCO (Professional Air Traffic Controllers Organization), *1980s:* 30, 36–37, 36 (ill.)
Patent medicines. *See* Pharmaceuticals
Patent Office, *1910s:* 132
Patents, *1900s:* 3
Pathe's Weekly, 1910s: 2
Patman, Wright, *1930s:* 74
Patou, Jean, *1910s:* 107; *1920s:* 87, 92
Patriotism, *1900s:* 45; *1910s:* 96–97
    Supreme Court and, *1940s:* 44
    war bonds, *1940s:* 33
Patterson, Floyd, *1950s:* 171

Patterson, Frederick Douglas, *1940s:* 49, 49 (ill.)

Patton, George S., *1940s:* 74 (ill.)

Pavlov, Ivan, *1900s:* 118

Paul, Alice, *1910s:* 81–82, 95, 95 (ill.)

Pauling, Linus, *1980s:* 114

Pavlova, Anna, *1910s:* 2, 9

Paxton, Tom, *1960s:* 113

Payne-Aldrich Act, *1920s:* 24

Payne-Aldrich Tariff Act, *1900s:* 34

Payne, Donald, *1990s:* 100

Payroll tax deductions, *1940s:* 33, 64

Payton, Walter, *1980s:* 180–81

PCP, *1980s:* 64

PEA. *See* Progressive Education Association

Peabody Museum, *1960s:* 148

Peace activism. *See* Antiwar protests

Peacekeeping, international, *1990s:* 69–70

Peacekeeping, UNESCO, *1940s:* 52

Peace negotiations, *1900s:* 72–73

Peace negotiations, Vietnam, *1970s:* 78

Peace talks, *1960s:* 69, 79

Peacock, Michon, *1970s:* 14

Peanuts, 1950s: 2

Pearce, Louise, *1910s:* 135, 144

Pearl Harbor attack, *1940s:* 24, 64, 70, 71 (ill.), 72–73

Pearl Jam, *1990s:* 22

Peary Land, *1900s:* 123

Peary, Robert Edwin, *1900s:* 119, 123, 123 (ill.)

Pecora, Ferdinand, *1930s:* 76

Peek, George N., *1920s:* 75

"Peg o' My Heart," *1910s:* 19

Pei, I. M., *1990s:* 3

Pellagra, *1900s:* 100, 110–11; *1910s:* 112, 114, 126; *1920s:* 122

Penguin paperbacks, *1940s:* 11

Penguins, global warming, *1990s:* 150

Penicillin, *1920s:* 120–21; *1930s:* 111; *1940s:* 108–11, 118–19; *1950s:* 115, 123

Penicillin B, *1940s:* 108

Penn, Arthur, *1960s:* 10

Penney, James Cash, *1900s:* 25, 25 (ill.); *1920s:* 37

Penn State, *1960s:* 179

Pennsylvania railroad, *1960s:* 25

Pennsylvania Station, *1910s:* 100

Pennies (coins), *1900s:* 79

Penrod, 1910s: 11

Penzias, Arno, *1970s:* 144, 144 (ill.)

People magazine, *1970s:* 3

People's Church, Kansas City, Missouri, *1940s:* 86

The People's Court, 1990s: 15

People's Hospital, *1900s:* 100

People's Liberation Armed Forces in South Vietnam, *1960s:* 79

People's Republic of China. *See* China

People's Temple cult, *1970s:* 99, 116, 117 (ill.)

People's World, 1930s: 7

People United to Save Humanity (PUSH), *1970s:* 98, 103

PepsiCo, *1970s:* 26

Pepsi-Cola Company, *1900s:* 23, 37

Perez, Tony, *1960s:* 173

Perey, Margaret, *1930s:* 140

Perfume, *1950s:* 94

Pergonal, *1960s:* 134

Periodicals, *1900s:* 2, 5

Periodic table, *1930s:* 140, 143

Perisphere, *1930s:* 106–07

Perkins, Anthony, *1950s:* 176

Perkins, Frances, *1930s:* 73, 73 (ill.); *1940s:* 39, 69, 69 (ill.)

Permanent Investigations Subcommittee, *1950s:* 80

Pernocton, *1930s:* 116

Perot, H. Ross, *1960s:* 29, 29 (ill.); *1980s:* 58; *1990s:* 67, 67 (ill.)

Perrine, Charles, *1900s:* 118

Perry, Fred, *1940s:* 170

Pershing, John J., *1910s:* 70–71, 71 (ill.), 75, 77–78

Persian Gulf War, *1990s:* 64, 66–68, 69 (ill.)
    See also Gulf War Syndrome

Personal computers, *1970s:* 42–45, 141, 146; *1980s:* 33, 42–44; *1990s:* 28–29, 33, 58
    Hewlett Packard Company, *1980s:* 30

IBM, *1980s:* 146–47
revolution, *1980s:* 158–61
See also Computers
Personal income. *See* Income, personal
Personality disorders, *1940s:* 113
Person to Person, 1950s: 7
Pesotta, Rose, *1930s:* 31, 31 (ill.)
Pesticides, *1960s:* 98; *1970s:* 140, 143, 152–53
Peter and Gordon, *1960s:* 10
Peter Ibbetson, 1930s: 22
Peter, Paul and Mary, *1960s:* 113
Peterson, Oscar, *1950s:* 15
Pet rocks, *1970s:* 99
Petroleum. *See* Oil
Petroleum industry, *1900s:* 20, 29
See also Oil and gas industry
Pets, in the workplace, *1990s:* 38
Pettibone, George, *1900s:* 30
Petticoat Junction, 1960s: 19
Petting parties, *1920s:* 102
Petty, Richard, *1960s:* 170
P-59A Airacomet, *1940s:* 138
PGA Championship, *1920s:* 165–66; *1980s:* 182
PGA Player of the Year, *1980s:* 182–83
PGA Player of the Year award, *1970s:* 175
PGA (Professional Golfer's Association), *1910s:* 155–56, 170; *1920s:* 165–66; *1930s:* 164; *1940s:* 168; *1970s:* 160, 174; *1980s:* 171, 181–83
PGA Senior Championships, *1990s:* 179
Phantom of the Opera, 1980s: 12–14 13 (ill.)
Pharmaceutical companies, AIDS drugs, *1990s:* 126
Pharmaceuticals, *1900s:* 103–04; *1910s:* 112, 115, 126–28
Pharmacology, *1900s:* 104
Phenobarbital, *1920s:* 108
Phenotypes, *1900s:* 119
Philadelphia, 1990s: 128
Philadelphia Athletics, *1900s:* 138–39; *1910s:* 157, 161–63; *1930s:* 158

Philadelphia Eagles, *1950s:* 173
Philadelphia Flyers, *1970s:* 173
Philadelphia Giants, *1900s:* 146
Philadelphia, Pennsylvania, professional basketball, *1900s:* 147–48
Philadelphia Phillies, *1920s:* 156; *1980s:* 174
Philadelphia 76ers, *1960s:* 176–77; *1980s:* 177
Philadelphia SPHAs, *1910s:* 165
Philadelphia Warriors, *1950s:* 168; *1960s:* 176
Philanthropy, *1910s:* 33, 36
Carnegie, Andrew, *1900s:* 24, 40–41, 78, 118
Mellon, Andrew, *1900s:* 25
Rockefeller, John D., *1900s:* 40, 115
Southern schools and, *1900s:* 55
Straus, Nathan, *1900s:* 101
Philco TV Playhouse, 1950s: 30
Philharmonic Hall, *1960s:* 2
Philip Morris, *1950s:* 30; *1960s:* 41
Philip Morris Tobacco Company, *1990s:* 71
Philippines, *1900s:* 58, 72; *1940s:* 65, 72; *1980s:* 75
Philosophy, *1910s:* 95
Phocomelia, *1960s:* 136
Phoenix Coyotes, *1990s:* 176
Phoenix Suns, *1960s:* 176
Phonofilm, *1900s:* 122; *1920s:* 142
Photoelectric effect, *1900s:* 119
Photofacsimile machines, *1900s:* 118
Phonograph records, *1970s:* 156
Phonographs, *1900s:* 78, 119; *1930s:* 30
Photographs, color, *1900s:* 2
Photography, *1900s:* 13; *1910s:* 2, 9
Mars, *1960s:* 143
of ocean floor, *1960s:* 142
Photoheliograph, *1900s:* 133
Photon, *1920s:* 132
Photoplay, 1920s: 19
Photo-Secession, *1900s:* 13
Photovoltaic cells, *1950s:* 136
Physical abuse, children, *1980s:* 112

Physical fitness, *1910s:* 54, 56, 121; *1950s:* 128 (ill.), 131
Physicians
    African American, *1900s:* 105–07; *1940s:* 115–17
    foreign-trained, *1960s:* 120
    group practice, *1910s:* 114, 118–20
    health insurance and, *1940s:* 117–18
    house calls by, *1960s:* 128–30, 129 (ill.)
    salaries, *1980s:* 137
    shortages of, *1940s:* 111, 115–16, 120–21
    standards for, *1900s:* 103
    women, *1900s:* 108–09, 108 (ill.)
    See also Doctors
Physics, *1910s:* 132, 139–40, 146; *1930s:* 143–47
    basic forces, *1980s:* 146
    Nobel Prize, *1900s:* 119, 133; *1970s:* 150
Physiology, Nobel Prizes in, *1970s:* 135
Piaget, Jean, *1920s:* 109
Picabia, Francis, *1910s:* 12
Picasso, Pablo, *1900s:* 2; *1910s:* 2, 12; *1980s:* 3
Picketing, *1900s:* 59
Pickford, Mary, *1900s:* 3, 11; *1910s:* 3, 7, 7 (ill.), 13 (ill.), 15; *1920s:* 3
Pictorial photography, *1900s:* 13
Pierce-Arrow, *1920s:* 34; *1930s:* 41
Pierce v. *Society of Sisters of the Holy Names, 1920s:* 53
Pierrette's Wedding, 1980s: 3
Piersall, Jimmy, *1950s:* 176
Pigeons, 1910s: 8 (ill.)
Piggly Wiggly, *1910s:* 42
Pike, F. H., *1900s:* 101
Pilatus, Rob, *1980s:* 17
Pinckney, William, *1990s:* 92
Pine Ridge Reservation, *1970s:* 109–10
Pinero, Arthur Wing, *1910s:* 19
Pinkerton Detective Agency, *1930s:* 29
Pink Floyd, *1970s:* 2

Pinkham Company, *1910s:* 127
Pinky, 1960s: 105
Pins and Needles, 1930s: 22
Pinter, Harold, *1960s:* 18
Pioneer IV, 1950s: 154
Pioneer space probes, *1970s:* 140–41
Pippen, Scottie, *1990s:* 171
Piscator, Erwin, *1940s:* 20
Pissarro, Camille, *1910s:* 12
Pittman, Robert, *1980s:* 17–18
Pittsburgh Crawfords, *1930s:* 157, 160
Pittsburg Ironmen, *1950s:* 168
Pittsburgh Penguins, *1990s:* 177
Pittsburgh Pipers, *1960s:* 177
Pittsburgh Pirates, *1900s:* 138–39; *1910s:* 161; *1920s:* 157; *1950s:* 159; *1960s:* 164
Pittsburgh Steelers, *1970s:* 161, 171 72; *1980s:* 181
Pittsburgh Sun, 1920s: 145
Pizza Hut, *1950s:* 91
The Place of Science in Modern Civilization, 1910s: 149
Plague, *1900s:* 100
Plague, bubonic, *1900s:* 111–12, 111 (ill.)
Planck, Max, *1900s:* 118
Planet Hollywood restaurant, *1990s:* 92
Planets, *1910s:* 137; *1980s:* 146; *1990s:* 138
Plank, Eddie, *1910s:* 163
Planned Parenthood, *1990s:* 130
Planned Parenthood Federation, *1920s:* 102; *1940s:* 109; *1950s:* 141
Planned Parenthood Foundation of America, *1910s:* 117
Planned Parenthood v. *Danforth, 1970s:* 90
Plasma, *1900s:* 101
Plastic Man, *1940s:* 10
Plastics, *1910s:* 146
    in furniture, *1950s:* 91
Plato, *1980s:* 55
Platoon system, *1940s:* 167
Playboy, 1950s: 2, 95
Plays, *1910s:* 5
"Please Mr. Postman," *1960s:* 13

Pledge of Allegiance, *1950s:* 69

Plessy v. Ferguson, 1900s: 72; *1950s:* 48, 56–57

PLO (Palestine Liberation Organization), *1970s:* 71, 75

P. Lorillard, *1960s:* 41

PLTA (Professional Lawn Tennis Association), *1940s:* 170

Pluggers, 1900s: 16

Pluto, *1930s:* 130

Plutonium, *1940s:* 130–31, 145–46

Plymouth, *1920s:* 25, 34; *1930s:* 40

Pneumocystis carinii, 1980s: 127

Pneumonia, *1910s:* 114, 122–26; *1990s:* 126

Pocket Books, *1940s:* 11

Pocket calculators, *1970s:* 140

Podoloff, Maurice, *1940s:* 162

Poetry, *1910s:* 5, 11–12

Poetry, 1910s: 12

The Poetry Journal, 1910s: 12

Pogroms, *1910s:* 98

Poindexter, John, *1980s:* 69, 87, 89

Poiret, Paul, *1910s:* 107; *1920s:* 92

Poisonous gases, *1910s:* 135, 151

Poison Prevention Packaging Act of 1970, *1970s:* 122

Poitier, Sidney, *1960s:* 7, 7 (ill.), 97, 105

Poland, *1930s:* 69

Polanski, Roman, *1960s:* 80

Polar ice, *1960s:* 143

Polaroid film, *1930s:* 2

Polaroid Land Camera, *1940s:* 131

Police
  America as world police, *1990s:* 68–69
  Columbine High School shootings, *1990s:* 50
  in schools, *1990s:* 46
  shows, *1990s:* 16–18
  See also Los Angeles Police Department

The Police (rock group), *1980s:* 19

Police strikes, *1910s:* 25

Polio, *1900s:* 109; *1920s:* 119; *1930s:* 110–13, 122; *1940s:* 108–12, 121–23, 123 (ill.); *1950s:* 114–16, 123

Polio vaccine, *1960s:* 120, 145

Political consciousness, *1960s:* 5

Political machines, *1900s:* 66–67

Political protests, *1960s:* 36
  See also Antiwar protests

Political reform, *1900s:* 67

Political scandals, *1920s:* 67

Politics. *See* Government, politics and law

Politics versus arts, *1980s:* 8–9

Pollard, Fritz, *1980s:* 169

Pollard, Jim, *1950s:* 170

Pollock, Jackson, *1930s:* 10; *1940s:* 8–9, 9 (ill.); *1950s:* 5, 7–9, 7 (ill.)

Poll taxes, *1910s:* 82; *1940s:* 104

Pollution, *1960s:* 94, 98, 123, 126, 130; *1970s:* 90, 122; *1980s:* 140–42, 164–65; *1990s:* 138

Pollyanna, 1910s: 7

Poltergeist, 1980s: 7

Polyester clothing, *1970s:* 99

Polygraphs, *1920s:* 131, 141

Polyphenylalanine, *1960s:* 146

Polystyrene containers, *1990s:* 92

Poole, Ernest, *1910s:* 11

Pop Art, *1960s:* 5, 7, 15–17, 16 (ill.)

Popcorn, Faith, *1990s:* 97, 97 (ill.)

Pop culture, *1920s:* 103–04

Pope Pius XII, *1940s:* 86; *1950s:* 46

Popeye the Sailor, *1930s:* 18

Pop music, *1960s:* 11; *1970s:* 2

Popular culture, *1900s:* 4

Population, *1900s:* 22; *1910s:* 91

Population, school age, *1980s:* 48

Porgy and Bess, 1920s: 6; *1930s:* 3, 20, 22–23

Porky Pig, *1930s:* 3

Porky's Hare Hunt, 1930s: 3

Pornography, *1950s:* 2, 95, 107

Porter, Cole, *1920s:* 3

Porter, Edwin Stanton, *1900s:* 7, 11, 78; *1910s:* 2

Porter, James A., *1940s:* 10

Porter, William Sydney, *1910s:* 3

Portland, Oregon World's Fair, *1900s:* 79

Poseidon 3, 1960s: 143

Positron, *1930s:* 144

Possessed, 1930s: 6

Postal workers, strikes, *1970s:* 26

Post, Emily, *1920s:* 91, 91 (ill.)

The Postman Always Rings Twice, 1930s: 15

Postmodern architecture, *1960s:* 99

Postwar economy, *1940s:* 27, 89, 99–01

Post, Wiley, *1930s:* 136

Potato hybrids, *1900s:* 122

Potsdam, Germany, *1940s:* 79–80

Potter, Clare, *1930s:* 102

Potvin, Denis, *1980s:* 183

Pound, Ezra, *1910s:* 12; *1920s:* 13; *1940s:* 2–3

Poverty, *1910s:* 2; *1980s:* 30, 122
  health care and, *1960s:* 123
  malnutrition and, *1960s:* 121
  settlement houses and *1900s:* 47–48
  war on, *1960s:* 68, 70, 82, 85

Povich, Maury, *1990s:* 14

Powell, Adam Clayton, *1940s:* 79

Powell, Colin, *1990s:* 67, 67 (ill.), 69

Power plants, nuclear, *1950s:* 25, 136

Powers, Francis Gary, *1960s:* 76

Powers, Jimmy, *1950s:* 176

Poynter, Nelson, *1940s:* 13–14

Prairie Style, *1900s:* 5, 96; *1930s:* 93

Praise the Lord (PTL), *1980s:* 97, 116

Prayer in schools, *1960s:* 46; *1980s:* 48, 51, 58; *1990s:* 44

"The Preacher and the Slave," *1910s:* 94

The Preakness, *1910s:* 172; *1920s:* 166

Preakness Stakes, *1930s:* 165

Precisionism, *1920s:* 18

Prefabricated housing, *1920s:* 87, 101

Pregnancy
  employment and, *1970s:* 27
  ultrasound tests and, *1950s:* 115

Pregnancy termination. *See* Abortion

Prejudice, *1920s:* 66

Prelude to War, 1940s: 14

Premature babies, *1960s:* 121

Preminger, Otto, *1950s:* 15

Prenatal care, *1910s:* 112, 126

Prendergast, Maurice, *1910s:* 8

The Preppy Handbook, 1980s: 96, 107

Prep Schools, *1900s:* 48

Preschool programs, *1970s:* 105

Prescription drugs. *See* Pharmaceuticals

"Preservation of Democracy," *1940s:* 48

Presidential candidates, *1900s:* 24; *1970s:* 81

Presidential elections, *1900s:* 58; *1910s:* 68, 83–85; *1940s:* 68; *1950s:* 83–86, 145–46; *1960s:* 69, 71; *1970s:* 81; *1980s:* 73, 76
  McCarthy, Eugene in, *1960s:* 73
  1960, *1960s:* 19–20, 68, 82–84
  1964, *1960s:* 85
  1968, *1960s:* 86–89
  Nixon, Richard in, *1960s:* 19–20, 68, 73
  televised debates, *1960s:* 19–20, 68, 83–84, 83 (ill.)
  Wallace, George C. in, *1960s:* 73, 88

Presidential power, *1900s:* 68, 70; *1930s:* 77

Presidential pardons, Iran contra scandal, *1990s:* 64

Presidential Succession Act, *1940s:* 65

President's Commission on the Status of Women, *1960s:* 94

President's Committee on Civil Rights, *1940s:* 45, 104

President's National Advisory Committee on Women, *1970s:* 102

Presidents, tenure limited, *1950s:* 68
  See also specific Presidents

Presley, Elvis, *1950s:* 3, 7, 7 (ill.), 15; *1960s:* 10; *1970s:* 3; *1990s:* 5, 26

Prestone, *1920s:* 24

Preven Emergency Contraceptive Kit, *1990s:* 117

Preventive health examinations, *1910s:* 112

Price Control Bill, *1940s:* 24

Price controls, *1940s:* 24, 27; *1950s:* 39–40

Price-fixing, steel, *1960s:* 24, 37

The Price is Right, 1950s: 64

Price, Leontyne, *1960s:* 2

Price Tower, *1950s:* 97 (ill.)

The Pride of St. Louis, 1950s: 176

Pridgett, Gertrude, *1900s:* 5, 14

Primary elections, *1900s:* 58

Primordial soup, *1960s:* 150–51

Prince Edward County, Virginia, *1960s:* 46

Princeton Invitation Meet, *1930s:* 168–69

Princeton University, *1910s:* 46

Princeton University Institute for Advanced Studies, *1930s:* 130

Princeton University's Physics Colloquium, *1910s:* 140

Prince Valiant, 1930s: 11

The Principles of Mathematics, 1900s: 118

Principles of Rural School Administration, 1920s: 47

The Principles of Scientific Management, 1910s: 149

Print media, *1900s:* 5

Prisoners
  convicts, *1910s:* 87, 126
  war, *1910s:* 78

Prison riots, *1970s:* 92–93

Private schools, *1990s:* 47, 51, 54–55

Proctor and Gamble, *1930s:* 12; *1960s:* 39; *1980s:* 131

Production Code (films), *1960s:* 5, 9

Production methods, *1900s:* 34–36, 35 (ill.), 36 (ill.), 91

Product labeling, *1900s:* 32

Product safety, *1900s:* 60
  See also Food safety regulations

Professional Air Traffic Controllers Organization (PATCO), *1980s:* 30, 36–37, 36 (ill.)

Professional athletes, *1900s:* 141

Professional Bowlers Association, *1990s:* 164

Professional Golfer's Association (PGA), *1910s:* 155–56, 170; *1920s:* 165–66; *1930s:* 164; *1940s:* 168;

1970s: 160, 174; *1980s:* 171, 181–83

Professional Lawn Tennis Association (PLTA), *1940s:* 170

Programming languages, *1960s:* 152; *1970s:* 44–45

Progressive, 1900s: 62

Progressive education, *1910s:* 48, 50–51, 54–56; *1920s:* 46, 48, 51, 55–56; *1930s:* 46, 49, 51, 56–58, 60; *1940s:* 47, 54

Progressive Education Association (PEA), *1910s:* 47, 50, 54; *1930s:* 46; *1940s:* 44

Progressive Movement, *1910s:* 29, 32, 114, 125

Progressive Party, *1910s:* 83–84; *1930s:* 74–76

Progressives, *1900s:* 46–49, 62

Progressives, in education, *1970s:* 50

Progressive taxation, *1940s:* 33

Prohibition, *1910s:* 25, 69, 82–83; *1920s:* 24, 64–65, 67, 72–74, 86, 103; *1930s:* 18, 30, 68, 71, 85, 88, 92

Project Bumper, *1940s:* 139

Project Gemini, *1960s:* 146, 158

Project Independence, *1970s:* 32

Project Mercury, *1960s:* 146, 156–58

Project Ozma, *1960s:* 150–51

Project Soyuz, *1960s:* 159

Project Vostok, *1960s:* 144, 156–58

Prokofiev, Sergei, *1920s:* 2

Prokofiev, Sergey, *1910s:* 16

Prolactin, *1920s:* 109

Proletarian fiction, *1930s:* 12–14

Prometheus, 1910s: 3

Promontory Apartments, Chicago, Illinois, *1940s:* 92

Promoters, in boxing, *1940s:* 165–66

Prontosil, *1930s:* 120

Propaganda, *1940s:* 13–14

Proposition 48, student athletes, *1980s:* 58–60, 59 (ill.)

Proposition 209, *1990s:* 59–60

Prostitution, *1910s:* 69

Protease inhibitors, *1990s:* 125

Protein, dietary, *1910s:* 112

Protein, synthetic, *1960s:* 146
Protestant Church, *1910s:* 97–98
Protestantism, *1940s:* 99–101; *1950s:*
    91, 95
Protestants, *1930s:* 100
Protests, *1930s:* 74
Protocols, *1990s:* 146
Proton, *1930s:* 143
Protosil, *1940s:* 118
Proulx, E. Annie, *1990s:* 5
Providence Steamrollers, *1950s:* 168
Prudhoe Bay, *1970s:* 34–35
Pryor, Richard, *1970s:* 7, 7 (ill.)
Psychiatry, *1910s:* 116; *1940s:* 110,
    113, 120, 125
Psychoanalysis, *1900s:* 131–32; *1910s:*
    135, 146–47; *1930s:* 114, 123
Psychoanalytic Institute, *1930s:* 114
Psychobiology, *1910s:* 116
Psychological Types, 1920s: 108
Psychology, *1900s:* 123, 131–32,
    1960s: 50, 125
Psychology, behavioral, *1940s:* 113
Psychology education, *1970s:* 63
Psychosurgery, *1940s:* 123–24
The PTL Club, 1970s: 102
PTL Network, *1970s:* 102
PTL (Praise the Lord), *1980s:* 97, 116
Public Broadcasting Act, *1960s:* 31–32
Public Citizen, *1970s:* 30
Public education, *1910s:* 46, 48–49
Public Education in the United States,
    1920s: 55
Public Enemy, *1990s:* 23
The Public Enemy, 1930s: 83
Public health, *1900s:* 102, 105
    biological sciences and, *1910s:*
        144–45, 145 (ill.)
    education, *1910s:* 56, 117
    government and, *1910s:* 124–26
    laboratories, *1910s:* 125
    medical checkups, *1910s:* 51, 112
    physical fitness, *1910s:* 54, 56, 121
    U.S. Public Health Service, *1910s:*
        113–16, 121, 126
Public Health Service, *1930s:* 113;
    1940s: 109, 121; *1960s:* 121; *1970s:*
    137

Public Health Service, AIDS preven-
    tion and, *1980s:* 124
Public Health Service Division of
    Industrial Hygiene, *1910s:* 113
Publicity Act, *1910s:* 66
Public Law 584, *1940s:* 45, 52
Public Law 601, *1940s:* 81
Public libraries, *1900s:* 2, 24; *1910s:* 2,
    94
Public radio, *1960s:* 114
Public schools, *1940s:* 52
    versus Catholic schools, *1960s:*
        57
    See also Schools
Public television, in schools, *1970s:* 59
Public Television Laboratory, 1960s: 31
Public Works Administration (PWA),
    1930s: 78–79, 98
Public works bill, *1960s:* 24
Publishers' Weekly, 1990s: 18
Puccini, Giacomo, *1900s:* 2
Puerto Rican nationalists, *1950s:* 68, 81
Puerto Rico, *1900s:* 72
Pulitzer, Joseph, *1900s:* 16
Pulitzer Prizes, *1910s:* 11, 16; *1950s:* 9
    A Chorus Line, 1970s: 15
    drama, *1920s:* 9
    fiction, *1920s:* 13; *1960s:* 18
    Of Thee I Sing, 1920s: 6
    O'Neill, Eugene, *1920s:* 7
    Warren, Robert Penn, *1940s:* 12
    Wharton, Edith, *1900s:* 7
    Wilson, Edward O., *1970s:* 144
Pullman Company, *1900s:* 24
Pulp fiction, *1920s:* 19; *1930s:* 14
Pulp Fiction, 1990s: 4, 7, 9
Pulp magazines, *1940s:* 13
Pulsars, *1960s:* 150
"Pulse Transfer Controlling Device,"
    1960s: 36
Punk fashions, *1970s:* 99
Punk music, *1990s:* 5
Punk rock, *1970s:* 2, 5, 13–14
Pure Food and Drug Act, *1900s:* 3, 21,
    33, 59, 65, 101, 105; *1910s:* 112,
    127; *1930s:* 27, 121
Pure science, versus applied, *1940s:*
    133

Puritanism, in performing arts, *1900s:* 14–15

PUSH. *See* People United to Save Humanity

Push-through tabs, *1970s:* 140

"Put Your Hand in the Hand (of the Man from Galilee)," *1970s:* 13

Puzo, Mario, *1970s:* 2, 7, 18

Puzzled America, 1930s: 12

PWA (Public Works Administration), *1930s:* 78–79, 98

Pyrex, *1910s:* 133

Q

Quacks, medical, *1900s:* 114

Quadricycle, *1900s:* 124

Quaker Oats, *1930s:* 12

Quaker Oats Company, *1900s:* 23

Quant, Mary, *1960s:* 98, 111–12

Quantum theory, *1900s:* 118

Quarks, *1960s:* 146

Quarry, Jerry, *1970s:* 160

Quasars, *1960s:* 149; *1980s:* 147

Quebec conference, *1940s:* 76

Quebec Nordiques, *1990s:* 176

Queen Latifah, *1980s:* 24

Quigley, Joan, *1980s:* 78

Quilts, AIDS, *1980s:* 123; *1990s:* 127 (ill.)

Quimby, Harriet, *1910s:* 132, 135, 138–39

Quinlan, Karen Ann, *1970s:* 123–24, 127–28, 128 (ill.)

Quotas
    educational, *1970s:* 65
    employment, *1970s:* 42, 49
    for minority medical students, *1940s:* 116–17

Quo Vadis, 1950s: 106

QVC Network, *1980s:* 103

R

Rabies, *1900s:* 100; *1960s:* 121

Race relations, *1930s:* 77–78

Race relations, O. J. Simpson trial, *1990s:* 83–88, 86 (ill.)

Racial discrimination
    Africa and, *1910s:* 91
    Bethune, Mary McLeod on, *1940s:* 90
    education, *1910s:* 47, 49, 51, 60–62, 61 (ill.), 62 (ill.); *1970s:* 48
    employment, *1970s:* 26, 42
    in federal government, *1940s:* 86, 103
    in housing, *1940s:* 100
    Jim Crow Laws, *1910s:* 69, 82, 96
    in medical schools, *1940s:* 115–17
    in military, *1940s:* 104
    race riots, *1910s:* 91
    racism, *1910s:* 14, 36, 96
    in sports, *1940s:* 153
    in steel industry, *1960s:* 68
    in voting, *1960s:* 75
    See also African Americans; Civil Rights movement

Racism, *1900s:* 71–72, 71 (ill.), 85–86; *1920s:* 66, 82–83; *1960s:* 68; *1970s:* 48–49, 166–67; *1980s:* 52; *1990s:* 29, 44, 80, 93
    McDuffie, Arthur, *1980s:* 84–85
    in minstrel shows, *1900s:* 13
    in Olympics, *1900s:* 153
    in plays, *1900s:* 3
    school reading, *1980s:* 56
    South Africa, *1980s:* 62
    in sports, *1900s:* 140–41, 143
    See also African Americans; Civil Rights movement; Ku Klux Klan

Radar, *1940s:* 130, 142–43; *1960s:* 143

Radiation belt, *1950s:* 137

Radiation hazards, *1970s:* 155–57

Radiation therapy, *1940s:* 110; *1950s:* 129–31; *1960s:* 120

Radio, *1900s:* 79, 81, 118–20, 122, 127–29, 128 (ill.)
    public, *1960s:* 114
    television and, *1940s:* 18

Radio active-potassium dating system, *1950s:* 148–49

Radioactivity, *1900s:* 118

Radio broadcasting, *1910s:* 3, 5, 20–21; *1990s:* 3–5, 11–13

Radiocarbon-dating method, *1940s:* 131

Radio communications, *1910s:* 134, 147–48
    short-wave, *1910s:* 133
    Titanic, 1910s: 151

Radio City Music Hall, *1930s:* 2, 98

Radio Corporation of America (RCA), *1900s:* 129; *1910s:* 21, 133; *1920s:* 7, 24–25, 36, 38; *1930s:* 130, 134, 147; *1950s:* 142

Radio dramas, *1950s:* 2

Radio emissions, *1950s:* 136

Radioimmunoassay (RIA), *1970s:* 126

Radio industry, *1920s:* 35–36
    Federal Communications Commission, *1920s:* 34
    FM radio, *1920s:* 128
    impact on music, *1930s:* 18–20
    impact on sports, *1930s:* 154
    photograph transmission, *1920s:* 128
    presidential elections and, *1920s:* 145
    programming, *1920s:* 7, 36, 144–45; *1930s:* 2–3
    receivers, *1920s:* 144–45, 144 (ill.)
    transmitters, *1920s:* 24
    Zenith, *1920s:* 24

Radio pagers, *1950s:* 143

Radios, CB, *1970s:* 99

Radiosonde, *1930s:* 144

Radios, transistor, *1950s:* 136

Radiotelephones, *1910s:* 133

Radio tubes, *1910s:* 136

Rad Lab (MIT), *1940s:* 130, 142–43

Radon, *1980s:* 140–41

Raggedy Ann dolls, *1910s:* 91

Ragtime, *1900s:* 2, 5–7, 13–14, 78

Raiders of the Lost Ark, 1980s: 7, 9

Rail Passenger Service Act of 1970, *1970s:* 39

The Railroad Control Act, *1910s:* 25

Railroad industry, *1950s:* 24

Railroad Labor Board, *1920s:* 24

Railroads, *1900s:* 32–33, 64–65; *1910s:* 30, 38, 76; *1920s:* 24–25, 30; *1930s:* 139–40; *1960s:* 25
    administration, *1910s:* 25
    deregulation, *1980s:* 35
    safety, *1910s:* 86–87
    war goods, *1910s:* 25

Railroad strikes, *1940s:* 24

Railway Rate Regulation Act, *1900s:* 32–33

Rain, artificial, *1940s:* 143

Rainey, Ma, *1900s:* 5, 14

Rainfall, global warming, *1990s:* 139

The Rainmaker, 1990s: 20

Rain Man, 1980s: 9

Raising Hell, 1980s: 24

Ramadan War, *1970s:* 31–32

Ramones, *1970s:* 2, 14

Randolph, A. Philip, *1920s:* 25

Randolph, Joyce, *1950s:* 17, 18 (ill.)

Random access memory (RAM), *1980s:* 146–47

Rand, Sally, *1930s:* 2, 106

Ranger 8, 1960s: 143

The Range Rider, 1950s: 107

Rankin State Prison Farm, *1910s:* 126

Ransom, John Crowe, *1930s:* 14

Rapid transit, *1900s:* 20

Rap music, *1980s:* 23–24; *1990s:* 3, 5, 7, 23, 111

Rapp-Condert Committee, *1940s:* 51

Rationing, *1940s:* 24–25, 30–31, 87

Rationing, of gas, *1970s:* 27

Rauschenberg, Robert, *1960s:* 16

Ray, Man, *1920s:* 2–3, 13

Rayon, *1910s:* 90; *1950s:* 90

Raytheon Company, *1950s:* 136

Razors, *1900s:* 78, 18–119

RCA Building, *1930s:* 98

RCA (Radio Corporation of America), *1900s:* 129; *1910s:* 21, 133; *1920s:* 7, 24–25, 36, 38; *1930s:* 130, 134, 147; *1940s:* 87; *1950s:* 142; *1960s:* 37, 143

"Reach Out I'll Be There," *1960s:* 14

Reading, *1950s:* 47, 60–61, 90; *1980s:* 48

Reading, Oprah's Book clubs, *1990s:* 3, 18–19

Reagan, Nancy, *1980s:* 63, 78, 96, 102

Reagan, Ronald, *1950s:* 176; *1960s:* 63, 87; *1970s:* 94; *1980s:* 75 (ill.), 80 (ill.); *1990s:* 106, 116, 126
  AIDS, *1980s:* 123
  arts funding cuts, *1980s:* 5, 8
  assassination attempt, *1980s:* 68, 78
  bilingual education, *1980s:* 61
  church versus state, *1980s:* 50–51, 54, 58
  communism, *1980s:* 70–71, 74–75
  conservatism, *1980s:* 98
  consumerism, *1980s:* 104
  creationism, *1980s:* 48, 54, 58
  deregulation, *1980s:* 35
  drug crisis, *1980s:* 109
  economics of, *1980s:* 31–32, 71, 81–85
  education, *1980s:* 50
  foreign policy, *1980s:* 70–71, 74–75
  homeless crisis, *1980s:* 111–12
  inauguration, *1980s:* 96
  Iran-Contra scandal, *1980s:* 68–69
  labor unions, *1980s:* 36–37
  military build-up, *1980s:* 70–71, 74–81, 99, 113
  NASA, *1980s:* 152, 154
  national debt, *1980s:* 31–32, 81–85
  school lunch programs, *1980s:* 48
  Social Security System, *1980s:* 30
  South Africa and, *1980s:* 62
  televised addresses, *1980s:* 30

Real estate, *1940s:* 87, 100–03

Realism, in literature, *1900s:* 6, 8; *1940s:* 12

Reality television, *1990s:* 13–18

Realms of Being, 1910s: 95

Reapportionment, *1920s:* 79

Reattachment, of limbs, *1960s:* 120, 122, 127

Recalls, automobiles, *1960s:* 25

Recessions, *1960s:* 26; *1970s:* 27

Reconstruction Finance Corporation (RFC), *1930s:* 26, 68, 70, 76; *1940s:* 37

Reconstruction, postwar, *1940s:* 25, 27, 35, 38–39, 52

Reconstructive surgery, *1910s:* 128

Recording industry, *1900s:* 14; *1950s:* 136, 138, 152

Record players, *1970s:* 156

Records (music), *1940s:* 131

Red baiting, *1930s:* 60

Red Baron. *See* Richthofen, Manfred von

Red Cross. *See* American Red Cross

Red decade, *1930s:* 104

Redding, Otis, *1960s:* 12, 15

Red Harvest, 1920s: 19

Red Hot Peppers, *1920s:* 3

The Red Network, 1930s: 60

Redon, Odilon, *1910s:* 12

Red rider, *1930s:* 47, 61

Red scare, *1910s:* 79–80, 121; *1920s:* 49, 70–71
  See also Cold war

Reeb, James, *1960s:* 101–02

Reebok, *1980s:* 96

Reed, John, *1910s:* 7, 7 (ill.), 98

Reed, Lou, *1970s:* 13

Reed v. *Reed, 1970s:* 98

Reed, Walter, *1900s:* 104, 104 (ill.)

Reed, Willis, *1960s:* 177; *1970s:* 169

Reeve, Christopher, *1990s:* 117–19

Reeves, Martha, *1960s:* 15

Reform movement, *1910s:* 68, 120–23

Refrigerators, *1910s:* 134, 144; *1930s:* 141, 141 (ill.)

Refugees, *1940s:* 65

Regan, Donald, *1980s:* 78

Regents of the University of California v. *Bakke, 1970s:* 42, 64–65

Regionalism
  in art, *1930s:* 4–5, 8
  in fiction, *1930s:* 14

Regionalist fiction, *1940s:* 12

Regional theaters, *1960s:* 2, 114

Regret (horse), *1910s:* 172

Rehnquist, William, *1990s:* 63

Reidpath, Charles, *1910s:* 174
Reincarnation, *1980s:* 118
Reinhardt, Adolph "Ad," *1940s:* 9
Relativity, theory of, *1900s:* 119, 123, 133; *1960s:* 146
The Relief, 1910s: 113
Religion, *1900s:* 87–88; *1930s:* 98–100; *1940s:* 86–87; *1970s:* 101–02, 113–16
    church attendance, *1940s:* 89, 99–01
    fundamentalism, *1920s:* 102–03
    intolerance, *1920s:* 66
    radio station of, *1920s:* 91
    revival, *1940s:* 99–01
    in school, *1920s:* 47, 87; *1940s:* 45, 47, 60
    socialism and, *1940s:* 91
Religion in schools. *See* Church versus state
Religious groups, censorship and, *1980s:* 54–56, 97, 115–16, 116 (ill.)
Religious television. *See* Televangelism
Rely tampons, *1980s:* 122, 131
Remington Arms Company, *1930s:* 130
The Remington Honor Medal, *1910s:* 119
Remington-Rand Corporation, *1950s:* 43, 136, 145
Renaissance Ballroom, *1930s:* 161
Renaissance Unity church, *1990s:* 97
Renault, *1960s:* 30
Renfrew Center, *1980s:* 122–23
Renoir, Pierre Auguste, *1910s:* 12
Reno, Janet, *1990s:* 67, 67 (ill.), 83
Repetitive stress injury (RSI), *1980s:* 139
Repression, of sexual desires, *1900s:* 131–32
Republican Party, *1910s:* 38, 68, 83; *1920s:* 66–67
The Republic of South Africa, *1980s:* 27, 62
Republic of Vietnam, *1990s:* 64
Republic Steel, *1930s:* 27
A Requiem for a Nun, 1950s: 9

Research
    corporate laboratories, *1900s:* 118
    grants, *1950s:* 47
    medical, *1900s:* 100–02, 109; *1910s:* 119, 125; *1950s:* 114–15; *1970s:* 137
    National Science Foundation, *1950s:* 54
    scientific, *1900s:* 118, 120–21
    in space, *1970s:* 146
Reservoir Dogs, 1990s: 7
Resident cavity magnetron, *1940s:* 142
Resignation, Nixon, Richard, *1970s:* 71, 73, 82–83, 88
Resnik, Judith A., *1980s:* 152
"Respect," *1960s:* 15
Resta, Dario, *1910s:* 160
Restaurants, fast food, *1950s:* 92, 97
Resuscitators, infants, *1950s:* 115
Retail industry, *1910s:* 41–42; *1960s:* 26, 33–35, 34 (ill.)
Retail stores, *1900s:* 25
Retail trade, *1920s:* 36–37, 86
Retirement benefits, temporary employees, *1990s:* 36
Retraining, *1960s:* 82
Retton, Mary Lou, *1980s:* 171, 189, 188 (ill.)
Return of the Jedi, 1980s: 2, 9, 12
Reuther, Walter P., *1930s:* 38, 39 (ill.), 59; *1950s:* 28, 28 (ill.), 32, 33 (ill.)
Revascularization, *1960s:* 127
Revenue Act, *1920s:* 65; *1940s:* 33
Reverse discrimination, *1970s:* 49, 52, 64–65
Reverse discrimination, in schools, *1990s:* 45
Revival meetings, *1920s:* 91
Revlon, *1950s:* 102
Revolta, Johnny, *1930s:* 164
Revson, Charles, *1950s:* 102
Revues, *1920s:* 9–10, 86
Reynolds, Debbie, *1950s:* 13
Reynolds, James, *1900s:* 88
Reynolds Metals, *1950s:* 36

RFC. *See* Reconstruction Finance Corporation

Rhapsody in Blue, 1920s: 3, 6

Rheumatoid arthritis, *1910s:* 116; *1930s:* 110

Rh factor, *1920s:* 113; *1930s:* 115

Rhode Island, *1990s:* 117

Rhodes, Dusty, *1950s:* 167

Rhumba Bowl, *1930s:* 163

Rhythm and blues, *1940s:* 17

RIA (Radioimmunoassay), *1970s:* 126

Ribonucleic acid (RNA), *1960s:* 151

Rice, Alice Hegan, *1900s:* 5

Rice, Elmer, *1920s:* 2–4

Rice, Grantland, *1920s:* 162

Rice, Jerry, *1980s:* 181; *1990s:* 164, 175

Rice, Tim, *1970s:* 2

Richard Pryor Live, 1970s: 7

Richardson, J. P. "The Big Bopper," *1950s:* 3; *1960s:* 10

Richardson-Merrill, *1960s:* 125, 136–37

Richards, Renee, *1970s:* 161

Richards, Theodore, *1910s:* 133, 137, 137 (ill.)

Rich Man, Poor Man, 1970s: 10, 23

Richter, Charles, *1930s:* 143, 145

Richter Scale, *1930s:* 143, 145 (ill.)

Richthofen, Manfred von, *1910s:* 138

Rickard, Tex, *1920s:* 161

Rickenbacker, Eddie, *1910s:* 138

Rickenbacker, Edward V., *1920s:* 29, 29 (ill.)

Ricketts, Howard Taylor, *1900s:* 101

Rickey, Branch, *1940s:* 153–54, 157, 162

Ride, Sally K., *1980s:* 150–51 150 (ill.)

Riegels, Roy, *1920s:* 149

Rigby, Cathy, *1970s:* 178 (ill.)

Riggin, Aileen, *1920s:* 151, 167

Riggs, Bobby, *1940s:* 170; *1970s:* 130, 160, 163–64, 176

Right-to-die, *1970s:* 123–24, 127–28

Right to privacy, *1970s:* 88–89

Riis, Jacob, *1900s:* 113, 113 (ill.); *1910s:* 69, 85

Riley, Richard W., *1990s:* 48, 48 (ill.), 55

Rio, 1980s: 18

Riots

    Anti-Riot Act, *1960s:* 115

    Atlanta, *1900s:* 44, 59

    Brownsville, Texas, *1900s:* 79

    police, *1970s:* 98

    prison, *1970s:* 92–93

    race, *1900s:* 85; *1910s:* 91; *1940s:* 24, 86, 104; *1960s:* 46, 69, 95, 101 (ill.), 102–03

    Rodney King incident, *1990s:* 64

Ripken, Carl, Jr., *1980s:* 168, 175 (ill.); *1990s:* 163, 165, 169

Risberg, Swede, *1910s:* 162; *1920s:* 155

The Rise of David Levinsky, 1910s: 11

Ritchie, Lionel, *1980s:* 24

Ritter, Joseph E., *1940s:* 60

Rivera, Diego, *1930s:* 10

Rivera, Geraldo, *1990s:* 13, 15

Rivers, Thomas Milton, *1920s:* 113

R. J. Reynolds, *1960s:* 41

R. J. Reynolds Tobacco Company, *1990s:* 71

RKO Studios, *1940s:* 3

RNA (ribonucleic acid), *1960s:* 151

Road construction, *1910s:* 66, 142

Road maps, *1900s:* 78

Road rage, *1990s:* 107

Roads, *1920s:* 30–31

    condition of, *1900s:* 91

Robbins, Harold, *1970s:* 9

Robbins, Jerome, *1940s:* 17

The Robe, 1950s: 106

Roberts, Glenn "Fireball," *1960s:* 170

Robertson, Alice, *1920s:* 64

Robertson, Marion Pat, *1980s:* 97, 116

Roberts, Oral, *1980s:* 115

Robinson, David, *1990s:* 172

Robinson, Edward G., *1930s:* 16

Robinson, Frank, *1950s:* 164; *1960s:* 169, 169 (ill.), 173; *1970s:* 160, 163; *1980s:* 168

Robinson House, Williamstown, Massachusetts, *1940s:* 90

Robinson, Jackie, *1920s:* 157, 160; *1940s:* 153, 157, 157 (ill.), 161; *1950s:* 159, 164

Robinson, Joseph T., *1920s:* 78

Robinson, Smokey, *1960s:* 13

Robinson, Sugar Ray, *1940s:* 152, 165–66; *1950s:* 158, 172

Robison, James, *1980s:* 116

Robots, computerized, *1980s:* 159

Robustelli, Andy, *1950s:* 174

Rochester Royals, *1950s:* 169

Rock and Roll Hall of Fame, *1980s:* 3

Rock and roll music, *1950s:* 15–16; *1960s:* 3, 6–13, 108; *1990s:* 3, 5

Rockefeller Center, *1930s:* 2, 89, 98, 114

Rockefeller Foundation, *1910s:* 33; *1920s:* 122

Rockefeller Institute, *1930s:* 111; *1940s:* 139

Rockefeller Institute for Medical Research, *1900s:* 100; *1920s:* 112

Rockefeller Institute Hospital, *1910s:* 112

Rockefeller, John D., *1900s:* 40, 64, 115; *1910s:* 32 (ill.)

Rockefeller, John D., Jr., *1930s:* 98

Rockefeller, Nelson, *1960s:* 82, 85, 87; *1970s:* 70, 93

Rockefeller Plaza, *1930s:* 147

Rockefeller Sanitary Commission, *1900s:* 115; *1910s:* 126

Rocketry, *1920s:* 129; *1930s:* 135

Rockets, *1940s:* 131, 133, 139

Rocket science, *1910s:* 136

Rock festivals, *1960s:* 12

Rock music, *1970s:* 2, 11–12, 14 *See also* Punk rock

Rock musicals, *1960s:* 18–19

Rockne, Knute, *1910s:* 168; *1920s:* 151, 153, 153 (ill.)

"Rock the Boat," *1970s:* 15

Rockwell, George Lincoln, *1960s:* 101

The Rocky Horror Picture Show, 1970s: 3, 19

Rocky Mountain spotted fever, *1900s:* 101

"Rock Your Baby," *1970s:* 15

Roddenberry, Gene, *1990s:* 139

Rodgers, Jimmie "Singing Breakman," *1930s:* 18

Rodgers, Richard, *1940s:* 17

Rodin, Auguste, *1910s:* 12

Rodman, Dennis, *1990s:* 171

Roe v. *Wade, 1970s:* 70, 73, 75, 89–91, 106, 122; *1980s:* 104

Roffe, Diann, *1980s:* 168

Rogan, Wilbur "Bullet," *1920s:* 160

The Rogers Commission, *1980s:* 152, 154

Rogers, Ginger, *1920s:* 10; *1930s:* 18, 89

Rogers, Richard, *1920s:* 8

Rogers, Roy, *1930s:* 18

Rogers, Will, *1910s:* 5, 18; *1920s:* 9; *1930s:* 78

Rogue River Bridge, *1930s:* 138

Rolex, *1980s:* 104

Rolling Stone, 1960s: 3, 7

The Rolling Stones, *1960s:* 5, 10–11, 95

Rollins College, *1930s:* 59

Rollins, William Herbert, *1900s:* 100

"Roll On, Columbia," *1930s:* 3

Roman Catholic Church. *See* Catholicism

Romances (comic books), *1940s:* 10

Romances (novels), *1900s:* 5

The Romantics, *1980s:* 18

Romeo Void, *1980s:* 18

Rommel, Erwin, *1940s:* 75

The Ronettes, *1960s:* 11

Room 222, 1970s: 21

Roosevelt, Alice, *1900s:* 93

Roosevelt, Eleanor, *1920s:* 50; *1930s:* 50, 73, 73 (ill.), 88

Roosevelt, Franklin D., *1910s:* 28, 85; *1920s:* 50, 65, 76; *1930s:* 26, 76, 89, 98, 146; *1940s:* 66–67, 69, 69 (ill.); *1950s:* 71, 77, 116, 127; *1980s:* 39
    air travel and, *1930s:* 136
    architecture and, *1930s:* 98
    atomic bomb and, *1930s:* 131, 144–47
    banking industry and, *1930s:* 41–42

baseball and, *1930s:* 153

on baseball during war, *1940s:* 161

Beard, Charles A. and, *1930s:* 50

business incentives, *1940s:* 30

communism and, *1930s:* 60

death of, *1940s:* 86–87

declaration of war, *1940s:* 24, 64

election of, *1930s:* 68, 70, 74

on equal rights, *1940s:* 103

European invasion strategy, *1940s:* 75–76

on films, *1940s:* 13

Fireside Chats, *1930s:* 2, 68, 76

first televised address, *1930s:* 106, 147

foreign policy, *1930s:* 80–81

fourth term, *1940s:* 64

Great Depression and, *1930s:* 34–43

Japanese internment camps, *1940s:* 64

Landon, Alf and, *1930s:* 72

National Foundation for Infantile Paralysis, *1930s:* 111

polio and, *1940s:* 121

red rider and, *1930s:* 47

re-election of, *1930s:* 69

Stalin, Joseph and, *1940s:* 79

support of allies, *1940s:* 64

war against crime, *1930s:* 83–85

World War I veterans and, *1930s:* 76

World War II and, *1930s:* 69; *1940s:* 70–75

Yalta conference, *1940s:* 76

See also Manhattan Project; New Deal

Roosevelt, Theodore, *1900s:* 3, 58, 61, 63, 63 (ill.), 68, 69 (ill.), 70; *1910s:* 68, 83–84; *1930s:* 76

African Americans and, *1900s:* 78

anthracite coal strike and, *1900s:* 26–27

antitrust laws and, *1900s:* 34, 64–65, 74

on college football, *1900s:* 139, 152

environmental conservation, *1900s:* 68

on foreign affairs, *1900s:* 72–74

peace talks, *1900s:* 59

presidential power, *1900s:* 68, 70

on sports, *1900s:* 140

Square Deal of, *1900s:* 32

Root Glass Company, *1910s:* 91

Root, Jack, *1900s:* 138

Roots, 1970s: 3–5, 23, 23 (ill.), 108

Roots: The Next Generations, 1970s: 23

Rorschach, Hermann, *1920s:* 121–22

Rorschach test, *1920s:* 121–22, 121 (ill.)

Roseanne, 1980s: 16

Rose Bowl, *1900s:* 138; *1920s:* 149, 153

Rose, Mauri, *1940s:* 158

Rosenberg, Ethel, *1950s:* 68, 71, 78–79

Rosenberg, Julius, *1950s:* 68, 71, 78–79

Rosenquist, James, *1960s:* 16

Rosenthal, Ida Cohen, *1920s:* 94

Rosenwald, Julius, *1930s:* 62

Rose, Pete, *1960s:* 164, 173; *1970s:* 161; *1980s:* 169

Rose, Ralph, *1900s:* 153

Rose, Reginald, *1950s:* 31

Rosewall, Ken, *1970s:* 176; *1980s:* 185

"Rosie the Riveter," *1940s:* 97 (ill.)

Ross, Barney, *1930s:* 162

Ross, Diana, *1960s:* 14; *1970s:* 20; *1980s:* 21

Ross, Edward Alsworth, *1910s:* 29, 29 (ill.)

Rossellini, Roberto, *1950s:* 106

Rossi, Bruno, *1940s:* 133

Ross, Katharine, *1960s:* 9

Ross, Nellie Taylor, *1920s:* 65

Rossner, Judith, *1970s:* 10

Rotary Club, *1900s:* 20, 78

Roth, Henry, *1930s:* 13

Rothko, Mark, *1930s:* 10; *1940s:* 2, 8–9; *1950s:* 8

Roth, Phillip, *1950s:* 9

Roth v. *United States, 1950s:* 106

Rotten, Johnny, *1970s:* 14–15

Rough Riders, *1900s:* 63

Route 66, *1950s:* 40

Rowan & Martin's Laugh-In, 1960s: 3, 19

Rowling, J. K., *1990s:* 21

Royal and Ancient Golf Club of St. Andrews, Scotland, *1910s:* 159

Royal Dutch/Shell, *1930s:* 43

The Roy Rogers Show, 1950s: 107

Rozelle, Pete, *1960s:* 179; *1970s:* 160

RSI (Repetitive stress injury), *1980s:* 139

Rubber, *1940s:* 24, 133

    synthetic arteries, *1950s:* 115

Rubella, *1960s:* 120, 123, 131–33, 132 (ill.), 145

Rubell, Steve, *1970s:* 99, 113

Rubik's Cube, *1980s:* 96, 103

Rubin, Jerry, *1960s:* 115

Ruby, Harry, *1910s:* 17

Ruby, Jack, *1960s:* 104

Ruckelshaus, William, *1970s:* 87

Rudolph, Wilma, *1960s:* 181

Ruel, Muddy, *1920s:* 158

Rue, Warren de la, *1900s:* 133

RU-484, *1990s:* 116

Rugg, Harold, *1930s:* 60

"Rule of Reason," *1920s:* 33

Run-D.M.C., *1980s:* 2, 24; *1990s:* 23

Running, *1900s:* 152; *1970s:* 125–26, 129–30

Runnin' Wild, 1920s: 11, 86

Runyon, Damon, *1930s:* 165

Rupp, Adolph, *1960s:* 176

Rural community banks, *1900s:* 32

Rural education, *1940s:* 44

Rural schools, *1910s:* 46

R.U.R. (Rossom's Universal Robots), 1920s: 8

Rushdie, Salman, *1980s:* 10

Russell, Bertrand, *1900s:* 118; *1940s:* 50, 51 (ill.)

Russell, Bill, *1950s:* 168; *1960s:* 169, 169 (ill.), 176–77

Russell, Cazzie, *1960s:* 177

Russell, Henry, *1910s:* 137, 137 (ill.)

Russell, Jane, *1950s:* 102

Russia, *1910s:* 75

    ballet, *1910s:* 9

Triple Entente, *1910s:* 77

U.S aid to, *1910s:* 67

See also Soviet Union

Russian American Jews, *1910s:* 96

The Russian Symphony Orchestra, *1910s:* 3

Russo-Japanese War, *1900s:* 72–73

Rutan, Richard, *1980s:* 147

Ruth, Babe, *1910s:* 154–55, 157–58, 163 (ill.), 164; *1920s:* 149–50, 152–53, 153 (ill.), 155–57; *1930s:* 152, 158; *1960s:* 172

Rutherford, Ernest, *1900s:* 118; *1910s:* 140

Ryan, Leo, *1970s:* 116

Ryan, Nolan, *1980s:* 175

Rydell, Bobby, *1960s:* 10

Ryder, 1920s: 3

Ryder, Albert Pinkham, *1910s:* 12

Ryder Cup, *1920s:* 149; *1980s:* 183

Ryun, Jim, *1960s:* 165

S

Saarinen, Eero, *1940s:* 92; *1950s:* 91, 96, 104

Saarinen, Eliel, *1910s:* 101; *1920s:* 97, 99

Sabin, Albert B., *1930s:* 113; *1940s:* 122; *1950s:* 115–16, 129; *1960s:* 120

Saccharin, *1960s:* 135

Sacco, Nicola, *1920s:* 83

Sachs, Eddie, *1960s:* 171

Sackler, Howard, *1910s:* 166

Sadat, Anwar, *1970s:* 71

Safe City, U.S.A., *1980s:* 112

Safe driving day, *1950s:* 91

Safety

    automobiles, *1960s:* 25, 29

    consumer, *1960s:* 29, 82; *1970s:* 30

    driving, *1970s:* 26

    labor reform, *1910s:* 69

    regulations, *1910s:* 24

    in ultrasonic equipment, *1970s:* 123

    See also Workers' compensation

Safety caps, *1970s:* 122

Safety razors, *1900s:* 78, 118

SAG (Screen Actors Guild), *1980s:* 74, 80

Sailors, *1910s:* 113

Saint Lawrence Seaway, *1950s:* 137

"The Saint Louis Blues," *1910s:* 7

Sakel, Manfred J., *1920s:* 109

Saks Fifth Avenue, *1920s:* 37, 86

"Salads, Sandwiches, and Desserts," *1960s:* 16

Salaries. *See* Wages and salaries

Salazar, Ruben, *1970s:* 98

Salinger, J. D., *1950s:* 9

Salk, Jonas E., *1940s:* 122; *1950s:* 115–16, 119, 128–29, 128 (ill.)

Salt-N-Pepa, *1980s:* 24

SALT (Strategic Arms Limitation Treaty), *1970s:* 80–81

SALT II arms-control treaty, *1980s:* 68

Salvation Army, *1900s:* 82, 90 (ill.); *1920s:* 90

Sampras, Pete, *1990s:* 179, 180 (ill.)

Sam's Club, *1980s:* 44

Sam, Vilbrun Guillaume, *1910s:* 72

San Antonio Spurs, *1960s:* 178

Sanatoriums, *1910s:* 129

Sanctuary, *1950s:* 9

Sandburg, Carl, *1910s:* 10

Sande, Earl, *1930s:* 152, 165

Sanders, Barry, *1990s:* 174 (ill.), 175

Sanders, Tom, *1960s:* 177

San Diego Chargers, *1960s:* 180

San Diego Padres, *1960s:* 174

San Diego Rockets, *1960s:* 176

Sandys, Edwina, *1970s:* 9

SANE (Committee for a Sane Nuclear Policy), *1980s:* 113

Sanford and Son, *1970s:* 108

Sanford Stakes, *1910s:* 155; *1920s:* 166

The San Francisco Ballet, *1980s:* 22

San Francisco Bay Bridge, *1930s:* 89, 139

San Francisco, California, *1900s:* 3
    bubonic plague in, *1900s:* 111–12
    earthquake, *1900s:* 21
    Human Be-In, *1960s:* 95

San Francisco Examiner, *1910s:* 20

San Francisco 49ers, *1950s:* 173; *1980s:* 169, 171, 181

San Francisco Giants, *1960s:* 164; *1980s:* 168

San Francisco State University, *1960s:* 57

San Francisco Warriors, *1960s:* 176–77

Sanger, Margaret, *1910s:* 24, 66, 91, 113, 117, 117 (ill.); *1920s:* 102, 108; *1930s:* 117; *1950s:* 141, 141 (ill.)

Sanitary codes, *1910s:* 144

Sanitary pads, *1910s:* 127

Sanitation, *1910s:* 126, 144

San Simeon, *1910s:* 91

Santa Clara, *1930s:* 163–64

Santayana, George, *1910s:* 95, 95 (ill.)

Santo, Ron, *1960s:* 173

Saperstein, Abe, *1920s:* 160; *1940s:* 162

Saperstein, Al, *1930s:* 161

Sappho, *1900s:* 2

Sara Lee, *1950s:* 90

Saratoga Cup, *1910s:* 172

Saratoga Springs, *1930s:* 165

Sarazen, Gene, *1910s:* 171 (ill.); *1920s:* 151–52, 165–66; *1930s:* 164

Sargent, Francis, *1970s:* 49

Sargent, John Singer, *1900s:* 3; *1910s:* 8

Sarnoff, David, *1900s:* 128; *1910s:* 5, 20; *1920s:* 7, 7 (ill.), 36

SAR (Sons of the American Revolution), *1900s:* 45

Sassoon, Vidal, *1960s:* 94

The Satanic Verses, *1980s:* 10

SATC (Students' Army Training Corps), *1910s:* 53

Satellites, *1950s:* 137, 141; *1960s:* 144, 158 (ill.)

SAT (Scholastic Aptitude Test), *1980s:* 50, 59

SAT scores, *1970s:* 57–59

The Saturday Evening Post, *1900s:* 20; *1940s:* 86; *1950s:* 126

Saturday Night Fever, *1970s:* 3, 16, 17 (ill.)

Saturday Night Massacre, *1970s:* 87

Saturn, *1910s:* 137, 140
Saunders, Clarence, *1910s:* 42
Saunders, Wallace, *1900s:* 2
Saving Private Ryan, 1990s: 4, 10–11
Savings and loan associations, *1980s:* 30, 33, 37, 39
Savings bonds, *1940s:* 24
Savio, Mario, *1960s:* 62–63, 62 (ill.)
"Say Say Say," *1980s:* 19
Scandals
    Medicaid, *1960s:* 131
    Twenty-One, 1950s: 3, 19
Scariest Police Shootouts, 1990s: 18
Scarlet fever, *1920s:* 112, 114
Scarlett: The Sequel to Margaret Mitchell's Gone With the Wind, 1990s: 20
Scepticism and Animal Faith, 1910s: 95
Schaefer, Vincent, *1940s:* 131, 143
Schenley Distillers Corporation, *1940s:* 108
Schenley Industries, *1960s:* 25
Schick, Bela, *1910s:* 132
Schick Dry Shaver Inc., *1930s:* 88
Schindler's List, 1990s: 2, 4, 10, 11 (ill.)
Schizophrenia, *1920s:* 109; *1940s:* 113, 122
Schizophrenia, genome mapping, *1990s:* 144
Schlafly, Phyllis, *1970s:* 98, 103, 103 (ill.), 105–06, 109
Schlessinger, Laura, *1990s:* 4, 7, 7 (ill.), 12
Schlitz Playhouse of Stars, 1950s: 30
Schmeling, Max, *1930s:* 152–55, 161–62
Schmidt, Joe, *1950s:* 174
Schmitz, Jonathan, *1990s:* 2, 15
Schnabel, Julian, *1980s:* 12
Schneiderman, Rose, *1910s:* 40
Schoenberg, Arnold, *1930s:* 20; *1940s:* 18
Scholarships, *1960s:* 59
Scholastic Aptitude Test (SAT), *1980s:* 50, 59
Schollander, Don, *1960s:* 181
School and Society, 1910s: 47

School and Society in Chicago, 1920s: 47, 53
School and University Program for Research and Development (SUPRAD), HarvardUniversity, *1960s:* 51
"School Days," *1900s:* 16
School integration. *See* Desegregation
School lunch program, *1940s:* 49, 55
Schools, *1980s:* 54
    alcohol abuse, *1980s:* 49, 63–64
    consulting firms, *1990s:* 44
    curriculum, *1980s:* 48
    discipline, *1980s:* 48
    drugs, *1980s:* 48–50, 63–65
    ethnic makeup, *1980s:* 61
    high, *1970s:* 48, 57
    inner-city, *1970s:* 51, 53
    lunch programs, *1980s:* 48
    math, *1980s:* 49
    nongraded, *1910s:* 46
    preschools, *1970s:* 105
    private, *1990s:* 47, 51, 54–55
    racial makeup of, *1990s:* 45, 47
    regulations, *1910s:* 47
    safety, *1990s:* 46
    sciences, *1980s:* 48
    secondary, *1910s:* 46, 48
    shortages, in Atlanta, Georgia, *1900s:* 40
    shortages of, *1950s:* 62–63
    smoking, *1980s:* 49, 64
    spanking in, *1970s:* 49
    students searches, *1980s:* 48
    students with AIDS, *1980s:* 123, 126, 129
    television in, *1970s:* 59
    truancy, *1910s:* 51
    violence, *1980s:* 50, 63–65; *1990s:* 49–56
    weapons in, *1990s:* 44
    women, *1910s:* 58–60
    See also Education; Universities and colleges
Schriner, Dave, *1930s:* 166
Schroeder, William, *1980s:* 132
Schulberg, Budd, *1950s:* 14
Schuller, Robert, *1980s:* 115

Schultz, Dave, *1970s:* 173

Schultz, "Dutch," *1930s:* 82

Schuster, Max Lincoln, *1920s:* 101

Schwab, Charles Michael, *1900s:* 25, 25 (ill.)

Schwarzkopf, Norman, *1990s:* 67

Schwartz, Stephen, *1970s:* 2

Schwarzchild, Karl, *1910s:* 133

Schwarzchild, Martin, *1960s:* 149

Schwerner, Michael, *1960s:* 102

Schwimmer, Rosika, *1920s:* 82

Schwyzer, Arnold, *1900s:* 100

Science, 1980s: 126; *1990s:* 138

Science and technology, *1900s:* 117–36; *1910s:* 131–52; *1920s:* 127–46; *1930s:* 129–49; *1940s:* 129–49; *1950s:* 135–55; *1960s:* 141–62; *1970s:* 139–58; *1980s:* 145–65; *1990s:* 137–60
  chronology, *1900s:* 118–19; *1910s:* 132–33; *1920s:* 128–29; *1930s:* 130–31; *1940s:* 130–31; *1950s:* 136–37; *1960s:* 142–43; *1970s:* 140–41; *1980s:* 146–47; *1990s:* 138–39
  government-funded research, *1940s:* 132–33
  headline makers, *1900s:* 122–23; *1910s:* 136–37; *1920s:* 132–33; *1930s:* 134–35; *1940s:* 134–35; *1950s:* 146; *1960s:* 146–47; *1970s:* 144; *1980s:* 150; *1990s:* 142
  in medicine, *1970s:* 129
  overview, *1900s:* 120–21; *1910s:* 134–35; *1920s:* 130–31; *1930s:* 132–33; *1940s:* 132–33; *1950s:* 138–39; *1960s:* 144–45; *1970s:* 142–43; *1980s:* 148–49; *1990s:* 140–41
  stocks in, *1960s:* 33
  student achievement, *1980s:* 48

Science fiction, *1950s:* 16

Science fiction films, *1900s:* 2; *1970s:* 19

Scientific American, 1920s: 145

Scientific method, in archaeology, *1940s:* 136

Scientific method, in education, *1900s:* 47

Scientific psychology, *1900s:* 123

Scientific research, *1900s:* 118, 120–21

SCLC (Southern Christian Leadership Conference), *1960s:* 72, 74

Scobee, Francis R., *1980s:* 152

Scopes, John T., *1920s:* 47, 59, 59 (ill.), 103

Scopes Monkey Trial, *1920s:* 58–60, 59 (ill.), 103

Scotch tape, *1920s:* 129

Scott, David, *1970s:* 145

Scott, George C., *1960s:* 10

Scott, James, *1910s:* 17

Scrap drives, *1940s:* 31

"Scrapple from the Apple," *1940s:* 17

Screen Actors Guild (SAG), *1980s:* 74, 80

Screen Directors' Guild, *1940s:* 3

Screenland, 1920s: 19

Screenplays, novelization of, *1970s:* 10

Screen Romances, 1920s: 19

Scriabin, Aleksandr, *1910s:* 3

Sculley, John, *1970s:* 43 (ill.)

Sculpture, *1910s:* 3, 12; *1930s:* 10

SDI. *See* Strategic Defense Initiative (SDI)

SDS (Students for a Democratic Society), *1960s:* 64

Seabiscuit, *1930s:* 165

Seafloor spreading, *1960s:* 154

Sealab, 1960s: 145, 154

Seale, Bobby, *1960s:* 115

Sea mines, *1910s:* 135

Seaplanes, *1910s:* 138

Searches, students, *1980s:* 48

Search for Freedom, 1970s: 60

Search for Tomorrow, 1950s: 2

Searle Pharmaceutical Company, *1960s:* 155

Searles, Charles, *1970s:* 8

Sears Roebuck, *1910s:* 56

Sears, Roebuck, and Company, *1930s:* 62

Sears, Roebuck catalog, *1900s:* 93, 96; *1920s:* 25, 37

Seattle Pilots, *1960s:* 174

Seattle Slew, *1970s:* 161

Seattle SuperSonics, *1960s:* 176

Seaver, Tom, *1960s:* 173

Second Amendment, *1990s:* 106–07

Second April, 1920s: 2

Secondary schools, *1910s:* 46, 48; *1980s:* 50, 54

Secondary smoke, *1970s:* 122

Secondhand clothing, *1970s:* 118

Second-hand clothing stores, *1960s:* 111

Second New Deal, *1930s:* 69, 71

Second Sonata for Piano, Concord, Mass., 1910s: 16

Secretarial work, *1910s:* 49, 59

SEC (Securities and Exchange Commission), *1930s:* 26

Securities and Exchange Commission (SEC), *1930s:* 26

Sedition Act, *1900s:* 24; *1910s:* 19, 76

Seed, Richard, *1990s:* 134

Seeger, Pete, *1960s:* 113

Segregation, *1900s:* 61, 72, 85–86; *1910s:* 19, 60–62, 61 (ill.), 62, 90, *1920s:* 65; *1960s:* 68
    educational, *1900s:* 41, 53–54, 106–07; *1970s:* 48–49, 51–54, 84
    gender, *1940s:* 55
    history of, *1960s:* 53
    racial, *1940s:* 45, 47, 58 (ill.), 59–61, 65, 104, 116, 157
    in schools, *1930s:* 46–47, 50, 62
    in sports, *1900s:* 140–41, 145–46, 148; *1930s:* 160
    Texas Western and, *1960s:* 176
    Wallace, George C. on, *1960s:* 73, 89
    See also Integration

Seinfeld, 1990s: 2

Seismographs, *1900s:* 118; *1930s:* 143

Seldes, Gilbert, *1920s:* 12

Selections of Nineteenth-Century Afro-American Art, 1970s: 8

The Selective Character of American Secondary Education, 1920s: 46

Selective Service Act, *1910s:* 76, 91, 98

Selena, *1990s:* 5, 25

Seles, Monica, *1990s:* 164, 181

Self-discovery, in the arts, *1940s:* 4–5

Self-expression, in fashion, *1970s:* 116–19

Selfridge, Thomas, *1900s:* 79, 126

Selig, Bud, *1920s:* 154

Selma, Alabama, *1960s:* 69, 94

Semiconductors, *1960s:* 152

Senate Permanent Investigations Subcommittee, *1940s:* 82

Sennett, Mack, *1910s:* 15

The Sense of Beauty, 1910s: 95

Separate but equal doctrine, *1900s:* 72; *1940s:* 59–61; *1950s:* 48, 57–60; *1960s:* 59

Serbia, *1910s:* 66; *1990s:* 69–70

Sergeant York, 1940s: 13

Serology, *1920s:* 113

Serrano, Andres, *1990s:* 8

Service industries, *1960s:* 39

Servicemen's Readjustment Act. *See* GI Bill

Sesame Street, 1970s: 2, 6

Settlement houses, *1900s:* 47–48, 82, 87

Sevareid, Eric, *1950s:* 18

Seventh-Day Adventists, *1900s:* 101

Seven-Up, *1960s:* 41

The Seven Year Itch, 1950s: 7

Sex and violence
    in blaxploitation movies, *1970s:* 20
    on television, *1970s:* 22

Sex change operations, *1950s:* 136

Sex discrimination
    African Americans, *1910s:* 36, 49
    in colleges, *1900s:* 50
    education, *1910s:* 49
    Equal Rights Amendment, *1910s:* 95
    voting rights, *1910s:* 67, 69, 80–82, 81 (ill.), 84, 90, 93, 95
    wages and salaries, *1910s:* 93

white slave trafficking, *1910s:* 69, 87

Sex education, *1900s:* 41, 132; *1910s:* 51, 117; *1950s:* 46; *1980s:* 54–58, 126

Sexism, *1980s:* 52

Sex Pistols, *1970s:* 3, 14

The Sex Side of Life, 1920s: 108

Sexual abuse, children, *1980s:* 112

Sexual activity, AIDS and, *1990s:* 128

Sexual activity, of adolescents, *1940s:* 98

Sexual Behavior in the Human Female, 1950s: 140

Sexual Behavior in the Human Male, 1950s: 140

Sexual behavior studies, *1950s:* 140

Sexual harassment
    Bill Clinton/Paula Corbin Jones, *1990s:* 62–63, 76
    The Citadel, *1990s:* 57
    Clarence Thomas/Anita Hill, *1990s:* 64, 87, 87 (ill.)

Sexually transmitted diseases (STDs), *1910s:* 113–14, 121; *1940s:* 108; *1950s:* 115; *1960s:* 120

Sexually transmitted diseases (STDs), AIDS, *1980s:* 123–24, 130

Sexual orientation. *See* Gay rights

Sexual revolution, *1960s:* 133–35, 134 (ill.), 155; *1970s:* 111–12

S-42, *1930s:* 137

Shadid, Michael, *1970s:* 131

Shadows of Evening, 1920s: 2

Shaft, 1970s: 20

Shahn, Ben, *1930s:* 8

Shakespeare, William, *1920s:* 3; *1980s:* 55

Shakur, Tupac, *1990s:* 3, 7, 7 (ill.), 24

Shall We Dance?, 1930s: 18

Shamanism, *1980s:* 117

"The Shame of the Cities," *1900s:* 67

Shanghai Surprise, 1980s: 21

The Shangri-Las, *1960s:* 11

Shaping Educational Policy, 1960s: 50

Shapiro, Robert, *1990s:* 86

Shapley, Harlow, *1910s:* 139

Share-Our-Wealth Society, *1930s:* 73

Sharkey, Jack, *1930s:* 152, 154, 161

Sharpton, Al, *1980s:* 72

Shatner, William, *1960s:* 19 (ill.)

Shaw, Artie, *1930s:* 20

Shaw, Irwin, *1970s:* 10

Shaw, Louis, *1920s:* 129

Shawn, Ted, *1910s:* 3, 9–10

Shaw, Wilbur, *1940s:* 158

Shea Stadium, *1960s:* 29

Sheboygan Redskins, *1950s:* 169

Sheehan, Patty, *1990s:* 179

Sheeler, Charles, *1920s:* 18; *1930s:* 4, 10

The Sheik, 1920s: 16

Sheindlin, Judy, *1990s:* 15

Shell, Art, *1980s:* 169

Shell shock, *1910s:* 122, 147

"She Loves You," *1960s:* 11

Shenandoah, 1920s: 140

Shepard, Alan B., *1970s:* 145, 174

Shepard, Alan B., Jr., *1960s:* 142, 144, 156–57

Shepard, Matthew, *1990s:* 93, 102

Shepard, Sam, *1980s:* 15

Sheppard-Towner Maternity and Infancy Protection Act, *1920s:* 111, 117–18

Sheraton Corporation, *1960s:* 41

Sherley Amendment, *1910s:* 112, 127

Sherman Antitrust Act, *1910s:* 31, 66; *1920s:* 154

Shiite Muslims, *1980s:* 69

Shinn, Everett, *1910s:* 8

Shipbuilding, *1940s:* 29

Shipping Act of 1894, *1910s:* 76

Shipping industry, *1960s:* 24

Ships
    ambulance, *1910s:* 113
    Morse Code, *1910s:* 132
    steam, *1910s:* 24

The Shirelles, *1960s:* 11

Shirtwaists, *1900s:* 93–94

Shock entertainment, *1990s:* 3–5, 11–16

Shockley, William, *1950s:* 142; *1970s:* 48

Shock therapy. *See* Electroconvulsive therapy

Shoemaker, Willie, *1950s:* 159
Shoes, *1980s:* 96
    athletic, *1970s:* 30
    women's, *1950s:* 90
Shogun, 1970s: 9
Shootings
    Butte, Montana, *1990s:* 44
    Carruth, Rae, *1990s:* 175
    Columbine High School, *1990s:*
      45, 50, 51 (ill.)
    Grayson, Kentucky, *1990s:* 44
    gun manufacturers, *1990s:* 93
    Jonesboro, Arkansas, *1990s:* 45
    mass, *1990s:* 94
    San Diego State University, *1990s:*
      45
    schools, *1990s:* 44, 49–56
    University of Iowa, *1990s:* 44
    West Paducah, Kentucky, *1990s:*
      45
"Shop Around," *1960s:* 13
Shopping centers, *1950s:* 90
Shopping complexes, *1990s:* 92
Shore, Dinah, *1950s:* 5, 15, 18, 30
Shore, Eddie, *1930s:* 166
Shore, Ernie, *1910s:* 163
Shortages
    goods, *1940s:* 31, 88–89, 93–96
    physicians, *1940s:* 111, 115–16,
      120–21
    teachers, *1940s:* 44–46, 57
Short-wave radio, *1910s:* 133
Show Boat, 1910s: 18; *1920s:* 10
Shrager, Ian, *1970s:* 99, 113
Shubert, Jacob J., *1910s:* 18
Shubert, Sam S., *1910s:* 18
Shuffle Along, 1920s: 11
Shula, Don, *1990s:* 164, 175
Shultz, Charles, *1950s:* 2
Shuster, Joe, *1940s:* 10
Sick building syndrome, *1980s:*
    141–42
Side effects, drug, *1960s:* 136
Sidney Janis Gallery, *1950s:* 9
SIDS (Sudden infant death syn-
    drome), *1990s:* 116
Siebert, Babe, *1930s:* 166
Siebert, Earl, *1930s:* 166

Siegel, Jerry, *1940s:* 10
"The Sign," *1990s:* 26
Sikorsky Aero Engineering Company,
    1920s: 133
Sikorsky, Igor, *1910s:* 132; *1920s:* 133,
    133 (ill.), 140–41; *1930s:* 131
Silastic, *1960s:* 127
Silberman, Charles E., *1970s:* 52
Silent films, *1920s:* 16
Silent movies, *1900s:* 10–11; *1910s:* 13
The Silent Spring, 1960s: 98
Silicon chips, *1960s:* 142, 145; *1970s:*
    146
Silicon computer chips. *See* Micro-
    processors
Silicone gel breast implants, *1990s:*
    132
Silicone gel implants, *1960s:* 120
Silicon Valley, *1980s:* 42–44
"Silly Symphonies," *1930s:* 17
The Silver Chalice, 1950s: 106
Silver Connection, *1970s:* 16
Silver, price of, *1980s:* 30, 34
Simon and Garfunkel, *1960s:* 9
Simon, Neil, *1960s:* 18
Simon, Richard Leo, *1920s:* 101
Simon, William, *1970s:* 30, 30 (ill.)
Simpson, Nicole Brown, *1990s:* 2,
    14–15, 63, 85–86, 88
Simpson, O. J., *1960s:* 178–79; *1970s:*
    164, 164 (ill.); *1990s:* 2, 14–15, 66,
    85–86, 86 (ill.), 88
Sinatra, Frank, *1930s:* 3; *1940s:* 2, 7, 7
    (ill.), 14, 16; *1950s:* 5, 15; *1980s:*
    111
Sinclair, Harry, *1920s:* 79
Sinclair, Upton, *1900s:* 3, 65
Singing Cowboys, *1930s:* 18
"Sioux City Sue," *1940s:* 18
Sir Barton (horse), *1910s:* 155–56,
    172
Sirica, John J., *1970s:* 85–87
Sisler, George, *1920s:* 148, 156
SI (Sports Illustrated), 1960s: 182–83
Sissle, Noble, *1920s:* 11
SIS (Special Intelligence Service),
    1940s: 73
Sister Carrie, 1900s: 5–6, 8; *1980s:* 2

Sit-down strikes, *1930s:* 27, 39

Sit-ins, *1940s:* 90; *1960s:* 63–64, 94

Sixteenth Amendment, Constitutional, *1900s:* 21, 59; *1910s:* 66

60 Minutes, 1990s: 16–17, 120

The $66,000 Question, 1950s: 3, 19

Skating, figure, *1900s:* 139; *1960s:*
164; *1970s:* 179 (ill.)

Skeen, Buren, *1960s:* 171

Skiing, *1900s:* 139; *1980s:* 188

Skin cancer, *1910s:* 114, 124

Skinner, B. F., *1900s:* 129; *1940s:* 113,
113 (ill.); *1960s:* 51, 51 (ill.)

"Skin-over-skeleton" architecture,
1940s: 92–93

Skyjackings, *1960s:* 81

Skylab, *1970s:* 140–41, 145–48, 148
(ill.)

Skyscrapers, *1900s:* 79; *1910s:* 100;
1920s: 86, 89, 97–99, 98 (ill.)

Skytrain, *1970s:* 30

SLA. *See* Symbionese Liberation Army

Slackers Raid, *1910s:* 98

Slang, *1950s:* 109

Slaughterhouse Five, 1960s: 18

Sleep, 1960s: 15

Sleeping sickness, *1910s:* 144

Sleep, learning during, *1950s:* 114

Slepian, Barnett, *1990s:* 128–29

Slipher, Vesto, *1910s:* 137, 137 (ill.);
1920s: 132

Sloan, Alfred P., *1930s:* 40–41, 94

Sloan, John, *1910s:* 9; *1920s:* 17

Slogans, advertising, *1920s:* 18

Slums and the Suburbs, 1960s: 50

Small Business Administration, *1990s:*
37

Small business, versus big business,
1950s: 41–43

Smallpox, *1970s:* 123, 126; *1980s:* 122

Smart Set, 1910s: 11

"Smells Like Teen Spirit," *1990s:* 2, 23

Smith Act, *1940s:* 64

Smith, Al, *1910s:* 155

Smith, Alex, *1900s:* 139

Smith, Alfred E., *1920s:* 52, 69 (ill.),
74, 76–78; *1930s:* 92

Smith, Bessie, *1920s:* 2, 12

Smith, Billy, *1980s:* 183

Smith, David, *1900s:* 105; *1930s:* 10

Smith, Emmitt, *1990s:* 175

Smith, Hamilton, *1990s:* 138

Smith-Hughes Act, *1910s:* 47, 57–58

Smith, James, *1900s:* 105

Smith, Kate, *1930s:* 3

Smith-Lever Act, *1910s:* 57–58

Smith, Mamie, *1910s:* 3

Smith, Michael J., *1980s:* 152

Smith, Ozzie, *1980s:* 176–77

Smith, Perry, *1960s:* 80

Smith, Tommie, *1960s:* 182

Smith v. Allwright, 1940s: 64, 79

*Smith v. Board of School Commissioners
of Mobile County, 1980s:* 54–55

Smith, Willie, *1900s:* 139

Smog, *1960s:* 126

Smoking, *1900s:* 58; *1940s:* 109;
1970s: 122–23; *1980s:* 49, 64, 122,
126; *1990s:* 92, 94, 98, 116
advertising, *1950s:* 30–31
cancer links, *1950s:* 114–15, 122
heart disease, *1950s:* 122
user percentage, *1950s:* 25

Smoking and health, *1960s:* 120–25,
137–38

Smoot-Hawley Tariff, *1930s:* 26, 33,
68

Snead, Sam, *1930s:* 164; *1940s:* 168

Snider, Duke, *1950s:* 167

Snoop Doggy Dog, *1990s:* 23, 24 (ill.)

*Snow White and the Seven Dwarfs,
1930s:* 3, 17

Soap operas, *1950s:* 2

Sobell, Morton, *1950s:* 79

Soccer, *1900s:* 139; *1930s:* 167; *1990s:*
163, 166

Social activism. *See* Antiwar protests;
Environmentalism

Social change, writers and, *1930s:*
12–14

Social Christianity, *1900s:* 89

Social classes, disparity in, *1900s:* 4

Social Frontier, 1930s: 53

Socialism
Debs, Eugene and, *1900s:* 24
Goldman, Emma and, *1900s:* 83

labor unions and, *1900s:* 61
national health care and, *1940s:* 117–18
Socialist Party, *1910s:* 37, 66, 97
Socialist Party of America, *1900s:* 24, 78
Social justice, *1940s:* 6; *1970s:* 21, 100–01, 108–11
Social programs, *1980s:* 32
Social protest, *1960s:* 6–7, 36, 47, 69
  in art, *1960s:* 15
  on college campuses, *1960s:* 60–65, 61 (ill.), 62 (ill.)
  industrial wastes and, *1960s:* 130
  in music, *1960s:* 12
  in theater, *1960s:* 17–18
  See also Antiwar protests; Civil Rights movement
Social reconstructionism, *1930s:* 58
Social reform, *1900s:* 62
  See also Great Society
Social sciences, *1910s:* 149–50
Social Security Act (SSA), *1930s:* 27, 69, 71, 73, 78–80, 115; *1990s:* 121
Social Security System, *1980s:* 30
Social trends. *See* Lifestyles and social trends
Social welfare
  Addams, Jane, *1900s:* 47–48, 82
  Carnegie, Andrew, *1900s:* 78
  Christian services, *1900s:* 89, 90 (ill.)
  settlement houses, *1900s:* 47–48, 82, 87
Social welfare programs, *1970s:* 37
Social work agencies, Catholic, *1910s:* 90
Society of American Newspaper Editors, *1920s:* 25
Sociobiology, *1970s:* 144
Sociology, as educational discipline, *1960s:* 53–54
Soddy, Frederick, *1900s:* 118; *1910s:* 140
Soeurs, Callot, *1910s:* 107
Soft Cell, *1980s:* 18
Soft contact lenses, *1960s:* 120, 122; *1970s:* 122

Soft drinks, *1900s:* 23, 37, 79
Software, *1970s:* 44–45; *1990s:* 28
Software Publishing Corporation, *1980s:* 44
So Goes My Love, *1940s:* 3
Solanis, Valerie, *1960s:* 95
Solar eclipses, *1900s:* 133
Solar energy, *1950s:* 136; *1960s:* 143
Solar system, *1990s:* 138
Solar system age, *1960s:* 142
Solar systems, *1980s:* 146
Soldier Field, *1930s:* 152
Soldiers
  attacks on African Americans, *1910s:* 91
  medical care of, *1910s:* 114, 121–24, 123 (ill.), 128–29
Solomon R. Guggenheim Museum, *1950s:* 3, 9
Solvay conference, *1910s:* 132
Somalia, *1990s:* 68
Somebody in Boots, *1930s:* 13
Somebody Up There Likes Me, *1950s:* 176
Some Like It Hot, *1950s:* 12 (ill.)
"Someone to Watch Over Me," *1920s:* 6
"Something About the Way You Look Tonight," *1990s:* 26
"Somewhere Over the Rainbow," *1930s:* 3
Sonar, *1910s:* 135, 146
Songbooks, *1930s:* 7
Song of Solomon, *1970s:* 7, 10; *1990s:* 18–19
Songs, *1900s:* 16
"Sonny Boy," *1920s:* 7
Son of the Sheik, *1920s:* 16
Sons of the American Revolution (SAR), *1900s:* 45
Sony, *1950s:* 137
Sony Corporation, compact discs, *1980s:* 2
Sony Walkman, *1980s:* 2
Sorcerer I, *1960s:* 143
Sosa, Sammy, *1990s:* 165, 169, 171
Sotheby's, *1980s:* 10–11
Soul music, *1960s:* 13, 15

The Souls of Black Folk, 1900s: 40, 53;
1930s: 93
The Sound and the Fury, 1930s: 7
Sound barrier, *1940s:* 138
Sounder, 1970s: 20
Soundgarden, *1990s:* 21
Sound, in films, *1920s:* 5, 16–17, 129,
131, 141–43
The Sound of Music, 1960s: 9
Sound recordings, *1940s:* 131
Soundtracks, *1960s:* 9
Sousa, John Philip, *1920s:* 12
South, *1950s:* 43, 60–61
    authors of, *1940s:* 12
    black voting in, *1940s:* 104
    civil rights laws in, *1960s:* 69
    civil rights protests in, *1960s:*
      74–75, 94
    education in, *1900s:* 53–55, 54
      (ill.)
    Freedom Riders in, *1960s:* 68, 74,
      94, 102
    hookworm in, *1900s:* 114–15
    Jim Crow laws, *1900s:* 72, 85
    medical schools in, *1940s:* 116
    pellagra in, *1900s:* 110–11
    school integration in, *1960s:* 59,
      70; *1970s:* 51
    school segregation in, *1940s:* 59
    segregation, *1910s:* 49, 60–62, 61
      (ill.)
    tobacco growing in, *1960s:* 137–38
    violence in, *1960s:* 96
    voting rights in, *1960s:* 75
    Wallace, George C. in, *1960s:* 73
    womens' education, *1910s:* 59
    See also Desegregation
South Africa, *1980s:* 27, 62
South Boston High School, *1970s:* 54,
54 (ill.)
Southern Baptist Convention, *1940s:*
99
Southern Baptist Convention, apology
for racism, *1990s:* 93
Southern Christian Leadership Con-
ference (SCLC), *1960s:* 72, 74
Southern Education Board, *1900s:* 40,
54

Southern Europeans, *1910s:* 99
Southern fiction, *1930s:* 14
Southern Manifesto, *1930s:* 14
Southern Medical College Associa-
tion, *1900s:* 100–01
Southern Renaissance, *1920s:* 14
South Pole, *1910s:* 132
South Vietnam, *1960s:* 68, 78
South Vietnamese army. *See* Army of
the Republic of Vietnam (ARVN)
Soviet Union, *1950s:* 61–62
    Afghanistan and, *1980s:* 2, 68, 92
    arms race and, *1980s:* 75, 99
    atomic bomb, *1940s:* 65, 80, 146
    Cuban missile crisis and, *1960s:*
      68, 70; *1980s:* 113
    expansion of, *1940s:* 34–36
    Pacific campaign and, *1940s:* 78
    postwar, *1940s:* 27, 39, 66, 79–80
    relations with Cuba, *1960s:*
      76–77
    relations with United States,
      1960s: 2, 68, 75–77; *1970s:* 26,
      70, 72, 80–83
    space race and, *1960s:* 142, 144,
      156–59
    space exploration, *1970s:* 145–46
    See also Cold war
SPAB. *See* Supply Priorities and Allocations Board
Space, *1910s:* 136
Space exploration, *1930s:* 130; *1950s:*
75–77, 136–37; *1960s:* 142–44,
146, 156–60, 159 (ill.); *1970s:*
140–42, 145–48, 147 (ill.)
    Hubble Space Telescope, *1990s:*
      138, 141, 156–58, 157 (ill.)
    International Space Station,
      1990s: 141, 158–60
    Mir, 142
    NASA and, *1990s:* 141, 156–60
    probes, *1990s:* 141
    Sputnik 1, 1990s: 145
Space race, *1960s:* 142, 156–59
Space shuttles, *1980s:* 151–55, 153
(ill.)
    Atlantis, 1990s: 142
    Columbia, 1990s: 44

Discovery, 1990s: 138–39, 156, 158

Endeavor, 1990s: 138, 158

Space stations, *1970s:* 140–42, 145–48, 148 (ill.); *1990s:* 141–42, 158–60

Space vehicles, *1940s:* 131, 138

"The Spaniard That Blighted My Life," *1920s:* 7

Spanish-American War, *1900s:* 63, 68, 72

Spanish influenza. *See* Influenza

Spanking, in schools, *1970s:* 49

Spartacus, 1950s: 15

Speakeasies, *1920s:* 73, 88

"Speakeasy," *1930s:* 84 (ill.)

Speaker, Tris, *1910s:* 157, 163; *1920s:* 156

Special education, *1970s:* 56

Special Intelligence Service (SIS), *1940s:* 73

Special relativity, *1900s:* 133

Speed limits, *1970s:* 26

Speed of light, *1910s:* 136; *1930s:* 130

Speed skating, *1980s:* 192

Spellman, Francis, *1950s:* 91, 95, 95 (ill.)

Spero, Nancy, *1970s:* 9

Sperry-Rand Corporation, *1950s:* 42; *1960s:* 37

Spielberg, Steven, *1970s:* 5, 18–19; *1980s:* 2, 7, 7 (ill.), 111; *1990s:* 2, 11, 20

Spillane, Mickey, *1940s:* 11

Spinal meningitis, *1900s:* 101

Spindletop oil gusher, *1900s:* 20, 29

Spingarn Medal, *1920s:* 47

Spinks, Leon, *1970s:* 180

Spinks, Michael, *1970s:* 180

Spiral nebulae, *1910s:* 137

The Spirit of St. Louis, 1920s: 131, 138–39; *1930s:* 136

Spiritualism, *1990s:* 95, 108–09

Spirituality, *1970s:* 101, 112

Spiritual music, *1910s:* 17

Spitz, Mark, *1970s:* 160, 164, 164 (ill.), 178

Spock, Benjamin, *1920s:* 117; *1960s:* 99, 99 (ill.); *1980s:* 114

Sponable, E. I., *1920s:* 131, 142

Sports, *1900s:* 137–54; *1910s:* 153–77; *1920s:* 147–71; *1930s:* 151–70; *1940s:* 151–72; *1950s:* 157–78; *1960s:* 163–84; *1970s:* 159–80; *1980s:* 167–93; *1990s:* 161–85
  chronology, *1900s:* 138–39; *1910s:* 154–55; *1920s:* 148–49; *1930s:* 152–53; *1940s:* 152–53; *1950s:* 158–59; *1960s:* 164–65; *1970s:* 160–61; *1980s:* 168–69; *1990s:* 162–63
  in education, *1920s:* 60–61
  headline makers, *1900s:* 142–43; *1910s:* 158–59; *1920s:* 152–53; *1930s:* 156–57; *1940s:* 156–57; *1950s:* 162–63; *1960s:* 168–69; *1970s:* 164, *1980s:* 172–73; *1990s:* 166–67
  overview, *1900s:* 140–41; *1910s:* 156–57; *1920s:* 150–51; *1930s:* 154–55; *1940s:* 154–55; *1950s:* 160–61; *1960s:* 166–67; *1970s:* 162–63; *1980s:* 170–71; *1990s:* 164–65
  on television, *1940s:* 18, 153, 155
  top twenty athletes, *1990s:* 184

Sports cars, *1960s:* 31

Sports Illustrated, 1940s: 153; *1950s:* 159; *1960s:* 182–83; *1990s:* 167, 179

Sports utility vehicles (SUVs), *1990s:* 105

Sportswear, *1940s:* 91; *1970s:* 117–19
  See also Athletic shoes

Sprague, Edward Wharton, *1900s:* 101

Spreadsheets, *1970s:* 44, 141

Sprewell, Latrell, *1990s:* 164, 172

"Spring Comes to Murray Hill," *1930s:* 2

Springer, Jerry, *1990s:* 13–16

Springsteen, Bruce, *1980s:* 3, 7, 7 (ill.)

Spruce Goose, 1930s: 137 (ill.); *1940s:* 34

Sputnik, 1950s: 49, 54, 63, 71, 75–77, 137, 153–54, 153 (ill.)

Sputnik 1, 1990s: 145

Sputnik I, 1970s: 145

Spying. *See* Espionage

Spy missions, *1960s:* 76

Square Deal, *1900s:* 32

The Squaw Man, 1910s: 15

SSA. *See* Social Security Act

S.S. Johnson and Son, *1960s:* 31

Stadiums, *1960s:* 94

Stage Door, 1930s: 89

Stage Struck, 1930s: 18

Stagflation, *1970s:* 28, 38

Stagg, Amos Alonzo, *1900s:* 150

Stalin, Joseph, *1940s:* 75–76, 79–80

"Stamp Out Syphilis," *1930s:* 115

Stand and Deliver, 1980s: 52

Stand for Children, 1990s: 48

Standardization, manufacturing,
    1910s: 28

Standard Oil Company, *1900s:* 65;
    1910s: 24; *1920s:* 24, 38; *1930s:* 43;
    1940s: 38

Standard Oil Trust, *1910s:* 32

Stanford University, *1920s:* 153;
    1980s: 55, 62

Stanley Cup, *1920s:* 149; *1930s:* 165;
    1960s: 165; *1970s:* 161, 173; *1980s:*
    168, 172, 184; *1990s:* 176–77

Stanley, Francis, *1900s:* 91, 125

Stanley, Freeman, *1900s:* 91, 125

Stanley Steamer, *1900s:* 91, 125;
    1910s: 142

Stanwyck, Barbara, *1920s:* 10

Staphylococcus aureus, 1980s: 131

Star!, 1960s: 9

Starbucks, *1990s:* 98, 99 (ill.)

Stargell, Willie, *1970s:* 166

Starling, Ernest, *1900s:* 119

Star magnitudes, *1910s:* 136, 139

Starr, Bart, *1960s:* 181

Starr, Kenneth W., *1990s:* 63, 77

Starr, Ringo, *1960s:* 6, 6 (ill.), 11

Stars Over Broadway, 1930s: 18

"The Star Spangled Banner," *1930s:* 2,
    68

Star Trek, 1960s: 19; *1990s:* 139

Star Trek: The Motion Picture, 1960s:
    19 (ill.); *1970s:* 19

Star Wars, 1970s: 3, 5, 19

*Star Wars: Episode I–The Phantom
    Menace, 1990s:* 3, 10

Star Wars (military system). *See*
    Strategic Defense Initiative (SDI)

State asylums, *1910s:* 116

State boards of health, *1910s:* 125

State control, Cleveland Ohio public
    schools under, *1990s:* 45

State of the Union address, *1930s:* 69

State parks, *1930s:* 89

*Statistical Abstract of the United States,
    1940, 1930s:* 118

Statue of Liberty, *1900s:* 2, 46 (ill.)

St. Denis, Ruth, *1910s:* 3, 9–10, 13 (ill.)

STDs (sexually transmitted diseases),
    1960s: 120

STDs (sexually transmitted diseases),
    AIDS, *1980s:* 124, 130

Steamboat Willie, 1920s: 142

Steam cars, *1900s:* 91

Steamships, *1900s:* 78–79; *1910s:* 24

Stedd, Andrew, *1900s:* 40

Steele, Shelby, *1980s:* 101, 101 (ill.)

Steel industry, *1900s:* 20, 58, 64;
    1910s: 30, 38–39; *1950s:* 24-25;
    1960s: 24–25, 37, 68

Steel Workers' Organizing Committee,
    1940s: 24

Steenbock, Harry, *1920s:* 123

The Steerage, 11, 1900s: 12 (ill.)

Steffens, Lincoln, *1900s:* 67

Steichen, Edward, *1910s:* 9; *1960s:* 3

Steichen Photography Center, *1960s:* 3

Steinbeck, John, *1930s:* 4; *1980s:* 9

Steinberg, Joel B., *1980s:* 97

Steinem, Gloria, *1970s:* 2, 7, 7 (ill.)

Stein, Gertrude, *1900s:* 5; *1910s:* 12;
    1920s: 13; *1930s:* 22

Steinseiffer, Carrie, *1980s:* 192

Stella, Joseph, *1910s:* 9, 12; *1920s:* 2

Stellar energy, *1930s:* 144

Stellar evolution, *1910s:* 137

Stells Maris, 1910s: 7

Steppenwolf (rock group), *1960s:* 10

Sterilization
    involuntary, *1920s:* 80
    of Native Americans, *1970s:* 123

Sterling, Ross, *1930s:* 26

Stern, Catherine Brieger, *1930s:* 51

Stern, Elizabeth, *1980s:* 134

Stern, Howard, *1990s:* 3, 5, 13

Stern, Melissa Elizabeth, *1980s:* 135

Stern, William, *1980s:* 134

Steroids, *1960s:* 120

Steroids, athletes and, *1990s:* 164

Steunenberg, Frank, *1900s:* 21, 24, 29–30

Stevens, Nettie, *1900s:* 130

Stevenson, Adlai, *1950s:* 68–69, 71, 73, 73 (ill.), 83, 85; *1960s:* 83

Stevens, Tony, *1970s:* 14

Stewart, James, *1930s:* 16; *1940s:* 14; *1950s:* 13

Stewart, Martha, *1980s:* 101, 101 (ill.)

Stewart, Payne, *1990s:* 179

St. George, Utah, *1960s:* 121

Stickley, Gustav, *1900s:* 97; *1910s:* 102

Stieglitz, Alfred, *1900s:* 11, 13; *1910s:* 2, 9; *1920s:* 18

Stiles, Charles Wardell, *1900s:* 115; *1910s:* 126

The Sting, *1970s:* 18

Sting (singer), *1980s:* 3

St. John's College, Annapolis, Maryland, *1940s:* 53

St. Laurent, Yves, *1960s:* 94

St. Louis Bombers, *1950s:* 168

St. Louis Browns, *1910s:* 161; *1920s:* 148; *1950s:* 168

St. Louis Cardinals, *1910s:* 155; *1920s:* 149, 157; *1930s:* 152–53, 158; *1960s:* 173; *1980s:* 174, 181; *1990s:* 169

St. Louis Central Public Library, *1910s:* 94

St. Louis Hawks, *1960s:* 176

St. Louis Rams, *1990s:* 174

St. Louis World's Fair, *1900s:* 2, 20

St. Mary's Hospital, *1910s:* 119

St. Moritz, Switzerland Olympics, *1940s:* 153

Stock car racing, *1940s:* 158–59

Stockings, nylon, *1950s:* 90

Stockman, David A., *1980s:* 73, 83

Stock market, *1900s:* 21, 28; *1960s:* 24–26, 32–33, 32 (ill.); *1970s:* 26

Stock market crash, *1920s:* 27–29, 38–43, 42 (ill.), 87; *1930s:* 32, 72

   See also Great Depression

Stock market, insider trading, *1980s:* 31, 34, 38

Stockton, John, *1980s:* 178; *1990s:* 172

Stock trading, *1920s:* 38–43

Stokowski, Leopold, *1940s:* 2; *1960s:* 3

Stomach cancer, *1910s:* 114, 124; *1950s:* 114

Stomach ulcers, *1930s:* 110

Stone, Edward Durrell, *1950s:* 96

Stone, Oliver, *1990s:* 8–10

Stonewall Inn, *1970s:* 110

Stooges, *1970s:* 13

Stopes, Marie, *1920s:* 108

Stoppard, Tom, *1960s:* 18

Stovall, George, *1910s:* 161

Stoves, *1910s:* 102

The Strange Career of Jim Crow, *1960s:* 53

"Strange Fruit," *1940s:* 2

Strangers and Dangers, *1980s:* 112

Strasburg, Lee, *1930s:* 21

Strassmann, Fritz, *1930s:* 145

Strategic Arms Limitation Treaty (SALT), *1970s:* 80–81

Strategic Defense Initiative (SDI), *1980s:* 68, 70, 75–81, 91

Straus, Nathan, *1900s:* 101

Strauss, Richard, *1910s:* 16

Stravinsky, Igor, *1910s:* 16; *1930s:* 20; *1940s:* 16, 18

"Strawberry Fields," *1960s:* 12

The Strawberry Statement: Notes of a College Revolutionary, *1960s:* 64

Streaking, *1970s:* 98

Streamline Moderne design, *1930s:* 89, 96

Stream-of-consciousness, *1920s:* 14

Streep, Meryl, *1990s:* 20

A Streetcar Named Desire, *1940s:* 19

Streetcars, electric, *1900s:* 90–91

Street, Picabo, *1990s:* 165, 182, 184

Streetsboro, Georgia, *1900s:* 72

Street Scene, *1920s:* 3

Street style fashion, *1980s:* 107–08

Streisand, Barbra, *1960s:* 7, 7 (ill.)

Streptomycin, *1940s:* 108–09, 119

Strikes, *1900s:* 23, 61; *1920s:* 87;
    1930s: 26–27, 29, 31, 38–39; *1940s:*
    25, 40, 40 (ill.), 41

  agricultural, *1960s:* 25

  airlines, *1960s:* 24

  automobile industry, *1940s:* 24;
      1960s: 24–25

  baseball, *1980s:* 168, 174; *1990s:*
      163–64, 168

  Bunsen School, *1900s:* 40

  Clayton Antitrust Act, *1910s:* 31

  coal miners, *1900s:* 20, 23,
      26–27, 58; *1910s:* 24; *1940s:*
      24, 29, 40; *1950s:* 24; *1970s:* 27

  college students, *1960s:* 63

  communications industry, *1960s:*
      25

  doctors, *1970s:* 122–23

  football, *1980s:* 168, 178–81, 179
      (ill.)

  garment industry, *1900s:* 21, 86;
      1910s: 40–41

  musicians, *1940s:* 2

  newspaper, *1960s:* 24

  PATCO, *1980s:* 30, 37, 37 (ill.)

  police, *1910s:* 25

  postal workers, *1970s:* 26

  Pullman Company, *1900s:* 24

  railroads, *1940s:* 24; *1950s:* 24

  rubber industry, *1960s:* 25

  shipping industry, *1960s:* 24

  steel industry, *1910s:* 38–39;
      1950s: 24–25; *1960s:* 24

  student, *1940s:* 57

  teacher, *1940s:* 45, 57; *1960s:* 25,
      46–47

  teachers, *1970s:* 48

  telephone, *1940s:* 25

  textile workers, *1910s:* 24

  vaudeville performers, *1900s:* 2

"Strike Up the Band," *1920s:* 6; *1930s:*
    2

Strip mining, *1980s:* 36

Stroheim, Erich von, *1920s:* 3

Stroke, *1990s:* 126

Strong, Barrett, *1960s:* 13

Strong, Benjamin, *1900s:* 28; *1920s:*
    29, 29 (ill.)

Strong force, *1980s:* 146

Strug, Kerri, *1990s:* 183

STS (Space Transportation System).
    See Space shuttles

Stubbs, Levi, *1960s:* 14

Studebaker, John W., *1930s:* 54; *1940s:*
    44, 59

Student government, *1910s:* 47

Student loans, *1960s:* 59

Student protests, *1960s:* 47, 49

Students' Army Training Corps
    (SATC), *1910s:* 53

Students for a Democratic Society
    (SDS), *1960s:* 64

Student Volunteer Movement for For-
    eign Missions (SVMFM), *1910s:* 95

Studio 54, *1970s:* 99, 113

Studio One, *1950s:* 18, 31

Studio system, *1930s:* 15

Studying abroad, *1940s:* 52

Sturgeon, Theodore, *1950s:* 16

Sturtevant, Alfred, *1910s:* 137

Stutz, *1930s:* 41

St. Valentine's Day Massacre, *1920s:*
    68

Subatomic particles, *1960s:* 146

Submarines, *1900s:* 119, 131; *1960s:*
    142

  German warfare, *1910s:* 30, 68,
      75–77, 142–43, 151

  nuclear, *1950s:* 136

  sonar detection of, *1910s:* 146

  U.S., *1910s:* 151

"Subterranean Homesick Blues,"
    1960s: 113

Suburbs, *1920s:* 101; *1940s:* 100–03;
    1950s: 90, 99–102; *1970s:* 98

Subways, *1900s:* 20, 78

Sudden infant death syndrome
    (SIDS), *1990s:* 116

Suffrage, *1920s:* 77

  for African Americans, *1900s:* 58,
      85; *1940s:* 64, 87, 90, 104

  for women, *1900s:* 81, 86

Sugar Bowl, *1930s:* 163

Sugar Loaves, 1920s: 3

Sugar rationing, *1940s:* 24–25, 87

Suicide, *1980s:* 48, 64; *1990s:* 116–17, 126

Suicide, soldiers, *1910s:* 122

Sulfa drugs, *1930s:* 111, 120; *1940s:* 109–10, 118

Sulfaguanidine, *1940s:* 118

Sulfanimide, *1930s:* 111, 120

Sullivan, Ed, *1950s:* 17, 19

Sullivan, Henry Stack, *1940s:* 113, 113 (ill.)

Sullivan, James E., *1910s:* 174

Sullivan, John L., *1900s:* 148

Sullivan, Louis, *1900s:* 96; *1910s:* 100; *1920s:* 86

Sulzer weaving machine, *1950s:* 136

Summerall, Pat, *1950s:* 174

Summer, Donna, *1970s:* 7, 7 (ill.), 16

"Summer of Love," *1960s:* 95, 107

Summer Olympics, *1940s:* 168; *1970s:* 160–61, 163–64, 178–80

    Athens, Greece, *1900s:* 139

    London, England, *1900s:* 139

    Paris, France, *1900s:* 138

    St. Louis, Missouri, *1900s:* 138

Summitt, Pat, *1990s:* 163, 167, 167 (ill.)

Sumner, James B., *1920s:* 109, 129

The Sun Also Rises, 1920s: 3, 6, 14

Sun Bowl, *1930s:* 163

Sunday, Billy, *1910s:* 93, 98

Sunday, William "Billy," *1920s:* 91, 91 (ill.)

Sun Records, *1950s:* 3

Sunshine Biscuits, *1960s:* 41

Sunspots, *1900s:* 119, 122

Suntanning cream, artificial, *1960s:* 142

Superballs, *1960s:* 94, 108

Super Bowl, *1950s:* 173–74; *1960s:* 165–66, 169, 180–81; *1970s:* 160–61, 170–72; *1980s:* 173, 180–81; *1990s:* 173, 175

Superconducting magnets, *1960s:* 143

Superfly, 1970s: 20

Superfortress B-50, *1940s:* 131

Superfund, *1980s:* 148, 155

Superhero comics, *1940s:* 10

Superman (character), *1930s:* 12; *1940s:* 10

Superman (television show), *1940s:* 18

Superman: The Movie, 1970s: 19

Supermarkets, *1950s:* 91; *1960s:* 35

Supersonics, *1970s:* 149

Supply and demand, *1970s:* 38

Supply Priorities and Allocations Board (SPAB), *1940s:* 30, 93

SUPRAD (School and University Program for Research and Development), *1960s:* 51

Supreme Court

    antitrust actions, *1900s:* 64–65, 74

    court television, *1990s:* 14

    Hughes, Charles Evans, *1900s:* 62

    on interstate commerce, *1900s:* 61

    jury selection, *1950s:* 69

    justices, *1900s:* 67; *1910s:* 70, 84

    Marshall, Thurgood, *1950s:* 51, 57 (ill.)

    on narcotic drugs, *1910s:* 113

    National Endowment for the Arts, *1990s:* 4

    separation of church and state, *1990s:* 44

    Thomas, Clarence, *1990s:* 62, 87, 87 (ill.)

    Warren, Earl, *1950s:* 58, 68

    See also specific cases by name

Supreme Court Building, *1910s:* 94

Supreme Court nominees, *1980s:* 68–69, 72–73

Supreme Court of Arkansas, *1910s:* 46

Supreme Court Retirement Act, *1930s:* 69, 80

The Supremes, *1960s:* 14

Surfer's knee, *1960s:* 120

Surfing, *1900s:* 139; *1960s:* 108

Surgeon General, *1970s:* 122

Surgery, *1900s:* 100–02, 106 (ill.), 107; *1960s:* 122, 124

    advanced techniques, *1910s:* 128–29

    for cancer, *1910s:* 124

cerebral palsy, *1950s:* 115
equipment for, *1960s:* 121
heart, *1950s:* 114–16, 124–25;
   1960s: 124, 126–28
reconstructive, *1910s:* 128
sex change operations, *1950s:*
   136
Surrealism, *1940s:* 4
Surrogate mothers, *1980s:* 123, 125,
   134–35, 135 (ill.)
Suspension bridges, *1960s:* 142
Sutherland, Jock, *1930s:* 162
Sutton, May, *1900s:* 138
Sutton, Walter, *1900s:* 130
Suturing, *1910s:* 112
SUVs (sports utility vehicles), *1990s:*
   105
Svedberg, Theodor, *1920s:* 108
SVMFM (Student Volunteer Move-
   ment for Foreign Missions), *1910s:*
   95
Swaggart, Jimmy, *1980s:* 97, 115, 116
   (ill.)
"Swanee," *1920s:* 6
Swann v. *Charlotte-Mecklenburg Board
   of Education, 1970s:* 53
Swanson and Sons, *1950s:* 99
Swanson, C. A., *1950s:* 90
Swanson, Gloria, *1910s:* 15
Swarthmore College, *1930s:* 59
SWAT, Columbine High School shoot-
   ings and, *1990s:* 50
Sweatshops, *1910s:* 37, 39 (ill.), 40,
   85, 106
Sweet, Blanche, *1910s:* 15–16
Sweethearts of the Rodeo, *1980s:* 25
Sweet, Ossian, *1920s:* 82–83
*Sweet Sweetback's Baadasssss Song,
   1970s:* 20
Swimming, *1900s:* 139, 142; *1910s:*
   155; *1970s:* 160, 164, 178
Swimming, English Channel, *1950s:*
   158
Swine-flu, *1970s:* 123, 125, 135–38
The Swing Mikado, 1930s: 21
Swing music, *1930s:* 5; *1940s:* 15–16
Swoopes, Sheryl, *1990s:* 165
Swope, Herbert Bayard, *1920s:* 71

Symbionese Liberation Army (SLA),
   1970s: 98, 102
Symington, Stuart, *1960s:* 82–83
Symphonic orchestras, *1910s:* 16
Symphony No. 4, 1960s: 3
Syncopated music, *1920s:* 11
Syndicalism, *1900s:* 29
Synthesize (scientific), *1930s:* 143
Synthetic materials, *1930s:* 89, 141–42
Synthetic protein, *1960s:* 146
Synthetic rubber, *1940s:* 133
Synthetic yarns, *1950s:* 90
Syphilis, *1920s:* 115; *1930s:* 115,
   123–24, 124 (ill.); *1940s:* 109;
   1960s: 120; *1970s:* 123, 137
Syphilis tests, *1950s:* 115
Syracuse Nationals, *1950s:* 169; *1960s:*
   176
Szent-Gyorgyi, Albert, *1920s:* 123–24,
   123 (ill.)

T

Taber, Norman, *1910s:* 174
Table of elements. *See* Periodic table
Taft-Hartley Act, *1940s:* 25
Taft, Howard, *1920s:* 64
Taft, Robert, *1940s:* 117
Taft, Robert A., *1950s:* 73, 73 (ill.)
Taft, William Howard, *1900s:* 59, 63,
   63 (ill.), 71; *1910s:* 2, 42, 72,
   83–84, 141, 154, 161
Tailhook convention, *1990s:* 92
"Take Me Out to the Ballgame,"
   1900s: 16
"The Talented Tenth," *1900s:* 53, 82
Talese, Gay, *1960s:* 80
Tales of Tomorrow, 1950s: 17
Taliesin, *1910s:* 90
The Talisman, 1980s: 12
Talkathons, *1960s:* 108
Talk shows
   shock, *1990s:* 4, 13–18
   Winfrey, Oprah, *1990s:* 3, 5, 7, 7
      (ill.)
Talk Talk, *1980s:* 18
Tally's Electric Theater, *1900s:* 2
Talmadge, Gene, *1940s:* 44

Talmadge, Herman, *1950s:* 58

Taming of the Shrew, 1910s: 13 (ill.);
    1920s: 13

Tamiris, Helen, *1930s:* 22; *1940s:* 17

Tammany Hall, *1900s:* 66

Tampa Bay Lightning, *1990s:* 176

Tampons, toxic shock syndrome,
    1980s: 122, 125, 131

Tang, *1970s:* 145

Tanks, *1910s:* 135, 150

Tannenbaum, Frank, *1910s:* 98

Tape recordings
    sleep learning, *1950s:* 114
    Watergate and, *1970s:* 86–88

Tarantino, Quentin, *1990s:* 7, 7 (ill.),
    9

Target, *1960s:* 34

Tariff reductions, *1960s:* 24

Tariff regulations, *1900s:* 34

Tariffs, *1910s:* 27, 31–32, 83

Tarkenton, Fran, *1990s:* 175

Tarkington, Booth, *1910s:* 10; *1920s:* 2

Tarzan, *1930s:* 155

Tarzan, 1930s: 11

Tarzan of the Apes, 1930s: 11

Tate, Allen, *1930s:* 14

Tate, Sharon, *1960s:* 80

Taussig, Helen B., *1940s:* 112; *1950s:*
    119, 119 (ill.)

Tax cuts, *1970s:* 26

Taxes, *1980s:* 30, 32, 71, 84
    Catholic schools, *1950s:* 49
    corporate, *1950s:* 25
    for education, *1910s:* 53
    income, *1900s:* 21; *1910s:* 32, 66;
        1960s: 24
    low-income workers, *1910s:* 32
    poll, *1910s:* 82
    preparation services, *1960s:* 35
    research grants, *1950s:* 47
    tariffs, *1910s:* 27, 31–32, 83
    for war costs, *1940s:* 32–33
    on wealthy, *1910s:* 33

Tax Foundation, *1960s:* 24

Tax Reduction Act, *1960s:* 24

Taylor, Elizabeth, *1950s:* 13; *1980s:* 21

Taylor, Frank Bursley, *1910s:* 147

Taylor, Frederick, *1900s:* 35–36

Taylor, Frederick W., *1910s:* 28, 34,
    149

Taylor Grazing Act, *1930s:* 69

Taylorism, *1900s:* 35–36

Taylor, James, *1970s:* 11

Taylor, Joseph Deems, *1930s:* 22

Taylor, Laurette, *1910s:* 19

Taylor, Paul, *1960s:* 114

Taylor, William Desmond, *1920s:* 104

TCP/IP (Transmission Control Proto-
    col Internet Protocol), *1990s:* 146

Teacher Corps, *1960s:* 58

Teacher in Space Project, *1980s:* 152

Teachers, *1960s:* 46–47; *1980s:* 48–50,
    53–54, 64; *1990s:* 44, 48
    bilingual, *1970s:* 56
    Civil Rights movement, *1950s:* 91
    communist, *1940s:* 50–51
    educational level of, *1900s:* 41, 43
    labor unions, *1900s:* 40
    maternity leave, *1970s:* 98
    new methods, *1960s:* 54
    progressive education, *1910s:* 54
    red scare, *1950s:* 46, 49, 61–62
    roles, *1910s:* 48
    shortages, *1910s:* 47; *1940s:*
        44–46, 57
    in the South, *1900s:* 55
    strikes, *1940s:* 45; *1960s:* 25;
        1970s: 48

Teachers' College at Columbia, *1920s:*
    50

Teachers' salaries, *1930s:* 46, 53–56

Teachers, training of, *1920s:* 53–55

Teagarden, *1930s:* 2

Teamsters Union, *1930s:* 40 (ill.);
    1950s: 25, 27, 32–35, 33 (ill.), 34
    (ill.)
    traditionalists *vs.* progressives,
        1900s: 46–49
    training, *1910s:* 49–50, 54–56,
        58; *1950s:* 62
    unions, *1910s:* 46; *1940s:* 48
    women, *1910s:* 58

Teapot Dome Scandal, *1920s:* 67,
    77–79

Tebelak, Michael, *1970s:* 2

Technical education. *See* Vocational education

Technicolor, *1920s:* 128, 131, 143–44

Technicolor Company, *1920s:* 143–44

Technological innovations, *1900s:* 22

Technology. *See* Science and technology

Technology companies, versus manufacturing, *1980s:* 31

Technology, war and, *1910s:* 150–51

Teenagers. *See* Adolescents

Telecommunications Act, *1990s:* 58

Telecommunications Reform Act, *1990s:* 3, 17

Telegraphs, *1900s:* 128

Telegraph service, *1910s:* 25

Telephone, long-distance, *1940s:* 86

Telephones, *1900s:* 78
    automated answering, *1960s:* 143
    cordless, *1960s:* 143, 145
    long distance rates, *1960s:* 25
    medical information, *1960s:* 121
    overseas, *1960s:* 143

Telephone service, *1910s:* 25, 102, 133
    deregulation of, *1970s:* 27
    transatlantic cable and, *1950s:* 137–38

Telephone strike, *1940s:* 25

Telephony, *1900s:* 119, 122

Telescopes, *1900s:* 122, 133; *1910s:* 133–34; *1940s:* 131; *1960s:* 150; *1990s:* 138, 141, 156–58, 157 (ill.)

Teletubbies, 1990s: 93

Televangelism, *1970s:* 112–14; *1980s:* 96–97, 99, 115–16, 116 (ill.)

Television, *1910s:* 133; *1920s:* 129; *1940s:* 2, 19 (ill.), 18, 87, 153, 155; *1950s:* 4, 17–19; *1960s:* 4–6, 19–20; *1980s:* 16, 96, 101
    advertising, *1950s:* 28, 30–31, 116
    African Americans in, *1960s:* 106; *1970s:* 22–23, 108
    from books, *1970s:* 10
    color telecasts, *1950s:* 43
    Disney, *1950s:* 2
    educational, *1950s:* 49, 63–64, 64 (ill.); *1960s:* 31–32; *1990s:* 48
    effect on children, *1960s:* 46
    emergence of, *1950s:* 4
    Hispanic Americans and, *1970s:* 109
    martial arts on, *1970s:* 114
    McCarthy hearings, *1950s:* 68, 80–81
    news programs, *1990s:* 44
    presidential debates on, *1960s:* 19–20, 68, 83–84, 83 (ill.)
    public, *1960s:* 114
    public, in schools, *1970s:* 59
    versus movies, *1950s:* 4, 10, 13–15
    reality, *1990s:* 13–18
    religious, *1970s:* 102, 112–14
    shock, *1990s:* 4–5, 13–18
    science on, *1970s:* 144, 148
    soap operas, *1950s:* 2
    sports, *1950s:* 160, 175–76; *1960s:* 178–79; *1970s:* 160–62, 166, 170, 174, 176
    taped, *1950s:* 137, 142
    top shows, *1990s:* 16
    Western films, *1950s:* 107
    See also Children's television; Educational television

Television cameras, *1960s:* 143

Television industry, *1930s:* 134, 147
    cathode-ray, *1930s:* 130
    programming, *1930s:* 2–3
    sports on, *1930s:* 163

Televisions
    color, *1950s:* 138, 142
    transistorized, *1950s:* 137

Television sets, v-chips, *1990s:* 3

Telharmonium, *1900s:* 119

Teller, Edward, *1940s:* 135, 135 (ill.), 146; *1950s:* 139, 149

Temperance movement, *1900s:* 81, 86

Temple, Shirley, *1930s:* 5

Temporary employees, benefits for, *1990s:* 36

Temporary housing, *1940s:* 93

The Temptations, *1960s:* 13, 14 (ill.)

"The Ten," *1900s:* 8

The Ten Commandments, 1950s: 106

Tennessee Valley Authority (TVA), *1930s:* 54, 79

Tennis, *1900s:* 138; *1910s:* 156, 174–75, 175 (ill.); *1920s:* 149, 153, 169–70; *1930s:* 153, 167–68; *1940s:* 153, 170–71; *1950s:* 158, 161; *1960s:* 165; *1970s:* 161, 164, 176–77; *1980s:* 173, 185–86; *1990s:* 160–63, 165, 167, 167 (ill.), 179, 180 (ill.), 181

Tennis Association (WTA), *1990s:* 181

Tennis shoes. *See* Athletic shoes

Tennyson, Alfred Lord, *1910s:* 15

Tereshkova, Valentina V., *1960s:* 142, 158

Terminator 2: Judgment Day, 1990s: 10

Terramycin, *1950s:* 114

Terra Nostra, 1970s: 11

Terrell County, GA, *1950s:* 60

Territories, United States, *1900s:* 58, 72; *1940s:* 65, 72

Terrorism, *1990s:* 62, 80–83, 82 (ill.)

Terrorist attacks, *1970s:* 160, 178–80

Terry, Bill, *1930s:* 159 (ill.)

Terry, Luther L., *1960s:* 125, 125 (ill.), 137

Tesla, Nikola, *1900s:* 127

Tests, college entrance, *1900s:* 40; *1940s:* 44

Test scores, educational, *1970s:* 50, 52, 56–60

Test-tube babies, *1970s:* 123

Tetanus, *1910s:* 123

Tetanus vaccine, *1920s:* 109

Tet Offensive, *1960s:* 69, 71, 78

Texaco, *1900s:* 23; *1990s:* 29

Texaco Star Theater, 1940s: 18

Texas Christian University, *1930s:* 163–64

Texas Instruments, *1960s:* 33, 142; *1970s:* 140

Texas, petroleum industry in, *1900s:* 20, 29

Texas Rangers, *1970s:* 166; *1990s:* 160

Texas State Text Book Board, *1920s:* 47

Texas Textbook Committee, *1970s:* 59–60

Texas Western, *1960s:* 165, 176

Textbooks, *1910s:* 46
  censorship of, *1940s:* 45; *1950s:* 61; *1970s:* 59–60; *1980s:* 5, 9, 49–50, 54–58
  creationism in, *1970s:* 140
  new math in, *1970s:* 61

Textile industry, *1910s:* 24, 85

Textiles
  colorfast, *1940s:* 86
  shortages of, *1940s:* 88–89, 93–96

Thalidomide, *1960s:* 123, 125, 135–37

Thank God It's Friday, 1970s: 7

Thaw, Evelyn Nesbit, *1900s:* 67

Thaw, Harry, *1900s:* 67

Theater, *1900s:* 13–15; *1930s:* 21–22, 58; *1940s:* 18–20; *1960s:* 4, 7, 17–18, 54; *1980s:* 12–15, 13 (ill.), 15 (ill.)
  experimental, *1910s:* 5
  Little Renaissance, *1910s:* 4
  movements, *1910s:* 17–19, 18 (ill.)
  musical, *1910s:* 10, 18; *1920s:* 9–10
  New York City, *1910s:* 5; *1920s:* 8–9, 11
  Pulitzer Prizes, *1920s:* 9

Theater arts, *1960s:* 54

The Theatre Guild, *1910s:* 3

Theatrical circuits, *1900s:* 15

Theatrical Syndicate, *1900s:* 15

Theelin, *1920s:* 109

Theory of relativity, *1900s:* 119, 123, 133; *1910s:* 133, 135–36

"There's No Business Like Show Business," *1910s:* 6

Thermo-luminescence, *1960s:* 148

Thermonuclear bombs. *See* Hydrogen bombs

"They Can't Take That Away From Me," *1920s:* 6

They Knew What They Wanted, 1920s: 3

They Won't Forget, 1930s: 15

Thiamine, *1920s:* 123, 129

Thiebaud, Wayne, *1960s:* 16

Thieu, Nguyen Van, *1970s:* 76–79

The Thing, 1950s: 16

The Thin Man, 1930s: 15

Thiokol, Morton, *1980s:* 152–53

Third International Conference for Eugenics, *1920s:* 109

Third Reich, *1930s:* 89, 93, 142–43, 166–67

Third Symphony, 1910s: 16

This Side of Paradise, 1920s: 2, 6

Tho, Le Duc, *1970s:* 70

Thomas, Augustus, *1910s:* 19

Thomas, Clarence, *1990s:* 62, 87

Thomas, Danny, *1950s:* 17

Thomas, Isiah, *1980s:* 169

Thomas, J. Parnell, *1940s:* 82

Thomas, Martha Carey, *1900s:* 40; *1920s:* 61

Thomas Tally's Electric Theater, *1900s:* 9–10

Thompsan, Virgil, *1920s:* 12

Thompson, Hunter S., *1960s:* 80

Thompson, John, *1920s:* 128

Thompson, Tiny, *1930s:* 166

Thompson, William Hale, *1920s:* 53

Thomson, Bobby, *1950s:* 158, 166

Thomson, J. J., *1900s:* 119

Thomson Steel Works, *1900s:* 25

Thomson, Virgil, *1930s:* 20, 22

The Thorn Birds, 1970s: 9

Thorndike, Edward Lee, *1900s:* 44, 44 (ill.); *1910s:* 150; *1920s:* 109

Thorpe, Jim, *1910s:* 157, 159, 169, 173–74

"Those Oklahoma Hills," *1930s:* 3

3C-48, *1960s:* 149

3-D movies. *See* Films

369th Infantry, *1910s:* 96

Three Men and a Baby, 1980s: 9

Three Mile Island nuclear power plant, *1970s:* 35, 141, 154–57, 154 (ill.); *1980s:* 114 (ill.)

3M (Minnesota Mining and Manufacturing), *1920s:* 129

Thriller, 1980s: 2, 18–19

Throop College of Technology. *See* California Institute of Technology

Thurber, James, *1960s:* 53

Thyroid disease, *1960s:* 121

Tiant, Luis, *1960s:* 173

Tibbets, Paul W., *1940s:* 145 (ill.)

Tickertape machine, *1920s:* 40, 41 (ill.)

Ticks, *1900s:* 101

Ticks, Lyme disease from, *1970s:* 136

Ticler, Sophie, *1920s:* 12

Tiffany Glass Company, *1900s:* 83

Tiffany, Louis Comfort, *1900s:* 83, 83 (ill.); *1910s:* 103

Tilden, Bill, *1920s:* 95, 151, 153, 153 (ill.), 169; *1930s:* 155, 167–68; *1990s:* 179

Till, Emmett, *1950s:* 74, 74 (ill.)

Til Tuesday, *1980s:* 18

Tilzer, Albert Von, *1910s:* 5

Tilzer, Harry Von, *1910s:* 5, 17

Time, *1910s:* 136

Time, 1950s: 132; *1970s:* 26; *1980s:* 160; *1990s:* 93, 117

Time and motion studies, *1910s:* 28, 34

Time Inc, Warner Brothers Communications and, *1990s:* 28

"The Times They Are A-Changin'," *1960s:* 5–6, 113

A Time to Kill, 1990s: 5

Tin Goose, *1920s:* 34

"Tin Lizzies." *See* Model T automobiles

Tin Pan Alley, *1900s:* 16; *1910s:* 4, 17

Tireman, Loyd S., *1930s:* 51

Tires, *1910s:* 132, 141

"A-Tisket, A-Tasket," *1930s:* 7

Tissue culture, *1900s:* 100–01

The Titan, 1900s: 6

Titanic, 1900s: 128; *1910s:* 24, 66, 90, 132, 149; *1980s:* 146

Titanic, (movie) *1990s:* 3, 10

Title IX, *1970s:* 62–63, 62 (ill.)

Titov, Gherman S., *1960s:* 157

Tittle, Y. A., *1950s:* 175

Tizard, Henry, *1940s:* 142

Tjio, Joe Hin, *1950s:* 148

TLC Group, *1980s:* 31, 34

TM (Transcendental meditation), *1970s:* 114

Toast of the Town. See The Ed Sullivan Show

Tobacco Bowl, *1930s:* 163

Tobacco industry, *1950s:* 25, 30–31; *1960s:* 41, 137–38; *1980s:* 126
    See also Smoking

Tobacco industry, lawsuits, *1990s:* 71

Tobacco Industry Research Company, *1950s:* 122

The Today Show, 1950s: 2, 19

To Have and Have Not, 1940s: 6

Tokyo, Japan bombing, *1940s:* 72

Tolan, Eddie, *1930s:* 166, 168

The Toll of the Sea, 1920s: 128, 144

Tombaugh, Clyde William, *1930s:* 130

Tommy Dorsey Band, *1930s:* 3

Tommy guns, *1920s:* 128

The Tommyknockers, 1980s: 12

Toney, Fred, *1910s:* 161

The Tonight Show, 1950s: 3, 19; *1960s:* 2, 6

Tony Awards, *1960s:* 17; *1970s:* 15

Toomer, Jean, *1920s:* 10–11

Toothbrushes, *1930s:* 111, 131

Tooth decay, *1940s:* 109; *1960s:* 121

"Toot, Toot, Tootsie," *1920s:* 7

Top Gun, 1980s: 9

Top Hat, 1930s: 18

Toronto Huskies, *1950s:* 168

Toronto Maple Leafs, *1960s:* 165

Torresola, Griselio, *1950s:* 81

Torrio, Johnny, *1930s:* 81

Torture in Chile, 1970s: 9

Torvalds, Linus, *1990s:* 138

Tosca, 1900s: 2

Totalitarianism, *1940s:* 90

Toulouse-Lautrec, Henri de, *1910s:* 12

Tour de France, *1980s:* 169, 189; *1990s:* 166

Tourist attractions, *1930s:* 98

Tournament of Champions, *1940s:* 166

Tournament of Roses, *1900s:* 138

Tournament of Roses Parade, *1950s:* 142

Tower, John, *1980s:* 87

Townes, Charles, *1950s:* 136

Townsend, Francis Everett, *1930s:* 115, 115 (ill.)

Toxic shock syndrome (TSS), *1980s:* 122, 125, 131

Toxic wastes, *1970s:* 141, 143, 153–54; *1980s:* 155

Toyota, *1960s:* 30–31

Toys, *1950s:* 107; *1960s:* 94, 108

Toy Story, 1990s: 10, 147

Track and field, *1900s:* 143, 152; *1930s:* 153, 168–69; *1960s:* 164–65, 181–82

Tracks, educational, *1900s:* 49

Tractors, *1900s:* 119

Trade, *1990s:* 29
    deficits, *1970s:* 27, 72
    embargoes, *1970s:* 26, 70, 82

Trade education. *See* Vocational education

Trade embargo, Republic of Vietnam, *1990s:* 62

Trade Expansion Act, *1960s:* 24

Trade, free, *1940s:* 35

Trade rights, *1910s:* 85

Trade routes, *1910s:* 24

Traditionalism
    cultural, *1970s:* 100–01
    educational, *1970s:* 50, 59–60

Traditionalists, in education, *1900s:* 46–47

Traffic control, computerized, *1960s:* 143

Traffic lights, *1910s:* 133

Traffic Safety Act, *1960s:* 25

Tragic America, 1930s: 12

Trains, *1970s:* 39

Tranquilizers, *1950s:* 117, 131–32

Trans-Alaska Pipeline, *1970s:* 26, 34–35, 152

TransAmerica Corporation, *1920s:* 25

Transatlantic cable, *1950s:* 137–38, 143

Transatlantic flight, *1920s:* 25, 38, 129, 131, 137–39

Transbay Bridge Project, *1930s:* 138–39

Transcendental meditation (TM), *1970s:* 114

Transcontinental Air Transport, *1920s:* 25

Transcontinental flights, *1930s:* 130, 134, 136–38; *1970s:* 27, 30, 148

Transfusions, *1910s:* 113, 122

Transistors, *1940s:* 141
> computers, *1950s:* 144; *1960s:* 152
> invention of, *1950s:* 142–43
> radios, *1950s:* 136
> silicon-chip, *1950s:* 137

Transmission Control Protocol Internet Protocol (TCP/IP), *1990s:* 146

Transmitter, wireless, *1920s:* 24

Transplants, *1930s:* 110; *1960s:* 120–22
> cardiovascular, *1950s:* 114–15

Transportation, *1900s:* 81, 89–91, 120; *1930s:* 138–40
> *See also* Air travel; Aviation; Automobile industry; Railroads

Trans World Airlines (TWA), *1940s:* 130; *1950s:* 35–36, 91

Travel, air, *1970s:* 27, 30, 140–41, 148

Travolta, John, *1970s:* 3, 17 (ill.)

Treasury Annex building, *1910s:* 94

Treaties
> Native American, *1900s:* 58
> with Soviet Union, *1970s:* 80–81

Treaty of Versailles, *1910s:* 38, 67, 78; *1940s:* 70

Treemonisha, 1900s: 7; *1910s:* 17

Trench warfare, *1910s:* 69, 77

Trends, social. *See* Lifestyles and social trends

Treviño, Lee, *1970s:* 174, 174 (ill.)

Trials
> Chicago Seven, *1960s:* 114–15
> Menendez brothers, *1990s:* 15
> murder, *1900s:* 21, 29–30
> Simpson, O. J., *1990s:* 2, 14–15, 66, 85–86, 86 (ill.), 88
> televised, *1990s:* 14–15
> Thaw, Harry, *1900s:* 67
> war crime, *1940s:* 65

Triangle Shirtwaist Company, *1900s:* 59

Triangle Shirtwaist Factory, *1910s:* 40, 41 (ill.), 90, 106

Triangular diplomacy, *1970s:* 80–83

Trichinosis, *1900s:* 100

Tri-Cities Blackhawks, *1950s:* 169

Trieste, 1960s: 154, 155 (ill.)

Trimble, Richard, *1900s:* 28

Trinity College, *1920s:* 47

Trinity Test, *1940s:* 130

Triode vacuum tubes. *See* Audion

Triparanol, *1960s:* 123, 136

Triple Alliance. *See* Central Powers

Triple Crown, *1910s:* 155–56, 172; *1920s:* 156, 166–67; *1930s:* 165; *1940s:* 156; *1970s:* 161

Triple Crown (baseball), *1960s:* 173

Triple Entente. *See* Allied Powers

A Trip to the Moon, 1900s: 2

Trotskyites, *1940s:* 78

Trottier, Bryan, *1980s:* 183

Truancy, *1910s:* 51

Trucking, deregulation, *1980s:* 30, 35

Trucks, *1910s:* 91

True Blue, 1980s: 21

Truman Doctrine, *1940s:* 69

Truman, Harry S, *1940s:* 65, 69, 69 (ill.), 87; *1950s:* 24, 60; *1990s:* 121
> anticommunism and, *1940s:* 78
> assassination attempt, *1950s:* 68, 81
> on civil rights, *1940s:* 104
> desegregation of military, *1940s:* 60
> elections, *1950s:* 68, 71, 83
> end of war production, *1940s:* 25, 27
> Korean War, *1950s:* 68
> labor unions and, *1940s:* 41
> McCarthyism and, *1950s:* 79
> on national health insurance, *1940s:* 117–18
> nuclear weapons and, *1950s:* 149
> at Potsdam, *1940s:* 79–80
> reelection of, *1940s:* 65
> on segregation, *1940s:* 65

on Soviet containment, *1940s:* 34–36

    See also Atomic bombs

Trumbo, Dalton, *1940s:* 14–15; *1950s:* 15

Trump, Donald, *1980s:* 34, 34 (ill.)

Trump Plaza, *1980s:* 34

Trump: The Art of the Deal, 1980s: 34

Trump Tower, *1980s:* 34

Trusts, business, *1900s:* 25, 34, 60, 64

Trylon, *1930s:* 106–07

Tschmeak, Erich von, *1900s:* 129

TSS (Toxic shock syndrome), *1980s:* 122, 125, 131

Tuberculosis (TB), *1900s:* 100–01, 112–13; *1910s:* 114, 124, 129–30; *1920s:* 114–15; *1930s:* 121–22; *1940s:* 109; *1950s:* 114, 132

Tugwell, Rexford Guy, *1930s:* 35, 76

Tuition, *1910s:* 46, *1990s:* 16–17

Tularemia, *1920s:* 122–23

Tumor Cell Biology Laboratory, *1990s:* 125

Tumors, *1910s:* 124

Tuna, environmental concerns and, *1990s:* 28

Tunney, Gene, *1920s:* 149, 151–52, 161

Turkey, *1910s:* 77–78

Turing, Alan, *1940s:* 140–41

Turner Broadcasting, *1980s:* 38

Turner, Florence, *1910s:* 15

Turner, Ted, *1980s:* 96, 101, 101 (ill.)

Tuskegee Institute, *1900s:* 51–52, 53 (ill.), 63; *1910s:* 60, 62, 62 (ill.); *1940s:* 49; *1970s:* 137

TVA (Tennessee Valley Authority), *1930s:* 54, 79

TV dinners. *See* Frozen dinners

TV Guide, 1950s: 2, 17

Twain, Mark, *1980s:* 56

TWA (Trans World Airlines), *1950s:* 35–36, 91

    See also Trans World Airlines

Twenty-first Amendment, *1930s:* 68

Twenty-One, 1950s: 3, 19

Twenty-sixth Amendment, *1970s:* 98

20/20, 1990s: 17

Twiggy, *1960s:* 113

The Twilight Zone, 1950s: 17; *1960s:* 19

"The Twist," *1960s:* 94, 97, 108

"Twist and Shout," *1960s:* 11

Two Centuries of Black American Art, 1970s: 3

289 Gallery, *1910s:* 2

2 Live Crew, *1980s:* 24

2001: A Space Odyssey, 1950s: 145; *1960s:* 10

Tylenol, cyanide poisonings, *1980s:* 122, 125, 129

Typhoid, *1910s:* 117, 122–24

Typhoid fever, *1900s:* 104, 112

Typhoid Mary, *1900s:* 112

Typhus, *1940s:* 109

Tyson, Cicely, *1970s:* 20

Tyson, Mike, *1980s:* 168–69, 173, 173 (ill.); *1990s:* 163–64

U

UAW (United Automobile Workers), *1930s:* 27, 38–39; *1950s:* 28

U-boats, *1900s:* 119

UCLA (University of California at Los Angeles), *1960s:* 54, 167, 176

UFOs (Unidentified Flying Objects), *1950s:* 90

UFW. *See* United Farm Workers of America

U-Haul, *1960s:* 35

Ulcers, *1930s:* 110

Ultramicroscopes, *1900s:* 118

Ultrasound tests, *1950s:* 115; *1970s:* 123, 129

Ulysses, 1920s: 2, 14

UMW (United Mine Workers), *1930s:* 31, 37

    See also United Mine Workers

Unabomber, *1990s:* 63, 80–81

UNCED (United Nations Conference on Environment and Development), *1990s:* 152

UNCF (United Negro College Fund), *1940s:* 49

Uncle Tom's Cabin, 1930s: 13

Unconscious mind, *1900s:* 131–32

The Undersea Odyssey of the "Calyp-so," *1970s:* 144

The Undersea World of Jacques Cousteau, 1970s: 144

Underwood-Simmons Tariff Act, *1910s:* 31

Unemployment, *1930s:* 26, 33, 68; *1970s:* 27, 38–39, 42; *1980s:* 30; *1990s:* 28–29, 31
 automation and, *1960s:* 142–43

Unemployment benefits, *1950s:* 24

UNESCO, *1940s:* 45, 47, 51–52

Unidentified Flying Objects (UFOs), *1950s:* 90

Unification Church, *1970s:* 114–15

Uniforms, military, *1940s:* 93, 95

Union Carbide, *1920s:* 24

Union Pacific M-1000 Streamliner, *1930s:* 94

Unions, labor, *1970s:* 102; *1990s:* 41
 See also Labor unions

Union Steel Company, *1900s:* 25

Unisex clothing, *1960s:* 95, 110 (ill.), 111

Unitas, Johnny, *1950s:* 174–75

United Airlines, *1930s:* 88; *1950s:* 36

United Artists, *1910s:* 3, 6–7

United Automobile Workers (UAW), *1930s:* 27, 31, 38–39; *1950s:* 28

United Farm Workers of America (UFW), *1960s:* 25, 28

United Farm Workers (UFW), *1970s:* 102

United Federation of Teachers, *1960s:* 47

United Kingdom. *See* England

United Mine Workers of America, *1910s:* 29, 38

United Mine Workers (UMW), *1900s:* 20, 26–27; *1930s:* 31, 37; *1940s:* 25, 29, 40–41; *1960s:* 24–25

United Nations
 International Women's Year Conference, *1970s:* 99
 Vietnam in, *1970s:* 71
 Young, Andrew and, *1970s:* 71, 75

United Nations Atomic Energy Commission, *1910s:* 28

United Nations Conference on Environment and Development (UNCED), *1990s:* 152

United Nations Educational, Scientific, and Cultural Organization. *See* UNESCO

United Negro College Fund (UNCF), *1940s:* 49

United Rubber Workers, *1930s:* 27; *1960s:* 25

United States Air Force, *1920s:* 136–37

United States Armed Forces Institute. *See* U.S. Armed Forces Institute

United States Auto Club (USAC), *1960s:* 166, 170

United States Constitution, *1910s:* 50

United States Engineering Society, *1900s:* 119

United States Geological Survey (USGS), *1980s:* 163

United States Golf Association (USGA), *1940s:* 168

United States Lawn Tennis Association (USLTA), *1930s:* 167–68; *1940s:* 170

United States Outdoor Championship (golf), *1940s:* 170

United States Public Health Service (USPHS), *1910s:* 113–14, 126

United States Steel Corporation, *1900s:* 23, 25; *1910s:* 38–39; *1930s:* 27

United States Tennis Association, *1980s:* 185

United States v. *Richard M. Nixon,* *1970s:* 88

United Steel Workers of America, *1960s:* 24–25, 68

Unity space module, *1990s:* 159

UNIVAC, *1950s:* 136, 138, 140, 143–46, 144 (ill.)

Universal automatic computer. *See* UNIVAC

Universal News, *1960s:* 3

Universal Service program, *1990s:* 58

Universe
    expansion of, *1910s:* 133
    origin of, *1960s:* 151; *1990s:* 141
Universities and colleges, *1930s:* 47,
    58–59, 110; *1990s:* 44, 47, 125, 167
    academic freedom, *1940s:* 50–51
    academic requirements, *1900s:*
      49–53
    accelerated programs, *1940s:* 44
    admissions, *1970s:* 59, 63–65
    art museums at, *1960s:* 114
    business schools, *1900s:* 50
    College Entrance Examination
      Board, *1900s:* 40
    costs, *1950s:* 46
    curriculum, *1940s:* 46; *1960s:*
      53–54
    desegregation of, *1940s:* 58 (ill.),
      60; *1950s:* 46
    diploma mills, *1950s:* 47
    enrollment, *1920s:* 46–47, 61–62;
      1940s: 47, 56, 87
    entrance exams, *1940s:* 44
    G.I. bill, *1950s:* 26
    government-funded research at,
      1940s: 46–47
    independent, *1910s:* 47
    integration of, *1960s:* 46
    international relations courses,
      1940s: 47
    medical schools, *1940s:* 115–17,
      120–21
    military draft and, *1960s:* 49
    minorities and, *1970s:* 61–66
    modernization of, *1910s:* 53–54
    morals revolution in, *1960s:* 60
    overcrowding of, *1940s:* 56
    reform programs, *1920s:* 48–49
    social protest at, *1960s:* 60–65, 61
      (ill.), 62 (ill.)
    sports in, *1920s:* 60–61
    student draft, *1950s:* 60–61
    student loans, *1960s:* 59
    theaters in, *1960s:* 54
    tuition, *1910s:* 46
    veterans in, *1940s:* 47
    women in, *1940s:* 55

    See also Medical schools; names
      of specific universities
University of Alabama, *1960s:* 46–47,
    178–79
University of Arkansas, *1940s:* 60;
    1960s: 179
University of California at Berkeley,
    1920s: 149; *1930s:* 135; *1960s:* 47,
    49, 61–63, 61 (ill.), 62 (ill.)
University of California at Los Ange-
    les (UCLA), *1960s:* 54, 167, 176
University of California, Davis, *1970s:*
    49, 64–65
University of Chicago, *1900s:* 150;
    1920s: 24; *1930s:* 56, 60, 153, 162;
    1940s: 49–50, 53, 152, 167; *1960s:*
    64
University of Cincinnati, *1960s:* 175
University of Connecticut, *1950s:* 58
University of Florida, *1950s:* 46
University of Georgia, *1940s:* 44;
    1960s: 46
University of Illinois, *1960s:* 54
University of Iowa, *1990s:* 44
University of Kentucky, *1960s:* 165,
    176
University of Maryland, *1930s:* 65;
    1940s: 45, 60
University of Michigan, *1900s:* 150;
    1930s: 168; *1950s:* 90; *1960s:* 165,
    179; *1970s:* 48
University of Mississippi, *1960s:*
    46–47, 102
University of New Mexico, *1960s:* 178
University of Notre Dame, *1930s:* 162;
    1960s: 60, 165, 178–79
University of Oklahoma, *1940s:* 58
    (ill.), 60
University of Pennsylvania, *1920s:* 24;
    1990s: 44
University of Pittsburgh, *1930s:* 162
University of Rochester, *1950s:* 46
University of Southern California
    (USC), *1960s:* 53–54, 178–79
University of Tennessee, *1990s:* 167
University of Tennessee Lady Volun-
    teers, *1990s:* 163

University of Texas, *1960s:* 178–79;
1990s: 125

University of Texas Law School,
1950s: 46, 56

University of Utah Medical Center,
1980s: 122, 131

University of Wisconsin, *1960s:* 64

Unleaded gasoline, *1970s:* 26

Unmarried heterosexual couples,
1990s: 92

Unsafe at Any Speed, 1960s: 29

The Unsinkable Molly Brown, 1960s: 18

Upper Deck, 1920s: 18

Upset (horse), *1910s:* 155

Uranium, *1940s:* 131

Uranus, *1910s:* 137

Urban development, *1920s:* 31–32

Urbanization, *1910s:* 92

Urban landscapes, *1900s:* 6

Urban migration, *1900s:* 42

Urban schools. *See* Inner-city schools

Urease, *1920s:* 109

Urey, Harold C., *1930s:* 135, 135 (ill.)

Urology, *1910s:* 129

U.S.A., 1930s: 13

USAC (United States Auto Club),
1960s: 166, 170

USA for Africa, *1980s:* 2, 25

U.S. Amateur Championship, *1980s:*
183

U.S. Amateur (golf), *1920s:* 165

U.S. Armed Forces Institute, *1940s:*
44–45, 55

U.S. Army, *1900s:* 100, 114

U.S. Army Air Corps, *1930s:* 131

U.S. Army education, *1940s:* 57

U.S. Army Nurse Corps, *1900s:* 100

U.S. Army Signal Corps, *1940s:* 131

U.S. Atomic Energy Commission. *See*
Atomic Energy Commission

U.S. Bureau of Indian Affairs, *1970s:*
109–10

U.S. Census Bureau. *See* Census
Bureau

U.S. Chamber of Commerce, *1930s:*
46

U.S. Congress, *1910s:* 66, 70; *1960s:*
84–85

USC (University of Southern California), *1960s:* 53–54, 178–79

U.S. Davis Cup, *1920s:* 153; *1930s:*
153, 168

U.S. Defense Savings Bonds, *1940s:* 24

U.S. Department of Agriculture,
1910s: 148

U.S. Department of Commerce, *1930s:*
130

U.S. Department of Defense, *1940s:* 66

U.S. Department of Education, *1980s:*
50

U.S. Department of Energy, *1970s:* 30,
34

U.S. Department of Justice. *See*
Department of Justice

U.S. Department of Labor, *1910s:* 86

U.S. Department of the Interior,
1930s: 3

U.S. Federal Council of Churches,
1930s: 110

U.S. Federal Narcotics Control Board,
1920s: 108

U.S. Food and Drug Administration.
See Food and Drug Administration

U.S. Forest Service, *1900s:* 68

USGA (United States Golf Association), *1940s:* 168

U.S. Golf Association Open, champions, *1920s:* 165–66

USGS (United States Geological Survey), *1980s:* 163

U.S. Immigration and Naturalization
Service, *1920s:* 52

U.S. Information Agency, *1960s:* 114

U.S. Labor Department, *1920s:* 24

U.S. Lawn Tennis Association
(USLTA), *1910s:* 174–75

USLTA (U.S. Lawn Tennis Association), *1910s:* 174–75; *1930s:*
167–68; *1940s:* 170

U.S. Nationals (tennis), *1930s:* 156

U.S. Naval Academy, *1940s:* 60

U.S. Navy, *1930s:* 134, 137

U.S. Office of Education, *1930s:* 53;
1970s: 56–57

U.S. Open (golf), *1900s:* 139, 142; *1910s:* 159, 170, 172; *1980s:* 183; *1990s:* 179

U.S. Open (tennis), *1990s:* 181

U.S. Open Tennis Championships, *1970s:* 161, 177

U.S. Open Tennis Singles, champions, *1920s:* 169

U.S. Open Tennis Tournament, *1960s:* 165; *1980s:* 185–86

U.S. Patent Office, *1930s:* 131

USPHS. *See* United States Public Health Service

U.S. Public Health Service, *1910s:* 113–16, 121, 126; *1930s:* 113; *1940s:* 109, 121; *1960s:* 121

U.S. Public Health Service, AIDS prevention and, *1980s:* 124

USS *Atlantis II, 1960s:* 142

U.S. Senate Prohibition Committee, *1920s:* 65

U.S. Senior Players Championship, *1990s:* 179

USS *George Washington, 1960s:* 142

U.S. Shipbuilding, *1900s:* 25

USS *Lexington, 1940s:* 72

USS *Pueblo, 1960s:* 71

USS *Reuben James, 1940s:* 64, 72

U.S. Steel, *1900s:* 20, 58, 64; *1920s:* 38; *1940s:* 31; *1960s:* 37

U.S. Supreme Court
on Agricultural Adjustment Act, *1930s:* 78
on education, *1930s:* 47
on labor unions, *1930s:* 69
on National Industrial Recovery Act, *1930s:* 79
Roosevelt, Franklin D. and, *1930s:* 69

U.S. Supreme Court Building, *1930s:* 98

U.S. Surgeon General, *1970s:* 122

USS *Yorktown, 1940s:* 72

U.S. v. American Tobacco Company, 66

U.S. Women's National Open (golf), *1940s:* 156

U.S. Women's Open (golf), *1990s:* 179

Uterine cancer, *1910s:* 114, 124

U-2 spy plane, *1960s:* 76

V

Vaccinations, *1900s:* 100, 102; *1920s:* 109, 114–15; *1930s:* 111–13, 118, 122; *1940s:* 108–09, 122; *1950s:* 114–16; *1960s:* 120–22, 131–33, 132 (ill.), 145; *1990s:* 116, 128
AIDS, *1980s:* 124, 130
swine-flu, *1970s:* 137–38
typhoid, *1910s:* 117

Vacuum tubes, *1900s:* 118–19
in early computers, *1940s:* 141

The Vagabond King, 1920s: 3

Valens, Ritchie, *1950s:* 3; *1960s:* 10

Valentina, *1930s:* 93

Valentino, Rudolph, *1920s:* 16

Valium, *1960s:* 120, 122

Values education, *1980s:* 50

Valves, heart, *1950s:* 114, 116

Van Brocklin, Norm, *1950s:* 175

Vance, Cyrus, *1970s:* 94

Vance, Vivien, *1950s:* 19

Vancouver Canucks, *1980s:* 168

Vanderbilt, Amy, *1950s:* 90

Vanderbilt family, *1930s:* 102

van der Rohe, Ludwig Mies, *1950s:* 90, 96

van Doren, Mark, *1940s:* 53–54

van Gogh, Vincent, *1910s:* 12

Vanilla Ice, *1990s:* 23

Vanity Fair, 1910s: 12; *1920s:* 99–100

Van Peeble, Melvin, *1970s:* 20

Van Vechten, Carl, *1920s:* 10

Van Vogt, A. E., *1950s:* 16

Vanzetti, Bartolomeo, *1920s:* 83

Vardon, Harry, *1910s:* 170

Variety, 1920s: 42–43, 142

Variety shows, *1940s:* 18

Variety television shows, *1960s:* 19, 106

Vassar College, *1930s:* 134

Vatican Sacred Congregation of Religious Studies, *1950s:* 47

Vaudeville, *1900s:* 2, 13–15; *1910s:* 10

Vaughan, Victor Clarence, *1910s:* 117, 117 (ill.)

Vaughn, Hippo, *1910s:* 161

V-chips, *1990s:* 3, 17

Veblen, Thorstein B., *1910s:* 149

Vee, Bobby, *1960s:* 10

Veeck, Bill, *1950s:* 167

V8 engine, *1930s:* 88, 95, 130

Veins, transplantation of, *1950s:* 114

Velvet Underground, *1970s:* 13

Venereal diseases, *1900s:* 101; *1930s:* 123; *1970s:* 123
  See also Sexually transmitted diseases

Venice Biennale art exhibition, *1960s:* 113

Venter, J. Craig, *1990s:* 139, 142, 142 (ill.), 144

Venturi, Robert, *1960s:* 99, 99 (ill.)

Venus, *1910s:* 137; *1960s:* 143, 149

Verbatim Corporation, *1980s:* 44

Verdi, Giuseppe Fortunino Francesco, *1940s:* 3; *1960s:* 31

Verrazano Narrows Bridge, *1960s:* 142

Vertical integration, in business, *1900s:* 23

Very long baseline interferometry (VLBI), *1960s:* 149–50

Veterans, *1910s:* 47–48
  education for, *1940s:* 44–45, 55–57, 87
  G.I. bill and, *1950s:* 26
  housing, *1940s:* 100–02
  mental health and, *1940s:* 110
  return to family life, *1940s:* 98–99
  World War I, *1930s:* 76
  See also Soldiers

Veterans Affairs Department, *1990s:* 124

Veterans' educational benefits, *1960s:* 47

Veteran's Readjustment Act, *1960s:* 47

V-E (Victory in Europe) Day, *1940s:* 65

Viacom, Inc., *1990s:* 29

Vice-presidential candidates, *1970s:* 81

Vicious, Sid, *1970s:* 14

Vickers Vimy-Rolls-Royce, *1910s:* 139

Victoria (Queen), *1900s:* 78

The Victor Talking Machine company, *1910s:* 91

Victory in Europe (V-E) Day, *1940s:* 65

Victory in Japan (V-J) Day, *1940s:* 65, 77

Victrola, *1910s:* 91

Video games, *1950s:* 138, 150

Video Killed the Radio Star, 1980s: 2

Viet Cong, *1960s:* 79

Vietnamization, *1970s:* 76–78

Vietnam, Republic of, *1990s:* 62

Vietnam Veterans Memorial, *1980s:* 68, 82–83

Vietnam War, *1950s:* 69; *1960s:* 69, 77–80, 86–88, 88 (ill.), 96; *1970s:* 70–71, 77 (ill.)
  Agent Orange, *1970s:* 155
  Cronkite, Walter on, *1960s:* 6
  draft and, *1960s:* 49, 54–55
  economic impact of, *1970s:* 36–37, 76
  end of, *1970s:* 72, 76–80
  McCarthy, Eugene on, *1960s:* 73
  My Lai massacre, *1970s:* 70, 74
  Nixon, Richard and, *1960s:* 86–87
  prisoners of war, *1960s:* 29
  protests, *1970s:* 2, 6, 48
  See also Antiwar protests

The View, 1990s: 15–16

Viking 1, 1970s: 141

Villa, Francisco "Pancho," *1910s:* 70–71, 73–75, 74 (ill.); *1930s:* 162

Vines, Ellsworth, *1940s:* 170

Violence, *1960s:* 96–97
  in boxing, *1900s:* 148
  in college protests, *1960s:* 65
  demonstrations, World Trade Organization, *1990s:* 41
  in films, *1990s:* 4, 9–11, 10 (ill.)
  in football, *1900s:* 151–52
  racial, *1900s:* 71–72, 71 (ill.), 85; *1960s:* 47, 68–69, 94, 99, 101–03, 101 (ill.)
  in reality television, *1990s:* 13–18
  in schools, *1980s:* 63–65; *1990s:* 49–56
  shock documentaries, *1990s:* 16–18

television v-chip and, *1990s:* 3,
17
See also Sex and violence
Violent Crime Control and Law
Enforcement Act, *1990s:* 107
Violinists, *1910s:* 3
Vionnet, Madeline, *1920s:* 92
Vionnet, P. Madeleine, *1910s:* 107
Virgil, *1930s:* 46
Virginia Military Institute (VMI),
1990s: 56–57
The Virginian, 1900s: 5
Virology, *1920s:* 108, 113
Viruses, *1910s:* 112–13; *1950s:*
114–15, 123, 129; *1970s:* 122–23,
125
VISA, *1950s:* 37–38
VisiCalc, *1970s:* 43–44, 141
Visual arts, *1900s:* 5–6, 8; *1910s:* 2–4,
8–10, 8 (ill.), 12–13, 100; *1920s.* 5,
17–18; *1930s:* 4–6, 8–10; *1940s:* 4,
8–10; *1960s:* 5, 7, 15–17, 16 (ill.),
31, 113–14; *1970s:* 8–9
Haring, Keith, *1980s:* 6
increased sales, *1980s:* 4, 9–12
Kruger, Barbara, *1980s:* 6
obscenity/censorship, *1980s:* 5,
8–9
Vitamin A, *1910s:* 112; *1930s:* 141
Vitamin B$_1$, *1920s:* 123, 129
Vitamin B$_{12}$, *1940s:* 131
Vitamin C, *1920s:* 123–24, 129; *1930s:*
110, 141
Vitamin D, *1910s:* 113; *1920s:* 123,
128; *1930s:* 110
Vitamin deficiency, *1900s:* 110
Vitamin K, *1920s:* 124
Vitamins, *1910s:* 132; *1920s:* 111,
123–24, 129, 131; *1930s:* 140–41
See also specific vitamins
Vitaphone, *1920s:* 16, 142
Vivisection, *1900s:* 109, 130
V-J (Victory in Japan) Day, *1940s:* 65,
77
VLBI (Very long baseline interferome-
try), *1960s:* 149–50
VMI (Virginia Military Institute),
1990s: 56–57

Vocational education, *1900s:* 41, 49,
52; *1910s:* 56–58, 57 (ill.)
adult, *1910s:* 48
African Americans, *1910s:* 60–61
secondary schools, *1910s:* 48
trade schools, *1910s:* 46
Vocational Education Act of 1976,
1970s: 63
Vocational Rehabilitation Act, *1940s:*
44
Vocational Rehabilitation Act of 1973,
1970s: 56
Vogue, 1910s: 105
Voice coder, *1920s:* 129
Voiceprint machine, *1920s:* 129
Volcanos, *1980s:* 146
Volkswagen, *1960s:* 30–31, 95; *1990s:*
29
Volleyball, *1980s:* 192
Volstead Act, *1930s:* 85
Volstead National Prohibition Act,
1920s: 65, 72–74, 86
von Braun, Wernher, *1950s:* 141, 141
(ill.)
Vonnegut, Kurt, Jr., *1960s:* 18
Vorse, Mary Heaton, *1930s:* 14
Vostok I, 1960s: 144, 156
Vostok 2, 1960s: 157
Voting, *1920s:* 77
African Americans, *1910s:* 82
New York constitution, *1910s:* 67
women, *1910s:* 67, 69, 80–82, 81
(ill.), 84, 90, 93, 95
See also Suffrage
Voting age, *1970s:* 98
Voting rights, *1960s:* 75, 102
Voting Rights Act, *1960s:* 69, 75
Voting tests, *1940s:* 104
Vouchers, school, *1990s:* 47, 51,
54–55
Vought-Sikorsky Corporation, *1940s:*
130
Voyager, 1970s: 141
Voyager (airplane), *1980s:* 147
Vries, Hugo de, *1900s:* 118, 129
V-2 rocket, *1940s:* 139
Vukovich, Bill, *1950s:* 159

W

Waco, Texas, *1990s:* 62, 65, 67, 81

Wade, Bily, *1960s:* 171

Wage and price controls, *1970s:* 26, 28, 38–39

Wages and salaries, *1930s:* 27, 46, 53–56, 69; *1940s:* 167; *1960s:* 24; *1990s:* 29

    average, *1970s:* 41

    convict labor, *1910s:* 87

    for doctors, *1970s:* 132

    Ford Motor Company, *1910s:* 141

    freeze on, *1970s:* 38

    homeless population, *1980s:* 111

    minimum, *1950s:* 24; *1980s:* 31, 36

    in sports, *1970s:* 162–63, 165–66, 172

    United Mine Workers of America, *1910s:* 29

    Wilson, Woodrow, *1910s:* 84–85

    women, *1910s:* 93; *1970s:* 104–05; *1980s:* 96

Wagner Act, *1930s:* 29, 38, 78–80

Wagner, Honus, *1900s:* 143, 143 (ill.); *1910s:* 157, 163

Wagner, Robert, *1930s:* 120

Waiting for Lefty, 1930s: 21

Wake Island, *1900s:* 72; *1940s:* 72

Waksman, Selman A., *1940s:* 119

Walcott, "Jersey" Joe, *1940s:* 153; *1950s:* 158, 171

Walgreen, Charles, *1930s:* 60

Walgreen's, *1920s:* 36

Walker, Alice, *1970s:* 10; *1980s:* 7

Walker, Charles Joseph, *1910s:* 36

Walker, Chet, *1960s:* 177

Walker Cup, *1920s:* 148

Walker, Doak, *1950s:* 174

Walker, Jimmy, *1930s:* 98

Walker, Moses Fleetwood, *1900s:* 145

Walker, Sara, *1910s:* 36, 37 (ill.)

Walk Like an Egyptian, *1980s:* 19

Walk-out strikes, *1930s:* 38–39

"Walk This Way," *1980s:* 24

The Wall. *See* Vietnam Veterans Memorial

Wallace, Blondy, *1900s:* 150

Wallace, George C., *1960s:* 46–47, 73, 73 (ill.), 86–89; *1970s:* 48, 84–85

Wallace, Henry, *1940s:* 51

Wallace, John H., *1980s:* 56

Waller, Augustus, *1920s:* 116

Waller, David, *1930s:* 77

Waller, Fats, *1910s:* 3; *1970s:* 3

Waller, Robert James, *1990s:* 2, 20

Waller, Willard, *1940s:* 96

Wall Street, *1920s:* 24–25, 35, 38–43; *1980s:* 31

Wal-Mart, *1960s:* 34; *1980s:* 44; *1990s:* 40

Walsh, Bill, *1980s:* 181

Walsh, Ed, *1910s:* 161

Walsh, Lawrence E., *1980s:* 87–89

Walt Disney Pictures, *1990s:* 147

Walt Disney (television show), *1950s:* 2, 108

Walters, Barbara, *1990s:* 15

Walton, Bill, *1960s:* 175

Walton, J.C., *1920s:* 64

Walton, Sam, *1980s:* 44

Wambsganss, *1920s:* 148

Wanamaker, John, *1900s:* 129; *1910s:* 41–42, 56

Waner, Paul, *1940s:* 152

Wang, An, *1960s:* 29, 36

Wang Laboratories, *1960s:* 29, 36

Wanted: Dead or Alive, 1950s: 17

Wapner, Joseph A., *1990s:* 15

War

    civil liberties and, *1940s:* 78–79

    literature, *1940s:* 12

    movies, *1940s:* 5, 13–14

War Admiral, *1930s:* 165

War bonds, *1940s:* 32 (ill.), 33

War crimes, *1940s:* 65

Ward, Arch, *1940s:* 167

War debts, World War I, *1940s:* 38–39

Ware, Jimmy, *1970s:* 171 (ill.)

Warhol, Andy, *1960s:* 5, 7, 7 (ill.), 15–16, 95

War Industries Board (WIB), *1910s:* 28, 31, 76

War Labor Board, *1910s:* 76

War Labor Disputes Act, *1940s:* 40

War Mobilization and Reconversion Office, *1940s:* 153

Warm Springs Foundation, *1930s:* 122

Warner Bros., *1920s:* 142; *1930s:* 3, 15–16; *1950s:* 11

Warner Brothers Communications, *1990s:* 28

Warner Communications, *1980s:* 17

Warner, Glenn "Pop," *1910s:* 159

Warner, Harry, *1920s:* 142

Warner, Pop, *1900s:* 151

Warner, Sam, *1920s:* 142

Warning labels, on cigarette packages, *1960s:* 120–21, 138

The War of the Worlds, 1930s: 3, 21–22; *1940s:* 7; 1950s: *16*

War on Poverty, *1960s:* 68, 70, 82, 85

War Production Board (WPB), *1940s:* 24, 30, 93

Warren Commission, *1960s:* 94, 104

Warren, Earl, *1950s:* 58, 68, 73; *1960s:* 104

Warren, Mike, *1960s:* 175

Warren, Robert Penn, *1930s:* 14; *1940s:* 12; *1980s:* 3

War Revenue Acts, *1910s:* 33

Wars
    Middle East, *1970s:* 26, 31–32
    World War II, *1970s:* 40
    See also Vietnam War

Wartime production, *1940s:* 27, 30, 86

Washing machines, *1910s:* 102, 132

Washington, Booker T., *1900s:* 40, 51–53, 63, 63 (ill.), 78; *1910s:* 60–62

Washington Capitols, *1950s:* 169

Washington Post, 1970s: 85

Washington Press Club, *1940s:* 144

Washington Redskins, *1930s:* 164; *1940s:* 152; *1990s:* 175

Washington Senators, *1910s:* 159; *1920s:* 149, 158; *1930s:* 152; *1960s:* 164, 174; *1970s:* 166

Wasserman, August von, *1920s:* 115

Wassermann, Albert, *1920s:* 110

The Waste Land, 1920s: 2

Waterfield, Bob, *1950s:* 175

Watergate, *1970s:* 70, 73–75, 83–88; *1980s:* 32

Water heaters, *1910s:* 102

Waterloo Hawks, *1950s:* 169

Water Pollution Control Act amendments of 1972, *1970s:* 90

Waters, Muddy, *1940s:* 17

Water supply, *1910s:* 132

Watson, James, *1990s:* 130

Watson, James D., *1950s:* 147

Watson, John, *1900s:* 129

Watson, John B., *1910s:* 149; *1920s:* 103

Watson, Thomas J. Jr, *1950s:* 29, 29 (ill.); *1960s:* 37

Watson, Tom, *1970s:* 175; *1980s:* 183

Watson-Watt, Robert, *1940s:* 142–43

Watt, James, *1980s:* 30, 35

Watts, Los Angeles riots, *1960s:* 69, 103

Wayne, John, *1950s:* 13

WCTU (Women's Christian Temperance Union), *1900s:* 86

Weak force, *1980s:* 146

Weapons, in schools, *1990s:* 44

"We Are the World," *1980s:* 2, 24–25

The Weary Blues, 1920s: 3, 10

Weather, *1930s:* 130, 143

Weatherly, Joe, *1960s:* 171

Weathermen, *1960s:* 103

Weather patterns, architecture and, *1910s:* 100

Weathervane (clothing), *1940s:* 170

Weaver, Buck, *1910s:* 162; *1920s:* 154

Weaver, Robert, *1930s:* 79

Webb, Chick, *1930s:* 7

Webber, Andrew Lloyd, *1970s:* 2; *1980s:* 13–14

Weber, Joseph, *1960s:* 147

Weber, Max, *1910s:* 9

The Wedding March, 1920s: 3

Weddington, Sarah, *1970s:* 75, 75 (ill.), 88

Wedge (hairstyle), *1970s:* 118

Wegener, Alfred L., *1910s:* 147; *1930s:* 143

Weill, Kurt, *1930s:* 20; *1940s:* 18

Weiner, Lee, *1960s:* 115

Weiskopf, Tom, *1970s:* 174

Weismann, August, *1930s:* 142

Weiss, Carl A., *1930s:* 83

Weissmuller, Johnny, *1920s:* 95, 168;
   1930s: 11, 155

Welch, Joseph, *1950s:* 80

Weldman, Charles, *1930s:* 22

Welfare, *1970s:* 38; *1990s:* 41

Welfare capitalism, *1920s:* 75

Wellesley College, *1900s:* 51 (ill.);
   1930s: 92

Welles, Orson, *1930s:* 3, 21; *1940s:* 7,
   7 (ill.)

Wells, H. G., *1930s:* 21–22

Wells, Horace, *1930s:* 116

Wells, Mary, *1960s:* 13

Wells, Willie, *1920s:* 160

Welty, Eudora, *1940s:* 12

Wenner, Jann, *1960s:* 7, 7 (ill.)

"We're Off to See the Wizard," *1930s:*
   3

Wertz, Vic, *1950s:* 167

West Coast Hotel v. *Parrish, 1930s:* 27

Western Association (baseball),
   1900s: 138, 144

Western Electric, *1920s:* 131; *1940s:*
   25

Western Federation of Miners
   (WFM), *1900s:* 29–30

Western Golf Open, *1940s:* 152

Western music, *1930s:* 20

Westerns (comic books), *1940s:* 10

Westerns (films), *1900s:* 7, 11, 78

Westerns (literature), *1900s:* 9

Western Union, *1950s:* 24

Westinghouse Electric, *1900s:* 129;
   1950s: 25

West, Mae, *1930s:* 53

West, Nathanael, *1930s:* 5, 13

West Paducah, Kentucky high school
   shootings, *1990s:* 45

West Side Story, 1950s: 3

Wetherald, Richard, *1960s:* 154

WFM (Western Federation of Miners), *1900s:* 29–30

Whales, James, *1930s:* 15

Wham!, *1980s:* 19

Wham-O, *1950s:* 91; *1960s:* 94

Wharton, Edith, *1900s:* 7, 7 (ill.);
   1910s: 11

"What Am I Gonna Do About You,"
   1980s: 25

"What Friends Are For," *1980s;* 19

"What is the Matter with Teaching,"
   1920s: 54

What's Going On, 1960s: 13

What to Listen for in Music, 1930s: 20

WHA (World Hockey Association),
   1970s: 161, 172; *1980s:* 184

Wheeler, Benjamin, *1900s:* 40–41, 50

When Animals Attack, 1990s: 16

When Stunts Go Bad, 1990s: 17

When Worlds Collide, 1950s: 16

"Where Did Our Love Go," *1960s:* 1

Where's the Rest of Me?, 1980s: 78

Whip Inflation Now (WIN), *1970s:*
   26–27

Whipple, George Hoyt, *1920s:* 113,
   128; *1930s:* 110

Whirlaway, *1940s:* 152, 156

Whistler, James McNeill, *1910s:* 12

"White Christmas," *1910s:* 6

White, Edward H., *1960s:* 143, 146,
   158–59

White Fang, 1900s: 5, 7

Whitehead, Mary Beth, *1980s:*
   134–35, 135 (ill.)

Whitehead, Sara Elizabeth, *1980s:* 134

White House, *1900s:* 83; *1920s:* 2
   redecoration of, *1960s:* 94

White House Conference on Education, *1950s:* 47

Whiteman, Paul, *1920s:* 3, 12

White, Rollin H., *1900s:* 91

White Russian Army, *1910s:* 67

White, Ryan, *1980s:* 126, 126 (ill.)

White slave trafficking, *1910s:* 69, 87

White Sox, *1910s:* 157

White, Stanford, *1900s:* 67

White Star line, *1910s:* 151

Whitewater investigation, *1990s:* 63,
   76–77

White, William Allen, *1920s:* 71;
   1930s: 72

Whiting, Richard, *1910s:* 17

Whitman, Charles, *1960s:* 80

Whitman Company, *1930s:* 12

Whitney, 1980s: 6

Whitney, Harry Payne, *1910s:* 172

Whitney Museum of Art, *1950s:* 2, 9

Whitney, Richard, *1920s:* 42

Whittaker, Terry Cole, *1980s:* 100, 100 (ill.)

Whitten-Brown, Arthur, *1910s:* 133, 139

Whittle, Frank, *1940s:* 138

Whizz Comics, 1940s 10

WHO. *See* World Health Organization

The Who, *1960s:* 12

"Whoever's in New England," *1980s:* 25

Whooping cough, *1940s:* 108; *1950s:* 115

Who's Afraid of Virginia Woolf?, 1960s: 18

Who's That Girl, 1980s: 21

Who Wants to Be a Millionaire, 1990s: 16

WHO (World Health Organization), *1980s:* 122

"Why Did I Pick a Lemon in the Garden of Love"?, *1900s:* 16

Why Marry?, 1910s: 11

WIB. *See* War Industries Board

Wickersham Committee on Law Enforcement and Observance, *1930s:* 68

Wicks, Sidney, *1960s:* 175

Widerseim, Grace, *1900s:* 37

Wiener, Norbert, *1940s:* 141–42; *1950s:* 136

Wie, Virginia Van, *1930s:* 164

Wightman, Hazel Hotchkiss, *1910s:* 174–75

Wilcox, Howard "Howdy," *1910s:* 160

Wild Bill Hickok, 1950s: 107

Wildcatting, *1930s:* 42–43

The Wild One, 1950s: 110

Wild West Show, 1900s: 2

Wilhelm II, *1910s:* 78

Wilkins, Maurice H. F., *1950s:* 147

Willard, Jess, *1910s:* 155, 167; *1920s:* 152, 161

William H. Spencer High School, *1930s:* 46

Williams, Andy, *1950s:* 30

Williams, Bert, *1900s:* 15

Williams, Claude, *1910s:* 162; *1920s:* 155

Williams College, *1950s:* 46

Williams, Daniel H., *1900s:* 107

Williams, Hank, *1950s:* 2

Williams, Jesse Lynch, *1910s:* 11

Williams, Montel, *1990s:* 14

Williams, Nushawn, *1990s:* 117

Williamson, Marianne, *1990s:* 97, 97 (ill.), 108

Williams, Serena, *1990s:* 165, 167, 181

Williams, Ted, *1940s:* 153, 159, 161; *1950s:* 158; *1980s:* 176

Williams, Tennessee, *1940s:* 5, 19

Williams, Vanessa, *1980s:* 96, 101, 101 (ill.)

Williams, Venus, *1990s:* 160–63, 165, 167, 167 (ill.), 181

Willkie, Wendell, *1940s:* 13, 67

Wills, Helen, *1920s:* 149, 151, 170

Willys-Overland company, *1910s:* 141–42; *1920s:* 28

Wilmut, Ian, *1990s:* 134

Wilson, August, *1980s:* 7, 7 (ill.), 15

Wilson, Bill, *1930s:* 89

Wilson, Charles E., *1950s:* 29, 29 (ill.)

Wilson, E. B., *1900s:* 130

Wilson, Edward O., *1970s:* 144, 144 (ill.)

Wilson, Kemmons, *1950s:* 36

Wilson, Louis Blanchard, *1900s:* 100

Wilson, Richard, *1970s:* 109–10

Wilson, Robert W., *1970s:* 144

Wilson, Woodrow, *1910s:* 71, 71 (ill.); *1930s:* 76

   antitrust laws, *1910s:* 24

   Commitee on Public Information, *1910s:* 20

   education, *1910s:* 47, 52

   election of, *1920s:* 75–76

   elections, *1910s:* 68, 84

   foreign policy, *1910s:* 84

   Fourteen Points, *1920s:* 70

Huerta, Victoriano and, *1910s:* 73
inauguration, *1910s:* 26, 66–67
industry regulation and, *1920s:*
    27, 33
labor unions, *1910s:* 38
medicine, *1910s:* 121–24, 123
    (ill.)
New Freedom, *1910s:* 26–27,
    30–32, 84
peace plan/conference, *1910s:* 67,
    71, 78–79, 79 (ill.)
preparation for war, *1910s:* 66
re-election defeat, *1920s:* 66–67
road construction, *1910s:* 142
segregation, *1910s:* 96
tariffs, *1910s:* 31, 41
wages and salaries, *1910s:* 84–85
Wimbledon, *1900s:* 138; *1920s:* 153;
    1930s: 153, 156, 168; *1940s:*
    170–71; *1980s:* 168, 185–86; *1990s:*
    181
Wimbledon Championships, *1970s:*
    161, 176
Windows, *1990s:* 29
Windows software, *1980s:* 44, 161
Wind tunnels, *1930s:* 130
Winesburg, Ohio, 1910s: 11
Winfield, Paul, *1970s:* 20
Winfrey, Oprah, *1990s:* 3, 5, 7, 7 (ill.),
    14–19
Wings, 1920s: 135
The Winning Team, 1950s: 176
Winnipeg Jets, *1990s:* 176
Winter Garden Theater, *1910s:* 18;
    1950s: 3
Winter Olympics, *1970s:* 161, 177,
    180
WIN (Whip Inflation Now), *1970s:*
    26–27
Wireless communication, *1900s:* 2–3;
    1990s: 154–56
Wiretapping, *1970s:* 84
Wisconsin, *1900s:* 58
Wise, Stephen, *1940s:* 99
Wise, Stephen Samuel, *1930s:* 93
Wister, Owen, *1900s:* 5, 9
The Withers, *1910s:* 172
Witness, 1950s: 78

Witt, Mike, *1980s:* 175
The Wiz, 1970s: 3
The Wizard of Oz, 1930s: 3
W. M. Keck Observatory, *1990s:* 138
"Wobblies." *See* Industrial Workers of
    the World
Wolfe, Tom, *1960s:* 80; *1970s:* 113
Wollstein, Martha, *1900s:* 109
The Woman's Peace Party (WWP),
    1910s: 80
Women, *1980s:* 52
    advances for, *1900s:* 80–81, 86
    affirmative action, *1990s:* 47
    African Americans, *1910s:* 36
    airlines and, *1930s:* 88
    American College of Surgeons,
        1910s: 112
    artists, *1970s:* 8–9
    astronauts, *1970s:* 99; *1980s:* 150
    athletes, *1920s:* 151, 167, 168
        (ill.), 169–70
    authors, *1970s:* 10
    in basketball, *1900s:* 141
    business opportunities, *1990s:*
        36–38
    Cable Act, *1920s:* 86
    clothing, *1970s:* 116–19
    college-educated, *1910s:* 47, 58
    cosmetics and, *1920s:* 87
    deaths during childbirth, *1930s:*
        111
    discrimination, *1910s:* 36, 49
    education and, *1900s:* 40–41, 50,
        51 (ill.); *1930s:* 59–60; *1940s:*
        48, 55; *1970s:* 49–50, 61–65,
        62 (ill.), 99
    employment of, *1970s:* 39–42, 49
    equal pay, *1990s:* 31, 36–38
    Equal Rights Amendment, *1910s:*
        95; *1980s:* 96, 104–05
    in fashion design, *1940s:* 91
    fashions for, *1900s:* 91–94, 92
        (ill.); *1910s:* 105–07; *1920s:*
        86–87, 90, 92–95; *1930s:* 88,
        90, 92, 101–02, 141; *1940s:*
        88–89, 94–96, 94 (ill.); *1950s:*
        90, 101 (ill.), 102–03; *1960s:*
        97, 108, 109 (ill.)

fitness and, *1970s:* 130–31
in football, *1980s:* 59 (ill.)
garment industry, *1910s:* 39–41, 39 (ill.)
in government, *1940s:* 69
Harvard Divinity School, *1950s:* 47
Harvard University Law School, *1950s:* 46
in labor force, *1910s:* 26, 93, 102; *1920s:* 24; *1940s:* 28, 86, 89, 95–97; *1960s:* 27, 41–42
literature by, *1900s:* 8
marriage, *1910s:* 47
medical reform for, *1920s:* 116–17
in medicine, *1900s:* 107–09, 108 (ill.); *1940s:* 112, 134; *1960s:* 125; *1970s:* 126
minimum wage and, *1930s:* 27, 69
in ministry, *1920s:* 87
Miss America pageant, *1920s:* 86
in music, *1960s:* 7
owned businesses, *1960s:* 28
pilots, *1910s:* 132, 135, 138–39
in politics, *1970s:* 74, 99, 102
President's Commission on, *1960s:* 94
for racial civil rights, *1940s:* 90
retail industry and, *1910s:* 42
rights, *1910s:* 26; *1930s:* 73, 92, 134
role models, *1980s:* 139–40
roles of, *1900s:* 22, 40–41, 50, 83; *1940s:* 96–99; *1950s:* 90, 100, 102
in science, *1930s:* 143; *1940s:* 136–37
in space, *1960s:* 142, 157
special schools, *1910s:* 58–60
in sports, *1910s:* 174–75; *1930s:* 155–56, 166–67; *1940s:* 152, 154, 156, 162, 163 (ill.), 170; *1960s:* 181; *1970s:* 62, 62 (ill.), 160–61, 163–64, 175–78, 180
suffrage, *1920s:* 77
teachers, *1910s:* 58; *1930s:* 47

voting rights, *1910s:* 67, 69, 80–82, 81 (ill.), 84, 90, 93, 95
wages and salaries, *1910s:* 93; *1980s:* 96
white slave trafficking, *1910s:* 69, 87
See also Feminism; names of specific women
The Women's Bureau, *1920s:* 24
Women's Christian Temperance Union (WCTU), *1900s:* 86
Women's Equity Act of 1974, *1970s:* 63
Women's International League for Peace and Freedom, *1910s:* 80
Women's liberation. *See* Feminism
Women's Medical College of Pennsylvania, *1900s:* 107
Women's movement. *See* Feminism
Women's National Press Club Award, *1940s:* 91
Women's Professional Golfers' Association (WPA), *1940s:* 170
Women's rights movement. *See* Feminism
The Women's Room, 1970s: 10
Women, Students, and Artists for Black Art Liberation, *1970s:* 8
Women's studies, *1970s:* 62
Women's Tennis Association, *1970s:* 164
Women's Western Open (golf), *1940s:* 156
Wonder, Stevie, *1960s:* 13–14
Wooden, John, *1960s:* 175–76
Wood, Grant, *1930s:* 8–9
Woodruff, Robert W., *1940s:* 37
Wood, "Smokey" Joe, *1910s:* 163
Woodson, Carter Godwin, *1910s:* 51, 51 (ill.); *1920s:* 47
Woods, Tiger, *1990s:* 167, 167 (ill.), 177–79
Woodstock, 1960s: 12
Woodstock Music and Art Fair, *1960s:* 3, 5, 12
Woodward, Bob, *1970s:* 74, 74 (ill.), 85–86
Woodward, Bobbie, *1940s:* 95

Woodward, C. Vann, *1960s:* 53

Woolworth Building, *1910s:* 24, 94, 100

Word processing, *1970s:* 44

Word processors, *1960s:* 36–37, 142, 145

Workday, *1900s:* 20, 34; *1910s:* 141

Worker benefits, *1910s:* 37

Worker efficiency, *1910s:* 26, 149

Worker's compensation, *1900s:* 20; *1910s:* 67, 84–87, 120

Work hours, women and children, *1910s:* 83

Working conditions, *1900s:* 60

Working women, *1900s:* 93–94

Workmen's Compensation Act, *1910s:* 67

Work People's College, *1930s:* 59

Workplace, safety, *1910s:* 86–87

Works Progress Administration (WPA), *1930s:* 4, 8, 22, 54, 69, 79, 98, 164; *1940s:* 8

Work-study programs, *1960s:* 59

Workweek, 40-hour, *1940s:* 24

World Alpine Skiing Championship, *1980s:* 168

World Bank, *1940s:* 24–25, 27, 35, 37

World Championship (baseball), *1960s:* 169

World Championship Tennis (WTC), *1970s:* 176

World Cup, *1930s:* 167

World Cup (skiing), *1980s:* 168

World fairs, *1900s:* 2, 20, 79; *1930s:* 2, 88, 106, 132

World figure skating, *1950s:* 158

World Health Organization (WHO), *1970s:* 123, 126; *1980s:* 122

World Hockey Association (WHA), *1970s:* 161, 172; *1980s:* 184

World power, America as, *1910s:* 68

World's Deadliest Swarms, 1990s: 17

World Series, *1900s:* 138–39, 141, 144; *1910s:* 155, 157–59, 162–64, 163 (ill.); *1920s:* 148, 152; *1930s:* 152–53, 158; *1940s:* 153, 157, 159, 161; *1950s:* 158–61, 164, 166;
1960s: 164–66, 173–74; *1970s:* 166–67; *1980s:* 174, 176
of 1924, *1920s:* 158
Black Sox Scandal, *1920s:* 148, 153–55
champions, *1920s:* 157

World 600 stock car race, *1960s:* 170

World's Most Dangerous Animals, 1990s: 16

World's Scariest Police Shootouts, 1990s: 18

World Trade Center, *1930s:* 98

World Trade Center bombing, *1990s:* 62, 65, 83

World Trade Organization (WTO), *1990s:* 40

World War I
African Americans, *1910s:* 93, 96
airplanes for, *1910s:* 138–39
America's entry, *1910s:* 5, 25–26, 66, 68, 70, 75–78
antiwar groups, *1910s:* 19, 53, 96–98
armistice, *1910s:* 67, 78, 85
baseball and, *1910s:* 155
bonds, *1910s:* 33
conscientious objectors, *1910s:* 98
costs of, *1910s:* 25, 32–33
courses on, *1910s:* 47
Germany after, *1940s:* 70
journalists, *1910s:* 7
medical conditions, *1910s:* 121–24, 123 (ill.), 128–29
newspaper coverage, *1910s:* 5, 20–21
racism, *1910s:* 96
radio communications, *1910s:* 147–49
shell shock, *1910s:* 122, 147
technology and, *1910s:* 150–51
trench warfare, *1910s:* 69, 77
universities during, *1910s:* 52–53
weaponry, *1910s:* 138–39, 150–51

World War II, *1930s:* 69, 71; *1940s:* 66–67, 72–75, 101 (ill.)
arts and, *1940s:* 4
causes of, *1940s:* 38–39

education and, *1940s:* 46

Eisenhower, Dwight D., *1940s:* 68

end of, *1940s:* 25

entry into, *1940s:* 26, 64, 70–72, 71 (ill.)

fashion and, *1940s:* 93–95, 94 (ill.)

Hollywood and, *1940s:* 5

medicine and, *1940s:* 114, 118, 120–21, 130

mental illness and, *1940s:* 124–25

military intelligence in, *1940s:* 140–41

nuclear weapons and, *1950s:* 75

radar in, *1940s:* 142–43

religion and, *1940s:* 99–101

science and technology in, *1940s:* 132, 137–38

sports and, *1940s:* 154, 159–61, 167–68

women working during, *1970s:* 40

See also Atomic bombs

World War II films, *1990s:* 4, 11

World Wide Web, *1990s:* 33, 142, 145–50, 148 (ill.)

World Wide Web browsers, *1990s:* 138

Wouk, Herman, *1950s:* 2

Wounded Knee II, *1970s:* 109–10, 111 (ill.)

Wozniak, Steve, *1970s:* 43–44, 43 (ill.); *1980s:* 43, 160

WPA (Women's Professional Golfers' Association), *1940s:* 170

WPA (Works Progress Administration), *1940s:* 8

See also Works Progress Administration

WPB. *See* War Production Board

Wrestling, *1900s:* 139

Wright brothers, *1900s:* 20, 79, 118–19, 121, 123, 126–27, 126 (ill.)

Wright, Frank Lloyd, *1900s:* 5, 81, 96–97; *1910s:* 90, 100–01; *1930s:* 89, 93, 93 (ill.), 96; *1940s:* 86; *1950s:* 3, 96, 97 (ill.)

Wright, Marc, *1910s:* 174

Wright, Orville, *1910s:* 138

Wright, Richard, *1930s:* 13, 21; *1940s:* 5, 7, 7 (ill.), 13

Wright, Wilbur, *1910s:* 138

Wrigley Building, *1920s:* 86

Wrigley, Philip K., *1940s:* 29, 29 (ill.), 154, 162

Writing, *1930s:* 12–15

Writing, school, *1910s:* 46

WTA (World Tennis Association), *1990s:* 181

WTBS cable networks, *1980s:* 101

WTO (World Trade Organization), *1990s:* 40

WWP (The Woman's Peace Party), *1910s:* 80

Wyeth Laboratories, *1950s:* 131

X

Xerography, *1930s:* 131

Xerox, *1950s:* 137, 140; *1980s:* 160–61

X Factor, *1920s:* 118–19

X-1 aircraft, *1940s:* 130 (ill.), 139

X ratings (movies), *1960s:* 10

X-ray detectors, *1960s:* 150

X-ray machines, *1950s:* 114, 130 (ill.)

X rays, *1900s:* 100; *1910s:* 123, 129; *1930s:* 110, 122

Y

Yahoo! Inc., *1990s:* 33

Yale University, *1910s:* 46; *1930s:* 111, 162; *1960s:* 95, 178

Yalow, Rosalyn S., *1970s:* 126, 126 (ill.)

Yalta conference, *1940s:* 65, 76

Yamaguchi, Kristi, *1990s:* 165, 182

Yankees. *See* New York Yankees

Yankee Stadium, *1920s:* 148; *1930s:* 153, 156, 162

Yardbirds, *1960s:* 10

Yarns, synthetic, *1950s:* 90

Yastrzemski, Carl, *1960s:* 173

Yeager, Charles E. "Chuck," *1930s:*
139; *1950s:* 151
Yeager, Jeana, *1980s:* 147
Yellow fever, *1900s:* 100, 104, 113–14;
1930s: 110; *1940s:* 110, 114
Yellow Fever Commission, *1900s:*
100, 104, 114
Yellow journalism, *1900s:* 16
The Yellow Kid, 1900s: 16
"The Yellow Wallpaper," *1900s:* 83
Yeltsin, Boris, *1990s:* 62
Yersinia pestis, 1900s: 111
"Yesterday," *1960s:* 11
YMCA (Young Men's Christian Asso-
ciations), *1900s:* 89, 140–41, 146;
1910s: 95, 164–65
Yoga, *1980s:* 117
Yom Kippur War, *1970s:* 31–32
Yorkin, Bud, *1970s:* 22
Yosemite National Park, *1900s:* 69
(ill.)
Yost, Fielding, *1900s:* 150
"You Beat Me to the Punch," *1960s:*
13
"You Light Up My Life," *1970s:* 13
Young, Andrew, Jr., *1970s:* 71, 75, 75
(ill.)
Young, Clara Kimball, *1910s:* 16
Young, Coleman, *1970s:* 98
Young, Cy, *1910s:* 159, 161
Young, Denton "Cy," *1900s:* 138, 144
Young, Ella Flagg, *1900s:* 41
Young, Hugh Hampton, *1900s:* 100
Young, Joe, *1910s:* 17
Young, Lester, *1930s:* 20; *1940s:* 16–17
Young Men's Christian Associations
(YMCA), *1900s:* 89, 140–41, 146;
1910s: 95, 164–65
Young, Neil, *1980s:* 3, 26
Young, Sheila, *1970s:* 180
Youngstown Patricians, *1910s:* 169
Young Women's Christian Associa-
tions (YWCA), *1900s:* 89
Your Hit Parade, 1930s: 3

Youth
crime, *1950s:* 81, 91
fashion, *1950s:* 108 (ill.), 109–10
suicide, *1980s:* 48
values, *1950s:* 93, 102
Youth Suicide Center, *1980s:* 48
Yo-yos, *1960s:* 94, 108
Y2K, *1990s:* 139–41, 155
Yugoslavia, *1990s:* 71–72
Yuppies, *1980s:* 102–06
YWCA (Young Women's Christian
Associations), *1900s:* 89

Z

Zaharias, Mildred "Babe" Didrikson,
1940s: 152, 154, 156, 156 (ill.),
170; *1950s:* 161, 163
See also Didrikson, Mildred
"Babe"
Zale, Tony, *1940s:* 165
Zangara, Giuseppe, *1930s:* 83
Zangwill, Israel, *1900s:* 3
Zapata, Emiliano, *1910s:* 75
Zapruder, Abraham, *1960s:* 104
Zarya space module, *1990s:* 159
Zeckendorf, William, *1950s:* 43
Zenith Radio, *1920s:* 24
Zephyr, *1930s:* 96, 97 (ill.), 140
Zeppelin dirigibles, *1900s:* 118; *1920s:*
139–40
Zeppelin, Ferdinand von, *1920s:*
139–40
Zero gravity, *1970s:* 145
Ziegfeld, Florenz, *1900s:* 3, 79; *1910s:*
18, 18 (ill.); *1920s:* 9
Ziegfeld Follies, 1900s: 3, 79
Zimmermann, Arthur, *1910s:* 77
Zinjanthropus, *1960s:* 148
Zionism, *1930s:* 93
Zsigmondy, Richard, *1900s:* 118
Zuppke, Robert, *1910s:* 168
Zurich University, *1930s:* 141
Zworykin, Vladimir, *1920s:* 128, 143